Samuel Taylor Coleridge
An Annotated Bibliography of
Criticism and Scholarship, 1793-1975

Richard Haven and Walter B. Crawford, *General Editors*

In preparation:

Volume 2: 1900-1975
Edited by Walter B. Crawford and Edward S. Lauterbach

SAMUEL TAYLOR COLERIDGE
An Annotated Bibliography of Criticism and Scholarship

Volume 1: 1793-1899

Edited by
Richard and Josephine Haven
Maurianne Adams

G. K. HALL & CO., 70 LINCOLN STREET, BOSTON, MASS.
GEORGE PRIOR PUBLISHERS, LONDON, ENGLAND

Library of Congress Cataloging in Publication Data

Haven, Richard, 1924-
    Samuel Taylor Coleridge : an annotated bibliog-
raphy of criticism and scholarship.

    Includes indexes.
    CONTENTS: v. 1. 1793-1899.—
    1. Coleridge, Samuel Taylor, 1772-1834—Bibliog-
raphy. I. Haven, Josephine, joint author.
II. Adams, Maurianne, joint author.
Z8182.H26 [PR4483] 016.821'7 75-40487
 ISBN 0-8161-7829-1

Available for sale in the British Commonwealth from
George Prior Publishers, 2 Rugby St., London, England
ISBN (U.K.) 0-904000-97-4

This publication is printed on permanent/durable acid-free paper.
MANUFACTURED IN THE UNITED STATES OF AMERICA

Contents

Preface

The present volume, while intended as an independent work, is also the first part of a bibliography of writing on Coleridge from the first known appearance of his name in print until the present day. The second part, being prepared by Walter B. Crawford and Edward V. Lauterbach, and containing material from the twentieth century, is approaching completion and will be published by G. K. Hall & Co. in the near future. Both parts attempt to include not only all works exclusively concerned with Coleridge but also works on other subjects which contain substantial or significant material on Coleridge. Both parts include a large amount of material which has not appeared in any previous bibliography, and all material has been re-examined and annotated. Both parts are arranged chronologically by year and in the same format, but they are independently indexed.

II

The choice of the date 1900 to divide the two parts of the work was to some extent a necessarily arbitrary attempt at an equitable division of labor between two groups of researchers. It may, however, be justified on more substantive grounds as falling within a span of years which separates distinguishable periods of widespread interest in Coleridge and his work. In 1895, Julia Wedgwood explained what she saw as a declining interest in Coleridge and his work on the grounds that to most mid-Victorians he had seemed a figure more of their own time than of the past, and that he was suffering from a general reaction against Victorian Sages. That reaction or something like it continued for a generation. Coleridge was of course read and written about, and a few poems became part of the standard school syllabus and were the common property of literate Englishmen and Americans. But the Victorian's Coleridge largely disappeared. A generation later in the 1920's, a series of studies, among them those of Snyder, Wilde, Gingerich, and Howard, offered a somewhat different figure, and in 1927, J. L. Lowes' monumental The Road to Xanadu gave impetus to a revival of interest in Coleridge which has continued and increased to the present day.

PREFACE

Nineteenth century writing on Coleridge contains a substantial amount of criticism which deserves to survive. It contains also a substantial amount of biographical material, particularly in the various kinds of personal accounts and recollections of Coleridge which continued to appear throughout the century, often in memoirs and collections of letters. From the point of view of a modern scholar, however, the value of much of the work listed in this volume depends upon something other than intrinsic critical merit or significance as biographical data, and may be as much for the cultural or literary historian in general as for the student of Coleridge in particular. Many essays and reviews which contain little fresh information or insight, and many private letters and comments, reveal the response to his life and work of various kinds of readers--professional men of letters, thinkers, politicians, and private individuals. It is often a response not only to a particular work but to a kind of work, to attitudes and ways of thinking with which Coleridge was widely identified.

In his own day, Coleridge was known initially as a poet and, briefly, a radical lecturer and journalist. He then appeared often as a poet who had abandoned poetry for speculation. Where this aroused any concern, it was at first commonly cause for regret or sometimes contempt. But by the last years of his life, when he reigned as the 'Sage of Highgate', and through the first generation of Victorians, Coleridge had become a figure to be reckoned with on both sides of the Atlantic, not primarily as poet and critic, but as thinker, theologian, and political theorist. It was this Coleridge whom Mill described as one of the two seminal minds of the age and in whom the creed of the University of Vermont asked its students to swear belief. It was this Coleridge on whose decline Julia Wedgwood commented. Many of the issues once hotly debated in print, especially theological ones, are now forgotten, but an understanding of them and of Coleridge's role in them is important to an understanding of the time. That the Victorian image of the Sage may not seem to us to have been the 'real' Coleridge alters, but does not lessen, the significance for us of these discussions.

The various and changing responses to Coleridge in the nineteenth century may have a further value to critics and scholars in the twentieth, in which there has been not only a new cycle of interest in Coleridge's poetry but also a revived respect for him as a thinker, even in some quarters as again a sage or guru, and which has seen as well renewed attacks on claims made for his intellectual significance. One need not adopt the belief that history repeats itself-- and we have perhaps more cause to fear that it will not--to suggest that the responses of the nineteenth century may help us to clarify, even to modify, our understanding of those of our own.*

*Nineteenth century responses to 'The Ancient Mariner' are discussed by Richard Haven in Studies in Romanticism, XI (1972), 360-374. Various aspects of Coleridge's influence among the Victorians are traced by Maurianne Adams in Coleridge and the Victorians, unpublished 1967 Indiana University dissertation, which has been substantially revised for forthcoming publication.

PREFACE

III

Discussions of Coleridge during his own lifetime appeared most
frequently in reviews of his own work or of that of another writer.
There were in addition a number of short sketches or word portraits,
some of them satirical, and, especially after the publication of
"Christabel," a number of parodies. The reviews characteristically
offer illustrative extracts with relatively brief judgmental comments. The first extended and serious analysis of Coleridge's work,
and the first serious treatment of him as a thinker, was John Foster's 1811 defense of The Friend. In 1816, Talfourd offered a favorable general assessment of the then-published poetry, including
Remorse, in a survey of the present state of literature, but the
first full-scale treatment of the poetry was that by Lockhart (or
possibly Wilson) in 1819. Reviews of the various publications of
1816-17 often turned into broader discussions, frequently, and especially in those by Hazlitt, unfavorable. Later publications, Aids to
Reflection and On the Constitution of the Church and State, elicited few
reviews and Coleridge's name for some years appears more frequently
in general articles and in the retrospective essays of Lamb, Hazlitt,
and De Quincey. The withdrawal of his pension in 1831 caused a flur-
ry of comment, and after 1830 the editors of Fraser's Magazine adopted him as a sort of pretended patron and he appears in a number of
generally humorous but respectful pieces. A review of Poetical Works
in the Westminster Review in 1830 has achieved some slight notoriety
by claiming Coleridge as a Benthamite, but is much more significant
for its perceptive discussion of some of what have come to be known
as 'Conversation Poems'. James Marsh's important and influential
introduction to Aids to Reflection was published in America in 1829.
In England, the first extended treatment of Aids was an admiring but
rather wooly-minded 1832 essay by J. A. Heraud, who later liked to
claim priority as expositor and explicator of Coleridge's philosophy
and theology and was a prolific if somewhat pompous and obtuse com-
mentator.

The publication of a new edition of Poetical Works in 1834 elicited two important review articles, one by Coleridge's nephew, son-
in-law, and editor, Henry Nelson Coleridge, and the other by John
Wilson who had earlier savaged Coleridge in an 1817 review of Biographia Literaria. As the year of Coleridge's death, it also saw a
large number of obituary memoirs, many of them bestowing a kind of
fulsome recognition which he rarely received in print during his
lifetime. It was followed in the next few years by a flood of posthumous publications and recollections, both in books and in periodicals. While individual fragments, letters, marginalia, and reports
of lectures continued to appear throughout the century as did im-
proved editions, by 1840 the canon of Coleridge's work as known to
the Victorians was for the most part established. And by that date
too, many of the issues which were seen as central concerns during
the next twenty years had been introduced. Coleridge's opium addiction had never been a secret, but it and with it the question of

his moral character became a public issue with the publication of
Cottle's reminiscences and letters in 1837. The enthusiasm for Coleridge felt by some younger churchmen is reflected in essays by, among
others, John Sterling in 1828 and J. C. Hare in 1835. Mill's identification of Coleridge and Bentham as the seminal minds of the age oc-
curs in his essay on Bentham in 1838 and his companion essay on Coleridge followed in 1840. In 1838, the young W. E. Gladstone took
Coleridge as a starting point for his book The State in its Relations
with the Church. And in 1840 also, J. F. Ferrier mounted a full
scale attack on Coleridge as a plagiarist from German philosophers
and critics.

From 1840 to 1860, discussion of Coleridge as thinker, particularly as theologian, outweighs consideration of him as a poet. By
supporters and detractors alike, he was seen as chief initiator of a
new school and on both sides of the Atlantic he was hailed as prophet
and damned as heretic. Letters and memoirs give evidence of the
personal impact of his work, notably of Aids, on individual readers.
Comments on the poetry rarely diverge significantly from opinions offered earlier. An important exception is the first allegorical interpretation of "The Ancient Mariner" which appeared in Hogg's Weekly Instructor in 1850.

The years 1860-70 saw a drop in both frequency and intensity.
There are a number of brief notes and comments. The charge of plagiarism is repeated and extended by Stirling in 1867 and by C. M. Ingleby in 1870, though the latter, a professor from Birmingham, offered
a more balanced and favorable evaluation of Coleridge in two substantial articles in 1872. The first of Pater's various essays on
Coleridge, and the germ from which the rest derive, appeared in 1866,
and Swinburne's enthusiastic assessment of Coleridge as a poet, and
of "Christabel" in particular, was published in 1869.

In the remaining thirty years of the century, there continue to
be discussions of Coleridge's intellectual significance and influence, but he is rarely a center of controversy or an object of attack. There is more concern with the poetry and much more with biography. Important new editions of the poetry appeared in 1877 and
1893; there were many others which were essentially reprints and
many volumes of selections. The first book-length biographies since
Gillman's abortive effort in 1838 were published by H. D. Traill
(1884), Hall Caine (1887) and J. D. Campbell (1893). Alois Brandl's
Samuel Taylor Coleridge und die Englische Romantik appeared in German in 1886, and in translation by Lady Eastlake in 1887. E. H.
Coleridge's edition of Letters and his selections from the notebooks,
Anima Poetae, both 1895, presented a substantial quantity of new
primary material for the first time in fifty years. All this activ-
ity produced many reviews and other articles. It did not, however,
seem to stimulate any extensive reassessment of Coleridge. The impression is rather one of consolidation. When a memorial bust of
Coleridge was unveiled at Westminster Abbey in 1885, one report of

the event was entitled "The Canonization of Coleridge." For some
time to come, Coleridge was offered due reverence by many, and continued to inspire enthusiasm in a few.

IV

In collecting materials for this volume, we have attempted to
include all published references to Coleridge through 1834, the year
of his death, all books, articles, notes, and reviews exclusively or
primarily devoted to him since that date, and all substantial or significant discussions of him in published material primarily concerned
with other subjects. Existing bibliographies have provided a basis
but only a limited one. Anderson's 1893 list of periodical articles
in the British Museum appended to Campbell's biography was useful but
frequently inaccurate and obviously far short of complete. Haney's
1903 bibliography, recently reprinted, was an admirable work but
limited by available facilities for research. Modern bibliographies
have generally involved no new examination of nineteenth century materials. The two exceptions are William Ward's Literary Reviews in
British Periodicals, 1798-1820 (1972) and Lawrence Wynn's The Reputation of Samuel Taylor Coleridge Among His Contemporaries in England (1951 Princeton doctoral dissertation), which contain extensive
and invaluable listings of reviews, but are limited in chronological
coverage to the earlier period. The Coleridge section in NCBEL is a
product of fresh research but is for the most part confined to books
and non-review articles wholly devoted to Coleridge, and the number
of titles listed is about one seventh of that included here. We have
also consulted, where they exist, bibliographies of figures associ-
ated with Coleridge or whom we knew to have written on him.

Apart from re-examining and annotating material listed in existing bibliographies we have searched the files of some hundreds of
periodicals both British and American and looked at as many collections of essays and volumes of memoirs and letters as we could discover either by methodical research or serendipity. All material
has been read by at least one of the editors except for a few cases
where we have been forced to rely on an existing description of an
item which has since disappeared. Such cases are clearly indicated.

Although it has been our intention to provide a complete and not
a selective listing, we have adopted a policy involving some limita-
tions which seemed either sensible or inescapable.

1. Although there is need for a new descriptive bibliography,
    we have not attempted to provide one here. The publication
    of the Collected Works now in progress under the editorship
    of Kathleen Coburn involves the thorough re-examination of
    all primary texts by a number of specialist editors. It
    would be futile to try to duplicate their work, and such a
    bibliography may wait until the Collected Coleridge is

complete. In the meantime, the NCBEL offers an enumerative
bibliography, and Wise, if used with care and an awareness of
his forgeries, is still of value as a descriptive bibliography. We have omitted primary material with the following exceptions: we have included editions which contain new editorial matter, or memoirs, critical introductions, and the
like, and we have included items of posthumously published
manuscripts, marginalia, and correspondence where these contain biographical or editorial comment, or the other side of
the correspondence.

2. We have included reprints of articles and reviews contemporary with their original appearance. These gave some items a
wider circulation than they would otherwise have had, and may
be of particular interest in the case of British material reprinted in the United States. Moreover, since reprints did
not always acknowledge the original source, such listing
clarifies relationships which would not otherwise be clear.
We have also listed the first reprint of a periodical item in
a collected volume, and further reprints involving significant textual changes. We have not listed reprints in later
or in modern editions. To trace the publishing history of
frequently reprinted essays would require an inordinate
amount of space and was, we felt, unnecessary.

3. We have included material from continental periodicals known
to us through existing bibliographies and through references
which we have discovered. We have not, however, been able to
attempt a systematic search of the files of such periodicals.

4. Since the bibliography is arranged by date of publication,
material written in the nineteenth century but not published
until the twentieth will appear under its date of publication
in the second part of the bibliography. Such material consists for the most part of additional letters and journals.

In addition to material which we have consciously excluded, we
are aware that there must be much which we have missed inadvertently.
The nineteenth century saw a tremendous outpouring of books and periodicals: there were more than 30,000 different periodicals published in Britain alone, and there is as yet no comprehensive listing
of titles, to say nothing of contents. The situation with newspapers
is particularly difficult as not only are there indices only for The
Times and the New York Times, but in most cases complete files are
difficult or impossible to find. We have not, for example, been able
to locate a copy of the issue of the Morning Herald for 25 January
1813, supposedly containing a review of Remorse by Pasquin. We hope
that users who discover omissions will bring them to our attention.

We must finally acknowledge the inevitability of errors, both
human and otherwise. Since the discovery of one of our data cards

stuck by an aged mother in a milk bottle outside our Oxford door with
the notation 'only one pint today please', we have never been quite
certain what part of our work may have fallen into the hands of the
Oxford Cooperative Dairy. In order to minimize errors in transcrip-
tion, we have used a computer for the storage as well as the sorting
and indexing of material, but we have discovered that the 'decay' of
electrical impulses on magnetic discs and fluctuations in electric
current can occasionally do strange things to carefully collected
data. And we were bemused to discover that the higher harmonics of
the bark of our dog fell within the acoustical range by which our
teletype terminal communicated with the computer. We are certain
that we have eliminated such entries as "zzowptt", but we cannot be
absolutely confident that a lesser yip has not led to an error in one
of the coded entries by which the indices were prepared.

V

The bibliography is arranged chronologically by year and, within
each year, alphabetically by author. Anonymous items are ordered by
the title of the periodical in which they appeared. Editions and
other primary materials, where included, precede other entries for
the year of publication. Items are numbered sequentially, and index
references are to item, not page, numbers. A few items added after
the indices were written have been given the number of the preceding
item followed by a letter (e.g. 414A). In cases where an item was
moved or removed after the numbering was completed, the original number is retained to avoid confusion but with the note 'No Entry.'

In cases where a number of short items (such as queries and replies) form a sequence, these are separately indexed but are grouped
together as a single entry under the first published item.

For signed articles, authors' names, initials, or pseudonyms are
given as printed. Missing names when known are supplied in square
brackets. Subtitles, including those of periodicals, have been
omitted except in a few cases where they were sufficiently descriptive to obviate the need for an annotation. Where, as was common in
the nineteenth century, the title of a review repeats the full title-
page of the work, this has been reduced to a short title.

The requirements of computer programs have necessitated some de-
partures from the conventions of punctuation. We do not believe that
these will result in any loss of clarity.

PREFACE

Annotations

Annotations are intended to assist the user in determining what materials may be to his or her purpose and not as précis or as substitutes for the originals. The length of an annotation should not be taken to reflect the editors' judgment of the importance of an item. For the most part, familiar or easily accessible items are more briefly annotated than some of less intrinsic importance which are generally unknown or of which few libraries possess copies. In a very few cases, the title of an item obviates the need for annotation. In a few others, particularly some sequences of comments concerning easily established matters of fact, description seemed pointless and we have indicated only the character, not the content, of the material.

Cross references to works listed elsewhere in the bibliography are by year of publication, author, and where necessary, short title.

Reviews

Reviews are listed following the annotation. Reviews which offer further critical or scholarly comment, as distinct from mere descriptions or collections of extracts, appear as individual entries. In these cases, the item numbers are included in the list of reviews. Since within each year, items are arranged by author, anonymous reviews which appear as individual entries will generally precede the work to which they refer. Reviews of works in which Coleridge plays a minor part are included only if the review is directed to the Coleridge material.

Attributions

Authorities for the attribution of anonymous or pseudonymous items are given at the end of the entry. For reviews listed in sequence, the authority is given in parentheses following the review entry. As far as possible, attributions are based on the latest available research. In some cases, attributions are, as indicated, still controversial; in others, especially where an earlier authority such as Poole has had to be used, they are open to question.

Indices

There are four indices as follows:

1. Author-title. This has been extracted by computer and includes all authors (including those of reviews), and all titles (including those of reviews, reprints, where different, collective volumes, periodicals). Where authors' names appeared

PREFACE

in various forms, these have been regularized in the index.
Pseudonyms are listed but not identified in the index.

2. Proper names of persons and places mentioned in annotations.

3. Subject index. This is schematically rather than alphabetically arranged and is intended, perhaps in conjunction with
   Index 2, to enable users to compose, in effect, specialized
   indices for their particular needs. Users are asked to con-
   sult the explanatory note and outline which precede the subject index on p. 346.

4. Index of parodies, satires, and other Coleridgeana.

June, 1975

Acknowledgments

The preparation of this work would not have been possible without substantial financial support. Generous grants from the National Endowment for the Humanities enabled two of the editors to take sabbatical leaves in England and also helped to cover the costs of travel, research assistance, photocopying, computer time, and the like. The University Computer Center of the University of Massachusetts provided a number of grants for computer time as well as extensive technical advice and assistance. The Faculty Research Council of the University of Massachusetts provided a series of grants-in-aid and the Smith College Committee for Aid to Faculty Research made a summer grant available to one of the editors, along with significant financial assistance.

Equally important have been the very large number of individuals and institutions whose help we have had to enlist and whose patience we must often have taxed. At the inception of the project, George Whalley, compiler of the Coleridge section of the New Cambridge Bibliography, offered much valuable advice concerning both subject matter and the use of the computer. Walter and Esther Houghton of the Wellesley Index have kindly allowed us to draw upon their files of still unpublished material, from which many of our attributions derive. Such attributions reflect evidence in Wellesley Index files as of April, 1974 and users should check forthcoming volumes of the Index for cases where new evidence may have led to re-attribution. Katherine Paranya devoted a great deal of time, thought, and skill to the design of our computer programs and to the supervision of their application. Our student research assistants, Mary Blagdon, Mary Leggio Fisher, Peter Stevens, Ruthanne Adams, Lynne Agress, and Katherine Sorensen, have spent untold hours at what must often have been tedious tasks. We wish to extend our appreciation to Marilyn Gaull for the major role she played as copy editor when the manuscript reached completion. Our research has also been helped in important ways by K. M. D. Barker, H. Brogan, P. Cook, B. Cooney, K. Cowles, J. Duffy, J. Fahnestock, J. Farrell, C. Heller, E. Kaplan, R. Keefe, J. Kendall, E. G. H. Kempson, D. Kresh, G. Mansbridge, F. Merritt, R. S. Mullen, G. W. Murray, J. Ogden, A. Page, S. Rudin, C. Vickers, J. Weston, and C. Wogrin.

ACKNOWLEDGMENTS

Much of our work has been done in the Bodleian Library in Oxford, the British Museum Library, Houghton and Widener Libraries of Harvard University, the libraries of the University of Massachusetts and of Amherst, Smith, and Mt. Holyoke Colleges, the Library of Congress, the Boston Public Library, the Boston Atheneum, the Bristol Central Library, and the Keats Memorial Room, Hampstead. Members of the staffs of all of these have been more than generous in their assistance. We are in addition grateful to the following libraries and their staffs for making their collections available to us or, in cases where we were unable to make personal visits, answering our questions by mail: American Antiquarian Society; Andover-Harvard Theological Library; National Library of Australia; Bath Municipal Library; Belfast Library; Birmingham Public Library; Boston (Lincolnshire) Public Library; University of British Columbia Library; Library of the University of California at Berkeley; Cambridge University Library; Cornell University Library; Duke University Library; Edinburgh University Library; Ewart Library (Dumfries); Forbes Library (Northampton, Massachusetts); Huntington Library; National Library of Ireland; Jesus College (Cambridge) Library; Kansas University Library; McGill University Library; Manchester College (Oxford) Library; Manchester Public Library; University of Melbourne Library; Nantucket (Massachusetts) Atheneum; Newport (Rhode Island) Historical Society; New York Historical Society; New York University Library; Princeton University Library; Rice University Library; San Francisco Public Library; University of Texas Humanities Research Center; Toronto Public Library; Trinity College (Dublin) Library; Trinity College (Hartford) Library; Tufts University Library; Victoria College (Toronto) Library; National Library of Wales; Dr. Williams's Library; Wiltshire Archaeological Society; University of Wisconsin Library; Worcester (Massachusetts) Atheneum; Beinecke and Stirling Libraries of Yale University.

Sources of Attributions

Abbreviations in text for sources of attributions
of anonymous and pseudonymous titles

Atlantic Index

Atlantic Index Supplement 1899-1901.
Boston, New York. Houghton Mifflin
and Co. 1903.

Axon

Axon, W. E. A. 'Anna Jane Vardill
Niven'. Transactions of the Royal
Society of Literature. 2nd S.
XXVIII (1908), 57-88.

Blanck

Blanck, Jacob. Bibliography of American
Literature. Compiled for the Bibli-
ographical Society of America. 6
vols. New Haven. Yale University
Press. London. Oxford University
Press. 1955--.

Blunden

Blunden, Edmund. Leigh Hunt's Examiner
Examined. London. Harper and
Brothers. 1928.

B. Mus. Cat.

British Museum. Department of Printed
Books; General catalogue of printed
books; Photolithographic edition to
1955.... 263 vols. London. Trus-
tees of the British Museum. 1959-
1966.

Bull. of Bibliog.

Booth, Bradford A. 'A bibliography of
John Galt.' Bulletin of Bibliography
[Boston], XVI (1936), 7-9.

Calvert

Calvert, George. Miscellanies of Verse
and Prose. Baltimore. N. Hickman.
1840.

Sources of Attributions

Campbell   Collection of material collected by
                                  James Dykes Campbell and deposited in
                                  the Huntington Library, California.

Chambers   Chambers, E. K. Samuel Taylor
                                  Coleridge. Oxford. Clarendon Press.
                                  1938. Reprinted 1958, 1963.

Chorley   Chorley, Henry Fothergill. Autobiogra-
                                  phy, Memoir and Letters. Compiled
                                  by Henry G. Hewlett. 2 v. London.
                                  Richard Bentley and Son. 1873.

Coburn   Coburn, Kathleen, ed. The Philosophical
                                  Lectures of Samuel Taylor Coleridge.
                                  Hitherto Unpublished. London. The
                                  Pilot Press Limited. 1949.

Coghill   Coghill, Mrs. Harry. The Autobiography
                                  and Letters of Mrs. M. O. W. Oli-
                                  phant. Arranged and edited by Mrs.
                                  Harry Coghill. Edinburgh, London.
                                  W. Blackwood & Son. 1899.

Curry   Curry, Kenneth, ed. New Letters of
                                  Robert Southey. 2 vols. New York,
                                  London. Columbia University Press.
                                  1965.

Cushing   Cushing, William. Index to the Chris-
                                  tian Examiner I-LXXXVII 1824-1869.
                                  Boston. J. S. Cushing. 1879.

Cushing   Cushing, William. Index to the North
                                  American Review: Volumes I-CXXXV,
                                  1815-1877. Cambridge, Mass. John
                                  Wilson. 1878.

DAPL   Dictionary of Anonymous and Pseudon-
                                  ymous English Literature. Edited by
                                  Samuel Halkett, John Laing et al.
                                  9 vols. Edinburgh, London. Oliver
                                  and Boyd. 1926-1962.

Dall   Dall, Caroline Healy. Transcendentalism
                                  in New England. Boston. Roberts.
                                  1897.

Dendurent   Dendurent, H. O. 'The Coleridge Collec-
                                  tion in Victoria University Library,
                                  Toronto.' The Wordsworth Circle
                                  [Philadelphia], V (1974), 225-86.

SOURCES OF ATTRIBUTIONS

Dowden   Dowden, Wilfred S., ed. Letters of Thomas Moore. 2 vols. Oxford. Clarendon Press. 1964.

Duffy   Duffy, John, ed. Coleridge's American Disciples: the Selected Correspondence of James Marsh. Amherst. University of Massachusetts Press. 1973.

English Catalogue of Books   English Catalogue of Books. 8 vols. London. S. Low, Marston & Co. 1835-1904.

Erdman   Erdman, David V. 'A new discovery: the first review of Christabel.' Studies in English [University of Texas], XXXVII (1958), 53-60.

Everson   Everson, Ida G. George Henry Calvert, Literary Pioneer. New York. Columbia University Press. 1944.

Fahnestock   Fahnestock, Jeanne. Unpublished work based on Athenaeum files.

Fisch   Fisch, M. H. 'The Coleridges, Dr. Prati, and Vico.' Modern Philology [Chicago], XLI (1943-4), 111-122.

Graham   Graham, Walter. English Literary Periodicals. New York. Thomas Nelson & Sons. 1930.

Griggs   Collected Letters of Samuel Taylor Coleridge, ed. Earl Leslie Griggs. 6 vols. Oxford. Clarendon Press. 1956-1973.

Haldane   Haldane, E[lizabeth] S[anderson]. James Frederick Ferrier. Edinburgh, London. Oliphant Anderson & Ferrier. New York. Charles Scribner's. 1899.

Halliford   Halliford. Works of Thomas Love Peacock. Ed. by H. F. B. Brett-Smith and C. E. Jones. 10 vols. London. Constable; New York. Gabriel Wells. 1924-1934.

SOURCES OF ATTRIBUTIONS

SOURCES OF ATTRIBUTIONS

Hamilton   Hamilton, Walter. Parodies of the Works of English and American Authors. Collected and annotated by Walter Hamilton. 6 vols. London. Reeves & Turner. 1884-1889. (All references are to volume V, 1887).

Haney   Haney, John Louis. A Bibliography of Samuel Taylor Coleridge. Philadelphia. Privately printed. 1903. Reprinted Folcroft. The Folcroft Press Inc. 1969.

Hanson   Hanson, Lawrence. The Life of S. T. Coleridge: The Early Years. London. Allen & Unwin; New York. Oxford University Press. 1938. Princeton University Press. 1939. Reprinted New York. Russell & Russell. 1962.

Harrison   Harrison, James Albert, ed. The Complete Works of Edgar Allan Poe. 17 vols. New York. E. G. Sproul. 1902.

Haskell   Haskell, Daniel. The Nation. Volumes 1-105. New York. 1865-1917. Indexes of titles and contributors. 2 vols. New York. New York Public Library. 1951, 1953.

Hayden   Hayden, John Olin. The Romantic Reviewers 1802-1824. London. Routledge & Kegan Paul. 1969.

Hazlitt   Hazlitt, W. Carew. Memoir of William Hazlitt. 2 vols. London. Richard Bentley. 1867.

Hodder   Hodder, George. Memories of my time including personal reminiscences of eminent men. London. Tinsley Brothers. 1870.

Hort   Hort, Arthur Fenton. Life and Letters of Fenton John Anthony Hort. London, New York. Macmillan & Company. 1896.

Houtchens   Houtchens, Lawrence Huston and Carolyn Washburn Houtchens. Leigh Hunt's Dramatic Criticism 1808-1831. New York. Columbia University Press. 1949.

SOURCES OF ATTRIBUTIONS

Howe
    Howe, P. P., ed. The Complete Works of William Hazlitt. 21 vols. London and Toronto. J. M. Dent and Sons, Ltd. 1930-1934.

Hudson
    Hudson, Derek. Thomas Barnes of The Times, with selections from his critical essays never before reprinted. Cambridge. University Press. 1943.

Hutchinson
    Hutchinson, Thomas, ed. Lyrical Ballads by William Wordsworth and S. T. Coleridge, 1798. Edited with certain poems of 1798 and an introduction and notes by Thomas Hutchinson. London. Duckworth and Co. 1898.

Ireland
    Ireland, Alexander. List of writings of Hazlitt and Leigh Hunt. London. John Russell Smith. 1868.

Jackson
    Jackson, J. R. de J., ed. Coleridge: the Critical Heritage. London. Routledge & Kegan Paul. 1970.

Jerdan
    Jerdan, William. The Autobiography of William Jerdan. 4 vols. London. A. Hall. 1852-3.

Johnson
    Johnson, Catharine Bodham Donne. William Bodham Donne and His Friends. London. Methuen and Company. 1905.

Kempson
    Kempson, E. G. H. Archivist, Marlborough College, England.

Kitchin
    Kitchin, George. A Survey of Burlesque and Parody in English. Edinburgh. Oliver and Boyd. 1931.

Koszul
    Koszul, A. 'Coleridgiana'. Revue Anglo-Américaine [Paris], VII (1929-30), 247-253, 327-335.

L. C. Catalog
    Association of Research Libraries. Catalog of Books represented by Library of Congress Printed Cards. Ann Arbor, Michigan. Edwards Brothers, Inc. 1944--.

SOURCES OF ATTRIBUTIONS

Landré   Landré, Louis. Leigh Hunt (1784-1859). Contributions à l'histoire du romantisme anglais. 2 vols. Paris. Société d'Edition 'Les Belles-Lettres'. 1935-1936.

Little   Little, G. L. "Christabess: by S. T. Colebritche, Esq." Modern Language Review [Cambridge], LVI (1961), pp. 215-220.

Lohrli   Lohrli, Anne. Household Words: A Weekly Journal 1850-1859. University of Toronto Press. 1973.

McGuire   McGuire, Richard Len. The Monthly Magazine 1797-1843. Politics and Literature in Transition. Unpublished Ph. D. dissertation. Rice. Houston. 1968.

Masson   Masson, David. The Collected Writings of Thomas De Quincey. New and enlarged edition. 14 vols. Edinburgh. Adam and Charles Black. 1889.

Mineka   Mineka, Francis E. The Dissidence of Dissent: The Monthly Repository, 1806-1838. Chapel Hill. University of North Carolina Press. 1944.

Nangle   Nangle, Benjamin Christie. The Monthly Review. Second Series 1790-1815. Indexes of Contributors and Articles. Oxford. Clarendon Press. 1955.

NCBEL III   New Cambridge Bibliography of English Literature, ed. George Watson. Volume 3, 1800-1900. Cambridge University Press. 1969.

NUC   National Union Catalog, pre-1956 Imprints. London. Mansell. 1968--.

Nesbitt   Nesbitt, George Lyman. Benthamite Reviewing: the First Twelve Years of the Westminster Review, 1824-1836. New York. Columbia University Press. 1934.

Sources of Attributions

Partridge   Partridge, Eric. The French Romantics'
             Knowledge of English Literature
             (1820-1848). Paris. E. Champion.
             1924.

Pochmann   Pochmann, Henry A. German Culture in
             America. Philosophical and Literary
             Influences 1600-1900. Madison. Uni-
             versity of Wisconsin Press. 1957.

Poole   Poole, William Frederick. An Index to
             Periodical Literature. New York.
             C. B. Norton. 1853--

Potter Collection   Notebooks of clippings in the Keats
             Memorial Room, Heath Public Library,
             Hampstead, London.

Raysor   Raysor, Thomas Middleton, ed. Cole-
             ridge's Miscellaneous Criticism.
             Cambridge. Harvard University Press.
             1936.

Raysor, 1930, 1960   Raysor, Thomas Middleton, ed. Cole-
             ridge, Samuel Taylor. Shakespearean
             Criticism. 2 vols. Cambridge. Har-
             vard University Press. 1930. Lon-
             don. J. M. Dent; New York, Dutton.
             1960, 1964.

Reid   Reid, J. C. Coventry Patmore. London.
             Routledge & Kegan Paul. 1957.

Robinson, H. C.   Robinson, Henry Crabb. Diary, Reminis-
             cences and Correspondence, ed.
             Thomas Sadler. 2 vols. London.
             Macmillan; Boston. Fields, Osgood &
             Co. 1869.

Rogers   Rogers, Winfield H. Satire in English
             Prose Fiction 1806-1832. Unpublished
             Ph.D. dissertation. Harvard. Cam-
             bridge. 1932.

Sanders   Sanders, Charles R. Coleridge and the
             Broad Church Movement. Durham, N. C.
             Duke University Press. 1942. Lon-
             don. Cambridge University Press.
             1943.

Sources of Attributions

Schneider   Schneider, Elisabeth. 'The Unknown Reviewer of Christabel: Jeffrey, Hazlitt, Tom Moore'. PMLA [New York], LXX (1955), 417-432.

Schwartz   Schwartz, Lewis M. 'A New Review of Coleridge's Christabel'. Studies in Romanticism [Boston], IX (1970), 114-124.

Shaver   Shaver, Chester L. The Letters of William and Dorothy Wordsworth. Arranged and edited by the late Ernest de Selincourt. Second edition revised by Chester L. Shaver. Oxford. Clarendon Press. 1967--

Shine   Shine, Hill and Helen Brodwick Shine. The Quarterly Review under Gifford. Identification of contributors 1809-1824. Chapel Hill. University of North Carolina Press. 1949.

Simmons   Simmons, Jack. Southey. New Haven. Yale University Press. 1948.

Smith   Smith, Elsie. An Estimate of Wordsworth by His Contemporaries 1793-1822. Oxford. Basil Blackwell. 1932.

Snyder   Snyder, Alice D. Coleridge on Logic and Learning with Selections from his Unpublished Manuscripts. New Haven. Yale University Press. 1929.

Snyder, Blunden   Snyder, Alice D. 'American Comments on Coleridge a Century Ago'. Pp. 199-221 of Blunden, E. C. and Earl Griggs, eds. Coleridge: Studies by Several Hands on the Hundredth Anniversary of his Death. London. Constable. 1934. Reprinted New York. Russell and Russell. 1970.

St John-Stevas   Stevas, Norman St John Walter Bagehot. The Collected Works. The Literary Essays. Cambridge. Harvard University Press. 1965.

Sources of Attributions

Strout
    Strout, Alan Lang. 'A Bibliography of Articles in Blackwood's Magazine, 1817–1825'. Texas Technical College Library Bulletin. No. 5 [Lubbock, Texas], 1959. (Supersedes 'Samuel Taylor Coleridge and John Wilson of Blackwood's Magazine'. PMLA [New York], XLVII (1933), 100–128, but does not reprint evidence for all attributions.)

Tener
    Tener, Robert H. 'The Writings of Richard Holt Hutton: A Check-List of Identifications'. Victorian Periodicals Newsletter [Amherst, Mass.] No. 17, Sept. 1972; No. 20, June 1973.

Thompson
    Thompson, Robert Ellis. 'Professor George Allen, LL.D.'. Penn Monthly [Philadelphia], VII (1876), 562–583.

Watson, L.
    Watson, Lucy E. Coleridge at Highgate. London. Longman et al. 1925.

Watson
    Watson, Robert A., and Elizabeth Watson. George Gilfillan. London. Hodder and Stoughton. 1892.

Weatherford
    Weatherford, Willis Duke. Analytical Index to De Bow's Review with collaboration of Don L. Moore, N.p.N.d.

WI.
    The Wellesley Index to Victorian Periodicals, 1824–1900. ed. Walter E. Houghton. 4 vols., 2 published. Toronto. Toronto University Press. London. Routledge & Kegan Paul. 1966––. [Attributions which will appear in future volumes are drawn from Wellesley Index files.]

Whitmer
    Whitmer, Anne B. American Reaction to the Literary Criticism of Samuel Taylor Coleridge, 1830–1860. Unpublished Ph.D. dissertation. Ohio State University. Columbus. 1939.

Sources of Attributions

WPA   New York University. <u>American Periodi-</u>
                        <u>cal Index 1728-1870</u>. University Mi-
                        crofilms. 1960.

Zall   Zall, Paul. 'Sam Spitfire or, Coleridge
                        in <u>The Satirist</u>'. <u>Bulletin of the</u>
                        <u>New York Public Library</u>, LXXI (1967),
                        239-244.

Bibliography

1793

1 [MIDDLETON, THOMAS FANSHAW]. [Letter to the Editor]. <u>Country Spectator</u> [Gainsborough], No. 16 (22 Jan), pp. 125-32. Reprinted in his <u>Sermon and Charges</u>. London: Longman <u>et al.</u> (1824), p. ix.
   Letter includes sonnet to Cambridge mentioning Coleridge.

1794

2 ANON. 'The Fall of Robespierre'. <u>Critical Review</u>, 2nd Series XII, 206-2. Reprinted <u>Gazette of the United States</u>. [Philadelphia], VII, No. 117 (18 May 1795), [p. 2].
   Although subject not entirely suitable for drama, author shows promise of distinction.

3 _____. <u>The Observer, Part 1st being a transient glance at about forty youths of Bristol</u>. Bristol: J. Reed. Reprinted 'Coleridge and the "Forty Youths of Bristol"', <u>TLS</u>, No. 1393 (11 Oct 1928), p. 736.
   'S. T. Coler..ge' (pp. 14-15) praised for his scholarship and for his hatred of war and of the slave trade, but criticized for his manner of speech and appearance.

4 D. M. 'The Fall of Robespierre'. <u>Analytical Review</u>, XX, 480-1.
   Recent history a poor subject for drama, but Coleridge has been 'tolerably successful'.

1795

5 ANON. 'The Fall of Robespierre'. <u>British Critic</u>, V, 539-40.
   Language shows promise of distinction in tragedy.

6 _____. [Wedding Announcement]. <u>Bonner and Middleton's Bristol Journal</u>, No. 1110 (10 Oct), p. 3. Reprinted <u>Bristol Gazette</u>, No. 1433 (15 Oct 1795), p. 3; <u>Felix Farley's Bristol Journal</u>, No. 2432 (17 Oct 1795), p. 3.

1794-ANON.

(ANON.)
Notice of wedding of 'Mr. Coldridge [sic], of this city'.

7 ____. 'A Moral and Political Lecture Delivered at Bristol'. Critical Review, New Series XIII, 455.
Admirable style but defective argument.

8 HUCKS, J[OSEPH]. A Pedestrian Tour through North Wales. London: J. Debrett and J. Edwards.
Series of letters by one of Coleridge's companions on 1794 walking tour. Descriptions interspersed with social criticism. No explicit mention of Coleridge.

9 WRANGHAM, FRANCIS. Poems. London: J. Mawman.
Notes (p. v) that the 'very elegant translation' of 'Hendecasyllabi ad Brutonam' is by Coleridge.

1796

10 [AIKIN, JOHN]. 'Joan of Arc'. Monthly Review, XIX, 361-8.
Coleridge's contribution of some 400 lines contains 'much striking and varied imagery'.
Attribution: Nangle

11 ____. 'Poems on Various Subjects'. Monthly Review, XX, 194-9.
Makes good the expectations raised by Coleridge in Joan of Arc. Aikin singles out Monody on the Death of Chatterton and Religious Musings, finding the latter 'on top of the scale of sublimity'.
Attribution: Nangle

12 ANON. 'Conciones ad Populum...The Plot Discovered'. Analytical Review, XXIII, 90-2.
Coleridge agrees with Robespierre on ends but differs as to means.

13 ____. 'Poems on Various Subjects'. Analytical Review, XXIII, 610-12.
Despite occasional turgidity and deficient metre, poems show imagination and promise. Religious Musings valuable for ideas.

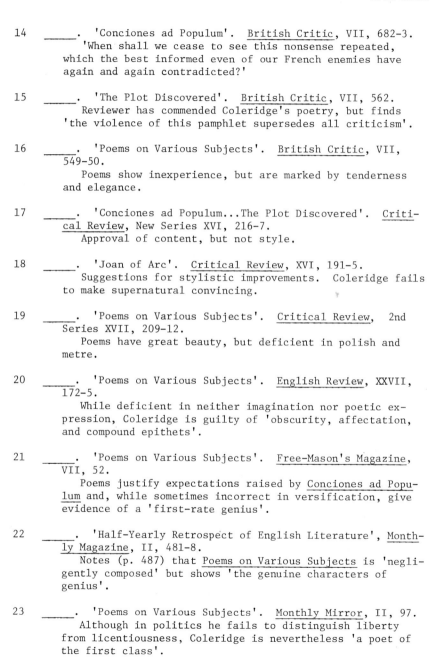

14   _____. 'Conciones ad Populum'. British Critic, VII, 682-3.
      'When shall we cease to see this nonsense repeated,
      which the best informed even of our French enemies have
      again and again contradicted?'

15   _____. 'The Plot Discovered'. British Critic, VII, 562.
      Reviewer has commended Coleridge's poetry, but finds
      'the violence of this pamphlet supersedes all criticism'.

16   _____. 'Poems on Various Subjects'. British Critic, VII,
      549-50.
      Poems show inexperience, but are marked by tenderness
      and elegance.

17   _____. 'Conciones ad Populum...The Plot Discovered'. Criti-
      cal Review, New Series XVI, 216-7.
      Approval of content, but not style.

18   _____. 'Joan of Arc'. Critical Review, XVI, 191-5.
      Suggestions for stylistic improvements. Coleridge fails
      to make supernatural convincing.

19   _____. 'Poems on Various Subjects'. Critical Review, 2nd
      Series XVII, 209-12.
      Poems have great beauty, but deficient in polish and
      metre.

20   _____. 'Poems on Various Subjects'. English Review, XXVII,
      172-5.
      While deficient in neither imagination nor poetic ex-
      pression, Coleridge is guilty of 'obscurity, affectation,
      and compound epithets'.

21   _____. 'Poems on Various Subjects'. Free-Mason's Magazine,
      VII, 52.
      Poems justify expectations raised by Conciones ad Popu-
      lum and, while sometimes incorrect in versification, give
      evidence of a 'first-rate genius'.

22   _____. 'Half-Yearly Retrospect of English Literature', Month-
      ly Magazine, II, 481-8.
      Notes (p. 487) that Poems on Various Subjects is 'negli-
      gently composed' but shows 'the genuine characters of
      genius'.

23   _____. 'Poems on Various Subjects'. Monthly Mirror, II, 97.
      Although in politics he fails to distinguish liberty
      from licentiousness, Coleridge is nevertheless 'a poet of
      the first class'.

3

1796-B

24   B. [Coleridge's Monody]. Monthly Magazine, II, 614.
        Letter praising Coleridge's Monody elicits comments from
     Crito (II, 695-6), A. B. C. D. (IV, 427), and finally Cole-
     ridge himself (V, 8).

25   [ENFIELD, WILLIAM]. 'Conciones ad Populum...The Plot Discov-
        ered'. Monthly Review, XIX, 80-1.
        Both pamphlets are 'replete with violent anti-ministeri-
     al declamation, but not vulgar'.
        Attribution: Nangle

26   GRACCHUS, CAIUS, pseud. [Letter to The Watchman]. Bristol
        Gazette, No. 1454 (24 March), p. [2].
        This letter, which Coleridge reprinted and answered in
     The Watchman, criticizes 'the inconsistency in the charac-
     ter of this philosopher'.

27   HEATH, CHARLES. Excursion down the Wye, from Ross to Mon-
        mouth. Monmouth. Printed and sold by him [C. Heath].
        Preface mentions Coleridge's 'beautiful poetry...deserv-
     ing [the] highest approbation'.

                              1797

28   ANON. ['Poems on Various Subjects']. Annual Register, XVII,
        265.
        Poems give proof of genius and taste. Particular men-
     tion of Monody on the Death of Chatterton, Song of the
     Pixies, and Religious Musings.

29   _____. 'Ode on the Departing Year'. Critical Review, XX,
        343-4.
        In attempting to imitate Pindar, Coleridge 'too fre-
     quently mistakes bombast and obscurity for sublimity'.

30   _____. 'Ode on the Departing Year'. Monthly Mirror, III,
        221.
        Although occasionally 'affected' and 'unintelligible', Ode
     'breathes genuine spirit of poesy'.

31   _____. 'Ode on the Departing Year'. Monthly Visitor, I, 188-
        90.
        A first-class poet, but as a politician 'we could wish
     him less violent'.

32   ____. 'Poems by S. T. Coleridge'. Monthly Visitor, II,
        169-80.
            'In a poet of such various yet uniform excellence, it
        would be tedious to seek for defects'. Prefers 1796 ver-
        sion of Ode to the Departing Year.

33   DYER, GEORGE. The Poet's Fate, a Poetical Dialogue. London:
        G. G. and J. Robinson.
            Note 33, on pantisocracy, describes Coleridge as 're-
        markable for a rich and powerful imagination'.

34   [HAMILTON, ALEXANDER]. 'Ode on the Departing Year'. Monthly
        Review, XXII, 342-3.
            Despite signs of extravagance and haste, poem shows true
        genius.
            Attribution: Nangle

35   LAMB, CHARLES. 'Lines Addressed, from London, to Sara and
        S. T. C. at Bristol, in the Summer of 1796'. Monthly Maga-
        zine, III, 54-5.
            Poem on visit to Clevedon.

36   LLOYD, CHARLES. 'Lines to S. T. Colridge [sic]'. Poems, by
        S. T. Coleridge, 2nd Ed. to which are now added Poems by
        Charles Lamb and Charles Lloyd. Bristol: J. Cottle; Lon-
        don: Messrs. Robinson, pp. 179-82.
            Forty-four lines addressed to 'My Coleridge'.

37   [NORGATE, THOMAS STARLING]. 'Half-Yearly Retrospect of the
        State of Domestic Literature'. Monthly Magazine, IV,
        118-21.
            Brief notice of Ode to the Departing Year (p. 120) which
        reveals 'ardent conception, and a great command of poetical
        language'.
            Attribution: McGuire

1798

38   [AIKIN, JOHN]. 'Half-Yearly Retrospect of Domestic Litera-
        ture'. Monthly Magazine, VI, 493-520.
            Auncient Mariner [sic] an exception to generally suc-
        cessful imitation of style of early poets in Lyrical Bal-
        lads.
            Attribution: Campbell, Athenaeum, No. 3236 (10 May
        1890), pp. 599-600.

39   [AIKIN, JOHN]. 'Lyrical Ballads'. Monthly Mirror, VI, 224-5.
        Briefly praises the language of nature as a corrective
    to the 'Della Cruscan' style.
        Attribution: E. Smith

40   No entry.

41   ANON. 'Lyrical Ballads'. Analytical Review, XXVIII, 583-7.
        The Ancient Mariner 'has more of the extravagance of a
    mad German poet, than of the simplicity of our ancient bal-
    lad writers'.

42   _____. 'Poems by S. T. Coleridge'. Critical Review, 2nd
    Series XXIII, 266-8.
        Reaffirms judgment of reviews of Poems on Various Sub-
    jects and Ode to the Departing Year. (Critical Review,
    1796, 1797).

43   _____. 'Literary Memoirs of Living Authors'. Gentleman's
    Magazine, LXVIII, 773-6.
        Review of Rivers (1798) facetiously compares Coleridge
    with Thelwall and Horne Tooke as democrats.

44   _____. 'Fears in Solitude'. Monthly Visitor, V, 417-20.
        Extensive quotation, with the comment that 'this publi-
    cation will not diminish the fame which he has already ob-
    tained'.

45   _____. 'Poems by S. T. Coleridge'. Scientific Magazine and
    Free-Mason's Repository, XI, 128.
        Notes Coleridge's acknowledgment of the value of criti-
    cisms of earlier editions.

46   [CANNING, GEORGE]. ['The New Morality']. Anti-Jacobin,
    No. 36 (9 July), pp. 282-7. Reprinted with title and Gill-
    ray's illustration in Anti-Jacobin Review, I (1798), 115.
    Reprinted Poetry of the Anti-Jacobin, London: J. Wright
    (1799), 220-40. Reprinted with additional notes Beauties
    of the Anti-Jacobin, London: J. Plymsell (1799), pp. 293-
    311.
        Satirical poem by Canning, Ellis and Frere. Canning's
    annotations in his copy, now in the British Museum, iden-
    tify the lines referring to Coleridge (282-7) as among
    those which he contributed. Title added in Anti-Jacobin
    Review in which poem was accompanied by Gillray's satirical
    engraving (Gillray, 1798, q.v.). Reprinted in The Beauties
    of the Anti-Jacobin with note attacking Coleridge and in-
    cluding charge subsequently repeated by others, that he has

(CANNING, GEORGE)
    abandoned his family and left the country. Hazlitt (1818)
    attributes note to John Gifford.

47   D. M. S. 'Fears in Solitude'. Analytical Review, XXVIII,
        590-2.
            Imagery sparse but free from extravagance.

48   FABRICIUS, PSEUD. 'The Anarchists--An Ode'. Anti-Jacobin
        Review, I, 365-7.
            A satirical poem. Eight lines on p. 366 are an attack
        on Coleridge, Southey, Lloyd, and Lamb.

49   GILLRAY, J[AMES]. 'New Morality--or--The Promised Installment
        of the High Priest of the Theophilanthropes, with the Hom-
        age of Leviathan and his Suite'. Anti-Jacobin Review, I.
        Frontispiece.
            A satirical engraving to accompany Canning's 'New Moral-
        ity' (1798). Gillray portrays Lloyd and Lamb as singing
        toads, Coleridge and Southey with asses' heads.

50   HUCKS, J. 'Lines Addressed to S. T. Coleridge'. Poems. Cam-
        bridge: B. Flower, pp. 145-51.
            Versified recollections of 1795 Welsh tour with Cole-
        ridge.

51   LLOYD, CHARLES. Edmund Oliver. 2 vols. Bristol: Bulgin and
        Rosser.
            Coleridge the model for the protagonist of this novel.
        Lloyd's exploitation of personal confidences led to es-
        trangement.

52   _____. 'To *******'. Blank Verse, By Charles Lloyd and
        Charles Lamb. London: John and Arthur Arch, pp. 7-13.
            Footnote on p. 9 identifies lines 32-41 as allusion to
        pantisocracy.

53   [RIVERS, DAVID]. 'Coleridge, S. T., Esq.' Literary Memoirs
        of Living Authors of Great Britain. 2 vols. R. Faulder.
        I, 105-7.
            Coleridge, whose 'fame as a poet has lately arisen with
        such splendour', has 'experienced the discouragement of
        disappointed hope' with the failure of The Watchman.
            Attribution: DAPL

1798–SOUTHEY

54 [SOUTHEY, ROBERT]. 'Lyrical Ballads'. Critical Review, 2nd
Series XXIV, 197–204.
The Ancient Mariner is 'absurd and unintelligible...a
Dutch attempt at German sublimity...a poem of little
merit'.
Attribution: Curry

54A [WORDSWORTH, WILLIAM]. 'Advertisement'. Lyrical Ballads.
Bristol: Biggs and Cottle; London. J. & A. Arch.
Includes a brief comment on The Ancient Mariner.

1799

55 ANON. 'Fears in Solitude'. Critical Review, 2nd Series XXVI,
472–5.
All three poems [Fears in Solitude, Frost at Midnight,
and France: An Ode] are 'very beautiful'. Coleridge has
not, as might appear, recanted his former principles.

56 _____. 'Fears in Solitude'. Monthly Mirror, VII, 36.
'The author's Fears are, perhaps, not highly honourable
to his feelings as a Briton'.

57 _____. ['Fears in Solitude']. New Annual Register, XIX, 310.
Serious sentiments and 'harmonious, elegant, and ani-
mated' poetry. Frost at Midnight singled out.

58 _____. ['Lyrical Ballads']. New Annual Register, XIX,
309–10.
Some passages 'entitle the author to a very respectable
rank among modern poets'.
Attribution: Nangle

59 _____. 'Lyrical Ballads'. Naval Chronicle, II, 328–30,
418–20.
Specifically mentions only The Ancient Mariner; the
first and fourth parts are reproduced. Lyrical Ballads
show uncommon merit and promise.

60 _____. 'Fears in Solitude'. New London Review, I, 98–100.
Fears in Solitude is ridiculous and France: An Ode reveals 'gross plagiarism' from Samson Agonistes. Frost at
Midnight is obscure, 'half poetry, half nonsense'. Coleridge nevertheless shows promise.

61 _____. 'Lyrical Ballads'. New London Review, I, 33-5.
Chiefly an attack on the Advertisement. Uses lines of
The Ancient Mariner as an example of obscurity.

62 [BURNEY, CHARLES]. 'Lyrical Ballads'. Monthly Review, XXIX,
202-10.
The Ancient Mariner 'is the strangest story of a cock
and a bull that we ever saw on paper but The Nightingale
sings a strain of true and beautiful poetry'.
Attribution: Bodleian copy

63 MOODY, CHRISTOPHER LAKE. 'Fears in Solitude'. Monthly Review, New Series XXIX, 43-7.
Fears in Solitude quoted and strongly recommended for
its truth.
Attribution: Nangle

64 [WRANGHAM, FRANCIS]. 'Fears in Solitude'. British Critic,
XIII, 662-3.
Objects to Coleridge's politics but finds Frost at Mid-
night 'entitled to much praise'.
Attribution: Hutchinson

65 _____. 'Lyrical Ballads'. British Critic, XIV, 364-9.
Considers the middle part of The Ancient Mariner too
long and confused in imagery. Suspects Coleridge is author
of whole volume.
Attribution: Hutchinson; Hanson

1800

66 ANON. 'The Piccolomini...The Death of Wallenstein'. Critical Review, New Series XXX, 175-85.
Translation unites fidelity and elegance, but is sometimes careless. Coleridge 'is the founder of a distinct
school in poetry'.

67 _____. Lyrical Ballads. Gazette of the United States
[Philadelphia], XVIII, No. 1455 (9 Aug), p. 1.
Attributes the whole of the 'elegant little collection'
to Coleridge and prints 'We Are Seven'.

68 _____. 'The History of Literature for 1800'. Historical,
Biographical, Literary and Scientific Magazine, II, 179.
'The translation of Wallenstein is...incomparably
excellent'.

1800-ANON.

69   ANON. 'Mr. Robert Southey'. Public Characters, I, 168-75.
        Includes a brief account of Southey's first acquaintance
      with Coleridge and of pantisocracy. Published in 1800
      though dated 1799.

70   [FERRIAR, JOHN]. 'The Piccolomini...The Death of Wallen-
        stein'. Monthly Review, XXXIII, 127-30.
        A 'languid translation'.
        Attribution: Bodleian copy

71   [HEATH, WILLIAM]. 'Lyrical Ballads'. Anti-Jacobin Review, V
        434 [misprinted as 334].
        The volume 'has genius, taste, elegance, wit and imagery
      of the most beautiful kind'. Ancyent Marinere warmly
      noticed.
        Attribution: Hayden

72   M. R. 'Present State of the Manners, Society, &c. &c. of the
        Metropolis of England'. Monthly Magazine, X, 35-8.
        Article on provincial society includes 'Coleridge, the
      exquisite poet' in a list of distinguished men born in
      Devon.

73   [SADLER, ROBERT]. The Haunted Farmer. Chippenham: J. M.
        Coombs.
        The motto on the title page of this political poem is
      adapted from lines 257-62 of The Ancient Mariner.
        Attribution: B. Mus. Cat.

74   WORDSWORTH, W. 'Note to The Ancient Mariner p. 155'.
        Lyrical Ballads, with other Poems. 2 vols. London: Long-
        man et al. I, 214-5.
        This second edition includes Wordsworth's criticism of
      The Ancient Mariner which was omitted in 1802 and there-
      after.

1801

75   ANON. The Spirit of the Farmers' Museum and Lay Preacher's
        Gazette. Walpole, New Hampshire.
        Introductory note to Wordsworth's 'Goody Blake and Harry
      Gill' (p. 116) praises the author of Lyrical Ballads and
      condemns the 'frenchpaste and tinsel of the childish Cole-
      ridges, Southeys and Merrys'.

76 _____. 'Wallenstein'. British Critic, XVIII, 542-4.
Finds the plays dull and tedious.

77 _____. 'The Drama'. Monthly Magazine, X, 611.
Flyleaf for volume dated 1800, but issued Jan 1801.
A brief notice of Coleridge's 'affected and unequal'
translation of Schiller.

78 DENNIE, JOSEPH. 'An Author's Evenings'. Port folio [Phila-
delphia], I, 263, 274, 324.
Excerpt (p. 263) from preface to Poems (1797) with a
comment that Coleridge's poetry is more admirable than his
politics. Article on Joan of Arc (p. 274) describes Coleridge and Southey as 'inflamed with French liberty', but
(p. 324) if they and Lamb would learn from Cowper it would
'spare us from flimsy poetry and abominable politics'.

79 ROBINSON, MARY. 'Mrs. Robinson to the Poet Coldridge [sic]'.
Memoirs of the late Mrs. Robinson. 4 vols. London: R.
Phillips. IV, 145-9. Reprinted Poetical Works of the late
Mrs. Mary Robinson. 3 vols. London: R. Phillips (1806).
I, 225-9.
Seventy-two lines addressed to 'thee, O favour'd child
of minstrelsy, sublimely wild' (lines 69-70).

79a STOCK, DR. JOHN. 'Foreign Literature'. Port folio [Phila-
delphia], I (1801), 37-8.
Review of Coleridge's translation of Schiller finds some
'almost Shakespearean' felicities.

80 [STODDART, JOHN]. 'Lyrical Ballads'. British Critic, XVII,
125-32. Reprinted Port folio [Philadelphia], I (1801),
188-9.
Identifies Coleridge as the 'friend' responsible for
The Ancient Mariner and other poems.
Attribution: Shaver

81 SURR, T[HOMAS] S[KINNER]. Splendid Misery, a Novel. 3 vols.
London: T. Hurst.
In his preface, Surr notes that the hero is modelled on
Wallenstein, and that he has borrowed a scene (Piccolomini
II, lines 80-109) from the translation of 'My School-
Fellow, Coleridge'.

82   THELWALL, JOHN. 'Lines, Written at Bridgwater, in Somerset-
      shire, on 27 July 1797'. Poems, Chiefly in Retirement.
      Hereford: W. H. Parker, pp. 126-32.
          Thelwall describes (pp. 129-30) Wordsworth and Coleridge
      gardening 'while, eager one propounds, and listens one,
      weighing each pregnant word, and pondering fit reply....'

                              1802

83   [BURNEY, CHARLES]. 'Lyrical Ballads'. Monthly Review,
      XXXVIII, 209.
          Reaffirms judgment in his review of first edition
      (1799).

84   [JEFFREY, FRANCIS]. 'Thalaba, The Destroyer. By Robert
      Southey'. Edinburgh Review, I, 63-83.
          Begins (pp. 63-71) with a long and indiscriminate attack
      on the style and supposed theories of the 'Lake Poets'.
      Attribution: WI

85   SEWARD, ANNA. 'To The Editor of The Poetical Register'.
      Poetical Register for 1801, I, 475-86.
          Discussion of Southey's Thalaba notes (p. 476) that 'the
      odd, but highly ingenious, and original poem, The Ancient
      Mariner, suggested much of the imagery'.

86   WARNER, RICHARD. A Tour Through the Northern Counties of Eng-
      land and the Borders of Scotland. 2 vols. Bath: R.
      Crutwell.
          Warner's glowing comments on Coleridge in Bristol (I,
      14) and Keswick (II, 100-01) aroused Coleridge's caustic
      comment (Griggs, Letters, II, 826).

                              1803

87   ANON. 'Poems by S. T. Coleridge. Third Edition'. Annual Re-
      view, II, 556.
          'Novel and picturesque personification, sometimes almost
      expanding into allegory, forms perhaps the most prominent
      and most beautiful feature of the highly figurative style
      of Mr. Coleridge'.

88   _____. 'An Author's Evenings'. Port folio [Philadelphia],
      III, 209-10.
          Love, misattributed to Wordsworth, reprinted and praised
      for its truth and beauty.

1804

89 CANTABR, pseud. 'On Sentiments exprest by Mr. Coleridge, in
the Preface to his Sonnets, Adverse to the Petrarcan
Model'. Monthly Mirror, XVII, 192.
    A sonnet begging Coleridge not to discard the 'Petrarcan
[sic] model'.

90 [DYER, GEORGE] E. R. 'Cantabrigiana. No. CXLVIII -
Mr. Coleridge'. Monthly Magazine, XVII, 125.
    Anecdote of a foolish student who thought himself supe-
rior to Coleridge since he had won two prizes at Cambridge
to Coleridge's one.
    Attribution: Griggs, Letters, II, 1091

91 [SCOTT, WALTER]. 'The Works of Thomas Chatterton'. Edinburgh
Review, IV, 214-30.
    Monody shows in many places the talent which he 'always
possesses, and sometimes chuses to display'.
    Attribution: WI

1805

92 ANON. 'The Lay of the Last Minstrel...by Walter Scott'.
Critical Review, 3rd Series V, 225-49.
    Scott's dialogue of spirits is compared (p. 229) with
'a certain frantic production entitled...The Ancient
Mariner'.

93 _____. 'Metrical Tales...by Southey'. Literary Journal, V,
157-65.
    Southey, Wordsworth and Coleridge miss 'the real senti-
ments and language of the common people' (p. 160).

94 VISCONTI. 'Present State of English Poetry'. Literary Tab-
let [Hanover, N. H.], III, 82. Reprinted: Literary
Miscellany [Cambridge, Mass.], II (1806), 369-74.
    Coleridge is 'the boast of many a vulgar mind, but, if
the Commons honor him, the Lords·reject, the Prince dis-
claims him'.

1806

95 ANON. 'Madoc, By R. Southey'. General Review of British and
Foreign Literature, I, 505-26.

1806–ANON.

(ANON.)
Begins with a very favourable estimate of Southey,
Wordsworth and Coleridge who are together credited with 'a
revivification of our poetical character'.

96 _____. 'For the Port folio'. Port folio [Philadelphia], II,
105–07.
Coleridge's Monody shows poetical genius despite 'erroneous' political views.

97 _____. 'Poems. By S. T. Coleridge'. Poetical Register for
1804, IV, 485.
'Not often equalled' for 'energy of thought, splendour
of diction and command of language'.

98 ROBINSON, MARY. 'Ode Inscribed to the Infant Son of S. T.
Coleridge, Esq.' Poetical Works of the Late Mrs. Mary
Robinson. 3 vols. London: Richard Phillips. I, 221–5.
Poem expressing hope that Derwent Coleridge will inherit
his father's genius.

1808

99 [JEFFREY, FRANCIS]. 'Poems, by the Reverend George Crabbe'.
Edinburgh Review, XII, 131–51. Reprinted in his Contributions to the Edinburgh Review. 4 vols. London: Longman
et al. (1844). III, 3–23.
Wordsworth, Southey, and Coleridge are contrasted (p.
133) with Crabbe as 'a misguided fraternity...labouring to
bring back our poetry to the fantastical oddity and puling
childishness of Withers, Quarles, or Marvel [sic]'.

100 [MANT, RICHARD]. The Simpliciad: A Satirico-Didactic Poem.
London: John Joseph Stockdale.
Satire on Coleridge and others.
Attribution: NCBEL

101 W. M. T. 'Essays on Literature and Humanity No. 1'. Cabinet,
III, 162–5.
Essay on sonnets discusses Coleridge among others.

1809

102   ANON. The American Poetical Miscellany. Philadelphia. Robert Johnson.
        Prints The Ancient Mariner with a vague but favourable comment and believes it 'to be from the pen of the Rev. Mr. Coleridge'.

103   [BYRON, LORD]. English Bards and Scotch Reviewers: A Satire. London: James Cawthorn.
        Coleridge is ridiculed in lines 139-48.

104   [DENNIE, JOSEPH, EDITOR]. 'New Periodical Paper'. Port folio [Philadelphia], Series 3, II, 104-07.
        Editorial discussion of the prospectus of The Friend.

105   JACKSON, EZEKIEL, pseud. 'Account of the Manuscripts of the late Sam Spitfire, Author'. Satirist, V, 538-44. Sequel to Jackson's 'Melancholy Exit', q.v.

106   JACKSON, EZEKIEL, pseud. 'Melancholy Exit of Sam. Spitfire, Author'. Satirist, V, 419-24.
        In this and its sequel ('Account of the Manuscripts...'), Spitfire resembles Coleridge only in being a Cambridge radical and pantisocrat.

107   [MANNERS, GEORGE]. 'The Bards of the Lake'. Satirist, V, 548-56.
        Sketch includes 'Breeches', a parody of Coleridge, as well as parodies of Wordsworth, Lamb, Lloyd, and Southey. Attribution: Zall

1810

108   ANON. 'Commentary on Coleridge's Three Graves'. Monthly Mirror, New Series VIII, 26-31, 98-105, 186-96.
        Detailed and sarcastic discussion of the poem, which had appeared in The Friend, ridiculing its 'simplicity' and condemning its moral effect.

109   [SCOTT, WALTER]. 'General View of Literature, of the Living Poets of Great Britain'. Edinburgh Annual Register, for 1808, I, 417-43. Reprinted Port folio [Philadelphia], VI, (1811), 555-68; Morgenblatt für gebildete Stände [Stuttgart], No. 148 (21 June 1811), p. 591; Ulster Register [Belfast], II (1817), 433-6.

(SCOTT, WALTER)
Possessed of 'exquisite talents', Coleridge (pp. 427–8) .
lacks 'perseverance' and 'sound sense'. Apart from a few
'unequalled' lines, his poetry mixes the terrible with the
disgusting, the tender with the ludicrous. He has now
'totally abandoned poetry for the mists of political metaphysics'.
Attribution: Curry

110   S. T. C., **pseud**. 'Walter Scott'. Courier, No. 4788 (15 Sept),
[p. 3]; No. 4791 (21 Sept) [p. 2]. Partially reprinted by
T. M. Raysor. Modern Language Notes [Baltimore], XLIII
(1928), 378.
Letter from 'S. T. C.' accusing Scott of plagiarism is
categorically repudiated at Coleridge's request, with report of his view of imitation.

1811

111   ANON. [Coleridge's Lectures]. Morning Chronicle, no. 13271
(20 Nov), unpaged; no. 13276 (26 Nov), unpaged; no. 13279
(29 Nov), unpaged, reprinted Courier, no. 5117 (30 Nov
1811) p. 4; no. 13288 (10 Dec), unpaged; no. 13291 (13 Dec),
unpaged, reprinted Courier, no. 5129 (14 Dec 1811) p. 4;
no. 13294 (17 Dec), unpaged.
Reports of lectures I, III, IV, VII, VIII, IX (1811–
1812), of which III, IV, VII and VIII are reprinted in Raysor (1930, 1960). Lecture VII is attributed by Raysor to
Henry Crabb Robinson.

112   _____. 'English Bards and Scotch Reviewers'. Port folio
[Philadelphia], 3rd Series V, 446.
'...the sighing and simpering Coleridge is thus brought
in contact with his subject' in Byron's lines on an ass.

113   [FOSTER, JOHN]. 'The Friend'. Eclectic Review, VII, 912–31.
Reprinted in his Contributions, Biographical, Literary and
Philosophical to the Eclectic Review, ed. Dr. Price, 2
vols. London: Ward (1844), I, 88–112; Critical Essays
contributed to the Eclectic Review by J. Foster, ed. J. E.
Ryland, 2 vols. London: Henry G. Bohn (1856), II, 1–24.
The difficulty of The Friend results from its mode of
publication and from Coleridge's manner of thinking and
writing, of which Foster gives a careful and sympathetic
analysis. This is the only serious review of the original
Friend and is, by a number of years, the first significant
discussion in print of Coleridge as a thinker.

114   [HUNT, LEIGH]. 'The Feast of the Poets'. Reflector, II,
       313-23. Reprinted his The Feast of the Poets with Notes,
       and Other Pieces in Verse. London: Cawthorn (1814),
       pp. 1-21. Reprinted London: Gale and Fenner (1815).
           This satirical poem contains a 5-line passage on Cole-
       ridge, to which Hunt added copious notes in the later edi-
       tions. Alterations in both text and notes reflect Hunt's
       changing and increasingly favourable view of Coleridge.

115   [JEFFREY, FRANCIS]. 'The Dramatic Works of John Ford'.
       Edinburgh Review, XVIII, 276-304. Reprinted his Contribu-
       tions to the Edinburgh Review. 4 vols. London: Longman
       et al. (1844), II, 284-314.
           Mentions (p. 283) Coleridge among others who copy the
       manners of 'older poets' but are 'remarkably and offensive-
       ly artificial'.

116   [ROBINSON, HENRY CRABB]. [Mr. Coleridge's Lectures on Poetry].
       Times, No. 8451 (19 Nov), p. 3.
           Coleridge is 'original in his views' and 'very different
       from critics in general'.
           Attribution: Raysor

117   SEWARD, ANNA. Letters...written between the years 1784 and
       1807. 6 vols. Edinburgh: Constable.
           Letters in IV and V discuss in detail the author's re-
       sponses to Coleridge's early poems, especially Ode to the
       Departing Year.

118   [SOUTHEY, ROBERT]. 'Bell and Lancaster's Systems of Educa-
       tion'. Quarterly Review, VI, 264-304. Reprinted and en-
       larged in The Origin, Nature, and Object of the New System
       of Education. London: Murray (1812).
           Mention (p. 285) of Coleridge's remarks on Lancaster in
       his 1808 lecture on education at the Royal Institute.
           Attribution: Shine

1812

119   [AMPHLETT, JAMES]. 'Mr. Coleridge'. Rifleman, No. 3 (19
       Jan), p. 21. Reprinted his Newspaper Press. London:
       Whittaker (1860), p. 13; reprinted by William E. A. Axon,
       Library, 3rd Series II (1911), 37-9.
           General discussion of the Shakespeare lectures of 1811-
       1812, with emphasis on lecture seven, 'one of the most in-
       tellectual treats which London has experienced for a number
       of years'.

1812-ANON.

120   ANON. 'Theatrical Examiner'. Examiner, No. 215 (9 Feb),
      p. 91.
           Coleridge is not 'worthy of poets he pretends to ana-
      lyze' in his lectures.

121   _____. 'Intelligence--Literary, Philosophical'. General
      Chronicle and Literary Magazine, IV, 310-12.
           Brief general comment on Coleridge's 1811-1812 lectures,
      with a detailed account of lecture IV.

122   _____. 'Ode, to the learned author of a celebrated work on
      The Art of Carving'. Rifleman, No. 24 (14 June), p. 197.
           Poem [to John Trusler] suggests that Coleridge should
      lecture on 'The Art of Starving'.

123   _____. 'The Rejected Bards--Genus Irritabile'. Satirist, or
      Monthly Meteor, XI, 375-83.
           Poem in which Coleridge is one of several poets sati-
      rized.

124   DYER, GEORGE. 'The Nightingale'. Poetics. 2 vols. London:
      J. Johnson, I, 141.
           Note refers to Coleridge's 'five lines' on the nightin-
      gale.

125   [JEFFREY, FRANCIS]. 'Rejected Addresses'. Edinburgh Review,
      XX, 434-51. Reprinted his Contributions to the Edinburgh
      Review. 4 vols. London: Longman et al. (1844), IV,
      470-86.
           While parody is 'unquestionably Lakish' it has none of
      Coleridge's special traits.

126   [SHELLEY, PERCY BYSSHE]. 'The Devil's Walk. A Ballad'.
      [Barnstable]. Reprinted his Poetical Works. 4 vols. Lon-
      don: Moxon (1839), III, 83-6.
           Imitation of The Devil's Thoughts, published as anony-
      mous broadside.

127   [SMITH, HORACE and JAMES SMITH]. 'Playhouse Musings, by
      S. T. C.' Rejected Addresses. London: John Miller,
      pp. 73-7.
           A parody of Coleridge's style.
           Reviewed: [F. Hodgson]. Monthly Review, LXIX, 288-98
      (attribution: Bodleian copy), reprinted Analectic Magazine
      [Philadelphia], New Series I (1813), 209-19; [John Wilson
      Croker]. Quarterly Review, VIII, 172-81 (attribution:
      Shine); Satirist, or Monthly Meteor, XI, 452-6; and
      no. 125.

128   T. T. 'Mr. Coleridge'. <u>Rifleman</u>, No. 4 (26 Jan), p. 30.
Only known account of Lecture XVI, on Milton, in 1811-12
series. Possibly by Thomas Talfourd.

1813

129   ANON. ['Remorse']. <u>Analectic Magazine</u> [Philadelphia], New
Series I, 533-4.
Review approves of moral and style but descriptive pas-
sages make play too long.

130   _____. 'Remorse'. <u>Belle Assemblée</u>, New Series VII, 81-5.
Brief, favourable account of performance, with extensive extracts. Finds poetry 'vigorous rather than elegant', action, simple, though varied, and characters, 'upon
the whole, natural'.

131   _____. 'Mr. Coleridge'. <u>Bristol Gazette</u>, Nos. 2400-3 (4, 11,
18, 25 Nov).
Partially reprinted <u>Courier</u>, Nos. 5486, 5510, 5512 (19
Nov, 17, 20 Dec 1813). Lecture I reprinted as 'On the
Characteristics of Shakspeare' in Nathan Drake, <u>Memorials
of Shakspeare</u>. London: Colburn (1828), pp. [73]-86; reviewed: <u>Athenaeum</u>, Nos. 21, 43, (4 April, 20 Aug 1828),
pp. 320-1, 673-5. Lecture VII reprinted <u>Athenaeum</u>,
No. 4246 (13 March 1909), pp. 316-7. Reprinted Raysor
(1930, 1960).
Reports of Coleridge's 1813 Bristol lectures on Shakespeare and on education.

132   _____. 'Remorse'. <u>Bristol Gazette</u>, XLVI, No. 2362 (4 Feb),
p. [4].
Factual summary without critical comment.

133   _____. 'Theatre, <u>First Impressions</u>'. <u>Bristol Gazette</u>,
No. 2403 (25 Nov), p. [4].
Brief discussion of imitation and parody in <u>Rejected
Addresses</u>. Doubts whether 'picturesque imagination and
sublime metaphysic' of Coleridge's poetry can be bur-
lesqued.

134   _____. 'Theatre--<u>Remorse</u>'. <u>Bristol Gazette</u>, XLVI, No. 2370
(8 Apr), p. [3].
Finds focus of play in an 'inward struggle of the soul'.

135   ANON. 'Theatre'. Bath Journal, LXX, No. 3584 (29 Mar), p. 3.
      Brief review of Remorse, chiefly a description of audi-
      ence.

136   _____. 'Drury Lane Theatre'. Bristol Mirror, XXXIX,
      No. 2225 (30 Jan), p. 4.
      Brief notice of favourable reception of Remorse.

137   _____. 'Remorse, A Tragedy, in Five Acts'. British Review,
      IV, 361-70.
      Success of play partly due to current popular interest
      in Spain. Despite many good passages, the plot is tedious
      and shallow and the characterization, weak.

138   _____. 'Remorse'. Cambridge Chronicle and Journal and Hun-
      tingdonshire Gazette, No. 2623 (29 Jan), p. 2.
      Brief notice of favourable reception of play.

139   _____. 'Remorse'. Country Magazine, and Quarterly Chronicle,
      for Hull, No. 2 (Apr), 184-8.
      Summary of plot, with the judgment that work has little
      to hold the playgoer, but much to delight the reader.

140   _____. 'Remorse'. Christian Observer, XII, 228-38. Reprint-
      ed Analectic Magazine [Philadelphia], II, 286-300.
      While theatres are places of 'impurity', some plays may
      be read. Such a one is Remorse, a highly moral, even re-
      ligious work and 'one of the best tragedies...since the
      time of Otway'.

141   _____. 'Remorse'. Critical Review, 4th Series III, 402-5.
      Reviewer objects to poor characterization and moral
      improbability, but play shows promise.

142   _____. 'Remorse'. Drakard's Paper, V, 29.
      Remorse an agreeable exception to 'idiotic affectation'
      of Lake Poets, and is Coleridge's best production.

143   _____. 'Theatrical Journal'. European Magazine, LXIII,
      137-8. Partially reprinted Analectic Magazine [Philadel-
      phia], New Series I (1813), 533-4.
      Review of Remorse praising characterization, style, and
      moral, and describing favourable reception of play.

144   _____. 'Theatrical Register. Drury Lane'. Gentleman's Maga-
      zine, LXXXIII, 179.
      Brief notice of Remorse describes Coleridge as well-
      known lecturer and as poet 'of genius'.

145   _____. 'Didascalia: Drury Lane Theatre'. Literary Panorama,
        XIII, 78-9, 462.
            Praises Coleridge's language but questions motivation of
        characters in Remorse.

146   _____. ['Remorse']. Morning Post, No. 13107 (25 Jan), p. 3.
            Review praises the play on all counts. A note in each
        of the next two issues (26, 27 Jan) promises further re-
        marks which, however, never appeared.

147   _____. 'Dramatic Register. Drury Lane'. National Register,
        VI, 62, 76-7.
            First notice a brief report of performance of Remorse.
        Second notes specific flaws in play and acting. Intricate
        plot better suited to reading than performance.

148   _____. 'New Tragedy at Drury Lane'. Republican, No. 4 (28
        Jan), p. 79.
            Brief review of Remorse confined to summary of 'labori-
        ously complex' plot.

149   _____. 'Drury Lane'. Satirist, XII, 187, 269-83.
            Ascribes Hazlitt's favourable review of Remorse in
        Morning Chronicle to Coleridge himself. Attacks Coleridge
        as Lake Poet and criticizes characterization and action in
        play. Qualified praise of performance.

150   _____. 'Theatrical Review'. Scourge, V, 174, 259-62.
            Plot summary and discussion of Remorse, followed in
        sequel by description of acting, which is praised, and
        play, which is condemned. A few good passages 'bloom like
        roses in a cabbage garden'.

151   _____. 'Dramatic Criticism'. Theatrical Inquisitor, II, 57-
        64. Cf review below by H., possibly same author.
            Remorse a failure in all respects. The plot is 'adapted
        from a romance entitled The Ring and the Well' (published
        1808 and bearing no resemblance to Remorse).

152   _____. 'British Mecaenases and Fashionable Writers'. Town
        Talk, IV, 257-62.
            Bitter comment (p. 258) on the 'unintelligible balder-
        dash' of 'the Coleridges, the Southeys, and the Wordsworths
        of the day'.

153   _____. 'Remorse'. Universal Magazine, XIX, 144-6.
            A sympathetic summary of plot with brief account of fa-
        vourable reception of the play.

21

154 [BARNES, THOMAS]. 'Theatrical Examiner'. Examiner, No. 266
       (31 Jan), pp. 73-4.
          Favourable review of Remorse.
          Attribution: Blunden

155 BONUCCI, JOSEPH ANTH[ON]Y. Reply to 'The Friend'. No. VII.
       Bristol: Evans. 12 pp.
          As a Neapolitan, Bonucci, in this brief pamphlet, takes
       exception to Coleridge's description of Neapolitans and
       Sicilians as 'cowardly' and cites a series of instances of
       Neapolitan courage.

156 CANDIDUS, pseud. 'Theatrical'. New York Columbian, IV,
       No. 1263 (9 Dec), p. 3.
          Review of New York performance of Remorse. Play a
       'striking exception' to the degenerate state of modern
       drama.

157 [CROLY, GEORGE?]. 'Drury-Lane Theatre'. Times, No. 8818 (25
       Jan), [p. 3].
          Reviewer of Remorse (possibly George Croly, Times drama
       critic) respects Coleridge's previous work, but finds major
       flaws in play. Plot followed by substantial discussion of
       Coleridge's shortcomings as dramatist.
          Attribution: H. C. Robinson

158 H. 'Remorse'. Theatrical Inquisitor, II, 111-16.
          'One of the best productions of a vicious and pedantic
       school'.

159 [HAZLITT, WILLIAM]. 'Drury Lane Theatre'. Courier, No. 5565
       (25 Jan), p. 3; Morning Chronicle, No. 13641 (25 Jan), p. 3.
          Flattering review offers plot summary followed by de-
       tailed discussion of characters and of Coleridge's powers of
       characterization, which bring him closer 'than almost any
       other writer' to Shakespeare. Howe came to accept Cole-
       ridge's hearsay attribution of the review to Hazlitt (Col-
       lected Letters III, 429) which would make this Hazlitt's
       first published discussion of Coleridge.

160 [HODGSON, F.]. 'Remorse...Second Edition'. Monthly Review,
       2nd Series LXXI, 82-93.
          Plot summary followed by general praise. Coleridge
       might take Otway as a model.
          Attribution: Ward; Nangle

161   KELLY, MICHAEL. <u>The Invocation, as Sung with Unbounded Ap-</u>
<u>plause by Mrs. Bland, at the New Theatre Royal Drury Lane,</u>
<u>in the Popular Tragedy of Remorse, Written by Coleridge</u>
<u>Esqr, the Music composed by Michl. Kelly, to which is added</u>
<u>the other Music performed in the same piece</u>. London:
Falkner & Christmas.

162   M. 'The Tragedy of Remorse'. <u>Republican</u>, No. 5 (13 Feb),
pp. 98-9.
Estimable work but unsuitable for stage.

162A [WILLIAMS, JOHN] Anthony Pasquin, <u>pseud</u>. [Review of <u>Remorse</u>].
<u>Morning Herald</u>, January.
No copy has been located of issue containing this re-
view, described by Coleridge in a letter as 'dirty malice'
(Griggs, III, 430). Griggs in a note questions authorship.

                              1814

163   ANON. 'Mr. Coleridge's Lectures upon Milton'. <u>Felix Farley's</u>
<u>Bristol Journal</u>, No. 3345 (16 April), partially reprinted
Raysor (1930, 1960).
Account of Lecture IV of Coleridge's 1814 series on
Milton.

164   _____. 'A Reply to the Most Popular Objections to Public
Schools, with particular reference to the Tyrocinium of
Cowper'. <u>Pamphleteer</u>, IV, 103-30.
Instances of those who have benefited from public
schools, giving (p. 114) brief but glowing eulogy of Cole-
ridge.

165   _____. 'Memoirs of Mr. Alexander Rae'. <u>Theatrical Inquisi-</u>
<u>tor</u>, V, 277.
Rae's performance in <u>Remorse</u> 'established his reputation'.

166   [BARNES, THOMAS] Strada, <u>pseud</u>. 'Mr. Coleridge'. <u>Champion</u>,
No. 64 (27 Mar), pp. 102-3.
Coleridge remarkable for poetry rather than prose.
Criticism of some views in <u>Friend</u> and defence of changes
in political views.
Attribution: Hudson

1814–COLERIDGE

167   [COLERIDGE, JOHN TAYLOR].   'Remorse'.   Quarterly Review, XI,
      177–90.
         Remorse exemplifies the interest of 'Lake Poets' in the
      origin and development of feeling and with minor feelings
      whose importance they exaggerate. Despite some merits,
      improbability, complexity, and difficulty makes play inef-
      fective on stage.
         Attribution: Graham

168   COSMO, pseud. 'Mr. Coleridge on the Fine Arts'. Bristol
      Gazette, Nos. 2443, 2445, 2447 (1, 15, 29 Sept.).
         Three heated letters referring to obscurity of three
      lectures and one letter of Coleridge's in Felix Farley's
      Bristol Journal.

169   OBERON, pseud. 'The Devil's Travels on Earth'. Theatrical
      Inquisitor, V, 186–9.
         Imitation of The Devil's Thoughts. Promised sequel did
      not appear.

170   [PEACOCK, THOMAS LOVE] P. M. O'Donovan, pseud. Sir Proteus:
      A Satirical Ballad. T. Hookham, Junr. and E. T. Hookham.
      pp. 18–22
         Comic note (pp. 18–22) on Coleridge.

171   WORDSWORTH, WILLIAM. The Excursion, being a portion of The
      Recluse, a Poem. London: Longman et al.
         Wordsworth's debt to Coleridge acknowledged in Preface
      (p. viii).

                              1815

172   ANON. 'Wiltshire Auxiliary British and Foreign Bible Soci-
      ety'. Salisbury and Winchester Journal, LXXX, No. 4090
      (14 Aug), p. 4.
         Coleridge is listed as a speaker at annual meeting at
      Devizes.

173   [HAZLITT, WILLIAM]. 'Theatrical Examiner'. Examiner, No. 403
      (17 Sept), pp. 601–2. Reprinted in his View of the English
      Stage. London: Robert Stodart (1818), pp. 152–6.
         Brief sarcastic comment on Remorse.

174   [HUNT, LEIGH]. 'Sketches of the Performers, The Tragic
      Actors'. Examiner, No. 371 (5 Feb), pp. 89-90.
      'Mr. Coleridge's Remorse has been the only tragedy with
      real poetry for the last fifty years'.
      Attribution: Houtchens

175   [NIVEN, ANNA JANE VARDILL] V. 'Christobell, A Gothic Tale'.
      European Magazine, LXVII, 345-6. Reprinted Fraser's Maga-
      zine, XI (1835), 55-6; Literary World [New York], XIII
      (1853), 25-6.
      Continuation of as yet unpublished Christabel.
      Attribution: Axon

176   [SIMOND, LOUIS]. Journal of a Tour and Residence in Great
      Britain. 2 vols. New York: T. and W. Mercein. Translat-
      ed as Voyage en Angleterre, pendant les années 1810 et
      1811. Paris: Treuttel et Würtz (1816).
      Originally published in English and republished in
      French. Includes description of meeting with Coleridge in
      1810, and criticism of Coleridge, Southey, and Wordsworth
      for 'whiggism'. Reviewed: no. 209.
      Attribution: 2nd edition (Paris, 1817).

177   TALFOURD, T[HOMAS] N[OON]. 'An Attempt to Estimate the Po-
      etical Talent of the Present Age'. Pamphleteer, V, 413-71.
      Discussion of Coleridge (pp. 458-61) centres on Remorse,
      Coleridge's most popular, but by no means his best work.
      Coleridge tries to combine a Shakespearean conception of
      character with classically formal logical utterance. His
      characters think like Shakespeare's but talk like Racine's,
      and the combination does not work. In 'spell poetry',
      examplified by The Ancient Mariner, he is 'far more potent
      than any writer of the present age'.

178   WORDSWORTH, WILLIAM. 'Stanzas Written in my pocket-copy of
      Thompson's Castle of Indolence'. Poems. 2 vols. London:
      Longman et al., I, 121-4.
      Of these eight stanzas, written in May 1802, the first
      four refer to Wordsworth, the next three to Coleridge.

                              1816

179   ANON. 'Christabel, &c ... Second Edition!!' Anti-Jacobin Re-
      view, L, 632-6.
      A sarcastic paraphrase of Christabel as 'absurd and stu-
      pid'. Kubla Khan and The Pains of Sleep are 'not wholly
      discreditable'.

1816-ANON.

180 ANON. 'Christabel' [etc.]. Augustan Review, III, 14-24.
   Reviewer confuses Coleridge with Wordsworth, sees him
   writing with Wordsworth's supposed faults (and credits him
   with The Idiot Boy, and with writing like Scott and Byron).

181 _____. 'Essays in Rhyme...by Jane Taylor'. Augustan Review,
   III, 459-73.
   Concludes with attack on Wordsworth and Coleridge who
   might learn from this book.

182 _____. 'The Poetic Mirror'. Augustan Review, III, 556-78.
   Review of Hogg's 1816 parodies, q.v. Attacks Coleridge
   for his 'bewildering metaphysics, made up of Kant and
   Berkeley, and Giordano Bruno', and 'the raving doggerel and
   wretched prose of Christabel', and quotes Hogg's parody.

183 _____. 'Christabel; Kubla Kahn [sic]'. British Lady's Magazine, IV, 248-51.
   The plot of Christabel admirable, but style 'most re-
   volting'. The other two poems wild and rhapsodical.

184 _____. ['Chaucer']. Champion, No. 177 (26 May), p. 166.
   Article includes a mildly favourable note on Coleridge.

185 _____. 'Christabel' [etc.]. Champion. No. 177 (26 May),
   pp. 166-7.
   Witty but unsympathetic summary and discussion of
   Christabel which is 'one of the most trifling, inconclu-
   sive, unsatisfactory performances, that was ever read'.
   Style and versification are 'slovenly and irregular...indo-
   lent experiments'.

186 _____. 'Christabel' [etc.]. Critical Review, 5th Series III,
   504-10.
   A very favourable review of Christabel with extended
   summary and quotation.

187 _____. 'Christabel'. Literary Panorama, New Series IV,
   561-5.
   Christabel combines 'the wilder graces of diction, with
   the most vigorous and speaking descriptions'. Kubla Khan
   is dismissed: 'a few stanzas' originating in circumstances
   not unusual.

188 _____. 'Siege of Corinth'. New Monthly Magazine, V, 148-9.
   Byron's note on Christabel facetiously mentioned.

189   ____. 'Literary Intelligence'. Portico [Baltimore], II, 421-2.
      Notes New York edition of Christabel... and observes that Coleridge's 'poetick powers have been in one uninterrupted state of suspended animation from 1797 to the present date'.

190   No entry.

191   ANON. 'Christabel [etc.]. Scourge and Satirist, XII, 60-72.
      A savage review which, between linking Coleridge initially with Hunt and finally with Byron, judges Christabel 'disgusting', Kubla Khan 'unintelligible' and The Pains of Sleep puerile.

192   B. N. [Letter to Editor]. Gentleman's Magazine, LXXXVI, 484.
      Says Coleridge's 'caprice of Christabel' earned £100.

193   [BYRON, LORD]. The Siege of Corinth. London: John Murray.
      In note to stanza XIX, Byron acknowledges resemblance to Christabel though written before he heard 'that wild and singularly original and beautiful poem'.

194   COLEBRITCHE, S. T., ESQ., pseud. Christabess. A Right Woeful Poem, translated from the Doggerel by Sir Vinegar Sponge. London: J. Duncombe.
      Vulgar parody, possibly by J. Duncombe, the publisher, in which Christabel ('Christabess') and Geraldine ('Adelaide') are daughters of a tinker and a sweep.
      Attribution: Little

195   [CONDER, JOSIAH]. 'Christabel [etc.]'. Eclectic Review, 2nd Series V, 565-72.
      Although Christabel is a 'mutilated statue', it does seize the imagination. Kubla Khan and The Pains of Sleep should not have been published.
      Attribution: Hayden

196   [CROKER, JOHN WILSON]. 'The Poetic Mirror'. Quarterly Review, XV, 468-75.
      Review of Hogg mentions (p. 473) parody of Christabel ('The Lady Isabelle') which is equally intelligible but less poetic.
      Attribution: Shine

1816–HAZLITT

197   [HAZLITT, WILLIAM]. 'Christabel [etc.]'. Examiner, No. 440
      (2 June) pp. 348–9.
          In spite of 'beauty both of thought, imagery, and versi-
      fication', the general effect of Christabel is 'obscure and
      visionary', and there is 'something disgusting at the bot-
      tom of his subject'. Kubla Khan is 'nonsense', a musical
      composition rather than a poem.
          Attribution: Howe

198   _____. 'A Lay-Sermon'. Examiner, No. 454 (8 Sept), pp. 571–
      3. Reprinted Port folio [Philadelphia],4th Series II
      (1816), 3–6. Reprinted his Political Essays. London:
      Hone (1819), pp. 118–24.
          Attack on Coleridge's principles and performance is
      ostensibly a review of The Statesman's Manual which Hazlitt
      has admittedly not yet read. In a sequel three months lat-
      er ('The Statesman's Manual') he continues his attack on
      Coleridge's 'nonsense', this time supporting it with exam-
      ples from the work.

199   _____. 'The Statesman's Manual'. Examiner, No. 470 (29 Dec),
      pp. 824–7.
          Sequel to Hazlitt's 'A Lay Sermon', q.v.

200   _____. 'The Statesman's Manual'. Edinburgh Review, XXVII,
      444–59. Reprinted in his Political Essays. London: Hone
      (1819), pp. 125–36.
          A broad attack on Coleridge in general and the work in
      particular.

201   [HOGG, JAMES]. The Poetic Mirror. London: Longman et al.
          Collection of parodies including 'Isabelle' (pp. 215–23)
      and 'The Cherub' (pp. 225–9), a parody of the style and
      metre, but not the story, of Christabel. Reviewed:
      nos. 182, 196.

202   [HUNT, LEIGH]. 'Mr. Coleridge and the Edinburgh Reviewers'.
      Examiner, No. 465 (24 Nov), p. 743.
          Argues that Moore's review of Christabel in the Edin-
      burgh Review was too harsh and that Coleridge's work was
      excellent before his political eclipse.
          Attribution: Landré

203   J. H. R. 'Pilgrimage of Living Poets to the Stream of Casta-
      ly'. Champion, No. 170 (7 April), p. 110.
          A satirical 'dream vision'.

204 [LAMB, CHARLES]. 'Christabel'. Times, No. 9839 (20 May),
     p. 3. Partially reprinted in Courier, No. 7391 (4 June
     1816), [p. 3]. Reprinted with discussion by David V. Erd-
     man in Studies in English [University of Texas], XXXVII
     (1958), 53-60.
         Neglected until Erdman rediscovered it, this very fa-
     vourable review helped significantly to balance the nega-
     tive criticism in other journals. The reviewer, probably
     Charles Lamb, considers the poem to be of 'indisputable
     originality'. Compares it with Burns's Tam o'Shanter, and
     discusses the 'moral beauty' of Christabel, the 'pictur-
     esqueness' of imagery, and the 'peculiar richness and vari-
     ety' of the metre.
         Attribution: Schwartz

205 [MATHEW, GEORGE FELTON] G. F. M. 'Christabel [etc.]'.
     European Magazine, LXX, 434-7.
         Christabel, as Byron says, is 'wildly original' and
     must be judged not by comparison but by its effect on its
     readers.
         Attribution: Tentative. Mathew **editor** of European
     Magazine

206 [MOORE, THOMAS?]. 'Christabel etc.'. Edinburgh Review,
     XXVII, 58-67.
         Sarcastic paraphrase of Christabel followed by dismissal
     of Coleridge's claims for a new metric. Kubla Khan and The
     Pains of Sleep are 'mere raving' and the whole publication
     is 'utterly destitute of value'. Concludes with attacks on
     Coleridge as a political opportunist.
         Attribution: WI. But the authorship of this notorious
     review has been long debated. W. S. Dowden in Letters of
     Thomas Moore (London, 1964) rejects arguments for Moore's
     authorship and supports H. Jordan in assigning it jointly
     to Jeffrey and Hazlitt.

207 [PEACOCK, THOMAS LOVE]. Headlong Hall. London: T. Hookham
     Junior.
         Novel in which Coleridge is satirized as Mr. Panscope,
     an incomprehensible philosopher.

208 [ROBERTS, WILLIAM]. 'Christabel [etc.]'. British Review,
     VIII 64-81. Reprinted American Monthly Magazine and Criti-
     cal Review [New York], I (1817), 12-16. Reprinted in his
     Life, Letters and Opinions. London: Seeleys (1850),
     pp. 56-7.
         Review of Christabel (pp. 64-71) and Maturin's Bertram
     much in favour of the latter. Sneers at and offers a

1816-ROBERTS

([ROBERTS, WILLIAM])
sarcastic paraphrase of Christabel which is unintelligible
and affected.

209 S. 'Journal of a Tour and Residence in Great Britain'. Portico [Baltimore], II, 181-94.
Review of Simond (1815). Sees Coleridge as rejected by
'the world' with 'general contempt'.

210 [SCOTT, WALTER]. 'Child Harold's Pilgrimage'. Quarterly Review, XVI, 172-208.
Notes (p. 204) instances reminiscent of 'the wild, un-
bridled, and fiery imagination' of Coleridge, who is worthy
of deference although he has too often 'wandered into the
wild and mystic'.
Attribution: Shine

211 SHELLEY, PERCY BYSSHE. 'To ---'. Alastor [etc.]. London:
Baldwin et al., pp. 53-5.
According to Mary Shelley's note, this poem ('Oh there
are spirits of the air') was addressed 'in idea' to Coleridge.

212 T. O. 'Christabel [etc.]'. Farrago: or the Lucubrations of
Counsellor Bickerton, Esquire, No. I (June), pp. 3-16.
Byron's praise of Christabel must have been ironic, as
the poem is a 'farrago of childishness and discord, degrad-
ed and degenerate'. Kubla Khan and The Pains of Sleep are
dismissed as neither better nor worse.

213 [WATKINS, JOHN and FREDERICK SHOBERL]. 'Coleridge, S. T.' A
Biographical Dictionary of the Living Authors of Great
Britain and Ireland. London: Henry Colburn, p. 70.
Short biographical sketch with list of works.
Attribution: B. Mus. Cat.

1817

214 'Mr. Coleridge's Second Lay Sermon'. Courier, No. 7642 (25
Mar), [p. 3].
Erdman (1961) identifies this favourable review as being
by Coleridge himself.

215 ANON. ['Biographia Literaria']. Atheneum [Boston], II, 65.
Biographia marred by metaphysical cloudiness.

SAMUEL TAYLOR COLERIDGE: AN ANNOTATED BIBLIOGRAPHY

216   ____. 'Sibylline Leaves...Biographia Literaria'. British
Critic, New Series VIII, 460-81.
    Comments unfavourably on Coleridge's poetry, prose
style, and unintelligible metaphysics, but commends criticism of Wordsworth. Half of the review devoted to Coleridge's criticism of reviewers and of Jeffrey in particular, taking Coleridge's part against Jeffrey.

217   ____. 'Zapolya'. Champion, No. 254 (16 Nov), p. 365.
    Despite some worthy passages in Zapolya, Coleridge's
style has been spoiled by his admiration for Bowles and for
the Della Cruscan.

217A   ____. 'The Edinburgh Review'. Courier, No. 7799 (24 Sept)
[p. 3].
    Discussion of attack on Edinburgh Review in Biographia,
leads to criticism of Coleridge's apolitical treatment of
Southey.

218   ____. 'A Lay Sermon'. Critical Review, 5th Series V, 581-6.
    Chiefly summary and extracts, commends Coleridge for
'integrity and purity of his principles'.

219   ____. 'The Statesman's Manual'. Critical Review, 5th Series
V, 42-8.
    England, unlike Germany, lacks an audience for such a
work.

220   ____. 'Sibylline Leaves'. Edinburgh Magazine, 2nd Series I,
245-50.
    Coleridge's poems differ strikingly from those of other
'Lake Poets'. Among best of modern time, they are charac-
terized by 'wildness and irregularity', and descriptions of
nature both accurate and able to convey emotion.

221   ____. 'Zapolya'. Edinburgh Magazine, 2nd Series I, 455-9.
    Modern drama generally weak and Coleridge no exception.
Remorse more suited to closet than stage. Zapolya fails as
drama and as a tale.

222   ____. 'Domestic Occurrences'. Gentleman's Magazine,
LXXXVII, 560.
    Mention of 'excellent address' given by Coleridge at the
London Philosophical Society.

1817-ANON.

223   ANON. 'House of Lords, May 12'. <u>Gentleman's Magazine</u>,
       LXXXVII, 548.
           Lord Grey read in debate <u>Anti-Jacobin</u> 1798 satire on
       Coleridge and others.

224   _____. 'Lay Sermon'. <u>Hone's Reformists' Register</u>, I, 406-7.
           Long quotation, with explanation of need to have it
       widely read because of the widespread economic distress,
       especially in Manchester.

225   _____. 'Biographia Literaria'. <u>Literary Gazette</u>, No. 29
       (9 Aug), pp. 83-5.
           Some passages 'instructive and entertaining'; others
       'absurd or disgusting'.

226   _____. 'Drury Lane'. <u>Literary Gazette</u>, No. 13 (19 April),
       p. 201.
           Review of revival of <u>Remorse</u> praises actors, 'but this
       strange and meagre mixture of lifeless insipidity and tur-
       gid rant, most successfully resisted their efforts'.

227   _____. 'Sibylline Leaves'. <u>Literary Gazette</u>, No. 27 (26
       July), pp. 49-51.
           Attack on Coleridge and his 'school' using <u>The Three</u>
       <u>Graves</u> as example of 'drivelling' and 'imbecility'.

228   _____. 'Zapolya'. <u>Literary Gazette</u>, No. 43 (15 Nov),
       pp. 307-8.
           <u>Zapolya</u> shows improvement over Coleridge's recent pro-
       ductions such as <u>Christabel</u>, but his 'liberties' seem to
       destroy poetry.

229   _____. 'To the Editor of the Monthly Magazine'. <u>Monthly</u>
       <u>Magazine</u>, XLIV, 108.
           Extracts from <u>The Fall of Robespierre</u> illustrate change
       in political opinions of Coleridge and Southey.

230   _____. 'New Publications in August [1817]'. <u>Monthly Maga-</u>
       <u>zine</u>, XLIV, 153-160. Reprinted <u>Analectic Magazine</u> [Phila-
       delphia], X (1817), 519.
           Unfavourable notices of <u>Biographia</u> (p. 154) and <u>Sybel-</u>
       <u>line [sic] Leaves</u> (p. 156). Coleridge's abandonment of
       'a good cause' to become one of 'the mercenaries of abused
       power' and the loss of the 'sterling genius' displayed in
       <u>Fire, Famine, and Slaughter</u> entitle him to pity, or con-
       tempt.

231 _____. 'New Publications in April'. Monthly Magazine, XLIII, 354-9.
Includes (p. 354) brief notice of the second Lay Sermon, like the first, an 'absurd rhapsody'.

232 _____. 'New Publications in December [1816]'. Monthly Magazine, XLII, 544-50.
Includes (p. 545) paragraph complaining of obscurity of The Statesman's Manual.

233 _____. 'Christabel [etc.]'. Monthly Review, Series II, LXXXII, 22-5.
Reviewer approves of The Pains of Sleep, ridicules Christabel and attacks Coleridge for lack of form, 'discordant...harmony' and 'execrable taste'. Questions account of composition of Kubla Khan which, as a poem, is 'below criticism'.

234 _____. 'A Lay Sermon'. Monthly Repository, XII, 299-300.
Objects to Coleridge's attack on, and misrepresentation of, Unitarianism.

235 _____. 'Biographia Literaria'. New Annual Register, XXXVIII, 145-62.
Three long extracts, with brief comment praising style and 'powers of mind' exhibited in this 'strange medley'.

236 _____. ['Biographia Literaria']. New Monthly Magazine, VIII, 50.
Accuses Coleridge of 'metaphysical jargon in the mystical language of the platonists and schoolmen, of Kant and Jacob Behmen'.

237 _____. 'Biographia Literaria'. Portico [Baltimore], IV, 417-27.
Defends Wordsworth's theory of poetic diction against Coleridge.

238 _____. 'Coleridge's Second Lay Sermon'. Times, No. 10101 (21 Mar), p. 3.
Reviewer hopes to make known both the work and the opinions which he cites.

239 _____. 'To the Editors of the Thanet Magazine'. Thanet Magazine, I, 55-7.
Comment on The Nightingale in response to earlier article.

1817-ANON.

240   ANON. 'Poets of the Present Age, Mr. Coleridge'. Ulster
      Register [Belfast], III, 35-8.
          More than half devoted to article acknowledging Cole-
      ridge's excellence in 'some fragments...and some lyric
      passages' which are 'unequalled' but finds most of his work
      'crude effusions'.

241   E. 'Biographia Literaria'. American Monthly Magazine and
      Critical Review [New York], II, 105-14.
          Dislikes Coleridge's poetry and metaphysics, but con-
      siders him interesting as a man.

242   H. T. 'Modern Poets. Defence of Coleridge'. Literary Ga-
      zette, No. 15 (3 May), p. 227.
          Comparison of Coleridge and Wordsworth. Coleridge 'all
      energy and fire', Wordsworth 'all imbecility and ice'.
      Letter from J. E. (No. 17, 17 May, pp. 257-8) cites Cole-
      ridge in defence of Wordsworth.

243   [HAZLITT, WILLIAM]. 'Biographia Literaria'. Edinburgh Re-
      view, XXVIII, 488-515. Partially reprinted Ulster Regis-
      ter [Belfast], III (1817), 249-50.
          Probably by Hazlitt though perhaps extensively revised
      by Jeffrey. Largely devoted to Coleridge's remarks on
      Southey and Burke, and to attacks on his supposed political
      apostasy. Long footnote (pp. 508-9), signed F. J. pre-
      sents Jeffrey's defence against Coleridge's criticism of
      him.
          Attribution: Howe

244   _____. 'The Courier and "The Wat Tyler"'. Examiner, No. 483
      (30 Mar), pp. 194-7. Reprinted his Political Essays.
      London: Hone (1819), pp. 200-12.
          Snide reply to Coleridge's letters in Courier of 17 and
      18 March supporting Southey against charges of apostasy
      made by Hazlitt in Examiner of 9 March.

245   _____. 'Death and Funeral of the Late Mr. Southey'. Exam-
      iner, No. 485 (13 April), pp. 236-7.
          A satirical obituary describing defence of Southey by
      'Dr. Paracelsus Broadhum Coleridge'.
          Attribution: Howe

246   _____. Semper ego auditor, pseud. 'Mr. Coleridge's Lay-
      Sermon'. Examiner, No. 472 (12 Jan), pp. 28-9. Reprinted
      in his Political Essays. London: Hone (1819), pp. 137-9.

([HAZLITT, WILLIAM])
 Describes Coleridge's 1798 sermon in Shrewsbury and
 contrasts it with the account (written by Hazlitt himself)
 of The Statesman's Manual in The Examiner.

247 _____. Vindex, pseud. 'Mr. Coleridge and Mr. Southey'.
 Examiner, No. 484 (6 Apr), p. 211.
 Vitriolic letter to the editor occasioned by Coleridge's
 supposed defence of Southey in The Courier.
 Attribution: Howe

248 _____. W. H. 'On Actors and Acting'. Examiner, No. 471 (5
 Jan), pp. 8-10.
 Contains a brief sarcastic reference to Coleridge's Lay
 Sermons.
 Attribution: Howe

249 HAZLITT, WILLIAM. 'What is the People?'. Champion, No. 250
 (19 Oct), p. 2. Reprinted Yellow Dwarf, Nos. 10, 11, (7,
 14 Mar 1818), pp. 74-7, 86-7.
 Mentions attack on Coleridge in Anti-Jacobin (Canning,
 'New Morality', 1798), which he attributes to Gifford, as
 instance of calumny by 'government writers'.

250 [LOCKHART, J. G.] 'On the Cockney School of Poetry, No. 1'.
 Blackwood's Magazine, II, 38-41.
 Attacks Leigh Hunt and compares him with 'a greater
 quack still (Mr. Coleridge)'.
 Attribution: Strout

251 [PEACOCK, THOMAS LOVE]. Melincourt, or Sir Oran Haut-ton.
 3 vols. London: Hookham.
 Coleridge is satirized in a minor character, Mr. Mystic,
 a transcendental philosopher.

252 [SMYTH, JOHN]. 'To the Reviewer of Coleridge's Biographia
 Literaria, in Blackwood's Magazine for October'. Black-
 wood's Magazine, II, 285-7.
 An attack on Wilson's review of Biographia Literaria.
 Attribution: Strout

253 S N D 'To S. T. Coleridge, Esq. On the Attack on the Unitarians Contained in his Second Lay Sermon'. Monthly Repository, XII, 213-6, 268-72.
 Two letters object to Coleridge's metaphysics and his
 misrepresentation of Unitarianism. Praises Religious Musings, written when Coleridge 'thought and felt with us'.

1817-S N D

(S N D)
Mineka's tentative attribution to Talfourd seems dubious.

254   [SOUTHEY, ROBERT]. 'Report of the Secret Committee'. Quarterly Review, XVI, 511-52.
     Contains (pp. 527, 536) two brief but favourable allusions to second Lay Sermon.
     Attribution: Shine; Curry

255   [WILSON, JOHN] H. M., pseud. 'Analytical Essays on the Early English Dramatists'. Blackwood's Magazine, II, 21-30.
     Mentions (p. 30) Coleridge's 'blind and blundering wrath' at apparent plagiarism from him in Edinburgh Review.
     Attribution: Strout

256   _____. Christopher North, pseud. 'Some Observations on the Biographia Literaria of S. T. Coleridge, Esq.--1817'. Blackwood's Magazine, II, 3-18.
     Savage attack on both the work and the man; Biographia Literaria is 'execrable': unfinished and obscure, it exhibits vanity and fancy without feeling or judgment. Concludes with account of Coleridge's life that drove him to consider a suit for libel.
     Attribution: Strout

1818

257   ANON. Prodigious!!! or, Childe Paddie in London. 3 vols. London: printed for the author.
     Coleridge is the subject (II, 134-43) of one of series of satirical character sketches.

258   _____. 'Nouvelles littéraires'. Les Annales Encyclopédiques [Paris], III, 93-100.
     Zapolya (pp. 97-9) shows great poetic talent and brilliant imagination, but is often metrically faulty.

259   _____. 'Lectures on Shakespeare'. Courier, No. 7907 (9 Feb), p. 2. Reprinted Raysor (1930, 1960).
     Enthusiastic account of Lecture I.

260   _____. 'Remarks on Mr. Hazlitt's Lectures'. Edinburgh Magazine, III, 2-12.
     Praises (pp. 4-5) Coleridge's criticism in Biographia Literaria while deploring his metaphysics.

1818-ANON.

261   _____. 'Zapoyla [sic], A Christmas Tale'. Edinburgh Observer, No. 10 (7 Feb), p. 237.
      Undistinguished, though 'less obscure than...some others
of his works'.

262   _____. 'Mr. Coleridge's Lectures'. Literary Gazette, No. 100
(19 Dec), p. 808. Reprinted Athenaeum, No. 3348 (26 Dec
1891), pp. 865-6; Coburn, Philosophical Lectures (1949).
      Brief account of first two philosophical lectures of
1818-19.

263   _____. 'The Devil's Walk by the Late Professor Porson?' Literary Journal, I, 15-6. Reprinted without comment Yellow
Dwarf, No. 19 (9 May 1818) p. 152.
      Fabrication that Porson composed the lines introduces
stanzas from The Devil's Thoughts.

264   _____. 'Mr. Coleridge'. Morning Chronicle, No. 15495 (19
Dec), unpaged. Reprinted Coburn, Philosophical Lectures
(1949).
      In reply to Mudford (1818), argues that Schlegel's 1801
essay seems to establish his priority as defender of
Shakespeare's judgment.

265   _____. 'Contemporary authors, an Estimate of the Literary
Character and Works of Mr. Coleridge'. Monthly Magazine,
XLVI, 407-9. Reprinted Atheneum [Boston], IV (1818),
435-7.
      Coleridge's performance has not matched his promises.
The Ancient Mariner his only work of genius; Christabel
'only fit for the inmates of Bedlam'; lectures show inability to 'at all understand' Shakespeare.

266   _____. 'New Publications in December [1817]'. Monthly Magazine, XLIV, 540-6. Reprinted Edinburgh Observer, I (1818),
237.
      Zapolya (p. 541) 'cannot add much to Mr. Coleridge's
fame'.

267   _____. 'State and Character of the Poetry of the Present
Age'. New Annual Register, XXXVIII, 43-50.
      Coleridge (p. 47) a 'subtle and metaphysical poet' but
lacks judgment and taste. Christabel the 'most absurd of
his poems'.

268   _____. 'Zapolya'. New Monthly Magazine, VIII, 544.
      Summary and brief favourable comment.

1818-ANON.

269   ANON. 'Lectures on Philosophy'. New Times, No. 5715 (17
      Dec), p. 2. Reprinted Coburn, Philosophical Lectures
      (1949).
          Report of Lecture I in 1818-19 series.

270   _____. 'On the Lake School of Poetry'. Portfolio [Edin-
      burgh], No. 3 (26 Nov), pp. 21-3.
          A defence of 'Lake Poets' for profundity of thought.

271   _____. 'Zapolya'. Theatrical Inquisitor, XII, 107-11.
          Summary with mixed judgment.

272   BROWN, THOMAS. Bath; A Satirical Novel, with Portraits. 3
      vols. London: Printed for the Author.
          Coleridge appears as 'Mr. Crazy', a man of 'infinite
      genius' but now 'muddy, obscure, delirious, confused,
      bloated and debilitated'.

273   F. 'On Literary Imitation'. New Monthly Magazine, X, 298-9.
          Byron in Siege of Corinth has 'unknowingly' used the
      same image as Coleridge.

274   [HAZLITT, WILLIAM]. 'The Fudge Family in Paris'. Yellow Dwarf,
      No. 17 (25 Apr), pp. 132-5. Reprinted in his Political Es-
      says. London: Hone (1819), pp. 343-56.
          Thomas Moore, as poet and patriot, compared with Words-
      worth, Southey, and Coleridge (p. 132) 'a maudlin method-
      istical lay preacher'.

275   _____. 'The Press--Coleridge, Southey, Wordsworth, and Ben-
      tham'. Yellow Dwarf, No. 1 (3 Jan), pp. 4-5.
          In abandoning their early political principles, the
      three poets have shown themselves neither wise nor honest.
          Attribution: Howe

276   _____. 'Mr. Coleridge's Lectures'. Yellow Dwarf, No. 8 (21
      Feb), pp. 60-1.
          Reference to Coleridge's treatment of Caliban leads to
      another attack on his political apostasy.
          Attribution: Howe

277   HAZLITT, WILLIAM. 'On the Living Poets'. Lectures on the
      English Poets. London: Taylor and Hessey, pp. 283-331.
          Concludes with assessment of Coleridge, some of whose
      work is 'dreary hash', but who is 'the only person from
      whom I ever learnt any thing'. Reviewed: [P. G. Patmore]
      A. Z., pseud. Blackwood's Magazine, III (1818), 71-7 (at-
      tribution: Strout).

278   [HAZLITT, WILLIAM] Peterkins, pseud. 'Mr. Wordsworth and the
      Westmoreland Election'. Examiner, No. 549 (5 July),
      p. 427.
          Includes jibe at Coleridge and Encyclopedia Metropoli-
      tana.
          Attribution: Howe

279   LAMB, CHARLES. 'To S. T. Coleridge, Esq.' Works. 2 vols.
      London: C. and J. Ollier, I, [v]-ix.
          Dedication recalls earlier joint publication and ex-
      presses present esteem.

280   [MUDFORD, WILLIAM]. 'Mr. Coleridge's Lectures'. Courier,
          No. 8174 (18 Dec), p. 2. Reprinted A. Koszul, Revue anglo-
      américaine [Paris], VII (1930), 330-1.
          Favourable review of the two opening philosophical and
      Shakespearean lectures. In the latter, Coleridge is
      thought the first to emphasize Shakespeare's 'judgment'.
          Attribution: A. Koszul

281   [NAPIER, MACVEY]. Hypocrisy Unveiled, and Calumny Detected:
      A Review of Blackwood's Magazine. Edinburgh: Francis
      Pillans.
          Blackwood's's treatment of Coleridge (p. 24) an instance
      of scurrilous writing, but Christabel and Byron's 'Para-
      sina' sin 'heinously against purity and decency'.
          Attribution: DAPL

282   OULTON, WALLEY CHAMBERLAIN. A History of the Theatres of
      London...from the Year 1795 to 1817 Inclusive. 3 vols.
      London: C. Chapple, I, 254-5.
          Outlines plot of Remorse, mistakenly thought to be taken
      from The Ring and the Well.

283   [PEACOCK, THOMAS LOVE]. Nightmare Abbey. London: T. Hook-
      ham.
          Mr. Flosky, a vain and unintelligible visionary, is the
      best known and most successful of Peacock's attempts at a
      satirical portrait of Coleridge.

284   [THELWALL, JOHN] A. S. 'Mr. Coleridge's alternate Lectures on
      the History of Philosophy; and on Six Plays of Shake-
      speare'. Champion, No. 311 (20 Dec), pp. 808-10. [Copies
      of this issue are dated both Sunday, 20 December, and Mon-
      day, 21 December. Only in latter does signature A. S. ap-
      pear]. Reprinted Raysor (1930, 1960).
          Criticizes Coleridge for changes in political opinions
      and lack of 'concentrating principle', but commends lec-

1818-THELWALL

([THELWALL, JOHN])
tures and gives detailed report of lecture on The Tempest.
    Attribution: Raysor

285   [WILSON, JOHN]. 'David Hume charged by Mr. Coleridge with
Plagiarism from St. Thomas Aquinas'. Blackwood's Magazine,
III, 653-7.
    Cites evidence in defence of Hume.
    Attribution: Strout

286   _____. Timothy Tickler, pseud. 'Letters of Timothy Tickler
to Various Literary Characters'. Blackwood's Magazine,
III, 75-7.
    Letter to Jeffrey criticizes him for treatment of Cole-
ridge.
    Attribution: Strout

287   _____. 'Some Remarks on the Use of the Preternatural in Works
of Fiction'. Blackwood's Magazine, III, 648-50.
    'Coleridge has perhaps the finest superstitious vein of
any person'. 'Christabel is the best model extant'...sur-
passing Scott's Lay of the Last Minstrel'.
    Attribution: Strout

288   _____. 'Works of Charles Lamb'. Blackwood's Magazine, III,
599-610.
    Comments (p. 603) on dramatic deficiencies and poetic
virtues of Remorse.
    Attribution: Strout

1819

289   ANON. 'Hazlitt's Essays, Criticisms, and Lectures'. British
Review, XIII, 313-39.
    Brief account (pp. 325-6) of Hazlitt on Coleridge.

290   _____. 'Mr. Coleridge's Lectures'. Courier, No. 8212 (1
Feb), p. 3. Partially reprinted A. Koszul. Revue anglo-
américaine [Paris], VII (1930), 334.
    A highly favourable review of Shakespeare lectures which
are contrasted with Hazlitt's 'glib nonsense'.

291   _____. 'The Friend'. European Magazine, LXXV, 141-2.
    General praise for The Friend coupled with lengthy re-
futation of Coleridge's claim that Ball was not adequately
recognized and rewarded.

292   . 'Memoir of S. T. Coleridge, Esq'. <u>European Magazine</u>,
LXXVI, 5-8. Portrait by Northcote.
Brief biographical sketch followed by strictures on un-
friendly critics.

293   . 'Remarks Philosophical and Literary on the Poetry of
the Nineteenth Century'. <u>Gentleman's Magazine</u>, LXXXIX,
397-400.
Coleridge and Wordsworth criticized (p. 398) for sins
against 'sound taste' and 'just and noble sentiments'.

294   . 'Biographia Literaria'. <u>Monthly Review</u>, LXXXVIII,
124-38. Partially reprinted <u>Fireside Magazine</u>, I (1819),
150.
Conventionally conservative disagreement with Coleridge's critical principles. Coleridge's criticism of
Wordsworth admirable in showing faults but completely unsuccessful in demonstrating virtues.

295   . 'Sibylline Leaves'. <u>Monthly Review</u>, LXXXVIII, 24-38.
Partially reprinted <u>Fireside Magazine</u>, I (1819), 115.
Sarcastic discussion of reasons for Coleridge's lack of
popularity, with critical comments. <u>The Ancient Mariner</u>
dismissed as unsuccessful and now forgotten experiment. A
few poems have some value.

296 [BYRON, LORD]. <u>Don Juan</u>. London: Thomas Davison (1819,
1821); Scott and Webster (1833).
Apparently annoyed by Coleridge's reported repetition
of a rumour, Byron attacked him as a 'drunk' in Canto I,
ccv (1819), followed this in III, xciii (1821) with lines
on pantisocracy and marriage, and finally, in the 'dedication' written 1819 but published 1833, made fun of his
metaphysical obscurity.

297 [DANA, R. H., SR.]. 'Hazlitt's <u>Lectures on the English
Poets</u>'. <u>North American Review</u> [Boston], VIII, 276-322.
Regrets (pp. 282, 320) Hazlitt's cursory treatment of
Coleridge, whose criticism of Wordsworth surpasses that
written on 'any other man of modern times'.
Attribution: Cushing

298 [GILLMAN, JAMES?] G. J. 'Character of Sir Thomas Brown [sic]
as a Writer'. <u>Blackwood's Magazine</u>, VI, 197-8.
As an example of Coleridge's marginalia, gives 1804 let-
ter to Sara Hutchinson, written on fly-leaf of edition of
Sir Thomas Browne.
Attribution: Haney

299   [HUNT, LEIGH]. 'A Tale for a Chimney Corner'. <u>Indicator</u>, I,
      73-80. Reprinted his <u>The Indicator and The Companion</u>.
      2 vols. London: H. Colburn (1834), I, 99-112.
            Comment (pp. 75-6) on <u>The Ancient Mariner</u>, 'that
      voyage...to the brink of all unutterable things'.

300   [LOCKHART, JOHN GIBSON?] Z. 'On the Cockney School of Poet-
      ry'. <u>Blackwood's Magazine</u>, VI, 70-6.
            Like Lamb, Coleridge allowed his 'fine, rich, overflow-
      ing monologues' to be 'plundered' by Hunt and Hazlitt.
            Attribution: Strout

301   _____. 'Essays on the Lake School of Poetry, No. III. --
      Coleridge'. <u>Blackwood's Magazine</u>, VI, 3-12.
            Generally favourable discussion marks significant de-
      parture from <u>Blackwood's</u> earlier treatment of Coleridge.
      Discusses <u>The Ancient Mariner</u> and <u>Christabel</u> at length,
      concludes that while Coleridge's powers may not be of the
      widest or highest kind, they are 'the most exquisite of
      powers'. In his command of 'wild, solitary, dreamy phan-
      tasies', and in his music, 'we think he stands absolutely
      alone among all the poets of the most poetical age'.
            Attribution: Strout's 1933 arguments in favour of
      Lockhart are still convincing though in 1959 he changed
      this attribution to John Wilson, following Wilson's editor
      J. F. Ferrier.

302   [LOCKHART, JOHN GIBSON]. 'The Mad Banker of Amsterdam'.
      <u>Blackwood's Magazine</u>, IV, 563-7.
            A satirical poem which singles out Coleridge's crani-
      ology (among others), and 'hubris' (p. 564) in trying to
      educate his 'Cockney auditors' by lecturing them.
            Attribution: Strout

303   _____. Dr. Peter Morris, pseud. <u>Peter's Letters to his Kin-
      folk</u>. 'Second Edition' [actually first]. 3 vols. Edin-
      burgh: Blackwood; London: T. Cadell and W. Davies. II,
      218-21.
            Letter 46 an important and favourable discussion of
      Coleridge's prose and poetry. Condemns <u>Blackwood's</u>, i.e.,
      Wilson's review of <u>Biographia</u>. Compares Coleridge with
      Wordsworth, and finds love poetry finest since Shakespeare.
      Coleridge responded warmly (<u>Collected Letters</u>, IV, 966-74),
      and in new ('third') edition Lockhart added eulogistic
      postscript. Letter 40 condemns ignorance of Coleridge
      among Scots. Reviewed: [J. G. Lockhart and John Wilson],
      <u>Blackwood's Magazine</u>, IV, 612-21, 745-52 (attribution:
      <u>WI</u>.).

304   M. 'Coleridge's Philosophical Lectures'. Champion, No. 313
       (3 Jan), p. 11. Reprinted Coburn, Philosophical Lectures
       (1949).
           Abstract of Lecture II of 1818-19 series.

305   [MOIR, D. M.]. Morgan O'Doherty, pseud. 'Christabel, Part
       Third'. Blackwood's Magazine, V, 286-91. Reprinted Wil-
       liam Maginn, Miscellanies: Prose and Verse. 2 vols.
       London: Sampson Low et al. (1885), I, 80-88.
           Geraldine revealed to be a man, and Christabel, preg-
       nant and awaiting disgrace, drowns her sorrows in wild-
       flower wine. Traditionally attributed to Maginn.
           Attribution: Strout

306   ____. Morgan O'Doherty, pseud. 'Letter from Mr. O'Doherty,
       enclosing three articles'. Blackwood's Magazine, V, 433-4.
           Coleridge 'a true genius and a true poet'.
           Attribution: Strout

307   ____. 'The Rime of the Auncient Waggonere'. Blackwood's
       Magazine, IV, 571-4. Reprinted William Maginn. Miscel-
       lanies: Prose and Verse. 2 vols. London: Sampson Low
       et al. (1885), I, 75-9.
           Parody of The Ancient Mariner traditionally attributed
       to Maginn.
           Attribution: Strout

308   [PATMORE, PETER GEORGE]. 'Notices of the acted drama in Lon-
       don'. Blackwood's Magazine, IV, 443-52.
           Notes (p. 445) 'force and originality' of Coleridge's
       Remorse.
           Attribution: Strout

309   Q. 'To the editor of the Monthly Magazine'. Monthly Maga-
       zine, XLVIII, 203-5. Reprinted as 'Mr. Coleridge'.
       Atheneum [Boston], IV, 435-7.
           Denials of accuracy of some biographical portions of
       Biographical Literaria, by one who 'knew Mr. Coleridge
       well' in Bristol. Coleridge was more of a democrat and rev-
       olutionary than he now admits

310   [TERROT, CHARLES HUGHES]. Common Sense: A Poem. Edinburgh:
       Brown.
           Attacks contemporary poets including Coleridge
       (pp. 8-9) from a neoclassic standpoint.
           Attribution: B. Mus. Cat.

1819-THELWALL

311 [THELWALL, JOHN]. 'Review of Literature etc.'. Champion,
     No. 314 (10 Jan), p. 29. Reprinted Raysor (1930, 1960).
         A brief, mainly enthusiastic review of Lecture III of
     1818-19 Shakespeare series.
         Attribution: Raysor

312 TURNER, SHARON. Prolusions on the Present Greatness of Brit-
     ain: on Modern Poetry: and on the present aspect of the
     World. London: Longman et al.
         Attacks German influence on English poetry (pp. 87-134),
     cites Christabel as instance, but does not include Cole-
     ridge among poets discussed individually.

313 W. 'Memoir of S. T. Coleridge, Esq.'. New Monthly Magazine,
     XI, 240-3. Portrait by Leslie.
         Inaccurate biographical sketch up to 1798.

314 [WILSON, JOHN]. P[hilip] K[empferhausen], pseud. 'Letters
     from the Lakes...Letter III'. Blackwood's Magazine, IV,
     735-44.
         Recounts Wordsworth's praise of Coleridge, 'the only
     man he knew in Britain entitled to lecture upon Shake-
     speare' (p. 742).
         Attribution: Strout

315 _____. 'The Missionary: A Poem. By the Rev. W. L. Bowles'.
     Blackwood's Magazine, VI, 13-18.
         Compares Bowles's sensibility with Coleridge's imagina-
     tion.
         Attribution: Strout

316 _____. '"Nugae Canorae", by Charles Lloyd'. Blackwood's
     Magazine, VI, 154-62.
         Brief reference to Coleridge (p. 154) among the 'sever-
     al great poets' of the age.
         Attribution: Strout

1820

317 ANON. 'Wordsworth's River Duddon'. Blackwood's Magazine,
     VII, 206-13.
         Ascribes the inspiration of Wordsworth's Duddon sonnets
     to Coleridge's plans for 'The Brook'.
         Attribution: Strout attributes the article to Wilson
     or Lockhart.

318 _____. 'Common Sense: A Poem'. British Review, XV, 31–44.
Review of Terrot's 1819 poem finds mention of Coleridge
and opium tasteless, but Christabelle [sic] fair game.

319 _____. 'To My Friend, Mr. Coleridge'. Battered Tar...A Poem,
with Sonnets. London: J. Johnston. [Date given in
B. Mus. Cat.]. Reprinted by Edward Dowden, Athenaeum,
No. 3434 (19 Aug 1893), p. 259.
Second sonnet begins 'Coleridge! when you your dose of
opium take....'

320 _____. 'Living Authors, A Dream'. Edinburgh Magazine, VII,
133–40.
Coleridge portrayed (pp. 139–40) as grand but obscure
talker. The rose at his window suited him better than the
volume of Boehme on his bookshelf.

321 _____. 'S[t]rictures on Messrs. Leigh Hunt, Coleridge, and
Company'. Literary Chronicle, No. 66 (29 July),
pp. 489–91.
Written in support of Hunt and critical of Coleridge for
his obscurity and vanity.

322 _____. 'Sibylline Leaves'. London Magazine [Gold's], II,
70–4.
Would-be humorous paraphrase of The Ancient Mariner.

323 _____. 'Contemporary Authors. -- No. 9, Wordsworth, and the
Lake School of Poets'. Monthly Magazine, L, 307–10.
Primarily concerned with changes of political views,
misquotes Biographia Literaria in support of attack on
Wordsworth's poetry.

324 _____. 'The Tragedies of the Last Age...A Short View of
Tragedy...by Mr. Rymer'. Retrospective Review, I, 1–15.
Reprinted as 'Essay on the Progress of Literature'. Lit-
erary and Scientific Repository and Critical Review [New
York], II (1821), 160–1. Possibly Talfourd.
Remorse (p. 15) 'a noble poem, but its metaphysical
clouds, though fringed with golden imaginations, brood too
heavily over it'.

325 B. T. 'Lines by Mr. Coleridge on the Queen'. Literary Chronicle, II, 424.
Correspondent finds On a Late Connubial Rupture 'nearly
as applicable now as then'.

45

1820-BYRONIUS

326   BYRONIUS, pseud. 'Longinus O'er a Bottle'. London Magazine
      [Gold's], I, 329-30.
         A satiric poem. Canto II, stanza 6 is on Coleridge and
      Christabel.

327   D. N. 'Essay on poetry, with observations on the living
      poets'. London Magazine [Gold's], II, 470-4.
         Coleridge and Wordsworth the leading poets of the day.
      Sibylline Leaves marked 'an aera in the annals of English
      poetry'.

328   [DEACON, W. F.] D. 'A Parody on Christabelle'. Déjeuné, I,
      105-8.
         Note says (p. 108) this 'has previously appeared in
      another work' which has not been identified.
         Attribution: Hamilton

329   DRAKE, NATHAN. Winter Nights. 2 vols. London: Longman et
      al.
         Passage in John Leyden's 'Scenes of Infancy' thought
      (I, 125) inferior to The Ancient Mariner, 'perhaps one of
      the most tremendous tales of supernatural horror in
      existence'.

330   G. 'The Literary Assise Court'. Déjeuné, I, 36-40.
         Satirical sketch. Coleridge ('Watchman' and 'Friend')
      defends himself against criticism by offering 'Christabess'
      (v 'Colebritch', 1816).

331   [GILLESPIE, THOMAS]. 'Brougham and Chalmers. On National
      Education'. Blackwood's Magazine, VII, 419-27.
         Praises Coleridge's educational principles in The
      Friend, and discusses his influence on Brougham and
      Chalmers.
         Attribution: Strout

332   [HARE, JULIUS CHARLES] J. C. H. 'A. W. Schlegel on Shake-
      speare's Romeo and Juliet; with Remarks on the character-
      istics of German criticism'. Ollier's Literary Miscellany,
      I, 1-46.
         Chides Coleridge (p. 8) for failing to publish lectures
      and 'discover' Shakespeare for his English audience as
      Schlegel had for Germany. Blames (p. 14) lack of self-
      control and self-denial.

333   [HAZLITT, WILLIAM] W. H. 'The Drama. No. XI'. London Maga-
       zine [Baldwin's], II, 685-90. Reprinted as 'Explanations--
       Conversations on the Drama with Coleridge' in his Criti-
       cisms and Dramatic Essays, of the English Stage. London:
       Routledge (1851), pp. [142]-56.
          Pretended conversation with Coleridge.

334   _____. 'General Reporter: The Drama'. London Magazine
       [Baldwin's], I, 432-40.
          Brief discussion of Remorse (p. 436), a 'meritorious
       tragedy' but over-metaphysical.
          Attribution: Howe

335   _____. T. 'Table-Talk. No. III. On the Conversation of
       of Authors'. London Magazine [Baldwin's], II, 250-62.
       Reprinted in his The Plain Speaker. London: Colburn
       (1826), pp. 49-76, 77-98.
          Contains anecdotes of Coleridge's conversation at
       Lamb's.

336   [HUNT, LEIGH]. 'Of Dreams'. Indicator , II, 9-16. Reprinted
       in his The Indicator. 2 vols. London: Colburn (1834),
       II, 123-37.
          Review of 'the beautiful poems' -- Christabel, Kubla
       Khan, The Pains of Sleep -- which 'have been too imagina-
       tive to be understood by the critics'. Extensive quotation
       and brief comment.

337   JACOBSEN, FRIEDERICH JOHANN. Briefe an eine deutsche Edel-
       frau. Altona: J. F. Hammerich.
          Letter 12 discusses critical persecution of Coleridge,
       praises Christabel and Shakespeare lectures, regards Love
       as best poem. Brief biographical sketch.

338   [LAMB, CHARLES] Elia, pseud. 'Christ's Hospital Five-and-
       thirty Years Ago'. London Magazine [Baldwin's], II,
       483-90. Reprinted Elia: Essays which have appeared under
       that signature in The London Magazine. London: Taylor and
       Hessey (1823), pp. 27-50.
          Pretended reply to Lamb's 'Recollections of Christ's
       Hospital' (1813) adopts view of schoolboy modelled on Cole-
       ridge, and describes Coleridge as youthful 'logician, meta-
       physician, bard'.

339   [LAMB, CHARLES] Elia, pseud. 'Two Races of Men'. London Magazine [Baldwin's], II, 623–5. Reprinted Elia: Essays which have appeared under that signature in The London Magazine. London: Taylor and Hessey (1823), pp. 51–9.
        Among 'men who borrow and men who lend', Coleridge appears as 'Comberbatch' who returns books 'enriched with annotations, tripling their value'.

340   [LOCKHART, JOHN GIBSON]. Peter Morris, pseud. 'Note from Dr. Morris, Enclosing a letter from Mr. Coleridge'. Blackwood's Magazine, VII, 628–31.
        Coleridge's letter (Collected Letters, IV, 966–70) with flattering comment.
        Attribution: Strout

341   PEACOCK, THOMAS LOVE. 'Four Ages of Poetry'. Ollier's Literary Miscellany, I, 183–200.
        Contains (pp. 195–6) brief sarcastic description of Coleridge.

342   RAPID, ROBERT, pseud. 'On the Conversation of Authors'. Déjeuné, I, 323–8.
        Brief satirical description (p. 326) of conversation between Coleridge and a carrier.

343   [SCOTT, JOHN?]. 'Blackwood's Magazine. They do but jest-- poison in jest'. London Magazine [Baldwin's], II, 509–21.
        Attack on Blackwood's criticism of Coleridge. Apparently forerunner of Scott's 'Mohock Magazine' (1820), q.v.

344   _____. 'The Mohock Magazine'. London Magazine [Baldwin's], II, 666–85.
        A major point (pp. 674–6) in this attack on Blackwood's is Lockhart's supposedly shabby treatment of Coleridge. Article led to Scott's death in duel with Lockhart's second.
        Attribution: Graham

345   [TALFOURD, THOMAS NOON]. 'Modern Periodical Literature'. New Monthly Magazine, XIV, 305–6. Reprinted Atheneum [Boston], VIII (1820), 103–4; reprinted in his Critical and Miscellaneous Writings. Philadelphia: Carey and Hart (1846), pp. 43–7.
        Attack on treatment of Christabel in Edinburgh Review (1816).

346 _____. 'Various Prospects of Mankind, Nature and Providence'.
Retrospective Review, II, 185-206. Reprinted Literary and
Scientific Repository [New York], II (1821), 150-70. Extract
on Coleridge reprinted Critical Review [New York], II
(1821), 161-2; reprinted in his Critical and Miscellaneous
Writings. Philadelphia: Carey and Hart (1846), pp.
pp. 73-82
     Article on Wallace's 1761 work includes (pp. 197-9)
discussion of Coleridge as poet, metaphysician, and teach-
er. Favourably compared with Wordsworth in range of
thought, and Shakespeare and Milton in music of language.

347 [WAINWRIGHT, THOMAS] Sam Quiz, pseud. 'Immortality in Em-
     bryo'. London Magazine [Gold's], II, 39-43, 151-4.
     Satirical sketches of Wordsworth ('Peter Bell'), Cole-
ridge ('Bard Bracy'), and Leigh Hunt, and a humourous
continuation of Christabel.
     Attribution: Dobell

348 [WARE, J.]. 'The Sea of the Poets'. Club-Room [Boston],
     No. 3 (April), pp. 87-103.
     Coleridge one of poets satirized (p. 95).

                         1821

349 ANON. 'Christabel and Other Poems'. Academic [Liverpool],
     No. 17 (15 Sept), pp. 339-41.
     'By far the most faulty of the Lake Poets!.

350 _____. 'Periodical Literature'. Literary and Scientific Re-
     pository [New York], II, 382-9.
     Quotes and criticizes Talfourd ('Various Prospects',
1820) for view of 'the unfortunate Christabel'.

351 _____. 'The Life of Wesley...by Robert Southey'. Monthly
     Review, XCVI, 26-43. Partially reprinted Monthly Reposi-
tory, XVI (1821), 595.
     Concludes with criticism of Coleridge's criticism of
Dr. Price and comparison in Price's favour.

352 _____. 'To Benjamin Bookworm, Esq.'. Salt-Bearer, No. 29,
     pp. 333-47.
     Reply to H. N. C. (1821) argues that as poet of love,
Coleridge is inferior to Scott, Campbell, Cornwall, and
Milman.

353   [BARBE, R. F. ST.] Simon Shatterbrain, pseud. 'Meteorologi-
      cal Observations Extraordinary'. Blackwood's Magazine, X,
      267-70.
          Coleridge's poems described (p. 269) as playful, mys-
      terious and puzzling.
          Attribution: Strout

354   CHASLES, PHILARÈTE E. 'Essai historique sur la poésie
      anglaise et sur les poètes anglais vivants'. La revue
      encyclopédique, [Paris], IX, 446-58.
          Coleridge (p. 447) briefly noted as having sacrificed
      great abilities.

355   [COLERIDGE, HENRY NELSON] Gerard Montgomery, pseud. 'On
      Coleridge's Poetry'. Etonian, I, 315-25. Reprinted 1822.
          Defence of Coleridge's poetry written by his nephew, a
      student at Eton. Coleridge at his best as love poet, 'the
      most genuine and original' since Shakespeare, and 'the
      greatest genius, in every respect, of the present day'.
          Attribution: Appendix to Etonian
          Reviewed: [William Sidney Walker]. Quarterly Review,
      XXV (1821), 102 (attribution: Shine).

356   HUNT, LEIGH. 'Sketches of the Living Poets. No. 4--Mr. Cole-
      ridge'. Examiner, No. 720 (21 Oct), 664-7. Reprinted
      Literary Gazette [Philadelphia], I (1821), 815-6.
          After biographical sketch, and brief comments on prose
      and poetry, Hunt adds that, having just reread The Ancient
      Mariner, what he has written may be 'nonsense' and poem is
      'very fine poetry'. See Hunt, 1819.

357   LLOYD, CHARLES. Desultory Thoughts in London. London:
      Charles and Henry Baldwyn.
          Twenty-two rather feeble stanzas (64-85) praise Cole-
      ridge and express gratitude for his 'fostering care'.

358   [LOCKHART, JOHN GIBSON] John Bull, pseud. Letter to the
      Right Hon. Lord Byron. London: William Wright. 64 pp.
      Reprinted with introduction and notes by Alan Lang Strout.
      University of Oklahoma Press (1947).
          Chides Byron for references to Coleridge's drinking and
      opium and describes The Ancient Mariner as 'Brunswick Mum'.

359   [MAGINN, WILLIAM]. 'Letter from Dr. Olinthus Petre'. Black-
      wood's Magazine, IX, 140-2.
          Criticizes Lamb for Jacobin tendencies abandoned by
      Coleridge.
          Attribution: Strout

360   [MOIR, D. M.] Morgan O'Doherty, pseud. 'Familiar Letter from
      the Adjutant, containing projects, promises, and imita-
      tions'. Blackwood's Magazine, IX, 131-40.
          Imagines how Byron would alter The Ancient Mariner and
      Christabel and adds parody of Kubla Khan (pp. 135-6).
          Attribution: Strout

361   ____. 'Vision by Moon-Light'. Blackwood's Magazine, IX,
      437-48.
          Romantic dream-vision of contemporary poets (Coleridge,
      pp. 442-3).
          Attribution: Strout

362   R. 'On Coleridge's "Friend"'. Edinburgh Magazine, VIII,
      51-4.
          This 'eloquent and admirable book' revives the philo-
      sophic and literary quality of 'the brightest days of our
      literature'.

363   [TALFOURD, THOMAS NOON]. 'Mr. Charles Lloyd's Poems'. Lon-
      don Magazine [Baldwin's], III, 406-13. Reprinted in Mod-
      ern British Essayists. Philadelphia: Carey and Hart
      (1848), VII, 94-8.
          Begins with lengthy comparison of Wordsworth and Cole-
      ridge in approximately the terms of Biographia Literaria.

364   WILSON, JOHN ILIFF. The History of Christ's Hospital. Lon-
      don: Taylor and Hessey.
          Biographical sketch of Coleridge included (pp. 227-36)
      among 'memoirs of eminent blues'.

365   [WILSON, JOHN?]. 'Lyndsay's Dramas of the Ancient World'.
      Blackwood's Magazine, X, 730-40.
          Remorse 'full of the deep metaphysics of passion', but
      barely approaches England's best works (p. 231).
          Attribution: Strout

                              1822

366   ANON. 'The Augustan Age in England'. Album, I, 183-234.
          Coleridge (pp. 216-7) more a metaphysician than a poet,
      but 'in neither capacity very pre-eminent'.

367   ____. 'Ecclesiastical Sketches'. Monthly Literary Register,
      XX, 88.
          Attacks both Wordsworth and Coleridge as poets of little
      range but great pretensions.

368 [CROWE, EYRE EVANS]. 'Hazlitt's Table-Talk'. Blackwood's
     Magazine, XII, 157-66.
          Brief comparison (p. 163) of Coleridge's social and fi-
     nancial status with that of Hazlitt.
          Attribution: Strout

369 [DOUBLEDAY, THOMAS] T. D. 'How Far is Poetry an Art?'.
     Blackwood's Magazine, XI, 153-9.
          Brief reference to Coleridge's description of Black-
     wood's (p. 154). Illustrates union of poetical and meta-
     physical talent (p. 156).
          Attribution: Strout

370 [HAZLITT, WILLIAM]. 'Table Talk V: On the Conversation of
     Authors'. New Monthly Magazine, V, 528-36. Reprinted in
     his Plain Speaker. 2 vols. London: Henry Colburn (1826),
     I, 74-97.
          Includes several recollections of Coleridge's
     conversation.

371 [JEFFREY, FRANCIS]. 'Memorials of a Tour on the Continent'.
     Edinburgh Review, XXXVII, 449-56.
          Coleridge 'by far the most original genius' of the Lake
     poets, has damaged reputation of group by publication of
     Christabel. Lake School now 'pretty nearly extinct'.
          Attribution: WI.

372 [MAGINN, WILLIAM] Paddy, pseud. 'Metricum Symposium Ambrosi-
     anum'. Blackwood's Magazine, XII, 79-83. Reprinted
     Noctes Ambrosianae. 5 vols. New York: Redfield (1854),
     I, 218-25.
          Drinking-song on contemporary poets hails (pp. 80-1)
     'mad Coleridge' and his unfavourable response to Maturin.
     Mackenzie's note describes (p. 221) Coleridge as an 'un-
     successful dramatist'.
          Attribution: Strout

373 [OLLIER, CHARLES] J[ohn] J[ohnes], pseud. 'London Chit-Chat'.
     Blackwood's Magazine, XI, 331-4.
          On misrepresentation of Coleridge and Wordsworth in The
     Edinburgh Review.
          Attribution: Strout

374 R. 'On the Poetry of Coleridge'. Literary Speculum, II,
     145-51. Portrait.
          Favourable estimate but chiefly devoted to Coleridge's
     use of repetition and 'pantomime' in attempt to be
     original.

375   No entry.

376   No entry.

377   No entry.

378   No entry.

379   No entry.

380   [WILSON, JOHN]. 'Wordsworth's Sonnets and Memorials'. Black-
      wood's Magazine, XII, 175-91. Reprinted in his Essays
      Critical and Imaginative. 4 vols. Edinburgh, London:
      William Blackwood (1855-58), I, 401-8.
          Coleridge and other contemporary poets deeply indebted
      to Wordsworth (p. 176).
          Attribution: Strout

381   Z. 'Memoirs of the Living Poets of Great Britain. Samuel
      Taylor Coleridge'. Imperial Magazine, IV, 1094-1103.
          Biographical sketch critical of Coleridge.

                              1823

382   AIKIN, LUCY. Memoir of John Aikin, M. D. 2 vols. London:
      Baldwin et al.
          Daughter of editor of Monthly Magazine recalls (I, 250),
      his interest in Coleridge's early work.

383   ANON. 'Original Communications. Strictures on the Poets of
      the Present Day. No. 7--S. T. Coleridge'. La Belle As-
      semblée, XXVII, 53-7.
          Coleridge's obscurity seen as result of failure to com-
      bine 'genius' with 'the straightforward industry of regu-
      lar application'. The Ancient Mariner the 'most singular'
      of Coleridge's poems.

384   _____. 'The Literary Police Office, Bow Street'. London
      Magazine [Baldwin's], VII, 157-62.
          Satire. 'Police' include Jeffrey and Gifford, and
      culprits are Coleridge, Wordsworth, and others.

385   _____. 'Recent Poetical Plagiarisms and Imitations'. London
      Magazine [Baldwin's], VIII, 597-604.
          The first of several instances is passage from Childe
      Harold said to be a plagiarism from Christabel.

1823-ANON.

386   ANON. 'Coleridge (S. T. Esq.)'. Public Characters of All
      Nations. 3 vols. London: Sir Richard Phillips. I, 393.
      Portrait.
          Brief, inaccurate biographical sketch.

387   _____. ['Remorse']. Saturday Evening Post [Philadelphia],
      II, No. 1 (4 Jan), p. 3.
          Advertisement with list of cast.

388   [COHEN, FRANCIS? (later Palgrave)]. 'Superstition and
      Knowledge'. Quarterly Review, XXIX, 440-75.
          Mentions (p. 451) Kubla Khan as instance of effect of
      'medicated potions' in producing a 'preternatural state of
      the body and of the mind'.
          Attribution: Shine, p. 85.

389   [DE QUINCEY, THOMAS] X. Y. Z. 'Death of A German Great Man'.
      London Magazine [Baldwin's], VII, 378-80. Reprinted in
      his Essays on Philosophical Writers and Other Men of Let-
      ters. 2 vols. Boston: Ticknor and Fields (1856), I,
      165-82.
          Herder (p. 373) 'the German Coleridge', but Coleridge,
      because of 'fineness and compass of understanding', has
      'greatly the advantage'. Reference to unfinished works
      and earliest volume of poems.

390   _____. 'Letters to a Young Man whose Education has been
      Neglected'; 'On the English Notices of Kant' [Letters I,
      V]. London Magazine [Baldwin's], VII, 84-90; VIII, 87-95.
      Reprinted in his Letters to a Young Man and other Papers.
      Boston: Ticknor, Reed, and Fields (1854), pp. [1]-17,
      68-87.
          Discussion of Coleridge's advice to prospective authors
      in Biographia, chapter XI, and of Coleridge's misunder-
      standing of Kant.

391   _____. 'To the Lakers'. London Magazine [Baldwin's], VIII,
      497-8. Reprinted in his Works...Author's Edition.
      15 vols., 2 supplements. Edinburgh: A. & C. Black
      (1871), XVI, 493-9.
          Humorous proposal for a guide to the Lakes to be written
      by Coleridge and others.

SAMUEL TAYLOR COLERIDGE: AN ANNOTATED BIBLIOGRAPHY

392 [HAZLITT, WILLIAM]. W. H. 'My First Acquaintance with
     Poets'. Liberal, III, 23-46. Reprinted in his Literary
     Remains. 2 vols. London: Saunders and Otley (1836), II,
     359-96.
          Hazlitt's famous account of Coleridge's visit to Shrop-
     shire and preaching at Shrewsbury.

393 [LOCKHART, J. G. and R. P. GILLIES]. 'Horae Germanicae.
     No. XVI. Wallenstein, Translated by Coleridge'. Black-
     wood's Magazine, XIV, 377-96.
          Coleridge's work best translation of foreign drama into
     English.
          Attribution: Strout

394 [LOCKHART, J. G.]. 'New Series of the Curiosities of Litera-
     ture'. Blackwood's Magazine, XIII, 163-73.
          Includes (p. 172) description of Coleridge's handwrit-
     ing.
          Attribution: Strout

395 [PATMORE, PETER GEORGE] Victoire, Count de Soligny, pseud.
     Letters on England. 2 vols. London: Henry Colburn.
          Letter XLVIII (pp. 78-85) describes Coleridge as 'per-
     haps...the first genius of his day in this country' al-
     though 'he has done--almost nothing'.
          Attribution: NCBEL
          Reviewed: [J. G. Lockhart]. Blackwood's Magazine,
     XIII (1823), 558-66 (attribution: Strout). Extract on
     Coleridge reprinted Album, VI (1823), 148-9.

396 [PRESCOTT, WILLIAM HICKLING]. 'The French and English Trage-
     dy'. North American Review [Boston], XVI, 124-56.
          Remorse is one of the four 'most meritorious tragedies
     of our own age' (p. 148). 'No man has painted in such
     visible coloring...the imaginative horrors of a dead and
     invisible world'.
          Attribution: Pochmann

397 [THOMSON, HENRY] Titus, pseud. 'Modern Dramas, and Dramatic
     Writers'. Blackwood's Magazine, XIV, 555-60.
          Coleridge's one tragedy is 'an excellently good one'
     although unfortunate in its acting (p. 557).
          Attribution: Strout

398 [WILSON, JOHN et al.]. 'Noctes Ambrosianae' Nos. VIII, XI,
     XII, XIV, XVI, XIX, XXI, XXXII. Blackwood's Magazine,
     XIII, 592-611; XIV, 236-48, 484-503; XV (1824), 367-90;
     XVI (1824), 231-50; XVII (1825), 366-84; XVIII (1825),
     378-92; XXI (1827), 473-89. Reprinted with Memoir and

1823-WILSON

([WILSON, JOHN et al.])
Notes by R. Shelton Mackenzie. 5 vols. New York: Redfield (1854). I, 218-25, 295-321, 346, 383, 407, 457-86;
II, 65, 98-116, 366.
Various Blackwood's writers (some of whom elsewhere
wrote significant criticism of Coleridge) mock and parody
his poetry, make jest of his plagiarism, illogic and conversation, and compare him unfavourably to Hogg and Pope.

1824

399   ANON. 'On the Poetry of Southey'. Knight's Quarterly Magazine, III, 156-64.
Includes comparison (p. 162) of Coleridge and Southey.

400   _____. 'Schiller's Life and Writings'. London Magazine, X,
149-63.
Footnote (p. 158) on Coleridge's admirable translation
of Wallenstein.

401   [DEACON, W. F.]. 'The Dream. A Psychological Curiosity. By
S. T. C.'. Warreniana...by the Editor of Quarterly Review.
London: Longman et al., pp. 93-108.
'Advertisement' (pp. 93-5) parodies Coleridge's note to
Kubla Khan. The poem parodies Christabel with echoes from
other poems.
Attribution: Hamilton

402   HAZLITT, WILLIAM. 'Preface and Critical List of Authors'.
Select British Poets. London: William C. Hall,
pp. 619-30.
Coleridge has 'produced nothing equal to his powers'.
The Ancient Mariner, Ode to the Departing Year, Fire, Fam-
ine and Slaughter and Genevieve receive brief comments.

403   JAJA, pseud. 'Memoirs of Samuel Taylor Coleridge, Esq.'.
Metropolitan Literary Journal, I, 231-9.
Biographical sketch. Coleridge 'great, yet not infal-
lible'. The early poems (1796-1797), especially Religious
Musings, basis for fame. Metaphysical speculation his be-
setting sin. Major concern is Coleridge's health, and relation of genius to 'physical derangement'.

404 MEDWIN, THOMAS. Journal of the Conversations of Lord Byron.
     2 vols. Paris: A. and W. Galignani.
          Records (I, 185-9; II, 6) Byron's comments on Christa-
     bel, Kubla Khan, Biographia Literaria, Coleridge's influ-
     ence on Scott, and on his own 'Siege of Corinth' and
     'Childe Harold'.

405 SHELLEY, PERCY BYSSHE. 'Letter to--[Maria Gisborne]'. Post-
     humous Poems. London: John and Henry L. Hunt.
          Lines 202-208 are Shelley's famous description of Cole-
     ridge as 'a hooded eagle among blinking owls'.

406 S. T. C., pseud. 'Sonnet'. Wasp, I, 47-8.
          An imitation.

                              1825

407 ANON. 'Aids to Reflection'. British Review, XXIII, 486.
          Work unreadable, instance of 'literary talent...entirely
     wasted'.

408 _____. 'Aids to Reflection'. Congregational Magazine, VIII,
     647-51.
          High praise tempered by criticism of the difficulty of
     Coleridge's manner of thinking and writing, which is ana-
     lysed and illustrated.

409 _____. 'A Parody on Christabelle'. Encyclopaedia of Anecdote
     and Wit. 2 vols. London: Duncombe, I, 49-51.
          The mastiff bitch is transformed into the devil and
     carries off the baron.

410 _____. 'The Spirit of the Age: or Contemporary Portraits'.
     Eclectic Review, New Series XXIII, 152-64.
          Review of Hazlitt's book discusses comparison of Godwin
     and Coleridge.

411 BARBAULD, ANNA LAETITIA. 'To Mr. S. T. Coleridge, 1797'.
     Works of Anna Laetitia Barbauld. 2 vols. London: Longman
     et al., I, 209-11.
          Forty-three lines exhorting Coleridge to escape 'maze of
     metaphysical lore' and exert himself for poetic fame.

412 CARLYLE, THOMAS. Life of Friedrich Schiller. London: Taylor
     and Hessey.
          Carlyle laments (p. 179, note) Coleridge's unfulfilled
     promise.

1825-HAZLITT

413   [HAZLITT, WILLIAM]. 'Mr. Coleridge'. The Spirit of the Age:
       or Contemporary Portraits. London: Henry Colburn,
       pp. 57-79. Rev. ed. Paris: A. W. Galignani (1825),
       pp. 57-75.
         Highly critical evaluation of Coleridge enlarged in the
       second edition.
       Reviewed: no. 417.

414   IRVING, EDWARD. 'Dedication, to Samuel Taylor Coleridge,
       Esq.'. For Missionaries after the Apostolical School.
       London: Hamilton, Adams, and Co., pp. vii-ix.
         A fulsome acknowledgement of Irving's debt to
       Coleridge.

415   [LOCKHART, J. G.]. 'Lord Byron'. Blackwood's Magazine,
       XVII, 131-51.
         Attempt to explain away Byron's 'ill-advised sarcasms'
       against Coleridge (p. 142).
       Attribution: Strout

416   [MAURICE, F. D.]. 'New School of Cockneyism'. Metropolitan
       Quarterly Magazine, I, 34-62.
         Coleridge called (p. 39) one of the 'first-rate men of
       genius'.
       Attribution: Sanders

417   P. P. 'Letter from an Absent Contributor on Hazlitt's Spirit
       of the Age'. London Magazine, New Series I, 182-9.
         Severe criticism (pp. 182-6) of Hazlitt's portrait of
       Coleridge.

418   PICHOT, AMÉDÉE. Voyage Historique et Littéraire en Angle-
       terre et en Écosse. 3 vols. Paris: Ladvocat et Charles
       Gosselin. Portrait (Leslie). Translated as Historical
       and Literary Tour of a Foreigner in England and Scotland.
       London: Saunders and Otley.
         Two letters (II, 363-94, 395-421) to Soulié and de La
       Martine emphasize Coleridge's mysticism, indolence, youth-
       ful reputation, and eloquence. Praises Coleridge's love
       poetry, and with reservations, The Ancient Mariner, which
       he translates. Long description of Remorse.

419   [WILSON, JOHN]. 'Analytical Essays on the Modern English
       Drama'. Blackwood's Magazine, XVIII, 119-30.
         Coleridge (p. 119) among poets of 'dramatic genius' in
       a generation of 'miserable' playwrights.
       Attribution: Strout

1826

420 ANON. 'Aids to Reflection'. British Critic, 3rd Series III, 239-80.
     'Gratitude' for Coleridge's support of church, but attack on him for his obscurity, reliance on German metaphysics, views on sin and redemption, and criticism of Paley.

421 _____. 'Aids to Reflection'. Quarterly Theological Review, III, 128-36.
     Praises Coleridge's intention but deplores obscurity. Quotes a number of aphorisms as deserving of the highest praise.

422 _____. 'Facetiae. Introductory Essay...by S. T. Coleridge, Esq.'. 'Vice, Venality, and Slander, A Newspaper Eclogue'. Wasp, I, 86-8, 153-4.
     A parody of Coleridge and of his poems.

423 KELLY, MICHAEL. Reminiscences of Michael Kelly, of the King's Theatre, and Theatre Royal Drury Lane. 2 vols. London: Henry Colburn.
     Kelly discusses (II, 309-10) his composition of the music for Remorse and Coleridge's favourable opinion of it.

424 [MAURICE, F. D.]. 'The Age of Folly'. Metropolitan Quarterly Magazine, II, 266.
     Coleridge's discussions of Wordsworth considered 'a model of friendly and impartial criticism.'
     Attribution: Sanders

425 [MOORE, THOMAS]. 'A Vision. By the Author of Christabel'. Times, No. 13058 (29 Aug), p. 2.
     A satire written in rough imitation of metre of Christabel. In a letter to The Times (31 August), Coleridge denied authorship.
     Attribution: Hamilton

1827

426 ANON. 'Wallenstein'. London Magazine [Baldwin's], New Series VII, 460-6.
     Considers (pp. 463-6) Coleridge's translation superior to that under review.

1827-ANON.

427   ANON. 'The Amulet'. <u>Monthly Review</u>, New Series VI, 347-60.
    <u>Conversational Dialogues</u> (i.e. <u>The Improvisatore</u>) noted
    (pp. 355-6) as praiseworthy in form but difficult in
    language.

428   _____. ['The Annuals']. <u>Monthly Repository</u>, New Series I,
    918-26.
    Favourable comment on 'Youth and Age'.

429   _____. 'The Plea of the Midsummer Fairies; Hero & Leander...
    by Thomas Hood'. <u>Monthly Review</u>, New Series, VI, 259-60.
    Criticizes Hood for dedicating 'Hero and Leander' to
    Coleridge.

430   [FAIRCHILD, SUMNER LINCOLN] L. 'Personal and Literary Charac-
    ter of S. T. Coleridge'. <u>Philadelphia Monthly Magazine</u>, I,
    57-60. Reprinted with revisions, naming author, in <u>Cabinet
    of Religion</u> [New York], II (1829), 622-6.
    Rhapsodic account of Coleridge's appearance and conver-
    sation, both unaffected by opium. His philosophy is incom-
    prehensible, but he is a model of domestic virtue, living
    in rural bliss with the 'wife of his bosom' (p. 59).

431   HARE, JULIUS CHARLES and AUGUSTUS WILLIAM. <u>Guesses at Truth
    by Two Brothers</u>. London: Taylor.
    Frequent allusions to, and brief essays on, Coleridge, by
    whose spirit 'most of my thoughts will appear to have been
    impregnated'. Subsequent editions (1838, 1847, 1848) add fur-
    ther Coleridge material. Reviewed: <u>Athenaeum</u>, No. 42
    (13 Aug 1828), pp. 656-8; [R. A. Willmott]. <u>Fraser's Maga-
    zine</u>, XIX (1839), 529-42 (Attribution: <u>WI</u>.).

432   [HERAUD, JOHN ABRAHAM]. 'Historical Romance'. <u>Quarterly Re-
    view</u>, XXXV, 518-66.
    Notes that Coleridge worked from a manuscript copy and
    this explains apparent errors in his translation of
    <u>Wallenstein</u>.
    Attribution: <u>WI</u>.

433   HOOD, THOMAS. 'To S. T. Coleridge, Esq.'. <u>Plea of the Mid-
    summer Fairies</u>. London: Longman <u>et al</u>., p. 67.
    Dedicatory sonnet prefixed to 'Hero and Leander'.

434   [MAGINN, WILLIAM]. 'Hebrew Tales...By Hyman Hurwitz'. <u>Quar-
    terly Review</u>, XXXV, 86-114.
    Quotes (pp. 113-4) from <u>Aids to Reflection</u>, 'a book full
    of passages of the most powerful eloquence'.
    Attribution: <u>WI</u>.

435 _____. Whitehall; or, The Days of George IV. London: Marsh.
Humorous novel in which Coleridge (pp. 231-2) delivers
a long and characteristically involuted monologue as his
dying words.
Attribution: Rogers

436 [MONTGOMERY, ROBERT]. The Age Reviewed: A Satire. London:
Carpenter.
Satirical portrait (pp. 139-40, 184).
Attribution: Rogers

437 [PICHOT, AMÉDÉE]. 'S. T. Coleridge. An Essay on Coleridge's
Life and Poetry'. The Living Poets of England. Specimens...with Biographical and Critical Notices. 2 vols.
Paris: Baudry, I, 413-9.
Summaries of The Ancient Mariner ('whimsical', 'over-
praised'), Remorse and Christabel ('incomplete effusion')
with judgment that Coleridge, but for indolence, might be
the greatest of modern poets.

1828

438 ANON. 'Coleridge and the Malmsey'. Atheneum [Boston], 2nd
Series IX, 166.
Anecdote of Coleridge at Rogers's dinner party.

439 _____. 'Aids to Reflection'. Christian Examiner and Church
of Ireland Magazine. [Dublin], VI, 42-53.
Reviewer feels unable to do justice to Coleridge's
thought and devotes essay to a discussion and defence of
Coleridge's apparent obscurity.

440 _____. 'Short Review of Books'. Foreign Review, II, 533-5.
Vigorous defence of Coleridge's character and genius
against Charles Coquerel (1828), whose insinuations are
compared with Hazlitt's.

441 _____. 'Coleridge's Aids to Reflection and Montgomery's
Omnipresence of the Deity'. Literary Chronicle, No. 474
(31 May), p. 1.
'A man who has read more, thought more, and felt more
than perhaps any one now living'.

1828-ANON.

442   ANON. 'Coleridge's Poems'. Literary Chronicle, No. 476
      (28 June), pp. 67-8.
         Reviewer of Poetical Works (1828) admires Coleridge as
      a poet of love and tranquillity. Attempts to distinguish
      Coleridge from Wordsworth in terms of attitude to nature.
      Harsh criticism of Hymn before Sunrise, The Ancient Mari-
      ner and Christabel. Editorial note (E. J. Dalby) disavows
      reviewer's reservations, and calls Coleridge 'the greatest
      man now living'.

443   _____. 'Poetical Works of S. T. Coleridge'. Literary Ga-
      zette, No. 605 (23 Aug), pp. 535-6. Reprinted Atheneum
      [Boston], 3rd Series I (1828), 111-4.
         Effusive, moralistic review speaks of Coleridge's in-
      fluence on 'modern bards' and praises him as 'the founder
      of our present noble and impassioned school of poetry'.

444   _____. 'Coleridge's Works'. London Weekly Review, II,
      369-70.
         Review of 1828 edition, argues against Coleridge's in-
      flated reputation as poet and thinker. Only Love and a
      few fragments from The Ancient Mariner and Christabel are
      likely to survive.

445   _____. 'The Poetical Works of S. T. Coleridge--oeuvres poé-
      tiques de S. T. Coleridge'. Revue encyclopédique [Paris],
      XL, 666-7.
         Coleridge little known in France, but a poet of tender
      passion and quiet feeling, whose treatment of nature re-
      calls Claude Lorrain.

446   _____. 'A Second Gleaning from the Anthologies of 1829'.
      Spectator, No. 22 (29 Nov), pp. 346-7.
         The Keepsake has published some epigrams of Coleridge's
      'which have lost their merit by being put into print'.
      The 'Laudes Italiae', however, 'are more discriminative
      and exquisite' than Virgil and Addison.

447   COQUEREL, CHARLES AUGUSTIN. Histoire abrégée de la littéra-
      ture anglaise. Paris: Janet, pp. 513-4.
         Brief comment finds Ancient Mariner impressive, but
      Coleridge generally obscure and, like Byron, indulging in
      horror and obscenity. Reviewed: no. 440.

448   [DANA, RICHARD HENRY]. 'The Course of Time'. The Spirit of
       the Pilgrims [Boston], I, 516-40. Reprinted in his Poems
       and Prose Writings. 2 vols. New York: Baker and Scrib-
       ner (1850), II, 344-79.
           Review of Pollok concludes (pp. 538-40) that Coleridge
       is the one living poet capable of writing a great religious
       poem in English.

449   HUNT, LEIGH. Lord Byron and Some of His Contemporaries.
       London: Colburn.
           Includes amiable portrait (pp. 330-4) of Coleridge as
       an old man, inspired and indolent.

450   [JEFFREY, FRANCIS]. 'Fall of Nineveh, A Poem. By Edwin
       Atherstone'. Edinburgh Review, XLVIII, 47-60.
           Crabbe, Coleridge and Wordsworth (p. 47) are 'burnt
       out'.
           Attribution: WI.

451   [LOCKHART, J. G.]. 'May Fair'. Quarterly Review, XXXVII,
       84-100.
           Praises (pp. 90-1) Coleridge's contributions to The
       Bijou, especially The Wanderings of Cain, which has the
       'noblest qualities' of The Ancient Mariner.
           Attribution: WI.

452   [MAURICE, F. D.]. 'Maria Edgeworth'. Athenaeum, No. 19
       (28 Mar), p. 289.
           Coleridge 'the first of living English philosophers'
       and a native definer of truths other have sought in Ger-
       many.
           Attribution: Sanders

453   [STERLING, JOHN]. 'An Appeal Apologetic from Philip Drunk to
       Philip Sober'. Athenaeum, No. 36 (2 July), pp. 567-8.
       Reprinted as 'On Coleridge's Christabel' in Essays and
       Tales by John Sterling Collected and Edited, with a Memoir
       of his Life. 2 vols. London: Parker (1848), I, 101-10.
           Defence of Christabel as tale of witchery in which
       every line has strong under-import; it is superior to 'The
       Lay of the Last Minstrel' for which it provided the germ.

1829

454   Aids to Reflection. First American, from the first London edition, with an appendix, and illustrations from other works
of the same author; together with a preliminary essay, and
additional notes, by James Marsh. Burlington [Vermont]:
Goodrich, lxi, 399 pp.
    Marsh's Preliminary Essay (pp. vii-liv) was the most
important single essay on Coleridge to be published in
America in the nineteenth century, exerting an influence
that extended from Emerson to John Dewey. Marsh found in
Coleridge an alternative to the 'prevailing theology' and
was the primary source of Coleridge's influence on American
transcendentalism.
    Reviewed: no. 478.

455   Poetical Works of Coleridge, Shelley, and Keats, Complete in
One Volume. Paris: Galignani. Portrait: J. T. Wedgwood.
Reprinted Philadelphia: Griff (1831).
    Biographical sketch of Coleridge (pp. v-xi) with praise
of Genevieve and The Ancient Mariner, but harsh criticism
of Coleridge's waste of talents on conversation and ephem-
eral prose.

456   ANON. 'Ugly Wives Fittest for Poets!'. Atlas, IV, 457.
    'W-- is wedded to the head of a gorgon, S-- is not much
better off, C-- has eloped from his mate...yet none have
excelled these writers in descriptions of female beauty'.

457   _____. 'Coleridge and the Germans'. Athenaeum, No. 101
(30 Sept), pp. 613-4.
    Attack on Carlyle's remarks in Foreign Review (1829),
q.v. Coleridge should be distinguished from the Germans,
who regard philosophy as an end, whereas to him it is a
means to religion and proper living.

458   _____. 'On the Genius of Professor Wilson'. Edinburgh Literary Gazette, II, 1-3.
    Begins with qualified praise for the 'Lake School', ad-
miration for Christabel and Genevieve.

459   _____. 'The Bijou; or Annual of Literature'. Literary Magnet. 3 vols. London: Poynton and Wright, III, 332-6.
    'The Wanderings of Cain one of the few commendable items
in The Bijou'.

460 _____. 'The Keepsake Reviewed'. Monthly Repository, New
Series III, 54, 875.
Coleridge's contributions in 1829 disappoint, but Poet's
Answer to a Lady's Question in 1830 is praised.

461 No entry.

462 _____. [untitled]. New Jerusalem Magazine [Boston], II,
81-3.
Passage from Biographia shows 'striking coincidence'
between Coleridge and Swedenborg.

462A _____. "Love. By S. T. Coleridge," Whitby Magazine, III
(1829), 111-6.
Text of poem, with warmly appreciative commentary.

463 BYRAN, DANIEL. 'Mother and Daughter Land'. New-York Mirror,
VII, [185]. Partially reprinted J. Dykes Campbell,
Athenaeum, No. 2949 (3 May 1884), pp. 566-7.
Lines of verse to Coleridge.

464 [CARLYLE, THOMAS]. 'Novalis Schriften'. Foreign Review, IV,
97-141. Reprinted in his Works. London: Chapman and Hall
(1899), XXVI, 1-55.
Carlyle distinguishes German and English readers (p. 98)
on the ground that Novalis has run to four editions, whereas The Friend and Biographia of 'our Coleridge', compara-
tively a 'slight business', are thought 'clearly unintelligible'. Coleridge a genius 'unable to see' the 'deep
thoughts' he originates.

465 CAMBRIDGE UNION SOCIETY. Laws and Transactions of the Union
Society. Cambridge: J. Hall, p. 56.
Topic for debate on 17 Feb, 1829: 'Will Mr. Coleridge's
Poem of The Ancient Mariner, or Mr. Martin's Act tend most
to prevent cruelty to animals?' Speakers include Richard
Monckton Milnes.

466 [HAZLITT, WILLIAM]. 'Memorabilia of Mr. Coleridge'. Atlas,
IV, 193. Reprinted Museum of Foreign Literature [Phila-
delphia], XIV (1829), 568.
Several brief comments attributed to Coleridge.
Attribution: Howe

1829–M. S.

467   M. S. 'Percy Bysshe Shelley'. Literary Phoenix [Birmingham],
      I, 14-8.
            Argues for vast superiority of Shelley to the 'insipid
      trash' of Coleridge and Wordsworth, who are seen as taste-
      less, childish and stupid.

468   [PEABODY, WILLIAM BOURNE OLIVER]. 'Lord Byron and his Con-
      temporaries'. North American Review [Boston], XXVIII,
      1-18.
            Coleridge's reputation for genius is based on his 'wild
      and powerful' Ancient Mariner (p. 17), and undercut by
      Christabel.
            Attribution: Cushing

468A [WATKINS, JOHN]. "Rhyme of the Ancient Mariner -- A Poet's
      Reverie," Whitby Repository, V (1829), 114-8, 140-2, 182-5,
      205-7, 263-6, 315-8.
            Text of poem, with favorable criticism and interpretive
      comments, concerning the ballad style, the poem's plain
      language, logical sequence of events, and general truth to
      life.
            Attribution: Cook and Ogden, Victorian Periodicals
      Newsletter, VIII (December 1975).

469   [WILLIS, N. P.?]. 'The Editor's Table'. American Monthly
      Magazine [Boston], I, 646-59.
            Review of Poetical Works (1828) chiefly devoted to Re-
      morse which, in spite of 'well-wrought workmanship', is
      poetical rather than dramatic.
            Attribution: editor was N. P. Willis

                              1830

470   ANON. The Real Devil's Walk. Not by Professor Porson. De-
      signs by Robert Cruikshank. London: Effingham Wilson.
      34 pp.
            Imitation of The Devil's Thoughts.

471   _____. 'The Westminster Review.--Writings of Coleridge'.
      Athenaeum, No. 116 (16 Jan), pp. 17-8.
            Criticism, perhaps by Maurice and Sterling, of 1830 re-
      view of Poetical Works for its dismissal of Coleridge's
      prose, 'the richest possession of our age'.

472   _____. 'A Visit to the Grand National Cemetery in the Year
      2000'. British Magazine, I, 337-44. Reprinted Museum of
      Foreign Literature [Philadelphia], XVII (1830), 123-7.
            Coleridge among notables commemorated in verse.

473 _____. 'On the Constitution of the Church and State'. Christian Examiner [Boston], X, 307-12.
Sympathetic paraphrase without critical comment.

474 _____. 'Du perfectionnement moral, ou de l'education de soi-
même'. Christian Examiner [Boston], IX, 70-107.
Review cites Coleridge (pp. 73-4) as, in spite of his
obscurity of style, one in 'possession of a treasure of
valuable truth...capable of doing a great service'.

475 _____. 'On the Constitution of the Church and State'. Edin-
burgh Literary Journal, III, 303-4.
Despite inability to complete or communicate his ideas,
Coleridge's influence on his age has been great.

476 _____. 'The Last of the Supernaturalists'. Fraser's Magazine, I, 217-35.
Passing reference to Coleridge's 'mysticism' and 'mad-
ness' (p. 217) in an essay on Blake.
Attribution: See discussion in WI.

477 _____. 'The Inventions of William Blake, Painter and Poet'.
London University Magazine, II, 318-23.
Blake, Flaxman, and Coleridge forerunners of 'more ele-
vated and purer system'. Notes similarities of thought.

478 _____. 'American Edition of Aids to Reflection'. New Jerusalem Magazine [Boston], III, 189-91.
Quotations from Marsh with statement (p. 189) on Coleridge's present stature, influence, and relation to New
Church.

479 _____. 'Poetical Works of S. T. Coleridge...1829'. Westminster Review, XII, 1-31.
Tentatively attributed by WI to W. J. Fox. Previously
attributed to Bowring or Mill (Graham; Nesbitt).
Written from an avowedly Benthamite point of view, this
is one of the first attempts at a serious consideration of
Coleridge's poetry in its own terms. It devotes particular
attention to 'meditative poems' and to the manner in which
they reproduce natural movements of thought and feeling,
'exhibitions of the writer's mind under certain circumstances or influences'.

480 _____. The Devil's Visit; A Poem from the Original Manuscript, with Notes by a Barrister. London: W. Kidd. Illustrated by Cruickshank.
Imitation of The Devil's Thoughts.

481 [BYRON, LORD]. 'The Devil's Drive'. Letters and Journals of
     Lord Byron. Ed. Thomas Moore. 2 vols. London: John Mur-
     ray, I, 471-4. Reprinted with 16 additional stanzas in
     Works of Lord Byron. Ed. Ernest Hartley Coleridge. Lon-
     don: John Murray (1898-1904), VII, 21-34.
        Imitation of The Devil's Thoughts written in 1813.

482 CHEEVER, GEORGE B[ARRELL]. Studies in Poetry. Embracing
     Notices of the Lives and Writings of the Best Poets in the
     English Language. Boston: Carter and Hendee.
        Coleridge's (pp. 279-91) poetical genius not inferior to
     Milton's. Praises 'wildness of fancy and richness of im-
     agery', and the 'elevated...moral character and rich
     philosophy' of his prose.

483 [EMPSON, WILLIAM]. 'Lord Leveson Gower's Poems and Transla-
     tions'. Edinburgh Review, LII, 231-61.
        Coleridge's translation of Wallenstein 'splendid, but
     very unequal'.
        Attribution: WI.

484 HALLAM, ARTHUR HENRY. Poems. London: Littlewood and Co.
        Note to 'Timbuctoo' (pp. 62-76) says lines 40-41 were
     suggested by a passage in The Friend. Lines 160-71 de-
     scribe Coleridge, 'that good old man, most eloquent', whom
     Hallam met.

485 [HERVEY, THOMAS KIBBLE]. The Devil's Progress. London:
     Lupton Relfe.
        Political satire imitated from The Devil's Thoughts.
        Attribution: B. Mus. Cat.

486 [MACNISH, ROBERT?] A Modern Pythagorean, pseud. 'Political
     Portraits'. Blackwood's Magazine, XXVII, 632-3.
        Coleridge, 'magician', one of thirty-four poets de-
     scribed in individual quatrains.
        Attribution: Macnish. 1838.

487 [MAGINN, WILLIAM]. 'The Election of Editor for Fraser's Maga-
     zine'. Fraser's Magazine, I, 496-508, 738-57.
        Coleridge parodied in a speech in verse (from Piccolo-
     mini II, iv) and another in prose (pp. 497, 503-4).
        Attribution: WI.

488 [MAGINN, WILLIAM possibly with J. A. HERAUD] Ned Culpepper,
     pseud. 'Mr. Edward Lytton Bulwer's Novels'. Fraser's
     Magazine, I, 509-32.

([MAGINN, WILLIAM possibly with J. A. HERAUD])
Bulwer chastised for ineffectual efforts to quote Coleridge's opinions.
Attribution: WI.

489   [MAGINN, WILLIAM]. 'Sacred Poetry. The Descent into Hell'. Fraser's Magazine, I, 341-52.
Use of archaic language is an 'insufferable liberty' in most writers, but 'Mr. S. T. may do so, and with impunity'.
Attribution: WI.

490   MARSHALL, W. 'Correspondence'. Court Journal, no. 42 (13 Feb), p. 109. Reprinted with additional comment and letter from Porson's nephew in John Bull, X, No. 479 (14 Feb), p. 53.
Letter from 'W. Marshall' of York claims authorship of The Devil's Walk.

491   MONTAGU, H. W. The Devil's Walk; A Poem, by Professor Porson. Edited with a biographical memoir and notes by H. W. Montagu. London: Marsh and Miller. 2nd edition, 1830.
Memoir discusses (v-viii) controversy over authorship and argues in favour of Porson. Second edition corrects the error on the basis of information received from Coleridge identifying his own and Southey's contributions and explains Porson's lighthearted hoax.

492   MOXON, EDWARD. 'Sonnet to Coleridge'. Sonnets. London: Bradley and Evans, p. 29. Reprinted Newcastle Journal, IV, No. 186 (21 Nov 1835), p. [4].
Feeble pastoral lament.

493   [PEACOCK, THOMAS LOVE]. 'Letters and Journals of Lord Byron, with Notices of his Life. By Thomas Moore'. Westminster Review, XII, 269-304.
Discusses Byron's attempt to secure favourable reviews in Edinburgh Review of Christabel, 'this most beautiful little poem'.
Attribution: Halliford Edition.

494   [RUSSELL, WILLIAM]. 'Aids to Reflection'. American Journal of Education [Boston], V, 161-81.
Criticizes Marsh for exaggerating Coleridge's significance, but respects Coleridge as 'a most potent antagonist' and one who 'cuts up error by the roots when he gets about it'.
Attribution: W. P. A. Index

495 WARNER, RICHARD. Literary Recollections. 2 vols. London:
       Longman et al.
           Includes (II, 153-4) brief account of visit to Coleridge
       in 1801 and of Coleridge in Bath in 1802, where he recited
       Christabel.

1831

496 The Friend...First American, From Second London Edition.
       Burlington [Vermont]: Chauncey Goodrich. viii, 510 pp.
           Marsh's preface (pp. v-viii) compares Coleridge with
       Tholuck and distinguishes him from Kant, whom he alters as
       Cudworth or More might have done.

497 ANON. 'On the Constitution of the Church and State'. Congrega-
       tional Magazine, XIV, 302-10.
           Admires Coleridge but criticizes his fragmentary work.
       Attacks Church and State as 'a mere farrago' of
       speculations.

498 _____. 'Extraordinary Case of the Royal Associates of the
       Royal Society of Literature'. Englishman's Magazine, I,
       263-7.
           Complaint about cancellation of pensions for the Royal
       Associates uses Coleridge as example, perhaps by Joseph
       Hardman [Griggs, XI, 855].

499 _____. 'On the Constitution of the Church and State' [etc.].
       Eclectic Review, 3rd Series VI, 1-28.
           Review-article chiefly concerned with Coleridge, whose
       digressive manner is illustrated by analysis of character-
       istic sentences.

500 No Entry.

501 _____. 'The King's Speech'. Fraser's Magazine, III, 655-65.
           Condemns withdrawal of pensions and commends Coleridge
       for refusing the 'insidious offer of the premier'.

502 _____. 'Coronation Lays, Picked up in the Crowd'. New
       Monthly Magazine, XXXII, 327-35.
           A series of parodies with brief satiric word portraits.
       Portrait of Ancient Mariner concerns cancellation of Cole-
       ridge's pension, followed by parody in the metre of
       Christabel.

503   ____. 'Progressive Changes in English Prose Writings...Recollections of another of Mr. Coleridge's Lectures'. Tatler, II, 893-4, 897-8. Reprinted Athenaeum, Nos. 3203, 3210 (16 Mar, 4 May 1889), pp. 345-6, 568. Reprinted Raysor, Coleridge's Miscellaneous Criticism (1936).
Reports on Lectures XIV ('by one of his auditors') and IX in 1818 series.

504   ____. [Coleridge's Pension]. Times, No. 14555 (3 June), p. 2. Partially reprinted Athenaeum, No. 188 (14 June 1831), p. 363.
A leading article opposing withdrawal of Coleridge's pension.

505   ____. [Pension List]. Times, No. 14554 (2 June), p. 2.
Two heated columns on withdrawal of Coleridge's pension.

506 [COLERIDGE, HENRY NELSON]. 'Popular Specimens of the Greek Dramatic Poets'. Quarterly Review, XLIV, 389-414.
Coleridge mentioned (p. 389) as combining virtues of German poetry with original genius and English taste.
Attribution: WI.

507 [DE QUINCEY, THOMAS]. 'Dr. Parr and his Contemporaries. No. IV'. Blackwood's Magazine, XXIX, 901-12. Reprinted in his Essays on Philosophical Writers and Other Men of Letters. 2 vols. Boston: Ticknor, Reed, and Fields (1854), II, [133]-275.
Compares Parr unfavourably with Coleridge.

508 GILLMAN, JAMES. [Coleridge's Pension]. Times, No. 14556 (4 June), p. 5.
Comment on Times article of 3 June.

509 [HERAUD, JOHN ABRAHAM]. 'Grant's Notes on Byron's "Cain"'. Fraser's Magazine, III, 285-304.
Includes Coleridge's comments on The Natural History of Enthusiasm and description of monologues on the subject of Will.
Attribution: WI.

510 [LAMB, CHARLES]. Satan in Search of a Wife...By an Eye Witness. London: Edward Moxon. Illustrations by Cruickshank.
Imitation of The Devil's Thoughts advertised as 'by the author of Elia'.

1831-LANDSEER

511   [LANDSEER, EDWARD]. [Illustrations for The Devil's Thoughts].
London: F. G. Harding.
Ten engraved plates, each with verse of poem.

512   [MAGINN, WILLIAM]. 'Coronation Coronal; or, Verses on the
Coronation of their Majesties, King William IV, and Queen
Adelaide, By the most Eminent Poets of the Day'. Fraser's
Magazine, IV, 375-86.
Parodies of Coleridge ('A Vision in a Dream', p. 382)
and others.
Attribution: WI

513   No entry.

513A   [MILL, JOHN STUART]. 'Attack on Literature'. Examiner,
No. 1219 (18 June), pp. 369-71. Reprinted Alexander, John
Stuart Mill: Literary Essays (1967).
Discussions of the cancellation of Coleridge's pension
and of the influence of a writer's audience.

514   PARIS, JOHN AYRTON. Life of Sir Humphry Davy. 2 vols. London: Henry Colburn and Richard Bentley.
Comments on Coleridge in three letters to Poole (I,
176, 293; II, 285-6).

515   [PEACOCK, THOMAS LOVE]. Crotchet Castle. London: T. Hookham.
Coleridge satirized as Mr. Skionar, a transcendental
poet.

516   PLANCHÉ, GUSTAVE. 'De la haine littéraire'. Revue des deux
mondes [Paris], IV, 605-14.
Anecdote of young Frenchman claiming translation of
'the old mariner' as an original poem (p. 608).

517   POE, EDGAR ALLAN. 'Letter to Mr. --'. Poems. New York:
Elam Bliss, pp. 2-29. Reprinted Southern Literary Messenger [Richmond, Va.], II (1836), 501-3.
Includes comment on Biographia Literaria and apostrophe
to Coleridge's 'towering intellect'.

518   [PRAED, WINTHROP MACKWORTH]. 'The Legend of the Teufel-Haus'.
The Gem. London: W. Marshall, pp. 39-48. Reprinted in
his Lillian and Other Poems. New York: Redfield (1852),
pp. 121-30.
Parody of Christabel.

518A [WILSON, JOHN]. 'An Hour's Talk About Poetry,' Blackwood's
      Vol. XXX (1831), 475-490.
          Although Coleridge's "Discourse" is perfect, he has
      failed, like all other English poets except for Milton, to
      produce a Great Poem.
          Attribution: WI.

1832

519 ANON. 'American Lake Poetry'. American Quarterly Review
     [Philadelphia], XI, 154-74.
         Attack on the style of the Lake Poets and on its influ-
     ence in America.

520 _____. 'Study of Greek Literature'. American Quarterly Reg-
     ister [Boston], IV, 273-90; V (1833), 33-46, 218-36.
         Flattering serial essay, clearly in response to review
     of Aids to Reflection in American Journal of Education,
     1830, q.v. Coleridge's classical education discussed as
     important influence on his style.

521 _____. 'Theological Library. Life of Wiclif' [sic].
     Fraser's Magazine, V, 177-97.
         Uses Church and State (p. 177) to argue the impossibil-
     ity of national churches.

522 _____. 'The Rambler. Authors Continued'. National Omnibus
     and General Advertiser, II, 201-2.
         Enthusiastic appraisal of Christabel, The Ancient Mari-
     ner, and Love. Coleridge a 'disciple of Kant' and 'a deep
     thinker'.

523 _____. 'English Bards. Samuel Taylor Coleridge'. The
     Shrine [Amherst, Massachusetts], I, 26-7.
         Undergraduate article emphasizes Coleridge's poetry and
     conversation, considers him 'the most remarkable genius of
     his age'.

524 BYRON, LORD. Works. With His Letters and Journal and His
     Life. Ed. Thomas Moore. 6 vols. London: John Murray.
         Letters reflect Byron's changing opinions of Coleridge
     between 1811 and 1821, and include his request to Moore to
     review Christabel favourably, his defence of that poem to
     Murray, and description of his recitation of it to Shelley.

525 GENEST, JOHN. Some Account of the English Stage from the
     Restoration in 1660 to 1830. 10 vols. Bath: H. E.
     Carrington.
         Three mentions of Drury Lane productions of Remorse
     (VIII, 354, 355, 500), a 'tolerable' tragedy.

1832-GREEN

526   GREEN, JOSEPH HENRY. <u>An Address Delivered in King's College,
<u>London</u>. London: B. Fellowes.
        A speech on professionalism and the importance of a
metropolitan college, grounded, according to Green's Preface, on Coleridge's <u>Church and State</u>, which is summarized.

527   [HERAUD, JOHN ABRAHAM, and WILLIAM MAGINN?]. 'Lord Byron's
Juvenile Poems'. <u>Fraser's Magazine</u>, VI, 183-204.
        Questions (pp. 187-8) Coleridge's criticism of Words-
worth's lines 'thou best philosopher'.
        Attribution: <u>WI</u>.

528   [HERAUD, JOHN ABRAHAM] Oliver Yorke, <u>pseud</u>. 'Oliver Yorke at
Home'. <u>Fraser's Magazine</u>, V, 22-34.
        Fictional dialogue with Goethe on redemption describes
Coleridge's intellectual penetration.
        Attribution: <u>WI</u>.

529   ____. 'Some Account of Coleridge's Philosophy'. <u>Fraser's</u>
<u>Magazine</u>, V, 585-97.
        Effusive but superficial assessment of second edition of
<u>Aids to Reflection</u> explains Coleridge's position in con-
trast with 18th century empiricism. In his 'Reminiscences'
(1834), Heraud claims this as the first serious discussion
of Coleridge's metaphysics.
        Attribution: Nesbitt; <u>WI</u>.

530   [MAGINN, WILLIAM?]. 'What is an Irish Orator? [By] S. T.
Coleridge, Esq.'. <u>Fraser's Magazine</u>, V, 721.
        Humorous description followed by parody 'The Irish
Orator's Booze, A Sonnet'.
        Attribution: <u>WI</u>

531   MICHELL, NICHOLAS. <u>Living Poets and Poetesses; A Biographical</u>
<u>and Critical Poem</u>. London: William Kidd.
        Political satire (pp. 55-9) parodies <u>Christabel</u> and
mocks <u>The Ancient Mariner</u>. Review with a defence of Coleridge by [John Wilson], <u>Blackwood's Magazine</u>, XXXI (1832),
957-64 (attribution: <u>WI</u>.).

532   [RIPLEY, GEORGE]. 'Professor Follen's Inaugural Discourse'.
<u>Christian Examiner</u> [Boston], XI, 373-80.
        Kant preferred to Coleridge (p. 375), who shares his
philosophy, but is his intellectual opposite.
        Attribution: Snyder, Blunden.

533   [WATTS, ALARIC A.].   A. A. W.   'Coleridge'.   Literary Souvenir.   London: Hurst, Robinson, p. 293.
          Poem.

534   WOLFF, O[SKAR] L[UDWIG] B[ERNARDT].   Die schöne Litteratur Europa's in der neuesten Zeit.   Leipzig: Breitkopf und Härtel.
          Coleridge the best English lyricist--after Moore (pp. 337-44).

1833

535   ANON.   'The British Association Meeting at Cambridge'.   Cambridge Quarterly Review, I, 118-37.
          Coleridge listed among the 'noblemen and gentlemen' attending.

536   _____.   'Dissecting Room First Subject. Coleridge'.   Critic, I, 14-15.
          Pokes fun at Christabel in effort to show Coleridge's reputation inflated.

537   _____.   'March of Humbug. No. 1--Coleridge'.   Critic, I, 15.
          Parody of Coleridge's Ode to the Rain entitled 'An Ode to the Mud'.

538   _____.   'Friendship's Offering and Winter's Wreath'.   Gentleman's Magazine, CIV, 439-40.
          Coleridge's hexameters are not suited to an English ear.

539   _____.   'The Annuals for 1834'.   Monthly Review, New Series III, 333-44.
          Coleridge's Hymn to the Earth cited as instance of publication of an author's 'refuse'.

540   _____.   'Poems and Prose Writings by Richard H. Dana'.   New England Magazine [Boston], V, 327-31.
          Dana resembles Coleridge and Wordsworth but imitates neither.

541   _____.   'To Coleridge, After Reading Some of his Darker Writings'.   Western Monthly Magazine [Cincinnati], I, 214.
          Poem praises Coleridge's poetry but deplores later 'darker' prose.

1833-COLERIDGE

542   COLERIDGE, HARTLEY. 'Dedicatory Sonnet, To S. T. Coleridge'
       Poems. London: Baldwin and Cradock; Leeds: F. E. Bing-
       ley, p. [4].
          Poem describes Hartley's debt to his father.

543   CUNNINGHAM, ALLAN. 'Coleridge'. Athenaeum, Nos. 316 (16 Nov)
       and 320 (14 Dec), pp. 759, 855. Reprinted in his Bio-
       graphical and Critical History of the British Literature
       of the Last Fifty Years. Paris: Baudry's Foreign Library
       (1834), pp. 76-8.
          Brief favourable comments on several poems and general
       poetic reputation.

544   [HEDGE, F. H.]. 'Coleridge's Literary Character'. Christian
       Examiner [Boston, New York], XIV, 108-29.
          Review article deals with Biographia Literaria, The
       Poetical Works, Aids to Reflection, and The Friend, and
       considers the discrepancy between Coleridge's merit and
       actual achievement. Coleridge a profound thinker though
       not a successful poet or critic. Discusses Coleridge's
       style, originality, and relation to Kant, Fichte, and
       Schelling.
          Attribution: Dall

545   M. M. 'Sketches of American Poets'. Shrine [Amherst, Massa-
       chusetts], II, 149-52.
          Undergraduate essay measuring American poets by yard-
       stick of Wordsworth and Coleridge.

546   [MAGINN, WILLIAM]. 'Gallery of Literary Characters. No.
       XXXVIII. Samuel Taylor Coleridge, Esq.'. Fraser's Maga-
       zine, VIII, 64. Portrait by Daniel Maclise. Reprinted
       with additional comments by the editor in A Gallery of
       Illustrious Literary Characters (1830-1838) Drawn by the
       Late Daniel Maclise, R.A. and Accompanied by Notices
       Chiefly by the Late William Maginn, LL.D. Ed. William
       Bates. London: Chatto and Windus (1874), pp. 178-85.
          Maginn's original sketch a brief and flattering word
       portrait crediting Coleridge with all of Hazlitt's ideas
       'worth reading or remembering' and with an influence 'now
       diffused throughout the literature of England'. Bates
       adds description of Coleridge the talker and judges his
       philosophy both turgid and derivative. In 1883 edition,
       Bates modifies this judgment and adds paragraph on Theory
       of Life.

SAMUEL TAYLOR COLERIDGE: AN ANNOTATED BIBLIOGRAPHY

547 _____. 'The Miller Correspondence'. Fraser's Magazine, VIII, 624-36.
A series of letters purporting to be by eminent men, including Coleridge.
Attribution: WI.

548 _____. 'The Two Round Spaces on the Tombstone; Being an Epitaph on the Late Sir James Mackintosh, By S. Taylor Coleridge, Esq.'. Fraser's Magazine, VII, 175-7.
Coleridge's poem on Mackintosh with discussion of its propriety, which is continued in 'Fraser's Papers' for March (VII, 367) and May (VII, 620).
Attribution: WI.

549 MONTGOMERY, JAMES. Lectures on Poetry and General Literature. Delivered at the Royal Institution in 1830 and 1831. London: Longman et al.
'The Bristol Youths', Southey, Coleridge, and Wordsworth are said (pp. 368-72) to have established a new era in English poetry.

550 [SEABURY, SAMUEL]. [Coleridge's Philosophy]. Churchman [New York], III, 449, 458, 462-3, 467.
Note approving of Coleridge's increasing influence drew from John McVickar two letters ('the Philosophy of Coleridge') expressing admiration for the man but doubts concerning his theology. Seabury replied ('Coleridge and German Philosophy') arguing that McVickar based his arguments not on Coleridge's own work but on his supposed German sources.
Attribution: Snyder

551 WILLARD, EMMA. Journal and Letters from France and Great Britain. Troy [New York]: N. Tuttle.
Describes visit to Coleridge in May, 1831 (pp. 311-2) and impressions of his conversation.

552 [WILSON, JOHN]. 'Spenser'. Blackwood's Magazine, XXXIV, 824-56.
Genevieve proves (p. 825) Coleridge's abilities in the 'region of the shadowy-sublime'.
Attribution: WI.

553 No entry.

554 No entry.

555 No entry.

SAMUEL TAYLOR COLERIDGE: AN ANNOTATED BIBLIOGRAPHY

1834

556 ANON. 'Biographical Memoir of the Late Samuel Taylor Coleridge'. Analyst, I, 148–52. Reprinted by B. Butler in Cambridge Chronicle, No. 3758 (31 Oct 1834), p.2.
　　Laudatory but uncritical biographical memoir with some discussion of Coleridge and Wordsworth on poetic diction.

557 _____. 'Decline of Poetry'. American Quarterly Review [Philadelphia], XV, 448–73.
　　An attack on the pernicious influence of the 'Lakers' who have 'corrupted the taste of nearly all the poets and critics of the day'.

558 _____. 'Samuel Taylor Coleridge'. American Quarterly Observer [Boston], III, 391–3.
　　Obituary notice.

559 _____. 'Memoir of Samuel Taylor Coleridge, Esq.'. Annual Register, LXXVI, 377–87.
　　Obituary memoir.

560 _____. 'Coleridge's Will'. Athenaeum. No. 364 (18 Oct), p. 788.
　　Selections 'of most personal interest'.

561 _____. 'Death of S. T. Coleridge, Esq.'. Christian Examiner [Boston], New Series III, 645.
　　Obituary memoir with high praise for Coleridge as theologian.

562 _____. 'Popular Information on Literature'. Chambers's Edinburgh Journal, I, 99–100.
　　Coleridge ranked, with Wordsworth, below Scott, Southey, and Campbell, his writings so little read that 'it is unnecessary to give any account of them'.

563 _____. 'Supper and Flight of the Poets'. Cambridge Quarterly Review, II, 19–33.
　　Satirical fantasy in which Coleridge is described.

564 _____. 'Samuel Taylor Coleridge'. Georgian Era: Memoirs of the most eminent persons who have flourished in Great Britain. 4 vols. London: Vizetelly, Branston and Co., III, 424–5.
　　Highly inaccurate account which values only Coleridge's love poetry.

565 _____. 'Coleridge's Poetical Works'. <u>Gentleman's Magazine</u>,
New Series II, 11-14.
Coleridge's failure to continue to write poetry explained by failure of audience to appreciate his work and
his refusal to 'pander to their desires'. General praise
for Coleridge as poet.

566 _____. 'Samuel Taylor Coleridge, Esq.'. <u>Gentleman's Maga-
zine</u>, New Series II, 544-9, 661-3.
Obituary memoir, and text of will.

567 _____. 'The Poetical Works of S. J. [sic] Coleridge'. <u>King</u>,
I, 30.
Very brief but favourable notice.

568 _____. 'Coleridge'. <u>London Literary Gazette</u>, No. 928
(1 Nov), p. 739.
Brief note on Coleridge's definition of the four classes
of readers.

569 _____. 'The Poetical Works of S. T. Coleridge'. <u>London Literary Gazette</u>, No. 904 (17 May), pp. 339-42.
Coleridge unequal and publishes whatever comes into his
head. <u>The Ancient Mariner</u> the most perfect of his poems.

570 _____. 'Literary Notices'. <u>Literary and Theological Review</u>
[New York], I, 691-2.
Coleridge's intellectual virtues more than compensate
for his obscurity. Comments on Withington (1834).

571 _____. 'Life of Friedrich Schiller'. <u>New England Magazine</u>
[Boston], VI, 165-6.
Of the 'four most eminent living poets' Coleridge alone
now derives no benefit from Tory patronage.

572 _____. 'A New Theory of Comets'. <u>New England Magazine</u> [Bos-
ton], VII, 276-88.
Brief comment on Coleridge's obscurity.

573 _____. 'Coleridge'. <u>Parterre</u>, I, 107-9.
Chorley's <u>Athenaeum</u> obituary combined with McLellan's
<u>Recollections</u> (1834) q.v.

574 _____. 'The Poetical Works of Samuel Taylor Coleridge'.
<u>Portico</u>, No. 5 (5 April), pp. 65-8.
Criticizes Byron's opinions of Coleridge and defends
both quantity and quality of Coleridge's work.

1834-ANON.

575   ANON. ['Coleridge's Estate']. Times, No. 15632 (11 Nov),
       p. 3.
           Value of Coleridge's estate less than £3000.

576   _____. 'Died'. Times, No. 15541 (28 July), p. 6.
           Obituary notice.

577   _____. 'Funeral of S. J. [sic] Coleridge, Esq.'. Times,
       No. 15548 (5 Aug), p. 2.

578   _____. 'Mr. Coleridge's Will'. Times, No. 15620 (28 Oct),
       p. 6.

579   BACON, FRANCIS. The Works of Francis Bacon, Lord Chancellor
       of England. New edition by Basil Montagu. 16 vols.
       London: Pickering.
           Preface (XVI, 12) speaks affectionately of Coleridge.

580   BOWLES, WILLIAM L. 'Coleridge a Private Soldier'. Athenaeum,
       No. 353 (2 Aug) pp. 613-4; reprinted Lady's Magazine and
       Museum, New Series V (1834), 178-9; Metropolitan Magazine,
       XI (1834), 23; Mirror, XXIV (1834), 138-9; Times, No.
       15555 (13 Aug 1834), p. 3.
           Describes Coleridge's enlistment and discharge. Bowles
       adds that he considers Religious Musings 'by far the most
       correct, sublime, chaste, and beautiful of his poems'.

581   BRANSBY, JAMES HEWS. 'Coleridge's Unitarianism'. Christian
       Reformer, 2nd Series I, 837-40.
           1798 letter, extracts from Religious Musings and com-
       ment on Birmingham sermon.

582   BUTLER, SAMUEL. ['Coleridge at Cambridge']. Analyst, I,
       227.
           College friend corrects anonymous 'biographical memoir'
       (Analyst, 1834) concerning Coleridge's academic honours at
       Cambridge.

583   [CALVERT, GEORGE HENRY]. 'To S. T. Coleridge'. Don Carlos.
       Baltimore: William & Joseph Neal.
             Dedicatory poem.
             Attribution: Blanck

584   [CHORLEY, HENRY FOTHERGILL]. 'Obituary of Samuel Taylor Cole-
       ridge'. Athenaeum, No. 353 (2 Aug), pp. 574-5. Reprinted
       as 'Death of Coleridge'. Times, No. 15548 (5 Aug, 1834),
       p. 2.
             Attribution: Hewlett

SAMUEL TAYLOR COLERIDGE: AN ANNOTATED BIBLIOGRAPHY

1834-G.S.

585 [COLERIDGE, HENRY NELSON]. 'The Poetical Works of S. T. Coleridge'. Quarterly Review, LII, 1–38. Partially reprinted
Mirror, XXIV (1834), 153–5. Reprinted Museum of Foreign
Literature [Philadelphia], XXV (1834), 560–76.
This review-article, sometimes seen as a turning-point
in criticism of Coleridge, was written, though not published, before Coleridge's death. Begins with extended
account of Coleridge, his conversational brilliance and
intellectual profundity, before discussing The Ancient
Mariner (citing Coleridge's own comments on the poem and
on David Scott's illustrations), Christabel, and the love
poems, comments on Coleridge's views on the epic, consideration of the fall of Jerusalem as a possible subject,
translation of Wallenstein, 'improvements' on Schiller,
refusal to translate Faust and plan for a poem on Michael
Scott. Obituary notice added by Lockhart.
Attribution: WI.

586 [CRAIK, GEORGE L.]. 'Coleridge's Poetical Works'. Printing
Machine, I, 275–9.
Review of Poetical Works expanded in his Sketches
(1845), q.v.

587 [CRAWFORD, L. M.] L. M. C. 'Thoughts on the Poet Coleridge'.
Metropolitan Magazine, XI, 142–6.
Purple eulogy including accounts of Thursday afternoons
at Highgate. Author identified in Sept 1834 issue, p. 32.

588 [DE QUINCEY, THOMAS]. 'Samuel Taylor Coleridge, by the English Opium-Eater'. Tait's Edinburgh Magazine, New Series I,
509–20, 588–96, 685–80; New Series II (1835), 2–10. Portrait engraved from J. Northcote. Partially reprinted
Mirror, XXIV (1834), 249–52; Times, No. 15598 (2 Oct 1834),
p. 3. Reprinted in his Literary Reminiscences, 2 vols.
Boston: Ticknor, Reed, and Fields (1854), I, 151–254.
Rambling, anecdotal and often inaccurate account of
Coleridge. Charges of plagiarism and discussion of Coleridge's use of opium which made it notorious, occupy, in
fact, a small part of the whole.

589 ENORT, pseud. 'Coleridge'. Mirror, XXIV, 208.
Anecdote concerning Coleridge's monopoly of
conversation.

590 G. S. 'Coleridge, The Poet, and Sir Charles Flower'. Times,
No. 15638 (18 Nov), p. 1.
Comparison of the estates of Coleridge and Flower.

81

1834-GREAT UNMENTIONABLE

591   GREAT UNMENTIONABLE, pseud. 'The Sheriff's Officer'. Comic
       Magazine, IV, 166-71. Reprinted Hamilton (1888).
       Parody of The Ancient Mariner.

592   HAYWARD, A. Faust: A Dramatic Poem, By Goethe, translated
       into English Prose, with notes etc. 2nd Edition, London:
       Edward Moxon.
           'Preface to the Second Edition' cites Coleridge's Wal-
       lenstein as illustration of the principles of translation
       (pp. xiii-xiv, xix-xx).

593   HEMANS, FELICIA DOROTHEA. 'On Reading Coleridge's Epitaph,
       Written by Himself'. Blackwood's Magazine, XXXVI, 801.
       Reprinted in her Poetical Works. London, New York:
       Frederick Warne (1897), p. 597.
           Sonnet.

594   HERAUD, JOHN A. An Oration on the Death of S. T. Coleridge,
       Esq. London: James Fraser (1834). 28 pp.
           Purple praise with detailed accounts of Coleridge's con-
       versation, exposition of Coleridge's philosophy. Argues
       that Coleridge's later principles appeared in his poetry,
       and attacks his critics, concludes with sonnet to
       Coleridge.
           Reviewed: Times, No. 15552 (9 Aug 1834), p. 5.

595   [HERAUD, JOHN ABRAHAM]. 'Reminiscences of Coleridge, Bio-
       graphical, Philosophical, Poetical, and Critical'.
       Fraser's Magazine, X, 379-403; Reprinted Museum of Foreign
       Literature [Philadelphia], XXVI (1834), 359-65.
           Eulogy with a biographical and critical sketch. 'In-
       tensity' of The Ancient Mariner superior to 'melodrama' of
       Christabel. Suggests that 'Christobell, a gothic tale'
       (1815) may have been by Coleridge himself.
           Attribution: WI.

596   J. 'Coleridge'. New Monthly Magazine, XLII, 55-63. Reprint-
       ed Museum of Foreign Literature [Philadelphia], XXV (1834),
       555-60.
           Obituary memoir.

597   [JERDAN, WILLIAM]. 'S. T. Coleridge'. London Literary Ga-
       zette, No. 916 (16 Aug), 537-8, 547.
           Discussion of Schiller, concluding with praise for
       Coleridge's translation and brief eulogy. Sequel is brief
       biographical sketch.
           Attribution: Jerdan. Autobiography

598   LANDOR, WALTER SAVAGE. 'Ode to a Friend'. Leigh Hunt's Lon-
      don Journal, I, 282. Revised in Leigh Hunt's London Jour-
      nal, II (1835), 113-4.
         Lines 25-30 of poem to Joseph Ablett describe Coleridge.

599   [LE GRICE, C. V.]. Cergiel, pseud. 'College Reminiscences of
      Mr. Coleridge'. Gentleman's Magazine, New Series II,
      605-7. Reprinted with postscript Penzance: R. D. Rodda
      (1842), 4 pp. Reprinted with additional note by Le Grice
      in Clement Carylon. Early Years. 4 vols. London: Whitt-
      taker (1843), II, 279-83. Reprinted Joseph Cottle. Rem-
      iniscences of Samuel Taylor Coleridge and Robert Southey.
      London: Houlston and Stoneman (1847), pp. 303-5.
         Objection to inaccurate accounts of Coleridge's academic
      achievement at Cambridge.

600   M. N. M. 'S. T. Coleridge. Eine biographische Skizze'.
      Magazin für die Litteratur des Auslandes [Berlin], No. 134
      (7 Nov), pp. 533-5.
         Conventional biographic survey.

601   [MAURICE, F. D.]. Eustace Conway, or The Brother and Sister.
      3 vols. London: Richard Bentley.
         Character of Kreutzner, a German philosopher, seems
      partly based on Coleridge.

602   MCLELLAN, HENRY B[LAKE]. Journal of a Residence in Scotland.
      With a Memoir by I[rving] McLellan, Jr. Boston: Allen and
      Ticknor.
         Account of 1832 visit to Highgate (pp. 230-2) describes
      Coleridge's appearance, and conversation on Dr. Chalmers,
      Irving, Pufendorf, and Allston.

603   [MUDFORD, WILLIAM] G[eoffrey] O[ldcastle], pseud. 'The Late
      S. T. Coleridge, Esq.'. Canterbury Magazine, I, II
      (1835), 121-31; 31-5. Partially reprinted as 'Sketches of
      Society: Coleridge'. London Literary Gazette, No. 922
      (20 Sept 1834), p. 645.
         Mudford's 1817 meeting with Coleridge and four letters
      from him, with later discussion of his skill at character
      writing.
         Attribution: DAPL; E. K. Chambers.

604 [PRAY, ISAAC?]. 'Quarterly Review and Lake Poets'. Pearl and
Literary Gazette [Boston], III, 194-5.
A reply, perhaps by Pray, the editor, to anonymous attack in American Quarterly Review, 1834 ('Decline of Poetry'). Coleridge 'the most remarkable genius of the age'.

605 [SORTAIN, JOSEPH]. 'The Poetical Works of S. T. Coleridge'.
British Critic, XVI, 393-417.
Review offers extensive paraphrase and quotation with
brief critical comments. Religious Musings is sublime;
Dejection, characteristic of Coleridge's 'peculiarities and
beauties'; The Ancient Mariner and Christabel, 'wild but
exquisitely beautiful sports of...fancy'. Sees difficul-
ties in finding an audience largely due to effort demanded
of readers.
Attribution: WI

606 [WATERSTON, ROBERT CASSIE]. 'Coleridge's Poems'. North
American Review [Boston], XXXIX, 437-8.
First comprehensive American evaluation: a general discussion of Coleridge's work, with consideration of many
individual poems. The Ancient Mariner 'displays the inner
life' and 'lays bare the subterranean springs of a human
soul'. Remorse reveals intimate relation between Coleridge's poetry and philosophy.
Attribution: Cushing

607 [WILSON, JOHN]. 'Coleridge's Poetical Works'. Blackwood's
Magazine, XXXVI, 542-70. Reprinted in his Essays Critical
and Imaginative. 4 vols. Edinburgh, London: William
Blackwood (1857), III [293]-343.
In marked contrast to his 1817 attack, Wilson here offers a uniformly flattering appraisal of Coleridge as a
man who 'was always a poet' and who, at his best, equalled
Shakespeare. Gives literal and impressionistic commen-
taries on a number of poems, expresses reservations about
Coleridge's odes, finds true sublimity in Hymn Before Sunrise, and argues that Christabel (a new species of poetry)
and The Ancient Mariner are the most individual expressions
of his imaginative genius. Discussion of the last incor-
porates substantial passages from Lockhart's 1819 review,
q.v.

608 WITHINGTON, LEONARD. 'On Emulation in Schools'. The Introductory Discourse and the Lectures delivered before the
American Institute of Instructors. Boston: Carter, Hendee
and Co., pp. 131-52.

(WITHINGTON, LEONARD)
Coleridge exemplifies (pp. 136-7) verbal ingenuity in metaphysics.
Reviewed: New England Magazine [Boston], VI (1834), 424-8.

609 _____. 'Present State of Metaphysics'. Quarterly Christian Spectator [New Haven], VI, 609-31.
Mainly an attack on Coleridge (and Kant), especially distinction of reason and understanding. Coleridge credited with poetic genius, but accused of insincerity, affectation, and obscurity. His influence on the young deplored.

1835

610 Specimens of the Table Talk of the Late Samuel Taylor Coleridge. ed. Henry Nelson Coleridge. 2 vols. London: John Murray. I, lxxxiii, [2], 267; II, xi, 372 pp. Portrait by T. Phillips.
Preface contains an extended discussion of Coleridge's conversation. Reviewed: Mirror, xxv (1835), 29-30, 62, 220-22. See also 613, 614, 616, 619, 620, 622, 624, 625, 627, 638, 641, 644, 646, 648, 652, 655, 660, 677, 683, 769.

611 [ADAMS, SARAH FLOWER] S. Y., pseud. 'An Evening with Charles Lamb and Coleridge'. Monthly Repository, New Series IX, 162-8. Reprinted Bertram Dobell. Sidelights on Charles Lamb. London: privately printed, New York: Charles Scribners (1903), pp. 296-312.
Includes description of Coleridge's appearance and conversation.

612 ANON. 'Letters, Conversations, and Recollections'. Athenaeum, No. 424 (12 Dec), pp. 927-8. No. 425 (19 Dec), pp. 941-2.
Extracts from Allsop. Coleridge a 'beautiful theorist' who 'dreamed away an existence'.

613 _____. 'Specimens of the Table-Talk of the Late Samuel Taylor Coleridge'. Athenaeum, No. 395 (23 May), pp. 387-8. No. 396 (30 May), 406-7.
Description of Coleridge's manner of conversation and the subtlety of his arguments.

614 _____. 'Specimens of the Table-Talk of the Late Samuel Taylor Coleridge'. American Monthly Magazine [New York and Boston], V, 454-7.
Brief comments on Christabel, The Friend, Pantisocracy, and Coleridge's influence on Mme. de Staël, followed by extracts.

1835–ANON.

615   ANON.   'Specimens of English Dramatic Poets. By Charles
      Lamb'. Athenaeum, No. 406 (8 Aug), p. 598.
         Sees Coleridge's influence as diminishing, Lamb's as
      increasing.

616   _____.   'Excerpts from Table Talk'. British Magazine, VII,
      720–3.
         Quotes theological selections which 'will have their
      weight with the country'.

617   _____.   'Biographia Literaria'. Biblical Repository [New
      York], V, 247.
         Announcement of 1834 New York edition exhorting the
      reader to study it. Commends criticism of Wordsworth.

618   _____.   'S. T. Coleridge in Company with Socinians and Athe-
      ists'. Congregational Magazine, New Series XI, 486–90.
         Coleridge's comments extracted from Cottle's On the
      Predictions and Miracles of Jesus Christ...By a Layman
      (1835). Although advertised in Cottle's Early Recollec-
      tions and listed in the English Catalogue of Books, no ex-
      tant copy of this work has been located.

619   _____.   'Specimens of the Table-Talk of the Late Samuel Taylor
      Coleridge'. Eclectic Review, 3rd Series XIV, 135–40.
         H. N. Coleridge's selections make Coleridge appear
      'fiery, coarse, and one-sided' in his views of Whigs and
      dissenters. Coleridge's criticism of older philosophy and
      theology thought valuable.

620   _____.   'Specimens of the Table-Talk of the Late Samuel Taylor
      Coleridge'. Knickerbocker [New York], VI, 155–8.
         Largely extracts, mentions 'exciting accounts' of Cole-
      ridge's conversation which have reached America.

621   _____.   'Coleridge'. Mirror, XXV, 111.
         Gillman's inscription for Coleridge's tombstone.

622   _____.   'Coleridge's Tischgespräche'. Magazin für die Lite-
      ratur des Auslandes [Berlin], Nos. 71–2 (15, 17 June),
      pp. 281, 286–8.
         Comments on Coleridge's monologue and fragmentary
      prose, followed by excerpts translated into German.

623   _____.   'Annual Biography and Obituary'. Monthly Review, New
      Series I, 196–211.
         Apologetically brief mention of the death of 'one of
      the greatest poets of modern times'.

624 _____. 'Specimens of the Table-Talk of the Late Samuel Taylor
Coleridge'. Monthly Review, New Series II, 250-61.
Adulatory description of Coleridge as philosopher, crit-
ic and talker.

625 _____. 'Specimens of the Table-Talk of the Late Samuel Taylor
Coleridge'. New England Magazine [Boston], IX, 217-20.
Considers Table Talk 'a good book', but disagrees with
Coleridge's political conservatism and defence of the
established church. Coleridge not a great philosopher but
a great poet.

626 _____. 'Letters from Germany. By S. T. Coleridge'. New
Monthly Magazine, XLV, 211-26.
Letters from Coleridge to Sara printed by a 'gentleman'
to whom Coleridge gave them in 1798.

627 _____. 'Specimens of the Table-Talk of the Late Samuel Taylor
Coleridge'. Western Monthly Magazine [Cincinnati], IV,
201-6.
Extracts and favourable comments.

628 [ANSTEY, JOHN]. 'Coleridge'. Dublin University Magazine,
VI, 1-16, 250-67.
Favourable survey of prose and poetry defends Coleridge
against imputations of plagiarism, especially from Shelvocke
in The Ancient Mariner. Argues in support of Church and
State.
Attribution: L. Watson. Poole gives Tuckerman.

629 BOWLES, REV. W. LISLE. 'Recollections of the Late William
Linley, Esq.'. Gentleman's Magazine, New Series III,
574-6.
Account (p. 575) of Coleridge's bringing Osorio to
to Bowles's cottage, and Sheridan's condemnation of it.

630 CANTABRIGIENSIS, pseud. 'Mr. Coleridge and Professor Airy'.
Times, No. 15736 (12 Mar), p. 5.
Contrasts granting of annuity to Airy, a member of the
Opposition, with the withdrawal of Coleridge's 'pittance'.

631 [CHEEVER, GEORGE BARRELL]. 'Coleridge'. North American Review [Boston], XL, 299-351.
'Veneration and love' inform this detailed but uncritical
discussion of Coleridge's character and work, focused on
but not confined to The Friend. Praises Coleridge's style

([CHEEVER, GEORGE BARRELL])
(denying obscurity), his critical, political, and philosophical essays, and, briefly, his poetry.
Attribution: Cushing.

632 CRAWFORD, MRS. [L. M.]. 'Stanzas on Visiting the Grave of
Coleridge'. Metropolitan Magazine, XII, 91.

633 DANIEL, GEORGE. The Modern Dunciad, Virgil in London, and
other Poems. London: W. Pickering.
Note [p. 38], added in this edition, describes Coleridge
and Wordsworth as deserving praise but provoking ridicule.
Reviewed: [John Wilson]. Blackwood's Magazine, XXXVIII
(1835), 289–301 (attribution: WI).

634 [EVERETT, A. H.]. 'Dr. Channing'. North American Review
[Boston], XLI, 366–406.
A discussion (pp. 371–2) of Coleridge's 'slender claims'
to his reputation as 'the first of philosophers'.
Attribution: Cushing

635 [FIELD, BARRON]. 'Samuel Taylor Coleridge'. Annual Biography
and Obituary, XIX, 320–78.
Derivative biographical sketch followed by discussion
of Coleridge's obscurity, his unpublished works, and his
treatment by the reviews.
Attribution: L.C. Catalog

636 [FORSTER, JOHN]. 'Charles Lamb. His Last Words on Cole-
ridge'. New Monthly Magazine, XLIII, 198–206. Reprinted
Museum of Foreign Literature [Philadelphia], XXVI, 508–13.
Lamb's eulogy of Coleridge and account of their
friendship.
Attribution: NCBEL III

637 FULLER, MARGARET. 'Philip Van Artevelde'. Western Messenger
[Louisville], I, 399–408.
Mentions (p. 405) Coleridge and Byron as literary gen-
iuses who lack talent for drama.

638 [HARRISON, I. B.]. 'Coleridge's Table Talk'. Southern Lit-
erary Messenger [Richmond, Virginia], I, 458, 481.
Brief favourable notice.
Attribution: Duffy

639   [HARE, JULIUS CHARLES] J. C. H. 'Samuel Taylor Coleridge and
       the English Opium-Eater'. British Magazine, VII, 15-27.
       Attack on De Quincey's spiteful, petty, and distorted
       account in Tait's (1834-5). Points out inaccuracies, but
       argues that Coleridge's achievement would remain even if
       allegations were true.
       Attribution: Haldane

640   [HERAUD, JOHN ABRAHAM]. 'Coleridgeiana'. Fraser's Magazine,
       XI, 50-8. Reprinted Museum of Foreign Literature [Phila-
       delphia], XXVI (1835), 359-65.
       Prints Coleridge's will with comment, and other short
       items.
       Attribution: WI.

641   _____. 'Coleridge's Table-Talk'. Fraser's Magazine, XII,
       123-35.
       Attacks De Quincey's charges of plagiarism. Discusses
       Coleridge's views on gnosticism and logic, and contrasts
       Coleridge with Irving on the Trinity.
       Attribution: WI.

642   _____. 'Monologues of the Late Samuel Taylor Coleridge,
       Esq.'. Fraser's Magazine, XII, 493-6, 619-29. Portrait
       by Leslie.
       Two ostensibly verbatim transcripts on 'life', and
       'logic'.
       Attribution: WI.

643   _____. 'Ode on the Death of Samuel Taylor Coleridge'.
       Fraser's Magazine, XI, 58. Reprinted in Mirror, XXV
       (1835), 27-8.
       Attribution: WI.

644   [HUNT, LEIGH]. 'Coleridge's Table Talk'. Leigh Hunt's Lon-
       don Journal and the Printing Machine, II, 175-6.
       Describes Coleridge's conversation, of which Table Talk
       gives misleading impression.
       Attribution: Landré

645   [JEFFREY, FRANCIS]. 'Memoirs of the Life of...James Mackin-
       tosh'. Edinburgh Review, LXII, 205-55. Reprinted in his
       Contributions to the Edinburgh Review. 4 vols. London:
       Longman et al (1844), IV, 501-37.
       Comparison of Mackintosh and Coleridge (pp. 242-7) with
       bitter attack on Coleridge's politics and theology.

646   [JERDAN, WILLIAM].   'Coleridge's Table Talk'.   London Literary
      Gazette, No. 957 (23 May), pp. 331-2, 340-2.
          Circumstances of Coleridge's election to the Royal Soci-
      ety, with anecdotes, many repeated in his Autobiography
      (1853), Men I have Known (1862).

647   KAUFMAN, A., JR.   Böckshammer on the Freedom of the Human
      Will.   Translated from the German with additions by A. '
      Kaufman, Jr.   Andover [Massachusetts]:   Gould and Newman.
      199 pp.
          Preface (p. xii) recommends Coleridge's works as 'the
      best introduction to the study of German philosophy'.

648   [LOCKHART, JOHN GIBSON].   'Specimens of the Table-Talk of the
      Late Samuel Taylor Coleridge'.   Quarterly Review, LIII,
      79-103.   Reprinted Museum of Foreign Literature [Phila-
      delphia], XXVI (1835), 443-53.
          Favourable account of some opinions in Table Talk,
      chiefly concerned with Shakespeare.
          Attribution: WI.

649   MACKINTOSH, ROBERT JAMES.   Memoirs of the Life of the Right
      Honourable Sir James Mackintosh.   2 vols.   London: Edward
      Moxon.
          References to Coleridge passim including comments on
      his supposed responsibility for Mackintosh's rift with Fox
      (I, 326), The Friend (II, 195-6), and Moore's view of
      Coleridge (II, 436-7).

650   [MAGINN, WILLIAM].   'Contemplations of Coleridge in a Cavalry
      Regiment'.   Fraser's Magazine, XI, 422-3.
          Poetical satire with additional anecdotes.
          Attribution: WI.

651   _____.   O[liver] Y[orke], pseud.   'The Fraserians'.   Fraser's
      Magazine, XI, 1-27.   Engraving by Maclise.
          Brief discussion of Coleridge and Irving (pp. 4-5).
      Recollections of Coleridge by Hood and Cornwall (pp. 15-
      16).
          Attribution: WI.

652   [MERIVALE, HERMAN].   'Specimens of the Table-Talk of the Late
      Samuel Taylor Coleridge'.   Edinburgh Review, LXI, 129-53.
          Critical review by habitué of Coleridge's Highgate
      gatherings.   Gives description of Coleridge's talk and
      critique of views on theology, politics, and criticism.

([MERIVALE, HERMAN])
Examples of supposed plagiarism from Goethe. Coleridge
original nonetheless.
Attribution: WI.

653 [MILL, JOHN STUART] A. 'Tennyson's Poems'. Westminster Review, XXX, 402-24. Reprinted in his Early Essays...Select-
ed from the Original Sources by J. W. M. Gibbs. London:
G. Bell (1897), pp. 239-67.
Comparison of poetic concentration in Tennyson and Coleridge. Tennyson's versification less exquisite (p. 414).

654 [POE, EDGAR ALLAN]. 'Critical Notices'. Southern Literary
Messenger [Richmond, Virginia], I, 456-8.
Favourable notice of Cheever (1835) praises clarity of
Coleridge's thought.
Attribution: Snyder (Blunden).

655 [PUTNAM, GEORGE] P. G. 'Coleridge's Table Talk'. Christian
Examiner [Boston, New York], XIX, 204-15.
Mostly quotations. Comments on Coleridge's anti-
Benthamism, unitarianism, and obscurity.
Attribution: Snyder (Blunden).

656 [REDE, W. L.]. 'Coleridge's Remorse'. New Monthly Magazine,
XLIII, 86-7. Reprinted Mirror, XXV, 80.
Familiar anecdote of Sheridan's objections to the line
'drip, drip, drip' in Osorio.
Attribution: WI.

657 [ROBINSON, FREDERICK JOHN]. [Presidential Address]. [Annual
Report of the] Royal Society of Literature 1835. London:
H. J. Valpy, pp. 19-45.
Eulogy (pp. 23-31) of Coleridge: biographical memoir
of poet and philosopher who had died since last annual
meeting.

658 STYLES, ROBERT. 'On the Death of S. T. Coleridge'. Poems.
London: G. Mann, p. 38.
Obituary poem. Reviewed, reprinted: New Monthly Maga-
zine, XLVI (1836), 373.

659 SUMNER, WILLIAM H. 'Coleridge'. New-York Mirror, XIII,
180-1.
Essay in purple prose emphasizes German influence on
Coleridge, and his profound effect on his contemporaries.

660 [THOMPSON, THOMAS PERONNET]. 'Specimens of the Table-Talk of
     S. T. Coleridge'. Westminster Review, XXII, 531-7. Re-
     printed in his Exercises, Political and Others. 6 vols.
     London: Effingham Wilson (1842), III, 248-54.
        Coleridge's opinions those of a renegade and 'Tory
     sophist'.

661 TUCKER, GEORGE. 'A Discourse on the Progress of Philosophy'.
     Southern Literary Messenger [Richmond, Va.], I, 402-21.
        Coleridge's poetry (p. 408) obscured by philosophy.

662 [WALLACE, WILLIAM]. 'Printing Machine'. British and Foreign
     Review, I, 190-217.
        Comments on Craik's 1834 review and finds Coleridge too
     metaphysical in his poetry and insufficient in his
     metaphysics.
        Attribution: WI.

663 [WHITMAN, MRS. SARAH HELEN] Helen, pseud. 'A Brief Argument
     for Womanly Independence in Thought and Action'. American
     Monthly Magazine [New York and Boston], VI, 472-6.
        Remarks in Table Talk on the perfect woman quoted
     (p. 472) and challenged.
        Attribution: Snyder (Blunden).

664 [WILSON, JOHN]. 'Wordsworth's New Volume of Poems'. Black-
     wood's Magazine, XXXVII, 699-722.
        Wordsworth a greater melodist and harmonist than
     Coleridge.
        Attribution: WI.

665 [WILLIS, N. PARKER] N. P. W. 'Pencilling by the Way'. New-
     York Mirror, XII, 324. Reprinted in his Pencillings by the
     Way. New Orleans: Burnett & Bostwick (1854), pp. 507-8.
        Prints Coleridge's marginalia in Procter's copy of his
     own Dramatick Sketches, which Willis saw in London.

666 WORDSWORTH, WILLIAM. 'Extempore Effusion, upon reading, in
     The Newcastle Journal, the notice of the Death of the Poet,
     James Hogg'. Newcastle Journal, IV, no. 188 (5 Dec), p. 3.
     Reprinted: Athenaeum, No. 424 (12 Dec 1835), pp. 930-1.
        Two lines (17-18) on the death of Coleridge.

1836

667   No entry.

668   The Literary Remains of Samuel Taylor Coleridge. Collected
      and edited by Henry Nelson Coleridge. 4 vols. London:
      William Pickering (1836-1839); photoreprint, New York: AMS
      Press (1967).
         Two prefaces. The first (I, vii-xiv) on problems of
      Coleridge's unpublished work. The second (III, ix-xvi) on
      his theological position, particularly Biblical inspiration.
         Reviewed: [Calvert, George Henry]. New-York Review,
      II (1838), 96-111 (attribution: Calvert, Miscellanies.
      1840, p. 3); Dublin University Magazine, X (1837), 257-73.
      See also 679, 705, 727, 740, 742, 769, 774, 775, 790.

669   The Poetical and Dramatic Works of Samuel Taylor Coleridge
      with a Life of the Author. London: John Thomas Cox.
      lxxix, 403 pp.
         'Life' (pp. [vii]-lxviii) is largely a pastiche from
      Biographia Literaria, Hazlitt, Lamb, etc.

670   'A Letter from Wales by the Late S. T. Coleridge'. New Month-
      ly Magazine, XLVII, 420-4. Reprinted Gentleman's Magazine,
      New Series, V (1836), 242-4.
         Letter of 1794 plus a fragment on the study of history
      and philosophy written by Coleridge at Cambridge.

671   A'BECKETT, SIR WILLIAM. 'Coleridge, Samuel Taylor'. Univer-
      sal Biography. 3 vols. London: G. F. Isaac and Co.,
      I, 853.
         Brief, inaccurate sketch mentions 'wildness and
      eccentricity'.

672   [ALLSOP, THOMAS]. Letters, Conversations and Recollections.
      2 vols. London: Edward Moxon. xii, 234; iv, 240 pp.
      2nd edition London: Groombridge and Sons (1858). xii,
      251 pp. 3rd edition London: F. Farrah (1864).
         Letters and reports of Coleridge's conversation, chief-
      ly between 1818 and 1825, with some comments by Allsop.
      Inaccurate and often obtuse, Allsop remains, nevertheless,
      a primary source for Coleridge's later years. The 1858
      reprint adds preface defending his father by R[obert?]
      A[llsop]. In 1864, Thomas adds prefatory remarks, sup-
      pressed by Moxon in 1836, asserting consistency of Cole-
      ridge's early and later theological positions.

([ALLSOP, THOMAS])
Reviewed: <u>Leigh Hunt's London Journal</u>, II (1835),
457-9; <u>London Literary Gazette</u>, No. 987 (19 Dec 1835),
pp. 803-5; <u>Knickerbocker</u> [New York], VII (1836), 648;
<u>Mirror</u>, XXVII (1836), 137-9; <u>Monthly Review</u>, New Series I,
(1836), 87-101; <u>New Yorker</u>, No. 10 (28 May 1836), p. 157;
<u>Tait's Edinburgh Magazine</u>, New Series III (1836), 113-23;
<u>Economist</u>, XVI (1858), 595 (reprinted <u>Littell's Living Age</u>
[Boston], 3rd Series II (1858), 213). See also 612, 673,
680, 682, 685, 689, 694, 701, 1242.

673   ANON. 'Coleridge's Letters, Conversations and Recollections'.
<u>Atkinson's Casket</u> [Philadelphia], XI, 384.
A somewhat anti-American comment is extracted to quali-
fy 'so much unqualified approbation' of Coleridge.

674   _____. 'De Diabalo'. <u>American Monthly Magazine</u> [New York
and Boston], New Series I, 184-93.
'Gentleman's devil' of <u>The Devil's Thoughts</u> contrasted
(p. 186) with Goethe's Mephistopheles.

675   _____. '<u>Language, its connection with the present condition</u>
<u>and future prospects of man. By a Heteroscian</u>'. <u>American</u>
<u>Monthly Magazine</u> [New York and Boston], New Series I,
37-44.
Coleridge's prose (especially <u>Aids</u> and <u>Church and State</u>)
recommended (p. 43).

676   _____. 'Miscellaneous Sonnets...By William Wordsworth'.
<u>American Quarterly Review</u> [Philadelphia], XIX, 420-42.
Coleridge's <u>Improvisatore</u> (p. 432) in all respects 'the
finest <u>Prose</u> delineation of the passion of love'. Cites
prose extracts which Hartley Coleridge might well turn into
verse.

677   _____. 'Specimens of the Table-Talk of the Late Samuel Taylor
Coleridge'. <u>American Quarterly Review</u> [Philadelphia], XIX,
1-28.
Flattering but inconsistent biographical and critical
survey ('The Plato of his time' but 'we do not rank him
high as a philosopher'). His 'unfortunate mistake was in
not eradicating his early love for mystical theology'.

678   _____. 'Coleridge (S.-T.)' <u>Biographie universelle et porta-</u>
<u>tive des contemporains...depuis 1788</u>. 4 vols. Paris:
Chez l'Editeur, I, 1035-6.
Brief evaluation sees reputation based on youthful
promise rather than achievement.

SAMUEL TAYLOR COLERIDGE: AN ANNOTATED BIBLIOGRAPHY

679   ____. 'Literary Remains of Samuel Taylor Coleridge'. Examiner, No. 1497 (9 Oct), pp. 645-7. Reprinted Museum of
Foreign Literature [Philadelphia], New Series II (1836),
408-13.
    Complains of Coleridge's vanity and plagiarism, offers
marginalia on Jonson, Milton, Fletcher.

680   ____. 'Letters, Conversations, and Recollections'. Fraser's
Literary Chronicle, I, 81-4, 101-5, 119-22.
    Allsop an 'honest writer'. Reviewer uses material for a
defence of Coleridge and attacks those who failed to appreciate or support him, including Hazlitt, Irving, Jeffrey,
Brougham and Lord Russell.

681   No entry.

682   ANON. 'Recollections of Coleridge'. Monthly Repository, X,
122-4.
    Allsop's work contains interesting material but marred
by sentimentality and bad taste.

683   ____. 'Philosophy of the Present Time'. New Jerusalem Magazine [Boston], IV, 143.
    Extract from Table Talk with approving introductory
comment.

684   ____. 'The Exhibition at the Royal Academy'. Times, No.
16109 (13 May), p. 6.
    Mentions Sebastian Wyndam Arnald's bust of Coleridge.

685   ____. 'Letters, Conversations and Recollections of Samuel
Taylor Coleridge'. Western Literary Journal [Cincinnati],
I, 198-205.
    Allsop offers best insight into Coleridge's life so
far. Coleridge as poet preferred to philosopher.

686   [BANKS, PERCY WELDON] Morgan Rattler, pseud. 'The Books on
my Table. Of Hamlet'. Fraser's Magazine, XIV, 1-18.
    Reworks Coleridge's definition of genius to fit the
needs of this essay.
    Attribution: WI.

687   BROKENHURST, T. 'The Coleridge Papers'. Fraser's Literary
Chronicle, I, 184-5, 201-2, 217-8, 232-3, 248-9.
    Essays on Genial Criticism reprinted by one who knew
Coleridge well.

95

688 CARLYON, CLEMENT. Early Years and Late Reflections. London:
Whittaker and Co. Reprinted 4 vols (1843-1858).
Carlyon's meeting with Coleridge at Göttingen and their
walking tour in 1799. Describes manner and subjects of
Coleridge's conversation. Reviewed: Christian's Monthly
Magazine, I (1844), 143-55, 315-23, 652-5. See also 844.

689 C. J. H. 'On "Letters, Conversations, and Recollections of
S. T. Coleridge"'. British Magazine, IX, 369-73.
Instances of Allsop's misrepresentation of Coleridge's
theology.

690 [COOPER, THOMAS]. 'Sonnets'. Southern Literary Journal
[Charleston, S. C.], I, 313-8.
Condemns new schools of poetry, including that of Cole-
ridge and Wordsworth, 'the favourites of folly and naise-
rie'.
Attribution: Index of journal.

690A D. 'The Poets of Our Age, considered as to their Philosophic
Tendencies'. Westminster Review, XXV, 60-71.
Coleridge (pp. 37-38) had essentially poetic rather than
philosophic mind, and produced brilliant fragments rather
than coherent system.

691 DIBDIN, THOMAS FROGNALL. Reminiscences of a Literary Life.
London: John Major. Partially reprinted as 'Portraits'.
Gentleman's Magazine, New Series VI (1837), 253.
Account (pp. 253-7) of meeting with Coleridge at Sir
Thomas Bernard's and of Coleridge's conversation.

692 ENORT, pseud. 'The Late Mr. Coleridge'. Mirror, XXVII, 131.
Brief account of Coleridge and The Watchman.

693 ETHEE, pseud. 'Recollections of Coleridge'. Mirror for Magi-
strates, No. 1 (16 April), p. 3.
Describes meeting with Coleridge and his influence in
America.

694 [FELTON, CORNELIUS CONWAY]. 'Letters, Conversations, and
Recollections of S. T. Coleridge'. North American Review
[Boston], XLIII, 263-4.
Finds Coleridge's letters 'inferior...in every excel-
lence of style and thought' and Allsop 'indescribably
silly'.
Attribution: Cushing

695   [FULLER, MARGARET] M. F. 'Modern British Poets'. American
       Monthly Magazine [New York and Boston], New Series II,
       235-50, 310-33. Reprinted in her Papers on Literature and
       Art. New York, London: Wiley & Putnam (1846), pp. [58]-99.
           Coleridge infinitely suggestive (p. 326), meaningful to
       minds prepared for him and inexplicable to others.

696   [HERAUD, JOHN ABRAHAM]. 'The Last Portrait of Coleridge.
       Painted by Moses Haughton'. Fraser's Magazine, XIV, 179.
       Poem.
       Attribution: WI.

697   HUTCHINSON, HENRY. Retrospect of a Retired Mariner, in Nine
       Cantos, Written by Himself. London: Stockton (1836).
           Many mentions of Coleridge and Wordsworth, and their
       influence.

698   LANDOR, WALTER SAVAGE. A Satire on Satirists, and Admonition
       to Detractors. London: Saunders & Otley.
           Notes to lines 129 and 221 describe Coleridge and attack
       Blackwood's criticism.

699   [MAGINN, WILLIAM, with FRANCIS MAHONEY]. 'Parliamentary Re-
       port of the Proceedings...To Inquire into the Conduct...of
       Fraser's Magazine'. Fraser's Magazine, XIII, 1-79.
           Humorous sketch includes (pp. 23-5) a speech by Cole-
       ridge's ghost.
       Attribution: WI.

700   [POE, EDGAR ALLAN]. 'The Culprit Fay, and Other Poems'.
       Southern Literary Messenger [Richmond, Va.], II, 326-36.
           Joseph Rodman Drake, author of The Culprit Fay, and
       Fitz-Greene Halleck compared to Coleridge, who (p. 328)
       owed his 'almost magical pre-eminence rather to metaphysi-
       cal than poetical prowess'.
       Attribution: Harrison

701   _____. 'Recollections of Coleridge'. Southern Literary Mes-
       senger [Richmond, Va.], II, 451-3.
           Review of Allsop (1836) calls Coleridge 'little under-
       stood' and 'pitifully vilified'.
       Attribution: Harrison

702   [WILLMOTT, ROBERT ARIS]. 'S. T. Coleridge at Trinity, with
       Specimens of his Table Talk'. Conversations at Cambridge.
       London: John W. Parker, pp. 1-36. Reprinted Fraser's
       Literary Chronicle, I (1836), 291-2.
           Impressions of Coleridge's visit to Cambridge in 1833,
       followed by 30 pages of notes on his conversation.
       Attribution: NCBEL III.

1837

703   The Rime of The Ancient Mariner...Illustrated by David Scott.
Edinburgh: Alexander Hill; London: Ackermann & Co.,
16 pp. 25 plates. Reprinted Simpson (1883), q.v.
    Twenty-five 'poetic and dramatic' etchings which Cole-
ridge saw and liked.
    Reviewed: Monthly Repository, New Series XI (1837),
143–4; Art-Union, VII (1845), 313; and nos. 709, 949.

704   ANON. 'The Admirable Crichton'. Bentley's Miscellany, I,
416–8.
    Compares Crichton with Coleridge.

705   _____. 'The Literary Remains of Coleridge'. Church of England Quarterly Review, II, 24–56.
    General survey chiefly concerned with prose works and
development of ideas, including influence of Kant and
Schelling. More descriptive than critical.

706   _____. 'Cottle's Recollections of Coleridge'. Christian Observer, XXXVII, 594–611, 632–8.
    Passages from Cottle used as exempla of 'folly and mis-
ery of desultory literary adventure' in contrast with
'steady industry, in a...settled calling' and 'early set-
tled principles'. Sequel ('Horrors of opium: case of Mr.
Coleridge') treats Coleridge's opium addiction as object
lesson.

707   _____. 'Coleridge, Samuel Taylor'. The Penny Cyclopaedia of
the Society for the Diffusion of Useful Knowledge. London:
Charles Knight, VII, 343–5.
    Biographical sketch and generally unfavourable assess-
ment. Claims Alvar's soliloquy derived from Caleb
Williams.

708   _____. 'Cottle's Recollections of Coleridge'. Tait's Edinburgh Magazine, New Series IV, 341–8.
    Work valuable if indiscreet. A tragic Prometheus, soar-
ing yet enchained.

709   _____. 'Rime of the Ancient Mariner. Illustrated by David
Scott'. Tait's Edinburgh Magazine, New Series IV, 739.
    Poem 'a fable intended to teach the commonest and best
of morals--love for all sorts of created existence'. Illustrations 'worthy of the work'.

710 _____. 'Coleridge and Plagiarism'. Ward's Miscellany, I,
76.
Coleridge's On a Cataract an imitation rather than
translation of Stolberg's 'Unsterblicher Jüngling'.

711 _____. 'Nature'. Western Messenger [Louisville], II,
385–93.
Influence of Coleridge and Wordsworth (p. 387) briefly
discussed.

712 B. 'The Late S. T. Coleridge on the Schoolmen'. British Magazine, XI, 241.
Writer has Coleridge's copy of Cave's Historia Literaria
and prints marginal note.

713 BOWEN, F. 'Locke and the Transcendentalists'. Christian Examiner [Boston], XXIII, 170–94.
Coleridge and Carlyle (pp. 186–91) England's greatest
proponents of transcendentalism, a foolish German import.
Coleridge born for poetry, not philosophy.

714 [BULWER-LYTTON, EDWARD]. 'The Letters of Charles Lamb'.
Westminster Review, XXVII, 229–42.
Lamb's friendship with Coleridge. Coleridge's influence
more significant than that of Wordsworth.
Attribution: WI.

715 CHAMBERS, ROBERT. History of the English Language and Literature. Hartford: Edward Hopkins.
Coleridge's (pp. 203–4) genius blighted by 'study of
metaphysics and of German literature'.

716 [COOPER, JAMES FENIMORE]. Gleanings in Europe. England: By
an American. 2 vols. Philadelphia: Carey, Lea, and
Blanchard. I, 212–19, II, 179–82.
An account of dinner at Sotheby's with Coleridge and
later meeting at Highgate.

717 COTTLE, JOSEPH. Early Recollections; Chiefly Relating to the
Late Samuel Taylor Coleridge, during his long residence in
Bristol. 2 vols. London: Longman et al. xxxviii, 325;
346 pp. Portraits by Vandyke, Hancock. Revised as Reminiscences of Samuel Taylor Coleridge and Robert Southey.
London: Houlston and Stoneman (1847), xx, 516 pp.
Although very unreliable and somewhat obtuse, this account by Coleridge's one-time friend and publisher pre-
served first-hand information and often garbled letters,
chiefly for the years before 1807. Gives the first public

1837-COTTLE

(COTTLE, JOSEPH)
disclosure of Coleridge's opium addiction in a long moral-
izing account. Cottle widely attacked, and defended him-
self in preface bound into second issue (1839).
Reviewed: Athenaeum, No. 498 (13 May 1837), p. 343;
British Critic, XXII (1837), 257; British Magazine, XI
(1837), 668-9; Congregational Magazine, XX (1837), 520-8;
Eclectic Review, New Series II (1837), 137-64; Spectator,
No. 462 (6 May 1837), pp. 424-5; Hogg's Weekly Instructor,
IV (1846), 270-1. See also 706, 708, 723, 727.

718   'A Country Reader', pseud. 'Coleridge and Unitarianism'.
Christian Observer, XXXVII, 59-60.
Indignant letter concerning Coleridge's remarks in Table
Talk against Unitarianism.

719   D. L. 'Coleridge'. Ladies Companion [New York], VI, 221-2.
Brief sketch of Ancient Mariner and Christabel for
'lovers of romance', in a florid description of Coleridge.

720   [DE QUINCEY, THOMAS]. 'Sir Humphry Davy: Mr. Goodwin: Mrs.
Grant of Laggan'. Tait's Edinburgh Magazine, New Series
IV, 65-73, 169-76. Reprinted in his Literary Reminiscences; from The Autobiography of an English Opium-Eater.
2 vols. Boston: Ticknor, Reed, and Fields (1854), I,
37-61.
Reports (pp. 170-1) Coleridge's admiration for and criticism of Davy.

721   [EAGLES, JOHN] An Amateur, pseud. 'Exhibitions--British
Institution'. Blackwood's Magazine, XLII, 493-503.
Passage in Table Talk on Claude and Teniers quoted
(p. 502) and disputed.
Attribution: WI.

722   ENORT, pseud. 'Coleridge (To the Editor.)'. Mirror, XXIX,
4-5.
Mentions Gillman's proposed biography and submits copy
of Coleridge's 1794 prospectus for translations of Latin
poets.

723   FOSTER, JOHN. 'Early Recollections'. Eclectic Review, New
Series 4, II, 137-64. Reprinted in his Critical Essays
Contributed to the Eclectic Review. Ed. J. E. Ryland. 2
vols. London: Henry G. Bohn (1856), II, 455-83.
Chiefly biographical summary. Foster, an early defender
of The Friend (1811, q.v.) praises Cottle for honest por-
trayal of Coleridge's character.

724   [GILLIES, ROBERT PEARSE]. 'German Philosophy'. Fraser's
       Magazine, XV, 716-35.
            Editorial note justifies article on grounds that Cole-
       ridge's works assume knowledge of Kant.
            Attribution: WI.

725   [HERAUD, JOHN ABRAHAM]. 'One or Two Words on One or Two
       Books'. Fraser's Magazine, XV, 498-514.
            Landor's criticism of Blackwood's on Coleridge (1836)
       thought (pp. 499, 500) to be unwarranted.
            Attribution: WI suggests possibly in collaboration with
       William Maginn.

726   [KEMBLE, JOHN MITCHELL]. 'Cambridge, Article 6'. British and
       Foreign Review, V, 168-209.
            Discussion (pp. 179, 209) of education at Cambridge sup-
       ports Coleridge's theories.
            Attribution: WI.

727   [LOCKHART, J. G., and HENRY NELSON COLERIDGE]. 'Literary Re-
       mains of Samuel Taylor Coleridge...Early Recollections...
       By Joseph Cottle'. Quarterly Review, LIX, 1-32. Portrait
       by Leslie.
            Lockhart offers minor criticisms of the principles of
       inclusion in Literary Remains and a flattering assessment
       of Coleridge as critic. H. N. Coleridge's review of Cottle
       is a bitter attack on 'this forty-years deposit of Bristol
       garbage'.
            Attribution: WI.

728   [LOCKHART, JOHN GIBSON]. Memoirs of the Life of Sir Walter
       Scott, Bart. 7 vols. Edinburgh: Robert Cadell; London:
       John Murray and Whittaker and Co.
            Two letters of 1802 and 1810 (I, 351; II, 325-7) men-
       tion Coleridge. Journal for 1828 (VII, 126) describes his
       talking on Homer and Greek mysteries at Sotheby's.

729   MOULTRIE, JOHN. 'To the Anonymous Editor of Coleridge's Let-
       ters and Recollections'. Poems. London: William Picker-
       ing. 55 pp.
            Poem attacks Allsop.

730   PARTINGTON, CHARLES F. 'Coleridge, Samuel Taylor'. British
       Cyclopaedia of Biography. 10 vols. London: William S.
       Orr, I, 492-3.
            Brief, unremarkable biographical sketch.

731   [PEACOCK, THOMAS LOVE]. 'The Wise Men of Gotham. By S. T. C.,
       Esq., Professor of Mysticism'. Guide, No. 9 (18 June),
       p. 66. Reprinted in his Paper Money Lyrics and Other
       Poems. London: C. and W. Reynell (1837), pp. 22-5.
          Poem roughly imitating The Ancient Mariner.

732   [PRATI, GIOCCHINE DE'] Hermes, pseud. 'S. T. Coleridge--
       Garden Talk'. Shepherd, II, 31-2. Revised in his 'Auto-
       biography'. Penny Satirist, II, no. 77 (6 October 1838).
          Abbreviated account of introduction to Coleridge in
       1824 and of weekly meetings during 1824-26. Prati appar-
       ently introduced Coleridge to Vico (see Fisch, 1943).

733   ROSE, WILLIAM STEWART. Rhymes. Brighton. [No publisher].
          Note (p. 92) gives brief account of seaside walk with
       Coleridge, prints ms note from copy of Christabel (see
       Griggs, Letters, IV, 691).

734   [SMITH, J. E.?]. 'High Church Toryism of Coleridge'. Shep-
       herd, III, 91-2.
          Coleridge's greatness of mind contrasts with littleness
       of prejudices, as shown by opposition to Reform Bill and
       support of Established Church.
          Attribution: Smith, editor of Shepherd.

735   TALFOURD, THOMAS NOON. The Letters of Charles Lamb, with a
       Sketch of his Life. 2 vols. London: Edward Moxon.
          A memoir of Lamb with frequent mention of and letters to
       Coleridge. Reviewed: British and Foreign Review, V
       (1837), 430-1; London Literary Gazette, No. 1068 (8 July
       1837), pp. 430.

736   [WILLMOTT, R. A.]. 'An April Voyage'. Fraser's Magazine,
       XV, 599-621.
          Gratuitous references (p. 611) to Coleridge's lack of
       character, followed by attack (p. 620) on Moultrie's 1837
       sonnet, q.v.
          Attribution: WI.

                                1838

737   ALLEN, GEORGE. 'Reproductive Criticism'. New-York Review,
       II, 49-75.
          Coleridge's fragments 'the best guides' for students of
       art. Attacks Withington's 1834 essay.

738   ANON. 'Answers to Correspondents'. Christian Observer,
       XXXVIII, 71, 208.
           Two notes on date of composition of Religious Musings.

739   _____. 'State of the Stage'. Fraser's Magazine, XVII,
       156-70.
           Disagrees (p. 163) with Coleridge on Winter's Tale.

740   _____. 'The Literary Remains of S. Taylor Coleridge'. Lon-
       don Literary Gazette, No. 1109 (21 April), p. 248.
           Notice of Vol. III, which is 'written in a high mystical
       and metaphysical sentiment'.

741   _____. 'Modern Poets'. New-Yorker, VI, 211-2.
           Coleridge the equal of Shakespeare and Milton in devel-
       opment of 'the music of the English tongue'. Cornwall his
       closest rival as love poet.

742   [CALVERT, GEORGE HENRY]. 'The Literary Remains of Samuel
       Taylor Coleridge'. New York Review, II, 96-111.
           Chiefly extracts with brief favourable comments.
       Attribution: Calvert, 1840.

743   CHORLEY, HENRY F. The Authors of England. A Series of Medal-
       lion Portraits of Modern Literary Characters. London:
       Charles Tilt. Portrait from bust by S. Arnald, facing
       p. 37. Reprinted Museum of Foreign Literature [Philadel-
       phia], XXXIII, 89-92.
           Kindly, sometimes inaccurate sketch.

744   DE QUINCEY, THOMAS. 'Recollections of Charles Lamb'. Tait's
       Edinburgh Magazine, New Series V, 237-47; 355-66. Re-
       printed in his Literary Reminiscences; from The Autobiog-
       raphy of an English Opium Eater. 2 vols. Boston: Tick-
       nor, Reed, and Fields (1854), I, 62-134.
           Reports Lamb's comments on Coleridge and on The Ancient
       Mariner. Discusses (pp. 359-60) Coleridge's use of opium.

745   [DONNE, WILLIAM BODHAM]. 'The Works of Gray; edited by the
       Reverend John Mitford, 1836'. British and Foreign Review,
       VI, 397-420.
           'Hymn before Sunrise' instance of Romantic anthropo-
       morphism (p. 412).
       Attribution: WI.

746   [FELTON, CORNELIUS CONWAY]. 'Talfourd's Letters of Charles
       Lamb'. North American Review [Boston], XLVI, 55–71.
            Notes (p. 59) cogency of Lamb's criticism of Coleridge's
       'bombastic absurdities'.
            Attribution: Cushing.

747   FROST, JOHN. Select Works of the British Poets...from Falcon-
       er to Sir Walter Scott. With Biographical and Critical No-
       tices. Philadelphia: Thomas Wardle.
            Selections from Coleridge with inaccurate and obtuse bi-
       ographical and critical sketch (pp. 520–1).

748   GILLMAN, JAMES. The Life of Samuel Taylor Coleridge. In Two
       Volumes. Vol. I (only one published). London: Pickering.
            Almost entirely concerned with Coleridge's life before
       he came to Gillman's. Includes some then unpublished notes
       and letters, but draws little on personal knowledge of
       Coleridge.
            Reviewed: Literary Gazette, Nos. 1109, 1112 (21 April,
       12 May 1838), pp. 248, 289–91; Magazin für die Literatur
       des Auslandes [Berlin], No. 76 (25 June 1838), pp. 301–2;
       Metropolitan Magazine, XXII (1838), 65–74; Spectator, No.
       513 (28 April 1838), 396–7. See also 769, 802, 866, 1157.

749   GLADSTONE, W. E. The State in its Relations with the Church.
       London: John Murray.
            Summarizes (pp. 17–19) the 'beautiful and profound' ar-
       gument of The Constitution of Church and State and suggests
       modifications.

750   HALL, S. C. The Book of Gems. The Modern Poets...of Great
       Britain. London: Whittaker and Co.
            Brief biographical sketch (p. 50) with reprinted poems
       (pp. 51–9).

751   [HERAUD, JOHN ABRAHAM]. 'Coleridge's Friend'. Sunbeam, I,
       253, 344, 353, 360–1, 368.
            Series, probably by Heraud, the editor, purporting to
       constitute first review of The Friend, chiefly devoted to
       exposition of Coleridge's ideas on Being and Consciousness.

752   MACNISH, ROBERT. The Modern Pythagorean...with the author's
       life by his friend, D. M. Moir. 2 vols. Edinburgh: Wil-
       liam Blackwood and Sons; London: T. Cadell. Reprinted
       Tales, Essays, and Sketches. London: Henry G. Bohn (1844).
            Moir's memoir compares Coleridge and Macnish with ac-
       count of visit to Highgate and of Coleridge's conversation.

(MACNISH, ROBERT)
Notes Coleridge's impression that Maginn wrote Moir's imitations.

753 MATHEWS, MRS. [ANN]. Memoirs of Charles Mathews, Comedian. 4 vols. London: Richard Bentley.
Neighbour of Coleridge at Highgate describes (III, 188-98) dinner arranged by Coleridge, and prints a letter from Coleridge to Mathews.

754 [MILL, JOHN STUART]. A. The Works of Jeremy Bentham. London and Westminster Review, XXI, 467-506. Reprinted in his Dissertations and Discussions. 2 vols. London: John Parker & Son (1859), I, 330-392.
Companion piece to Mill's 1840 essay, q.v., begins with famous account of Bentham and Coleridge as 'the two great seminal minds of England in their age'.

755 PRINGLE, THOMAS. Poetical Works. Edited with a sketch of his life by Leitch Ritchie. London: E. Moxon.
Recounts (pp. cviii-cx) efforts to have Coleridge's pension restored.

756 RIPLEY, GEORGE, ED. Philosophical Miscellanies [of Victor Cousin], translated from the French. With Introductory and Critical Notices. 2 vols. Boston: Hilliard, Gray. Reprinted as Philosophical Essays. Edinburgh: Thomas Clark (1839).
Ripley recommends Marsh's notes to Aids (I, 40-2) and discusses Coleridge's popularity in America. His religious aims in large measure accomplished by Cousin.

757 [SHREVE, THOMAS H.] T. H. S. 'Talk and Talkers'. Hesperian [Columbus, Ohio], I, 18-22.
Coleridge's conversation more influential than his writing.

758 [STUART, DANIEL]. 'Anecdotes of the Poet Coleridge'. Gentleman's Magazine, New Series IX, 485-92, 577-90, New Series X, 23-7, 124-8. Partially reprinted as 'Anecdotes of the Late Mr. Coleridge'. Mirror, XXXII (1838), 107-9; 'Coleridge and the Press'. Hesperian [Columbus, Ohio], I (1838), 484-5.
Stuart's defence against 'misrepresentations' in Biographia Literaria and by Gillman and H. N. C. Account, with letters, of his acquaintance with Coleridge and letter from H. N. C. ('The Late Mr. Coleridge', 1838) rejecting Stuart's complaints was published with Stuart's reply,

([STUART, DANIEL])
which is repeated with further anecdotes in Stuart's 'Late
Mr. Coleridge'.

759 TUPPER, MARTIN FARQUHAR. 'Geraldine, A Sequel to Coleridge's
Christabel'. Geraldine...With Other Poems. London: Joseph Rickerby, pp. 3-52. Reprinted in his Ballads for the
Times. London: Arthur Hall, Virtue and Co. (1849),
pp. 121-52.
Serious but undistinguished attempt to complete Christabel. Reviewed: Eclectic Review, 4th Series V (1839),
40-50; [Dwight, John S.] J. S. D. Harbinger [Boston],
II (1845), 42-4 (attribution: table of contents). See
also 761.

760 [WILSON, JOHN]. 'Extracts from the Drawer of our Whatnot'.
Blackwood's Magazine, XLIV, 120-40.
General approval of Aids (pp. 135-40), but defends the
moral value of sensibility and Adam Smith's doctrine of
sympathy against Coleridge.
Attribution: WI.

761 _____. 'Tupper's Geraldine'. Blackwood's Magazine, XLIV,
835-52. Reprinted in his Essays Critical and Imaginative,
4 vols. Edinburgh, London: William Blackwood and Sons
(1857), III, 344-72.
Review is divided between discussion and appreciation of
Christabel and contempt for Tupper's 1838 attempt to complete it.

1839

762 Aids to Reflection. By Samuel Taylor Coleridge, with the Au-
thor's Last Corrections. Edited by Henry Nelson Coleridge.
To which is prefixed a Preliminary Essay by John M'Vickar,
Professor of Moral Philosophy in Columbia College, New
York. London: William Pickering; New York: Swords,
Stanford and Company. xlviii, 324 pp.
Unauthorized reprint. McVickar's replacement of Marsh's
1829 essay with his own explication of Coleridge and his
implication that he had H. N. C.'s approval led to con-
siderable controversy.

763 [ALDRICH, JAMES]. 'Original Letter of the Late Samuel Taylor
Coleridge'. New York Literary Gazette, I, 2-3.
Prints part of a letter of 31 May, 1822 to an American
admirer, prefaced by fulsome editorial praise of Coleridge.

([ALDRICH, JAMES])
Only known copy (in New York Public Library) lacks p. 3.
Attribution: WPA Index

764 ANON. 'The State and the Church'. British and Foreign Review, IX, 433-66.
Review of Maurice and Gladstone, who acknowledge debt to Coleridge (pp. 436-7).

765 _____. 'Hours with the Poets--Coleridge'. London Saturday Journal, II, 7-9.
Moralizing biographical account. Kubla Khan illustrates 'mental habits' of 'greatest of visionaries'.

766 _____. 'Thomas Carlyle's Miscellaneous Works'. London Weekly Review, I, 68.
Neither Coleridge nor Carlyle can provide the 'highest philosophy' but both are worth reading.

767 [CLEVELAND, HENRY RUSSELL]. 'Manuel du Graveur'. North American Review [Boston], XLIX, 118-45.
Comparison of engraving and translation (p. 135). Coleridge's Wallenstein 'a faithful representation of Schiller' and 'a beautiful English poem'.
Attribution: Cushing

768 [DE QUINCEY, THOMAS]. 'Lake Reminiscences from 1808 to 1830. By the English Opium-Eater. No. V.--Southey, Wordsworth, and Coleridge'. Tait's Edinburgh Magazine, New Series VI, 513-17. Reprinted in his Literary Reminiscences. 2 vols. Boston: Ticknor, Reed, and Fields (1854), II, 46-60.
Chiefly descriptive of area and Greta Hall, but criticizes Coleridge on political economy (pp. 515-17).

769 [DONNE, WILLIAM BODHAM]. 'The Life and Writings of Coleridge'. British and Foreign Review, VIII, 414-51.
Review of Table Talk, Literary Remains, and Gillman's Life. Careful evaluation of Coleridge's intellectual development. Comments on aesthetic, political and religious influence.
Attribution: WI.

770 [GALT, JOHN]. 'Coleridge and Wordsworth'. Diary Illustrative of the Times of George the Fourth. 4 vols. London: Henry Colburn, IV, 179-82.
Very unfavourable impression of Coleridge's abilities formed on basis of one visit.
Attribution: Bull. of Bibliog. (1936).

771   GRINFIELD, REV. THOMAS, M.A. 'Lines' [On Coleridge's Cot-
      tage]. Bristol Journal (June). Since no copy of the
      Bristol Journal has been located, the following reprint is
      the only known source. Reprinted Chilcott's Clevedon New
      Guide. Edited by J. Chilcott [1849], pp. 37-8.

772   [HERAUD, JOHN ABRAHAM]. 'The Ancient Mariner'. Sunbeam, II,
      129.
            Superstition the basis of The Ancient Mariner and its
      moral that of 'Heart-Leap Well' or Burger's 'Wild Hunter'.
      Attribution: Heraud edited Sunbeam. 772-4 exhibit his
      style and views.

773   _____. ['On the Constitution of the Church and State']. Sun-
      beam, II, 5-6.
            Lead article on new edition of Church and State and Lay
      Sermons, chiefly extracts from the latter.
      Attribution: See 772.

774   _____. [Literary Remains]. Sunbeam, II, 190, 198, 208-10.
            Three lead articles devoted largely to exposition of
      Essay on Faith.
      Attribution: See 772.

775   _____. 'Literary Remains of Samuel Taylor Coleridge'. Month-
      ly Magazine, New Series 3, II, 100-06, 218-21.
            A discussion, in Heraud's usual purple prose, of Cole-
      ridge's theological views. Statement that Coleridge
      was the only 'unitary' philosopher since Plato challenged by
      'Protheticus' ('Chartist Epic and Coleridge's Philosophy')
      who submitted a series of questions which Heraud answered
      in appended editorial note.

776   HERAUD, JOHN A. 'Response from America'. Monthly Magazine,
      II, 344-52.
            Review of Emerson and Alcott argues that Coleridge has
      'excited the American mind'.

777   MEDWIN, T[HOMAS]. 'Hazlitt in Switzerland: A Conversation'.
      Fraser's Magazine, XIX, 278-83.
            Minor comments on Coleridge.

778   [NEWMAN, JOHN HENRY]. 'The State of Religious Parties'.
      British Critic, XXV, 395-426. Reprinted in his Essays.
      Critical and Historical. 2 vols. London: Pickering
      (1871), I, 263-307.
            Review of fourteen theological works contains (p. 400)
      Newman's famous remark that Coleridge 'indulged a liberty
      of speculation which no Christian can tolerate'.

779   SHELLEY, PERCY BYSSHE. 'Peter Bell the Third'. Poetical
      Works of Percy Bysshe Shelley. Ed. Mrs. Shelley. London:
      Edward Moxon.
           Coleridge (line 373-97) the 'subtle-souled psychologist'
      who understands everything but his own mind.

780   STERLING, JOHN. 'Coleridge'. Poems. London: E. Moxon,
      pp. 153-5.
           Poem mourns Coleridge 'half-ruined, and all tottering,
      still divine'.

781   T. G. 'Coleridge's Cottage at Clevedon'. Felix Farley's
      Bristol Journal, XCV (20 July), 4.
           Note on location of 'Myrtle Cottage'.

781A W. H. C. 'Coleridge'. Western Literary Messenger [Cincin-
      nati], VII, 258-64.
           Coleridge judged as 'among the few remarkable writers
      of our time'. But article stresses weaknesses and
      failures.

                            1840

782   Works of Samuel Taylor Coleridge, Prose and Verse, Complete in
      One Volume. Philadelphia: Thomas, Cowperthwait & Co.
      xvi, 546 pp. Frontispiece. Portrait by A. Wivell. Fre-
      quently reprinted.
           Excludes posthumous publications as mere 'book-making'.
      Memoir presents Coleridge as one who wasted his genius in
      vague philosophy and perishable conversation.

783   [ALLEN, GEORGE]. 'Aids to Reflection. By Samuel Taylor Cole-
      ridge'. New-York Review, VI, 477-9.
           Discussion of Marsh's edition of Aids and its influence
      in introducing Coleridge's philosophy to America.
           Attribution: Thompson, Penn Monthly, 1876.

784   ALLEN, GEORGE. 'Dr. M'Vickar's Coleridge'. Churchman [New
      York], X, 1-2, 5-6, 9-10, 13-14, 17-18, 21-2.
           Allen, a former student of Marsh, and, like McVickar,
      an Episcopalian, argues that Marsh's introduction to Aids
      was true to its intent, and that McVickar presents it as
      'narrow, sectarian...an Episcopalian tract'. McVickar ar-
      gues (p. 30) for his approach. Editor (p. 30) supports
      him.

                            109

1840-ANON.

785   ANON. 'Popular Literature of the Day'. British and Foreign
       Review, X, 223-46.
          Coleridge on Maturin's Bertram used against Jack Shep-
       pard and Michael Armstrong, as examples of sensational
       literature.

786   _____. 'Further Particulars regarding Shakespeare and his
       Works. By J. P. Collier. 1839'. Gentleman's Magazine,
       New Series XIII, 273-5.
          Argues against Coleridge's emendations of Shakespeare
       and Beaumont and Fletcher.

787   No entry.

788   _____. 'The Discourse of Coleridge'. Mirror, XXVI, 357.
          Brief general description of Coleridge as talker.

789   _____. 'Les mémoires du diable'. Monthly Review, II, 98-108.
          Charges (p. 106) Southey with 'meanness and dishonesty'
       to claim The Devil's Walk.

790   _____. 'The Literary Remains of Samuel Taylor Coleridge...
       The Scriptural Character of the English Church...By the
       Rev. Derwent Coleridge'. New-York Review, VII, 403-29.
          Derwent accurately follows Coleridge's views, which were
       unlike those America takes as Coleridgean.

791   _____. 'Samuel Taylor Coleridge'. Yale Literary Magazine
       [New Haven], VI, 44-55.
          Biographical and critical essay attacks Coleridge's
       critics. Coleridge and Wordsworth the two most distin-
       guished modern English poets. Coleridge's philosophy 'no
       streamy mysticism' but a science.

792   _____. 'Coleridge und Mrs. Landon-Maclean'. Zeitung für die
       elegante Welt [Leipzig], No. 89 (7 May), pp. 355-6.
          Joint review finds Coleridge 'wild' and 'bizarre' with
       little trace of German influence.

793   C. W. 'Heresies of Samuel Taylor Coleridge'. Christian
       Teacher, New Series II, 71-82.
          Attacks Thomas Byrth, rector of Wallasey, for using
       Coleridge to support theological orthodoxy. Cites in-
       stances of Coleridge's heresies.

794   [COLERIDGE, HENRY NELSON]. 'Poems, By John Sterling'.
      Quarterly Review, LXVI, 156-62.
          A brief mention of Coleridge's influence on Sterling.
      Attribution: WI.

795   [DE QUINCEY, THOMAS]. 'Sketches of Life and Manners; from
      the Autobiography of an English Opium-Eater'. Tait's Edin-
      burgh Magazine, New Series VII, 629-37. Reprinted as
      'William Wordsworth' in his Literary Reminiscences; from
      the Autobiography of an English Opium-Eater. 2 vols. Bos-
      ton: Ticknor, Reed, and Fields (1854), II, 241-52.
          Describes (p. 634) Coleridge's estrangement from
      Wordsworth.

796   _____. 'Westmoreland and the Dalesmen: Society of the
      Lakes'. Tait's Edinburgh Magazine, New Series VII, 32-9.
      Reprinted in his Literary Reminiscences; from the Autobi-
      ography of an English Opium-eater. 2 vols. Boston:
      Ticknor, Reed, and Fields (1854), II, 116-40.
          Discussion of 'The Friend' (pp. 36-7), often its own
      worst enemy, and the response to it of some Lake dwellers.

797   DONNE, WILLIAM BODHAM. 'Hallam's Introduction to the Litera-
      ture of Europe'. British and Foreign Review, XI, 355-416.
          Improvement in quality of English drama criticism due
      in part to Coleridge's lectures, which 'furnished the
      groundwork of a deeply scientific analysis' (p. 408).

798   ELLIOTT, EBENEZER. 'A Defence of Modern Poetry'. Tait's
      Edinburgh Magazine, New Series VII, 309-14.
          Claims (p. 311) for Coleridge's poetry 'absolute and
      entire originality'.

799   [FERRIER, JAMES FREDERICK]. 'The Plagiarisms of S. T. Cole-
      ridge'. Blackwood's Magazine, XLVII, 287-99.
          Cites sources in Schelling for passages in Biographia
      Literaria and On Poesy or Art, and claims Maas as source
      of Chapter V of Biographia. Dismisses Coleridge's claim
      of 'genial coincidence'. Accuses Coleridge also of having
      borrowed 'some of the brightest gems in his poetic wreath'
      from Schiller, Stolberg, and Brun.
      Attribution: WI.

800   GREEN, JOSEPH HENRY. Vital Dynamics. The Hunterian Oration
      before the Royal College of Surgeons in London 14th Febru-
      ary 1840. London: William Pickering. xxx. 135 pp.
          Lecture, avowedly indebted to Coleridge. Attempts to
      develop and apply ideas from then unpublished Theory of
      Life.

801   [HORNE, R. H.]. 'Spirit of Modern Tragedy'. Monthly Chroni-
      cle, V, 108-26.
          Commends Coleridge's criticism and uses Coleridge on
      Shakespeare in corroboration of critical position (pp. 109,
      111, 120).
          Attribution: WI.

802   [MILL, JOHN STUART] A. 'Coleridge'. London and Westminster
      Review, XXXIII, 257-302. Reprinted in his Dissertations
      and Discussions. 2 vols. London: John W. Parker (1859),
      I, 393-466.
          Ostensibly a review article on Coleridge's prose works
      and Gillman's biography, this now classic essay argues that
      Coleridge was, with Bentham, one of the two 'seminal minds'
      of his age. Primarily concerned with political views of
      Church and State, its lasting value is in its explanation
      of two divergent ways of thought, their importance for the
      19th century, and the possibility of their reconciliation.
      Reviewed: no. 1166.

803   [MITCHELL, D. G.]. 'The Mirror, or Tablets of an Idle Man'.
      Yale Literary Magazine [New Haven], VI, 100-08.
          Dialogue concerning the 'Lake Poets' using Coleridge and
      Christabel and comparing Coleridge to his own Mad Ox.
          Attribution: Yale Library copy.

804   MONTAGU, BASIL. 'Monuments'. The Funerals of the Quakers.
      London: W. Pickering, pp. 56-83.
          Possession of a lock of Coleridge's hair leads to a
      eulogy.

805   RICHARDSON, DAVID LESTER. 'Samuel Taylor Coleridge'. Selec-
      tions from the British Poets. Calcutta: Baptist Mission
      Press, pp. ci-cv.
          Conventional anecdotal sketch. Rationalistic evaluation
      of Coleridge's metaphysics (derivative and confused) and
      brief favourable assessment of poetry.

806   [SPALDING, WILLIAM]. 'Recent Shakespearian Literature'.
      Edinburgh Review, LXXI, 446-93.
          Despite his eccentricities, Coleridge best qualified and
      most valuable of Shakespeare's critics.
          Attribution: WI.

807 [WELLS, SAMUEL] W. 'Predominance of Certain Organs in the
     British Poets'. American Phrenological Journal & Miscel-
     lany [Philadelphia], II, 166-70, 359-66.
         Phrenological analysis of Coleridge and his poetry.
     Attribution: Wells edited this journal.

                            1841

808 ANON. 'Mill and Hegel. Historic Criticism of the Gospel'.
     British and Foreign Review, XII, 515-42.
         Coleridge 'the greatest Christian philosopher of our
     age and country'. Quoted and compared with Strauss
     (p. 539).

809 _____. 'Literary Notices'. Boston Quarterly Review, IV,
     135-6.
         Brief favourable review of Confessions, possibly by
     Quarterly editor, Orestes Brownson, agrees with Coleridge's
     argument for plenary inspiration.

810 No entry.

811 _____. 'Confessions of an Inquiring Spirit'. Monthly Miscel-
     lany of Religion and Letters [Boston], IV, 44-7.
         Coleridge's views 'are familiar, in substance to most
     Christians, and acceptable to some'.

812 _____. The Rime of the New-Made Baccalere. Oxford: J. Vin-
     cent. 31 pp.
         Parody.

813 CARLYLE, THOMAS. On Heroes, Hero-Worship and the Heroic in
     History. Six Lectures. Reported, with Emendations and
     Additions. London: James Fraser.
         In 'the Hero as Poet' Coleridge's discussion of rhythm
     and melody used (pp. 146-7) to establish a definition of
     true poetry.

814 GILFILLAN, GEORGE. 'Late Samuel Taylor Coleridge'. Dumfries-
     shire & Galloway Herald and Advertiser, Unnumbered (11,
     18 Feb., 18 March), unpaged. Reprinted in his Gallery of
     Literary Portraits. Edinburgh: William Tate (1845),
     pp. 265-88.
         Descriptions of individual poems linked by purple prose.
     Reviewed: no. 1097.

1841-HENRY

815   [HENRY, CALEB SPRAGUE]. 'Confessions of an Inquiring Spirit.'
      New-York Review, VIII, 274.
            Quarrels with expression, not substance, of denial of
      plenary inspiration.
            Attribution: Duffy

815A [HORNE, R. H.?]. 'Shakespeare. A Suggestion'. Monthly
      Chronicle, VII, 481-8.
            Coleridge favourably compared with Lessing and Schlegel
      as critic of Shakespeare.
            Attribution: WI.

816   [PARSONS, T.] T. P. 'Coleridge's View of Swedenborg'. New
      Jerusalem Magazine [Boston], XIV, 468-78.
            Reprint, with comments, of Coleridge marginalia in
      Oeconomia Regni Animalis.

817   STEWART, ELIZA. 'Christabel, Continued from Coleridge by
      Eliza Stewart'. Smallwood's Magazine (June), 432-8.
            Only recorded copy, in the British Museum, destroyed
      during the war. Described in Nethercott (The Road to Try-
      ermaine, Chicago, 1939, pp. 39-40), as 'far more intelli-
      gent than any other attempted continuation, but Hamilton
      (1888) described it as 'very inferior'.

818   TUCKERMAN, H. T. 'Coleridge'. Southern Literary Messenger
      [Richmond, Va.], VII, 177-80.
            Eulogy regrets Coleridge's failure to write more, and
      traces his metaphysical background.

819   [WARE, W]. [Coleridge's Confessions of an Inquiring Spirit].
      Christian Examiner [Boston and New York], XXX, 121-5.
            After extensive quotation, charges Coleridge with awk-
      ward style and sham profundity.
            Attribution: Cushing

1842

820   EDITOR. 'Coleridge's Opinion of the Calumny so often heard
      against Swedenborg, that he was mad'. New Jerusalem Maga-
      zine [Boston], New Series III, 146-7.
            Extracts from Coleridge's marginalia on Swedenborg.

821   JOHNSON, EDWARD. Nuces Philosophicae; or the Philosophy of
      Things as developed from the Study of the Philosophy of
      Words. London: Simkin, Marshall, and Co.
            Discusses (pp. xvii-xviii) a passage from Aids as in-
      stance of meaningless language.

822 MAURICE, F. D. Kingdom of Christ. Second Edition. 2 vols.
     London: Rivington.
          Dedication, first published in this edition, character-
     izes Coleridge as thinker and expresses Maurice's debt.

823 [MOIR, GEORGE] W. W. W. W. pseud. 'Poetry'. Encyclopaedia
     Britannica. 7th edition. 21 vols. Edinburgh: A & C
     Black, XVIII, 140-73.
          Poetry defined primarily through works of Coleridge and
     Milton.
          Attribution: Table of Signatures, Vol. I, Encycl. Brit.

824 RIENZI, PSEUD. 'Wordsworth'. Yale Literary Magazine [New
     Haven], VII, 257-62.
          Coleridge shares with Wordsworth and Southey the 'empire
     of poetic mind in England'.

825 [STERLING, JOHN]. 'On Tennyson's Poems'. Quarterly Review,
     LXX, 385-416. Reprinted Essays and Tales by John Sterling.
     Ed. J. C. Hare. 2 vols. London: Parker (1848), I,
     422-62.
          Tennyson's use of supernatural compared unfavourably to
     that of Coleridge in Christabel.

826 T., L. F. 'Schiller'. United States Magazine [New York], XI,
     34-41.
          Mentions translation by Coleridge, a master poet whose
     metaphysics made him a 'python of oracles in another
     tongue'.

827 TAYLOR, HENRY. Edwin the Fair. London: John Murray.
          According to Taylor, character of Wulfstan the Wise
     based on Coleridge.

828 THEOR, PSEUD. 'Rime of the Ancient Pedlar-Manne'. Yale Lit-
     erary Magazine [New Haven], VII, 296-301.
          Undergraduate parody.

829 [WILBERFORCE, SAMUEL] S. W. 'Contributions of S. T. Cole-
     ridge to the Revival of Catholic Truths'. Christian's
     Miscellany [Leeds], II, 109-36.
          Introduction, extracts try to show Coleridge's contri-
     bution to revival of high church principles. Attacked by
     Sara Coleridge in introduction to Biographia (1847).
          Reviewed: Pioneer [Boston], I (1843), 48.
          Attribution: J. D. Campbell in Huntington Library ms.
     note.

1843

830   Aids to Reflection. Ed. Henry Nelson Coleridge.   2 vols. Lon-
       don: William Pickering, I, xviii, 325; II, xlix, 326-556 pp.
          Volume II contains Marsh's 'Preliminary Essay' (pp. xi-
       xlix), 'On Instinct' (pp. 328-34) by J. H. Green from
       Mental Dynamics (1847), and 'On Rationalism' (pp. 335-556)
       by Sara Coleridge, the last being Sara's Coleridgeian ex-
       tension of her father's position.

831   ANON. 'Life and Poetry of Coleridge'. Chambers's Edinburgh
       Journal, XI, 67-9, 74-5.
          Conventional biographical and critical sketch.

832   _____. 'Influence of German Literature'. Yale Literary Mag-
       azine [New Haven], VIII, 222-31.
          Undergraduate essay supports Coleridge's originality.

833   D. S. ['Coleridge and Zeno's Paradox']. Gentleman's Maga-
       zine, XIX, 479-81.
          Coleridge's solution to the puzzle given a century
       earlier by Jean-Pierre de Crousaz.

834   DE VERE, AUBREY THOMAS. 'Coleridge'. The Search After Pro-
       serpine...And Other Poems. Oxford: John Henry Parker;
       London: Rivingtons.
          Poem on Coleridge (pp. 160-1) as lonely visionary.

835   GRIFFIN, DANIEL. Life of Gerald Griffin. London: Simpkin
       and Marshall. Reprinted in Walter Donaldson. Recollec-
       tions of an Actor. London: John Maxwell (1865), p. 349.
          Attack on 'the Lakers', with parody of Christabel
       (p. 277).

836   GROVE, GEORGE, ED. Coleridgeiana. Memorials of a Great and
       Good Man. London: Lloyd, Wallis and Lloyd. Portraits.
          A privately assembled collection of articles and por-
       traits from periodicals.

837   H. J. 'A Concert of the Poets'. Chambers's London Journal,
       No. 105 (27 May), p. 167.
          Description of previously published humorous dream-
       vision. Original not located.

838   J. E. H. 'Samuel Taylor Coleridge'. Tait's Edinburgh Maga-
       zine, X, 148.
          Sonnet.

839   [LOCKHART, JOHN GIBSON]. 'Peregrine Bunce'. Quarterly Review, LXXII, 53-108.
      Recollection (pp. 65-6) of Hook and Coleridge drunk. Attribution: WI.

840   MURDOCK, JAMES. Sketches of Modern Philosophy, Especially Among the Germans. Edinburgh: Thomas Clark.
      Yale professor discusses (pp. 97-103) 'Coleridgeism' in the United States. Summarizes doctrines of Aids but finds Coleridge obscure.

841   ROBBERDS, J. W. Memoir of the Life and Writings of the Late William Taylor of Norwich. 2 vols. London: John Murray.
      Correspondence with Southey includes frequent reference to Coleridge.

842   TORREY, JOSEPH. Remains of the Rev. James Marsh. Boston: Crocker and Brewster. xii, 642 pp.
      Discusses passim Marsh's views of Coleridge and his effect on Coleridge's American reputation.

                              1844

843   ANON. 'Modern Poetry'. Athenaeum, No. 867 (8 June), pp. 525-6.
      Coleridge's desire to unite literature and life characteristic of the age.

844   No entry.

845   ANON. 'Religious Philosophy; or, A Statement of the Differences Between the Philosophy of Mr. Gladstone's Theory of the Relation Between Church and State, and that of the Late Mr. S. T. Coleridge'. Christian's Monthly Magazine, I, 143-155, 315-23.
      A defence of Coleridge and attack on Gladstone.

846   [BROWNING], ELIZABETH BARRETT. 'A Vision of Poets'. Poems. 2 vols. London: Edward Moxon, II, 1-59.
      Lines on Coleridge (p. 26) as visionary.

847   CHAMBERS, ROBERT. 'Samuel Taylor Coleridge'. Cyclopedia of English Literature. 2 vols. Edinburgh: William and Robert Chambers, II, 333-45, 514-6.
      Extracts with brief, favourable judgments on Coleridge's genius and eloquence.

1844–GRISWOLD

848   GRISWOLD, RUFUS WILMOT. The Sacred Poets of England and Amer-
       ica. New York: D. Appleton.
            Coleridge (pp. 384-9) a 'great genius' and major
       influence.

849   HERBST, OSWALD. 'Letters from England'. Tait's Edinburgh
       Magazine, XI, 641-5. Reprinted Eclectic Magazine [New
       York, Philadelphia], IV (1845), 25-9.
            Wordsworth (p. 644) far happier than Coleridge, 'who
       left poetry for philosophy'. Quotes him (p. 645) as re-
       gretting Coleridge's abandonment of 'his birth-right,
       poetry'.

850   HUNT, LEIGH. 'A Jar of Honey from Mount Hybla.   No. XII and
       Last'. Ainsworth's Magazine, VI, 487-93.
            Examples of Coleridge's fondness for 'sweet sounds'
       (p. 489).

851   _____. Imagination and Fancy; or, Selections from the English
       Poets, with an Essay, in Answer to the Question 'What is
       Poetry?' London: Smith Elder and Co.
            Dismisses Coleridge's prose but judges him 'the greatest
       master of his time' in 'pure poetry'.

852   _____. Poetical Works. London: Moxon.
            Regrets (pp. vii-viii) his neglect of Coleridge, the
       greatest name for 'quintessential poetry' since Milton.

853   [KENNEDY, T.]. 'Samuel Taylor Coleridge'. Yale Literary
       Magazine [New Haven], IX, 107-12.
            Undergraduate essay praises Coleridge's philosophy.
       Attribution: Yale Library copy

854   [LEWES, GEORGE HENRY]. 'Augustus William Schlegel'. Foreign
       Quarterly Review, XXXII, 160-81.
            Lewes sifts evidence of Coleridge's priority over
       Schlegel, argues he was a plagiarist (pp. 161-3).
       Attribution: WI.

855   _____. 'The Three Fausts. Goethe--Marlow--Calderon'. Brit-
       ish and Foreign Review, XVIII, 51-92.
            Coleridge applied organic criteria to Shakespeare but
       not to Faust. His criticism of Goethe unsympathetic and
       superficial (pp. 54, 61).

856   [MITCHELL, WILLIAM]. Coleridge and the Moral Tendency of His
       Writings. New York: Leavitt, Trow & Co. 118 p.
          Discusses Coleridge's relation to Plato, Boehme, Bruno,
       Schelling, Kant, and 'others of the mystic school'. All
       bad influences. Coleridge not really Christian and leads
       to 'Puseyism'. Reviewed: New Englander and Yale Review
       [New Haven], II (1844), 638.
          Attribution: Snyder

857   SCOTT, WILLIAM. 'Manuscript Fragments of S. T. Coleridge'.
       Christian Remembrancer, VII, 250-5.
          Marginalia from Vaughan's Life of Wycliffe with letter
       criticizing Coleridge's theology.

858   STANLEY, ARTHUR PENRHYN, ED. Life and Correspondence of
       Thomas Arnold. 2 vols. London: B. Fellowes.
          Remarks passim on Coleridge's stature as poet and
       thinker.

859   TENNYSON, A., pseud. 'A Fragment--Composed in a Dream'.
       Punch, VII, 21.
          Parody of Kubla Khan and Tennyson.

860   [WHIPPLE, EDWIN P.]. 'Complete Poetical Works of William
       Wordsworth'. North American Review [Boston, New York],
       LIX, 352-84. Reprinted in his Essays and Reviews. 2 vols.
       New York: D. Appleton (1849), I, 211-53.
          Discusses effect of French Revolution on political and
       poetical theories of Wordsworth and Coleridge (pp. 360-2)
       and (p. 380) Jeffrey's criticism.

861   [WILLMOTT, R. A.]. 'The Writings of the Late John Foster'.
       Fraser's Magazine, XXX, 684-702.
          Brief account of Foster's view of Coleridge's strengths
       and deficiencies, with passing reference to Cottle.
          Attribution: WI.

                                 1845

862   ANON. 'Genius'. Hogg's Weekly Instructor, I, 305-7, 321-3.
          Coleridge's genius (p. 306) restricted by opium.

863   _____. 'The Portrait Gallery. Samuel Taylor Coleridge'.
       Hogg's Weekly Instructor, I, 195-7.
          Biographical sketch with brief evaluations of Coleridge
       as poet, lecturer, philosopher, and theologian. Generally
       favourable, but philosophy too esoteric and theology a jum-
       ble of doubtful orthodoxy.

864   BALMER, ROBERT. 'Fragments of Conversation with the Late Rev.
      Robert Hall'. Academical Lectures and Pulpit Discourses.
      2 vols. Edinburgh: William Oliphant; London: Hamilton,
      Adams; Glasgow: David Robertson.
           Includes (I, 76-107) highly unfavourable views of Cole-
      ridge (whom Hall met in Bristol).

865   CRAIK, GEORGE L. Sketches of the History of Literature and
      Learning in England. 6 vols. London: Charles Knight.
      Revised as A Compendious History of English Literature.
      2 vols. London: Charles Knight (1861). Abridged as A
      Manual of English Literature. London: Charles Knight
      (1862).
           Coleridge (VI, 139-60) poet of 'imagination all compact'
      in contrast to the more homely Wordsworth. The two more
      alike in later poetry which includes some of Coleridge's
      best poems. At least nine editions of this work and
      abridged manual, the latter a school text, were published.

866   [DE QUINCEY, THOMAS]. 'Coleridge and Opium-Eating'. Black-
      wood's Magazine, LVII, 117-32. Reprinted in his Narrative
      and Miscellaneous Papers. 2 vols. Boston: Ticknor, Reed,
      and Fields (1853), II, 117-57.
           Review of Gillman contains anecdotes, recollections,
      and discussion of Coleridge and opium.

867   DE QUINCEY, THOMAS. 'On Wordsworth's Poetry'. Tait's Edin-
      burgh Magazine, New Series XII, 545-54. Reprinted in his
      Essays on the Poets. Boston: Ticknor, Reed, and Fields
      (1853), pp. 1-38.
           Comment (p. 547, n) on Coleridge's aversion to pain.

868   [FLETCHER, GEORGE] G. F. 'Shakespearean Criticism and Act-
      ing'. Westminster Review, XLIV, 1-77.
           Criticizes (pp. 57-60) Coleridge on the death of Juliet.
      Attribution: WI.

869   GRISWOLD, RUFUS WILMOT. Poets and Poetry of England in the
      Nineteenth Century. Philadelphia: Carey and Hart.
           Poems with brief biographical sketch (pp. 83-92) of
      'perhaps the most wonderful genius of the nineteenth cen-
      tury'. Reviewed: Graham's Magazine [Philadelphia], XXVI,
      (1845), 95.

870 HAWTHORNE, NATHANIEL. 'Star of Calvary'. Scenes in the Life
     of the Saviour. By the Poets and Painters. Ed. Rufus Wil-
     mot Griswold. Philadelphia: Lindsay and Blakiston,
     pp. 164-7.
          The second and third stanzas imitate The Ancient
     Mariner.

871 [MARTINEAU, JAMES]. 'Church and State'. Prospective Review,
     I, 283-321. Reprinted in his Miscellanies. Ed. T[homas]
     S[tarr] K[ing]. Boston: William Crosby and H. P. Nichols
     (1852), pp. 105-62.
          Coleridge's Church and State, one of several works con-
     sidered, compared favourably with Arnold's Fragment on the
     Church.

872 MAURICE, FREDERICK DENISON. 'Moral and Metaphysical Philoso-
     phy'. Encyclopaedia Metropolitana. 29 vols. London: B.
     Fellowes et al., II, 545-674. Revised in Modern Philoso-
     phy; or, A Treatise of Moral and Metaphysical Philosophy
     from the Fourteenth Century to the French Revolution.
     London: Griffin, Bohn, and Company (1862), pp. 664-72.
          Contrasts Coleridge with Bentham (pp. 673-4) defending
     Coleridge's Englishness and importance as a philosopher.

873 [METHUEN, THOMAS ANTHONY]. Πιστις, pseud. 'Retrospect of
     Friendly Communications with the Poet Coleridge'. Chris-
     tian Observer, No. 90 (May), pp. 257-63.
          Account of acquaintance with Coleridge beginning 1815
     with notes on Coleridge's conversation and theological
     views. Letters from Coleridge on pp. 81-2, 145-7, 585-9.

874 METHUEN, THOMAS ANTHONY. Clericus Bathoniensis, pseud.
     '"Thoughts on the Church", by the Late S. T. Coleridge'.
     Christian Observer, No. 90 (June), pp. 328-9.
          Report of Coleridge's comments.

875 [POE, EDGAR ALLAN]. 'More of the Voluminous History of the
     Little Longfellow War--Mr. Poe's Third Chapter of Reply to
     the Letter of Outis'. Broadway Journal, No. 12 (22 March),
     pp. 178-82.
          Accusation by "Outis" that Poe imitated The Ancient
     Mariner in The Raven quoted and refuted. Detailed discus-
     sion (pp. 179-80) of the metre of Coleridge's poem.

1845-THOMSON

876   [THOMSON, KATHERINE]. 'Literary Retrospect of the Departed
       Great. By a Middle-Aged Man'. Bentley's Miscellany,
       XVII, 83-8. Reprinted Littell's Living Age [Boston], IV
       (1845), 713-20.
           Two personal recollections, the second of a Royal In-
       stitute lecture.
           Attribution: WI.

877   [WHIPPLE, EDWIN P.]. 'The Poets and Poetry of England'.
       American Whig Review [New York], II, 30-58. Reprinted in
       his Essays and Reviews. 2 vols. New York: D. Appleton
       and Co. (1849), I, 284-354.
           Review of Griswold (1845), generally agrees with high
       opinion of Coleridge, but finds Table Talk 'mere rubbish'.

878   WHITE, JOSEPH BLANCO. The Life of the Rev. Joseph Blanco
       White, Written by Himself. Ed. John Hamilton Thom.
       3 vols. London: John Chapman (1849).
           References to Coleridge chiefly in letters from 1825 to
       1827.

879   [WILLMOTT, R. A.]. 'Glimpses of the Pageant of Literature'.
       Fraser's Magazine, XXXI, 17-31. Reprinted Eclectic Maga-
       zine [New York, Boston], IV, 266-79.
           Cites and answers (pp. 21-3) Coleridge's arguments for
       denying the existence of Homer.
           Attribution: WI.

                               1846

880   A'BECKETT, GILBERT ABBOTT. 'The Cockney Mariner'. Almanack
       of the Month, I, 136-44.
           Parody of The Ancient Mariner.

881   ANON. 'An Essay of the Ground and Reason of Punishment'.
       Democratic Review [New York, Washington], New Series XIX,
       90-103. Reviewed Daniel R. Goodwin. Bibliotheca Sacra
       [Andover, Mass.], IV (1847), 270-323.
           Coleridge is accused (p. 97) of making expediency the
       foundation of penal law. A long note in Bibliotheca Sacra
       (pp. 279-80) disagrees.

882   _____. 'The Humorous Writers of the Present Day'. Ecclesia-
       stic. I, 165-79.
           Instances of the ludicrous in Coleridge (pp. 172-4).

                               122

883 ____. 'Past and Present Condition of British Poetry'.
Fraser's Magazine, XXXIII, 577-90, 708-18.
Passing references to Coleridge's literary rank, impact
on Scott, and criticism of Tennyson (pp. 585, 587, 598,
715).

884 ____. 'Extracts from the Portfolio of a Man of the World --
1822'. Gentleman's Magazine, XXVI, 563-80.
Describes (pp. 570-4) meeting with Coleridge on 20 Feb
1822. Supposedly verbatim transcript of Coleridge's talk.

885 ____. 'The Poetical Works of S. T. Coleridge'. Hogg's Week-
ly Instructor, III, 113-6, 139-42.
Christabel is Coleridge's best poem and, with Youth and
Age and Lewti, exhibits a unique style. Fire, Famine, and
Slaughter compared with Burns's 'Tam O'Shanter'. Cole-
ridge's philosophy dismissed.

886 ____. 'Frederick von Schlegel'. Theologian, New Series II,
114-35.
Begins with a comparison of influence and theology of
Coleridge and Schlegel.

887 BOHN, HENRY G., ed. Piccolomini and the Death of Wallenstein.
2 vols. London: Henry G. Bohn.
Preface (I, iii-iv) argues for the influence of Coleridge's translation on Schiller's published text.

888 BURTON, JOHN HILL. Life and Correspondence of David Hume.
2 vols. Edinburgh: William Tait.
Refutes (I, 286-8) Coleridge's suggestion that Hume borrowed from Aquinas.

889 [COLTON, GEORGE H.] Earlden, pseud. 'American Poets No. 1.
The Poems of Alfred B. Street'. American Whig Review [New
York], III, 425-41.
Deprecates the effect on American imitators of metre of
Christabel (p. 432).
Attribution: Poole

890 [DIX, JOHN]. 'Reminiscences of Wordsworth, Coleridge, and
Charles Lamb'. Pen and Ink Sketches of Poets, Preachers,
and Politicians. London: David Bogue, pp. 122-39. Portrait. Reprinted in his Lions: Living and Dead. London:
Partridge and Oakey (1852), pp. 13-29.
Dix met Coleridge at Highgate. Describes his appearance
and conversation.

891 HAMILTON, SIR WILLIAM. The Works of Thomas Reid, D.D. Edin-
     burgh: Maclachlan, Stewart & Co.
          Hamilton (p. 890) attacks Coleridge as a plagiarist from
     Schelling and Maas.

892 HARE, JULIUS CHARLES. The Mission of the Comforter. 2 vols.
     London: John W. Parker.
          Collection of sermons dedicated to Coleridge by pupil
     'whom his writings have helped'. Preface includes discus-
     sion (pp. xii-xv) of Coleridge's theological influence and
     significance.

893 HOLMES, OLIVER WENDELL. Urania: A Rhymed Lesson. Boston:
     William Ticknor & Company.
          Lines on Coleridge, p. 28.

894 J. 'Religious Poetry (English) of the Seventeenth Century'.
     American (Whig) Review [New York], III, 250-8.
          Coleridge, Southey and Wordsworth seen as spiritual
     poets. Mentions Coleridge's admiration for Crashaw's
     'Lines on a Prayer Book'.

895 JAMESON, MRS. [ANNA]. 'Washington Allston'. Memoirs and Es-
     says. London: Richard Bentley, pp. 161-205.
          Includes (pp. 176-7) Allston's account of Coleridge in
     Rome. This reprinted in Flagg (1892).

896 MACKENZIE, ALEXANDER SLIDELL. Life of Stephen Decatur. Bos-
     ton: Charles C. Little and James Brown. [Library of
     American Biography. Conducted by Jared Sparks. Vol.
     XXI].
          Two accounts (pp. 123-5, 352-3) of Decatur's conversa-
     tion with Coleridge in Malta, concerning the occupation of
     Louisiana. Brief description (p. 125) of Coleridge.

897 MORELL, J. D. An Historical and Critical View of the Specu-
     lative Philosophy of Europe in the Nineteenth Century.
     2 vols. London: William Pickering.
          In 'mysticism in England', discusses Coleridge's use of
     Kant and Fichte, and his addition of faith to Kant's con-
     cept of reason. Reviewed: no. 939.

898 OLLIER, EDMUND. 'A Few Words about the Old English Ballads'.
     Ainsworth's Magazine, X, 412-20.
          Compares metre of The Ancient Mariner with 'The Ballad
     of Sir Cauline' and praises Genevieve, The Three Graves,
     and Christabel.

899 RYLAND, J. E., ed. Life and Correspondence of John Foster.
     2 vols. London: Jackson & Walford; New York: Wiley &
     Putnam.
        Frequent references to Coleridge including accounts of
     his conversation and lectures, primarily from correspond-
     ence. Reviewed: [Willmott, R. A]. Fraser's Magazine,
     XXXIV, (1846), 115-34 (attribution: WI.); [Andrew Preston
     Peabody]. North American Review [Boston], LXII (1846),
     141-64 (attribution: Cushing); Prospective Review, II
     (1846), 441-78.

900 SOUTHEY, ROBERT. Life of Wesley. Third Edition, With Notes
     by the Late Samuel Taylor Coleridge. Ed. Charles Cuthbert
     Southey. 2 vols. London: Longmans. Second American Ed-
     ition, with Notes by Rev. Daniel Curry. 2 vols. New York:
     Harper & Brothers (1847).
        Prints Coleridge's marginalia, to which Curry adds crit-
     ical comments. Reviewed: Reverend W. C. Hoyt. Methodist
     Quarterly Review [New York], XXX (1848), 406-36; London
     Quarterly Review I (1853), 38-68. See also 962.

901 TUCKERMAN, HENRY T. Thoughts on the Poets. New York: C. S.
     Francis, pp. 226-37. Reprinted as 'Essay on the Life and
     Writings of Coleridge'. Poems of Samuel Taylor Colerige.
     New York: C. S. Francis; Boston: J. H. Francis (1848),
     pp. i-xxiv.
        Discussion chiefly on shortcomings of Coleridge's prose.

902 [WHIPPLE, EDWIN P.] P., pseud. 'Criticism: Coleridge'.
     American Whig Review [New York], III, 581-7. Reprinted as
     'Coleridge as a Philosophical Critic' in his Essays and
     Reviews. 2 vols. New York: D. Appleton (1849), II,
     178-93.
        Coleridge praised as only true philosophic critic of
     his day and emancipator of English Shakespearean criticism
     followed by Carlyle, Macaulay, and Talfourd.

903 [WILLMOTT, ROBERT ELDRIDGE ARIS] M.A., pseud. 'A Postscript
     about John Foster, in a Note to Oliver Yorke'. Fraser's
     Magazine, XXXIV, 529-35.
        Notes (p. 534) points of comparison between Foster and
     Coleridge.
        Attribution: WI.

1847–Biographia Literaria...

1847

904   Biographia Literaria or Biographical Sketches of my Literary
Life and Opinions. Edited by Henry Nelson and Sara Coleridge. 3 vols. London: William Pickering. I, part I,
ii–clxxxviii, 112; Part II, iii, 112–369; II, vi, 447 pp.
    Sara Coleridge replies to Ferrier (1840) in preface to
Vol I (pp. v–clxxxix). H. N. C.'s "Biographical Supplement" consists of letters with biographical information
interspersed. Reviewed: nos. 906, 922, 934, 1018.

905   ANON. 'Presbyterian Meeting–House. Shrewsbury'. Christian
Reformer, 3rd Series III, 323–32. Reprinted in The Journal
of Margaret Hazlitt. Ed. Ernest J. Moyne. Lawrence: University of Kansas Press (1967), p. 165, n. 13.
    Account of Coleridge's candidacy (pp. 330–1) and de-
scription by Joseph Swanwick of his sermon at Wem.

906   _____. 'Biographia Literaria'. Literary World [New York],
II, 464, 503–4.
    Review of the 1847 edition commends defence against
charges of plagiarism. Sequel chiefly excerpts.

907   _____. 'Le lecture malgré lui. A Lay for Cantabs'. The Man
in the Moon, II, 80–1.
    Parody of The Ancient Mariner.

908   _____. 'The Rime of the Seedy Barristere'. Punch, XIII, 191.
    Parody of The Ancient Mariner.

909   _____. 'Cottle's Reminiscences of Coleridge and Southey'.
Spectator, No. 987 (29 May), pp. 519–21. Reprinted Littell's Living Age [Boston], XIV (1847), 123–5.
    Finds Coleridge here revealed in even worse light than
in Early Recollections (1837).

910   _____. 'Reminiscences of Coleridge and Southey, By Joseph
Cottle'. Times, No. 19697 (3 Nov), pp. 6–7. Reprinted
Essays from 'The Times'. London: John Murray (1852),
pp. 237–54.
    Chides Cottle for emphasis on weaknesses of a man who
was a 'moral dwarf' but an 'intellectual giant'.

911   _____. 'Poetry of Coleridge'. United States Magazine [New
York], XXI, 511–14.
    Defends the poet of many moods who 'wrote as he felt'
and offered glimpses of other worlds. Deplores use of
opium.

912 CARY, HENRY. Memoir of the Rev. Henry Francis Cary. 2 vols.
London: Edward Moxon.
Accounts of acquaintance with Coleridge and notes for
sketch of him (II, 299-300). Includes letters and marginalia in Selden's Table Talk.

913 COTTLE, JOSEPH. Reminiscences of Samuel Taylor Coleridge and
Robert Southey. London: Houlston and Stoneman. xx,
516 pp.
Extensively revised version, with many omissions and
some additions, of his Early Recollections (1837) q.v.
Reviewed: [John Abraham Heraud]. Athenaeum, No. 1024
(12 June 1847), p. 620 (attribution: Fahnestock); Benares
Magazine V (1851), 742-5. See also 909, 910, 922, 934,
955, 1157.

914 DE QUINCEY, THOMAS. 'The Nautico-Military Nun of Spain'.
Tait's Edinburgh Magazine, New Series XIV, 324-33, 369-76,
431-40. Reprinted as 'The Spanish Military Nun' in his
Narrative and Miscellaneous Papers. 2 vols. Boston:
Ticknor, Reed, and Fields (1853), I, 109-201.
Describes (p. 371) three levels of readers of The An-
cient Mariner: literalistic, psychological, and
moralistic.

915 GILFILLAN, GEORGE. 'George Crabbe'. Tait's Edinburgh Magazine, New Series XIV, 141-7. Reprinted in his Second Gallery of Literary Portraits. Edinburgh: James Hogg; London: R. Groombridge (1850), pp. 61-8.
Shelley and Coleridge (p. 142) 'attach themselves exclusively to the great' although 'half-mad, wholly miser-
able, and opium fed'. The Ancient Mariner compared with
The Tempest (p. 146).

916 GREEN, JOSEPH HENRY. Mental Dynamics or Groundwork of a Pro-
fessional Education. London: William Pickering.
Largely derived from Coleridge's unpublished ms. on
logic. Includes eulogy (p. 13) and frequent references.

917 HOWITT, MARY. 'An Old Man's Story'. Ballads and Other Poems.
London: Longmans et al; New York: Wiley and Putnam,
pp. 29-38.
An uninspired imitation of The Ancient Mariner.

918   HOWITT, WILLIAM. 'Samuel Taylor Coleridge'. <u>Homes and Haunts</u>
      <u>of the Most Eminent British Poets</u>. 2 vols. London: Rich-
      ard Bentley, II, 68-104. Illustration, W. and G. Meason,
      II, 68.
         Anecdotal account chiefly of early years.

919   JONES, W. A. <u>Literary Studies: A Collection of Miscellaneous</u>
      <u>Essays</u>. New York: Edward Walker. 2 vols in 1.
         Mostly favourable scattered comments on Coleridge's
      prose and sonnets.

920   [KNIGHT, CHARLES] C. K., <u>pseud</u>. <u>Half-Hours with the Best</u>
      <u>Authors</u>. 4 vols. London: C. Knight; New York: Wiley &
      Putnam.
         Selections, brief biographical sketch and scattered
      comments. Reviewed: <u>Literary World</u> [New York], II (1847),
      153-5, 161.

921   LESTER, JOHN W. 'S. T. Coleridge'. <u>Criticisms</u>. London:
      Longman, Brown, pp. 256-67. Second edition, revised.
      London: Longman, Brown (1848).
         Indiscriminate praise of Coleridge 'the dreamer'.

922   [NORTON, CHARLES ELIOT]. '<u>Reminiscences of...Coleridge</u>'.
      <u>North American Review</u> [Boston], LXV, 401-40.
         Review of Cottle (1847) and H. N. C.'s 'Biographical
      Supplement' (<u>Biographia</u>, 1847) but in effect a biographical
      monograph, drawing on other available sources. Makes much
      of Coleridge's indolence, failure to realize promise, and
      the problem of opium, suggesting excessive indulgence be-
      fore 1815 damaged his mind and later work. Article basis
      for memoir in <u>Poetical Works</u> (1854) q.v.
         Attribution: Cushing

923   PORTER, NOAH. 'Coleridge and his American Disciples'. <u>Biblo-</u>
      <u>theca Sacra</u> [New York], IV, 117-71.
         Acknowledges Coleridge's status as major poet and crit-
      ic. Discusses, as admirer though not disciple, Coleridge's
      services to theology, the flaws in his theology and meta-
      physics, and the benefits and dangers of his influence on
      Marsh and others in America.

924   WILLMOTT, ROBERT ARIS. <u>Bishop Jeremy Taylor</u>. London: John
      W. Parker. Reprinted London: Longman <u>et al</u>. (1864).
         Frequent references to Taylor's influence on Coleridge.

1848

925   Hints Towards the Formation of a More Comprehensive Theory of
Life. By S. T. Coleridge. Ed. Seth B. Watson, M. D.
London: John Churchill; Philadelphia: Lea and Blanchard.
94 pp.
     Preface (pp. 7-16) explains value of Coleridge's essay,
but questions conceptions of 'Life' and 'Nature'. Reviewed: [John Abraham Heraud]. Athenaeum, No. 1111
(10 Feb 1849), p. 139 (attribution: Fahnestock), reprinted
Eclectic Magazine [New York], XVI (1849), 572; Godey's
Lady's Book [Philadelphia], XXVIII (1849), 67. See also
929, 948, 1174, 1201.

926   ANON. The Devil's New Walk. A Satire. Boston: William D.
Ticknor.
     Imitation of The Devil's Thoughts.

927   _____. 'Essays and Tales, by John Sterling'. British Quarterly Review, VIII, 176-203.
     Mentions (p. 179) Coleridge's influence. Contrasts
(p. 187) Sterling's critique of Christabel (1838) with
Moore's in the Edinburgh Review (1816).

928   _____. 'On Tendencies towards the Subversion of Faith'.
English Review, X, 399-444.
     Discusses (pp. 416-23) Coleridge's influence on Ster-
ling, Hare, and Blanco White, all of whom are attacked.
Review of this article and of Hare's reply (Thou shalt not
bear false witness against thy neighbor. 1849) appeared
under the same title in the Eclectic Review (4th Series
XXV [1849], 656-69) and contains vigorous defence of Coleridge and his followers. Hare's pamphlet mentions Coleridge only once (p. 54).

929   _____. 'A New Fragment by Coleridge'. Literary World [New
York], III, 808-9.
     Review of Theory of Life; praise for Coleridge's poetic
talent but reservations about philosophical works.

930   _____. 'The Prolix Orator'. Punch, XV, 123.
     Humorous imaginary anecdote.

931   ANON. 'Coleridge and Shelley in the Vale of Chamouny'. Yale
Literary Magazine [New Haven], XIII, 276-8.
     Comparison of Coleridge's Hymn before Sunrise with Shel-
ley's 'Mont Blanc' preferring the former on religious
grounds.

932   [ATWATER, L.]. 'Coleridge'. Biblical Repertory and Princeton
      Review [Philadelphia], 2nd Series XX, 143-86.
          Notes Coleridge's great influence in America, and at-
      tempts evaluation of his work. After acknowledging Cole-
      ridge's achievement as poet and critic, devotes the second
      half of the article to a critique of his theology from a
      Presbyterian viewpoint.
          Attribution: Poole

933   CHANNING, WILLIAM HENRY. Memoir of William Ellery Channing.
      Boston: Wm. Crosby and H. P. Nichols; London: John Chap-
      man.
          Allston's brother-in-law met Coleridge in 1823 (II,
      218-20).

934   [CHRISTIE, W. D.]. 'Coleridge and Southey'. Edinburgh Re-
      view, LXXXVII, 368-92. Reprinted in Eclectic Magazine
      [New York], XIV (1848), 195-208; Littell's Living Age
      [Boston], XVII (1848), 310-20.
          Biographical sketch based largely on Cottle.
          Attribution: WI.

935   No entry.

936   COLLINS, W. WILKIE. Memoirs of the Life of William Collins,
      Esq., R. A. London: Longman et al.
          Includes letters from Coleridge (pp. 144-9) and account
      of evenings at Highgate (pp. 249-50).

937   E. T. T. Y., PSEUD. 'Overlooked Poem by Coleridge'. Gentle-
      man's Magazine, New Series XXIX, 160.
          Prings The British Stripling's War-Song under the title
      'The Volunteer Stripling' and notes original appearance in
      the Bath Herald.

938   HARE, JULIUS CHARLES, ed. Essays and Tales by John Sterling
      ...With a Memoir of His Life. 2 vols. London: John W.
      Parker.
          Memoir includes discussion of Coleridge's influence on
      Sterling, and Sterling's account of first meeting with
      Coleridge (xiv-xxvi). Reviewed: [R. A. Willmott].
      Fraser's Magazine, XXXVII (1848), 187-200 (attribution:
      WI.); Prospective Review, IV (1848), 272-96.

939 LORD, DAVID M. 'Morell's "Historical View of Speculative
     Philosophy"'. Theological and Literary Journal, I, 300-35.
     Revised as 'Coleridge's Philosophy of Christianity, an
     Atheistic Idealism'. Theological and Literary Journal, I
     (1848-9), 631-69.
         Attacks Morell's Historical View (1846), for its favour-
     able treatment of Coleridge. Revision associates Coleridge
     with Kant and Swedenborg and argues incompatibility of his
     philosophy with Christianity.

940 POE, EDGAR ALLAN. 'Rationale of Verse'. Southern Literary
     Messenger [Richmond, Va.], XIV, 577-85, 673-82.
         This revision of 'Notes upon English Verse' (Pioneer
     [Boston 1843]), adds (p. 673) a rejection of Coleridge's
     'nonsensical system' of metre in Christabel.

941 RICHARDSON, DAVID LESTER. Literary Chit-Chat. Calcutta:
     P. S. D. Rozario.
         Imaginary conversations. Condemns Coleridge's 'wretched
     prose' but praises the 'unsurpassed' Genevieve.

942 TALFOURD, THOMAS NOON. Final Memorials of Charles Lamb. 2
     vols. London: Moxon.
         Prints letters to Coleridge (I), and describes Lamb's
     'Wednesday Nights' with brief accounts of his 'dead com-
     panions' including (II, 195-205) Coleridge. Reviewed:
     British Quarterly Review, VIII (1848), 381-95.

943 TOOVEY, ALFRED DIXON. Biographical and Critical Notices of
     the British Poets of the Present Century, with Specimens
     of their Poetry. London: Kent and Richards.
         Includes (pp. 90-6) a brief and inaccurate biographical
     sketch. Praises Coleridge's 'tragedies' and dismisses The
     Ancient Mariner and Christabel.

944 [WHIPPLE, EDWIN P.]. 'Shakespeare's Plays'. North American
     Review [Boston], LXVII, 84-119. Reprinted in his Essays
     and Reviews. 2 vols. New York: D. Appleton and Co.
     (1849), II, 248-86.
         'In regards to principles' (p. 95) Coleridge 'probably
     the first critic of the century'. Fragments on Shakespeare
     valuable for 'suggestiveness'.

1849–Confessions of an Inquiring Spirit

1849

945   Confessions of an Inquiring Spirit. Edited by Henry Nelson
       Coleridge. London: William Pickering. xlii, 289 pp.
            J. M. Green's introduction (v–xlii) argues that despite
       derivations from Lessing, work is essentially original.
       Cites parallel passages and extracts from Coleridge's mar-
       ginalia on Lessing. Reviewed: nos. 961, 965, 986, 1028,
       1250.

946   Notes and Lectures upon Shakespeare and some of the old Poets
       and Dramatists with Other Literary Remains of S. T. Cole-
       ridge. Edited by Mrs. H. N. Coleridge. 2 vols. London:
       William Pickering. xv, 372; v, 371 pp.
            Scattered additions to a reprint of volumes I and II of
       the Literary Remains. Reviewed: no. 965.

947   ANON. 'Confessions of an Inquiring Spirit'. English Review,
       XII, 247–71.
            Attacks Coleridge's views on Biblical inspiration, seen
       as derived from Lessing and essentially identical with
       those of Froude. Influence on Sterling and comparison
       with Blanco White.

948   _____. 'Hints towards the Formation of a more Comprehensive
       Theory of Life'. Guardian, No. 166 (21 Mar), p. 193.
            Objects to Coleridge's figurative use of 'nature' and
       to 'mode of phraseology borrowed from the Eleatic philoso-
       phers'.

949   _____. 'The Monograms and Ancient Mariner of David Scott'.
       Hogg's Weekly Instructor, New Series III, 161–3.
            Scott's illustrations for The Ancient Mariner reveal
       affinity with Coleridge's attitude towards supernatural.

950   _____. 'William D. Gallagher'. Western Quarterly Review
       [Cincinnati], I, 135–72.
            Notes Coleridge's pronounced influence on Gallagher's
       poetry.

951   [DE VERE, AUBREY]. 'The Eve of the Conquest, and Other Poems,
       By Henry Taylor'. Edinburgh Review, LXXXIX, 352–80.
            In discussing (pp. 358–9) 'modern' narrative poetry,
       cites The Ancient Mariner as 'the subjective Odyssey of a
       psychological age'.
            Attribution: WI.

952   GRAHAM, WILLIAM S. Remains With A Memoir. Edited by George
       Allen. Philadelphia: J. W. Moore.
          Describes Graham's 'enraptured' discovery of Coleridge
       in 1841, and later views. Extensive remarks on Mitchell
       (1844) (pp. 253-68).

953   KNIGHT, CHARLES. Studies of Shakespeare. London: C. Knight.
          Concludes with an effusive tribute to Coleridge's
       Shakespeare criticism.

954   [LEWES, GEORGE HENRY]. 'Hegel's Aesthetics. Philosophy of
       Art'. British and Foreign Review, XIII, 1-49.
          Coleridge's vague and unsatisfactory distinction between
       poetry and prose unfavourably contrasted with that of J. S.
       Mill.
          Attribution: WI.

955   MILAND, JOHN. 'Trade Editions--Cottle's Life of Coleridge'.
       Notes and Queries, I, 55-6, 75.
          Query and anonymous reply concerning Times (1847)
       review.

956   [SMITH, WILLIAM HENRY]. 'Charles Lamb'. Blackwood's Maga-
       zine, LXVI, 133-50.
          Notes (p. 136) Coleridge's 'permanent and formative in-
       fluence'.
          Attribution: WI.

957   [WHELPLEY, JAMES D.] J. D. W., pseud. 'Life and Writings of
       Coleridge'. American Whig Review [New York], New Series
       IV, 532-9, 632-6.
          Sympathetic biographical account. Assessment of Cole-
       ridge's philosophy, especially in The Statesman's Manual
       and of his relation to Plato and to Kant.
          Attribution: Poole

                                  1850

958   Essays on his Own Times. By Samuel Taylor Coleridge. Forming
       a Second Series of The Friend. Edited by his daughter. 3
       vols. London: William Pickering. I, xciii, 292; II,
       viii, 293-676; III, x, 677-1034 pp.
          Introduction (I, ix-xciii) surveys Coleridge's political
       positions and finds his fundamental principles consistent.
       Discusses his views on Ireland and his work as journalist.
       Reviewed: no. 967.

959 ALLSTON, WASHINGTON. Lectures on Art, and Poems. Ed. Richard H. Dana, Jr. New York: Baker and Scribner.
Quotes (p. 9) Allston's remarks on the value to him of Coleridge's friendship in Rome.

960 _____. 'Sonnet on the Late S. T. Coleridge'. Lectures on Art, and Poems. New York: Baker and Scribner, p. 436. Reprinted Life and Letters of Washington Allston. New York: Scribner's (1892), p. 409.

961 ANON. 'Confessions of an Inquiring Spirit'. Christian Observer, L, 234-50.
Violent attack on Coleridge's views on inspiration. With Parker and Newman, he is one of 'Satan's agents'.

962 _____. 'Life of Wesley...With Notes by the Late S. T. Coleridge'. Christian Observer, L, 121-39.
Quotes and discusses Coleridge's notes.

963 _____. 'Samuel Taylor Coleridge'. English Churchman, VIII, 43-4.
Hare's view of Coleridge as religious philosopher challenged by quotations from Cottle and Foster, and on basis of influence on Sterling and White. Reply by Edwin E. Coleridge (p. 72) regrets these extracts and defends Coleridge.

964 _____. 'Autobiography of Leigh Hunt'. Eclectic Review, 4th Series XXVII, 409-24.
Criticizes (pp. 419-21) Hunt's view of Coleridge.

965 _____. 'Confessions of an Inquiring Spirit...Notes and Lectures upon Shakespeare. Examiner, No. 2189 (12 Jan), pp. 20-1. Reprinted Littell's Living Age [Boston], XXV (1850), 7-9.
Discusses Coleridge's indebtedness to Lessing and Schlegel and defends Coleridge's originality.

966 _____. 'Gems of Modern English Poetry. The Ancient Mariner'. Hogg's Weekly Instructor, New Series IV, 337-9.
Interprets poem as moral allegory of 'law and responsibility' and as analogue of the Fall. Sequel ('Gems of Poetry, Peter Bell', New Series V [1850], 321-3) compares The Ancient Mariner with 'Peter Bell'. While the 'leading theme' is the same, Wordsworth 'deals with but one half of it'.

967 _____. 'Literary Intelligence: Essays on his own Times'. Literary World [New York], VI, 572.
Brief announcement associates work with the 'German party in the English church.'

968 _____. 'The Autobiography of Leigh Hunt'. Times, No. 20585 (4 Sept), p. 7.
Quotes Hunt's disparaging remarks on Coleridge ('he would not work'), answered by Derwent Coleridge (Times, No. 20589--9 Sept, 1850--p. 6).

969 CHASLES, PHILARÈTE. 'Portraits Contemporains. Jeremie Bentham, Coleridge, Foscolo'. Études sur les hommes et les moeurs au xixe siècle. Paris: Amyot.
Meeting with Coleridge, 'le Novalis de l'Angleterre' in 1817. Describes (pp. 93-8) appearance, manner of speaking, and substance of his talk.

970 [CURTIS, REVEREND THOMAS]. 'Coleridge and Southey'. Christian Review, XV, 321-53. Reprinted in part in Littell's Living Age [Boston], XXVI, (1850), 420-1.
Personal impressions of Coleridge and comparison with Southey.
Attribution: Whitmer.

971 EMDEE, pseud. 'On Passages in Coleridge's Christabel and Byron's Lara'. Notes and Queries, I, 262-3, 324; II, 47.
Queries nature of Geraldine. 'C. B.' and C. Forbes reply with analogies with Spenser's Duessa, Scott's 'Eve of St. John' and a passage from folklore.

972 G. H. E. 'Schiller's Wallenstein. Translated by S. T. Coleridge'. Westminster Review, LIII, 348-65.
Attacks Coleridge's translation.

973 GILFILLAN, GEORGE. 'John Sterling'. Second Gallery of Literary Portraits. Edinburgh: James Hogg; London: R. Groombridge, pp. 395-420.
Coleridge's influence on Sterling (pp. 409, 413, 415).

974 HUNT, LEIGH. Autobiography of Leigh Hunt; with Reminiscences of Friends and Contemporaries. 3 vols. London: Smith, Elder and Co.
Humorous account (II, 223-9) of Hunt's impressions of Coleridge whose poetry was 'the finest of its time'.

975   [LOCKHART, JOHN GIBSON and ELWIN WHITWELL]. 'Life and Corre-
      spondence of Robert Southey'. Quarterly Review, LXXXVIII,
      197-247.
          General account of Coleridge in 1794 (p. 205) and brief
      comparison with Southey.
          Attribution: WI.

976   MAYOR, J. E. B. 'Coleridge'. Notes and Queries, II, 195-6.
          Two passages in Statesman's Manual as borrowed from
      Schiller and von Baader.

977   _____. 'Notes on Coleridge's Aids to Reflection. 2nd Edi-
      tion, 1831'. Notes and Queries, II, 228.
          Identifies references to Tertullian, Plato, Seneca, and
      Pindar.

978   SCOTT, WILLIAM B. Memoir of David Scott, R. S. A. Edinburgh:
      Adam & Charles Black.
          Seven illustrations, one from Ancient Mariner.
          Accounts (pp. 49-51, 58) of correspondence and meeting
      with Coleridge. Include description of Coleridge's ap-
      pearance, conversation, and opinion of Scott's drawings.

979   SCRYMGEOUR, DANIEL. Poetry and Poets of Britain. Edinburgh:
      Adam & Charles Black.
          Biographical and critical sketch (pp. 409-10). Dismis-
      ses Christabel and The Ancient Mariner (insufficient
      moral), but Coleridge the 'most imaginative' of modern
      poets.

980   SINGER, S. W. 'More Borrowed Thoughts'. Notes and Queries,
      II, 82-3, 156.
          Sources for To Mr. Pye and Job's Luck, comment by
      J. Bruce.

981   [SMITH, J. E.?]. 'Wildness and Extravagance'. Family Herald,
      VIII, 332-3.
          Attack on Coleridge, probably by Smith, the editor.
      Concludes from 'absurdity' and lack of moral purposes of
      The Ancient Mariner that Coleridge 'wrote it in a joke.'
      Also complains of Shakespeare idolatry. In later issues,
      Smith printed and replied to objections (pp. 362, 410,
      442).

982 SOUTHEY, ROBERT. Life and Correspondence of Robert Southey.
     Edited by his son Charles Cuthbert Southey. 6 vols. Lon-
     don: Longman et al. Photo reprint. Michigan (1970).
          Frequent references to Coleridge until 1819. Reviewed:
     [William Henry Smith], Blackwood's Magazine, LXIX (1851),
     349-67 (attribution: WI.); Christian Remembrancer, XIX
     (1850), 285-330. See also 990, 995.

983 TURNBULL, REV. ROBERT. 'Spirit and Form'. Christian Review
     [New York], XV, 543-72.
          Coleridge (p. 561) among 'prose writers who combine
     spirit and form in their highest perfection'.

984 [WILSON, JOHN] Christopher North, pseud. 'Dies Boreales. No.
     VI, Christopher Under Canvass'. Blackwood's Magazine,
     LXVII, 481-512.
          Dialogue on Othello draws on Coleridge (pp. 482, 484).
     Attribution: WI.

985 WORDSWORTH, WILLIAM. The Prelude. London: Edward Moxon.
          Entire poem is addressed to Coleridge.

                              1851

986 ANON. 'Coleridge on the Scripture'. Benares Magazine, VI,
     590-602.
          Summarizes Coleridge's Confessions which deserves to be
     more widely known. In reply, editor (VI, 602-27) criti-
     cizes Coleridge's views on scriptural inspiration. Aids
     the best of Coleridge's philosophical works.

987 _____. 'William Wordsworth'. Chambers's Papers for the
     People [Edinburgh, Philadelphia], V, 229-60. Largely re-
     printed by [George Searle Phillips] January Searle, pseud.
     in his Memoirs of William Wordsworth. London: Partridge
     & Oakey (1852), pp. 133-54.
          A fulsome account (pp. 236-47, 251) of Coleridge and
     Wordsworth.

988 _____. 'Samuel Taylor Coleridge. His Philosophy and Theolo-
     gy'. Eclectic Review, 5th Series I, 1-22. Reprinted with
     longer extracts as The Relation of Philosophy to Theology,
     to Religion. London: Ward and Co. (1851).
          Recommends, with copious extracts, Coleridge's later
     and posthumous prose.

1851-ANON.

989   ANON. 'Are the English a Musical People?' Fraser's Magazine,
      XLIII, 675-81. Reprinted in Littell's Living Age [Boston],
      XXX, (1851), 186-9.
         Discussion (pp. 675-7) of Coleridge's views on music.

990   [BOWEN, FRANCIS]. 'Life and Correspondence of Southey'.
      North American Review [Boston], LXXII, 1-33.
         Cites evidence (pp. 5, 28) of Southey's understanding of
      Coleridge.
         Attribution: Cushing.

991   CARLYLE, THOMAS. Life of John Sterling. London: Chapman and
      Hall; Boston: Phillips, Sampson and Co.
         Includes (Part I, Chapter 8, pp. 69-80) Carlyle's satir-
      ical portrait of Coleridge, often reprinted, usually in
      abridged form. Other comments passim on Coleridge's influ-
      ence on Sterling and his generation.
         Reviewed: British Quarterly Review, XV (1852), 240-53.
      See also nos. 994, 1007, 1014, 1015, 1017, 1019.

992   COLERIDGE, HARTLEY. Poems by Hartley Coleridge, with a Memoir
      of his Life by His Brother. 2 vols. London: Edward
      Moxon.
         Derwent's lovingly constructed memoir (I, ix-clxxxvii)
      includes many references to Coleridge. Sonnets of 1835 and
      1847 (II, 3, 58) are to and on Coleridge. Prints his Frag-
      ment of a Greek Grammar (I, clxxxviii-cxcviii).
         Reviewed: [John Abraham Heraud]. Athenaeum, No. 1220
      (15 Mar 1851), pp. 287-9 (attribution: Fahnestock).

993   COLLINS, MORTIMER. 'Coleridge's Christabel'. Notes and
      Queries, IV, 316, 410-11.
         Queries concerning continuation of Christabel and
      'Logosophia'.

993A C. [CUNNINGHAM, MR.] 'On Coleridge'. Witness [Edinburgh],
      XII (6 Aug), p. 3.
         A letter to the editor on Coleridge's anticipation of
      evolution.
         Attribution: Dendurent

994   [DIXON, WILLIAM HEPWORTH]. 'A Life of John Sterling, By
      Thomas Carlyle'. Athenaeum, No. 1251 (18 Oct),
      pp. 1088-90.
         Praises chapter on Coleridge.
         Attribution: Fahnestock

995   [DONNE, W. B.]. 'The Life and Correspondence of Robert Sou-
        they'. Edinburgh Review, XCIII, 370-402.
            Includes (pp. 377-8) account of Coleridge and panti-
        socracy.
            Attribution: WI.

996   GORTON, JOHN G. 'Coleridge, Samuel Taylor'. A General Bio-
        graphical Dictionary. A New Edition. 4 vols. London:
        Whittaker & Co., I, 133-4.
            Conventional sketch.

997   HANNA, THE REVEREND WILLIAM. Memoirs of the Life and Writings
        of Thomas Chalmers. 4 vols. New York: Harper and Broth-
        ers. Reprinted Edinburgh, London: Constable (1852).
            Account of 1830 visit (III, 265-7) and of Coleridge's
        conversation, including notion of Apocalypse.

998   H. G. T. 'Coleridge's Religious Musings'. Notes and Queries,
        III, 115.
            Ms. variant of lines 358-64.

999   [HORNE, R. H.]. 'Two Sonnets'. Household Words, No. 62
        (31 May), p. 252. Reprinted Littell's Living Age [Boston],
        XXX (1851), 175.
            The Good Great Man is 'the noblest [sonnet]...in the
        English language'.
            Attribution: Lohrli

1000 KERSHAW, J. H. 'Coleridge's Essays on Beauty'. Notes and
        Queries, IV, 175-6, 214.
            Request for information answered by Mortimer Collins.

1001 LEWES, GEORGE. 'Passage in Coleridge's Table-Talk'. Notes
        and Queries, III, 518.
            Requests name omitted from Table Talk for March 31,
        1832.

1002 [MASSON, DAVID]. 'Literature and the Labour Question'. North
        British Review, XIV, 382-420.
            Contrasts social view of literature with Coleridge's
        theory of 'pure literature'. Disparaging remarks
        (pp. 390-2) on opium.
            Attribution: WI.

1003 MEREDITH, GEORGE. 'The Poetry of Coleridge'. Poems. Lon-
        don: John W. Parker, p. 23.
            Youthful poetic effusion.

1004   MOIR, D. M. Sketches of the Poetical Literature of the Past
        Half-Century. Edinburgh, London: William Blackwood.
            Lecture II (pp. 59-115), on 'Lake School', includes
        discussion of The Ancient Mariner and Christabel, defends
        Coleridge's plagiarisms, especially in Hymn before Sunrise.
        Reviewed: Eclectic Review, 5th Series II (1851), 129-45.

1005   [SMITH, WILLIAM HENRY]. 'Southey'. Blackwood's Magazine,
        LXIX, 349-67.
            Influence of Coleridge's pantisocracy on Southey, ac-
        count of Coleridge's first meeting with his wife (pp. 359-
        61).
            Attribution: WI.

1006   TS. 'Coleridge's Opinion of Defore'. Notes and Queries, III,
        136.
            Coleridge's marginal note from Wilson's Memoirs...of
        Defoe.

1007   No entry.

1008   VENABLES, E. 'Origin of Present Penny Postage'. Notes and
        Queries, III, 6, 27.
            Anecdote with comment by C. W. D.

1009   WORDSWORTH, CHRISTOPHER. Memoirs of William Wordsworth.   2
        vols. London: Edward Moxon.
            Frequent mention of Coleridge. Important accounts of
        The Ancient Mariner (I, 15-6, II, 444), and the Fenwick
        notes of its composition (I, 107-8). Reviewed: Athenaeum,
        No. 1226 (26 April 1851), pp. 445-7.

                                1852

1010   Dramatic Works of Samuel Taylor Coleridge. A New Edition.
        Ed. Derwent Coleridge. London: Edward Moxon; New York:
        Ward, Lock and Co., xiv, 427 pp.
            Preface comments on Coleridge's dramatic works.

1011   The Poems of Samuel Taylor Coleridge. Ed. Derwent and Sara
        Coleridge. London: Edward Moxon. xxviii, 388 pp. Fron-
        tispiece: Portrait engraved by W. Holl from Robert
        Hancock.
            Preface by Sara (pp. vii-xiv) on text. Wordsworth's
        conversation with Dyce on composition of The Ancient Mari-
        ner (pp. 383-4) is reprinted in Poetical Works (1893),
        p. 594. Reviewed: Athenaeum, No. 1293 (7 Aug 1852),
        p. 841.

1012   ANON. Verdicts. London: Effingham Wilson. 70 pp.
            Poem includes passage (pp. 41-3) on Coleridge.

1013   _____. 'Coleridge the Table-Talker'. Colburn's New Monthly
        Magazine, XCIV, 281-90.
            Discusses effect of Coleridge's conversation, citing
        previously published accounts.

1014   _____. 'Carlyle on Sterling'. Christian Remembrancer,
        XXIII, 153-85.
            Coleridge gave 'serious impulses' to Sterling's mind
        (pp. 167-71) and 'will find his avenger' for Carlyle's
        caricature (p. 171).

1015   _____. 'John Sterling and his Biographers'. Dublin Universi-
        ty Magazine, XXXIX, 185-99.
            Carlyle has displaced Coleridge as influence on young
        university men. Sterling owed much to Aids.

1016   _____. 'Sterne and his Sentimentalism'. Englishman's Maga-
        zine, I, 151-67.
            Concludes with comparison of Coleridge and Sterne who
        both combined nobility with degradation.

1017   _____. 'Carlyle on Coleridge'. Knickerbocker [New York],
        XXIX, 90.
            Coleridge, though a great intellect, was often a bore.

1018   _____. 'Coleridge Biography'. Literary World [New York], X,
        404-6.
            A friendly review of new edition of Biographia Litera-
        ria, with excerpts.

1019   _____. 'John Sterling and Thomas Carlyle'. Monthly Christian
        Spectator, II, 21-30.
            Gives brief account of Coleridge's influence on
        Sterling.

1852-ANON.

1020   ANON. 'Samuel Taylor Coleridge'. National Magazine, I, 289-
        96. Portrait by Ezra Nye.
            Biographical sketch emphasizing Coleridge's weakness of
        character discusses both poetry and prose, compares Love
        with Tennyson's 'Gardener's Daughter' and considers rela-
        tion of Coleridge to Schlegel.

1021   _____. 'The Rime of the Ancient Ministere'. Punch, XXII,
        105-7.
            Political satire.

1022   [BAGEHOT, WALTER]. 'Hartley Coleridge's Lives of the Northern
        Worthies'. Prospective Review, XIV, 514-44. Reprinted in
        his Estimates of Some Englishmen and Scotchmen. London:
        Chapman and Hall (1858), pp. 330-66.
            Review compares father and son on many occasions empha-
        sizing dreaminess and conversation.

1023   [BAYNE, PETER]. 'The Portrait Gallery. Samuel Taylor Cole-
        ridge'. Hogg's Weekly Instructor, New Series IX, 129-33,
        152-7. Revised in his Essays in Biography and Criticism,
        Second Series. Boston: Gould and Lincoln (1858),
        pp. 108-48.
            Biographical sketch finds The Ancient Mariner a 'vivid
        and awful phantasmagoria', and Religious Musings comparable
        to Homer. Praises Coleridge's philosophy. Blames opium
        for his shortcomings.

1024   BONSALL. 'Coleridge's Notes on Pepy's Diary'. Notes and
        Queries, VI, 213-6.
            Marginalia.

1025   [BRADLEY, EDWARD] Cuthbert Bede, pseud. 'Wit Referred to by
        Coleridge'. Notes and Queries, VI, 590.
            Confuses S. T. C. with H. N. C.

1026   [BROWN, SAMUEL GILMAN]. 'De Quincey's Writings'. North Amer-
        ican Review [Boston], LXXIV, 425-45.
            Discusses De Quincey's comparisons of Coleridge and
        Wordsworth (pp. 431-3) and Coleridge and Goethe (pp. 435-6).
            Attribution: Cushing

1027   C. P. PH. 'Coleridge and Plato'. Notes and Queries, V, 317.
            Similarity of lines 69-70 of Lines on an Autumnal Eve-
        ning to epigram attributed to Plato.

1028   [CAIRNS, JOHN]. 'Infallibility of the Bible and Recent The-
        ories of Inspiration'. North British Review, XVIII,
        139–85.
            Review includes Confessions. Criticized Coleridge's
        views on inspiration and use of German metaphysics.
        Attribution: WI.

1029   CHICHESTER, FREDERICK RICHARD, EARL OF BELFAST. Poets and
        Poetry of the xixth Century. Course of Lectures by the
        Earl of Belfast. London: Brown, Green and Longman.
            In first lecture (pp. 13–27) praises Coleridge's de-
        scriptive power but notes his obscurity.

1030   COLERIDGE, HARTLEY. Lives of Northern Worthies. Edited by
        his brother. 3 vols. London: Edward Moxon.
            Editor includes and comments on Coleridge's marginalia.
        Reviewed: [Henry Fothergill Chorley], Athenaeum, No. 1278
        (24 April 1852), pp. 450–2 (attribution: Fahnestock). See
        also 1022.

1031   [DIX, JOHN]. 'Morning Party at Samuel Roger's'. Pen and Ink
        Sketches of Authors and Authoresses. London: Partridge
        and Oakey, pp. 137–71.
            Account of a party with Coleridge.

1032   H. C. K. 'Notes on Coleridge's Christabel'. Notes and Que-
        ries, V, 339–40.
            Literalistic explanation of conclusion to part II of
        Christabel.

1033   No entry.

1034   INGLEBY, C. MANSFIELD. 'Coleridge's Additions to Aids to Re-
        flection'. Notes and Queries, VI, 533.
            A request for information on Coleridge's unpublished
        mss.

1035   _____. 'Reason and Understanding according to Coleridge'.
        Notes and Queries, V, 535–6. Reprinted National Magazine
        [New York], I (1852), 273; New Series II, 255–6.
            An interchange with 'Casper' on Coleridge's views of
        understanding in animals.

1036   J. M. 'Coleridge's "Friend"'. Notes and Queries, V, 297,
        351, 427.
            Query concerning identity of Coleridge's 'munificent co-
        patron' (Wedgwood) answered by Ingleby.

1037   LE GRICE, CHARLES VALENTINE.   'Sonnet in Reminiscence of the
       Poet Coleridge'. Gentleman's Magazine, XXXVIII, 52.
       Poem by school friend.

1038   MITFORD, MARY RUSSELL. Recollections of a Literary Life. 3
       vols. London: Richard Bentley.
            Recalls (III, 15-19) arrangements for Coleridge's dis-
       charge from Dragoons, made at her father's house, and 1842
       visit to Cottle.

1039   RICHARDSON, DAVID LESTER. 'Samuel Taylor Coleridge'. Liter-
       ary Recreations, or, Essays, Criticisms and Poems. London,
       Calcutta: W. Thacker, Spink and Co., pp. 538-41.
            Praise for Love, The Ancient Mariner and Christabel, but
       a generally negative account. Accuses Coleridge of plagi-
       arism, vagueness, and confusing poetry with metaphysics.

1040   ROBERTS, EDWIN F. 'Rhapsody on Poetry'. Cabinet, I, 51-4.
       Brief rhapsodic comparison of Coleridge and Tennyson.

1041   [THOMS, W. J.]. 'Coleridge: Letters to Lamb and Notes on
       Samuel Daniel's Poems'. Notes and Queries, VI, 117-8.
       Letters and marginalia.

1042   [TULLOCH, JOHN]. 'Carlyle's Life of Sterling'. North British
       Review, XVI, 359-89.
            A vigorous defence of Coleridge as spiritual teacher
       against Carlyle's contemptuous portrait.
            Attribution: WI.

                              1853

1043   The Complete Works of Samuel Taylor Coleridge, With an Intro-
       ductory Essay upon his Philosophical and Theological Opin-
       ions. Ed. Professor [William Greenough Thayer] Shedd. 7
       vols. New York: Harper & Brothers. Frontispiece.
       A. Wivell portrait.
            Collection of Coleridge's published works, excluding
       The Watchman, and Essays on his Own Times. Based on the
       editions of Henry Nelson and Sara Coleridge and James
       Marsh. The only 'collected' edition until K. Coburn's
       Collected Works. Shedd's introductory essay, q.v., an
       important assessment. Reviewed: New England and Yale Re-
       view [New Haven], XI (1853), 643; Saturday Review, VII
       (1853), 338-40; Southern Literary Messenger [Richmond, Va.]
       XIX (1853), 256, 318-9, 448, 584. See also 1048, 1052,
       1054, 1055, 1058, 1071, 1083, 1091, 1096, 1098.

1044   Notes on English Divines by Samuel Taylor Coleridge. Ed. the
        Reverend Derwent Coleridge. 2 vols. London: Edward Mox-
        on. I, xvi, 356; II, vi, 356 pp.
            Arranged by Sara Coleridge. Mostly reprint from Liter-
        ary Remains.

1045   Notes, Theological, Political, and Miscellaneous by Samuel
        Taylor Coleridge. Ed. the Reverend Derwent Coleridge.
        London: Edward Moxon. xii, 415 pp.
            'Completes the publication of Coleridge's marginalia'.
        Reviewed: Guardian, No. 415 (16 Nov 1853), p. 768; Liter-
        ary Gazette, No. 1921 (12 Nov 1853), pp. 1091-3. See also
        1056.

1046   ALISON, SIR ARCHIBALD. History of Europe. Edinburgh, Lon-
        don: William Blackwood.
            Gives 'poetic character' of Coleridge, comparing him
        with Wordsworth.

1047   ANON. 'Obituary'. Christian Reformer, 3rd Series IX, 592-4.
            Obituary of W. D. Champion includes description of Cole-
        ridge's preaching at Bridgwater.

1048   _____. 'Complete Works of Samuel Taylor Coleridge'. Evan-
        gelical Review [Gettysburg], V, 125-6, 290.
            Series of laudatory comments on individual works.

1049   _____. 'The Original Ancient Mariner'. Gentleman's Maga-
        zine, New Series XL, 371-4. Summarized by 'Philo. Col.',
        Notes and Queries, 4th Series XII (1853), 439.
            Unconvincing argument for Paulinus of Nola as a source
        of The Ancient Mariner.

1050   _____. 'A Visit to the Residence of Coleridge the Poet at
        Highgate'. Home Companion, No. 30 (5 Nov), pp. 480-1.
            Inaccurate biographical sketch.

1051   _____. 'Coleridge and Maginn: Curious Blunder of a Critic'.
        Literary World [New York], XIII, 7-9.
            Explanation that Maginn's 1819 parody not part of orig-
        inal poem.

1052   _____. 'Coleridgiana. I. The New Edition of Coleridge'.
        Literary World [New York], XII, 263-5.
            Minor criticisms of Shedd's edition questions authen-
        ticity of Theory of Life.

1853-ANON.

1053   ANON. 'Coleridgiana'. Literary World [New York], XII, 10-11,
       349-50, 393, 433-4.
           Marginalia in Lamb's copies of John Bunell's Octavo,
       Donne's Poems, Reynold's God's Revenge Against Murder, Pet-
       vin's Letters and a work by Phillip de Commines.

1054   _____. 'Short Review and Notices of Books'. Methodist Quar-
       terly Review [New York], XXXV, 305-15.
           A review of Works (1853) defends against charges of
       'indolence' and emphasizes intellectual influence.

1055   _____. 'Complete Works of Samuel Taylor Coleridge'. National
       Era [Washington, D. C.], VII, 62.
           Notice comments on quality and value of Coleridge's
       work.

1056   [CHORLEY, HENRY FOTHERGILL]. 'Notes, Theological, Political
       and Miscellaneous. By Samuel Taylor Coleridge. Edited by
       the Reverend Derwent Coleridge'. Athenaeum, No. 1359
       (12 Nov), p. 1354.
           Regrets that Coleridge wasted his great powers in making
       notes.
           Attribution: Fahnestock

1057   CLEVELAND, CHARLES D[EXTER]. English Literature of the Nine-
       teenth Century. Philadelphia: E. C. and J. Biddle.
           School text combines (pp. 292-305) inaccurate biographi-
       cal sketch with fulsome praise of moral value of his
       writings.

1058   [ELLIS, G. E.]. 'Complete Works of Samuel Taylor Coleridge'.
       Christian Examiner [Boston, New York], LV, 307-8.
           Disagrees with Hare's praise in Mission of the Comforter
       (1846), although Coleridge instructive to minds 'when in a
       transition state' [sic].
           Attribution: Cushing

1059   [FOSDICK, WILLIAM] St. Thomas Aquinas, pseud. 'The Ancient
       Mariner'. Spirit of the Times [New York], XXIII, 243. Re-
       printed in his Ariel and Other Poems. New York: Bunce &
       Brother (1855), 225-42.
           Weak parody.

1060   [GILFILLAN, GEORGE] Apollodorus, pseud. 'Modern Critics.
       Jeffrey and Coleridge'. Critic, XII, 462-4. Reprinted in
       his A Third Gallery of Portraits. Edinburgh: James Hogg,
       London: R. Groombridge (1854), pp. 215-6.

1853-J. M. B.

([GILFILLAN, GEORGE])
Jeffrey and Coleridge polar opposites in criticism, the mechanical versus the impulsive. Chiefly devoted to Jeffrey, essay concludes with apostrophe to Coleridge.

1061   HETHERINGTON, WILLIAM H. 'Coleridge and his Followers'. Lectures Delivered Before the Young Men's Christian Association in Exeter Hall. London: James Nisbet, pp. 1-44.
Brief biographical sketch including account of interview. Discussion of Coleridge's philosophy and comments on Sterling and Gladstone.

1062   [HUTTON, R. H.]. 'The Theology of Coleridge and Maurice'. Inquirer, No. 573 (25 June), pp. [401]-2.
Critical of both men, but approves of unrecognized implications in their position which logically undermined Anglican doctrines.
Attribution: Tener

1063   INGLEBY, C. MANSFIELD. 'Coleridge As Prophet'. Notes and Queries, VII, 36.
Coleridge's insights into destiny of France reflected in events of 1830 and 1848.

1064   _____. 'Coleridge's Unpublished Mss'. Notes and Queries, VIII, 43; IX (1853), 496-7, 543-4, 591.
Attacks Green for his failure to publish Coleridge's unpublished work. Green's reply that mss were unpublishable seems inadequate to Ingleby.

1065   JERDAN, WILLIAM. Autobiography of William Jerdan. 4 vols. London: Arthur Hall, Virtue & Co.
Account of acquaintance with Coleridge (III, 34). Discussion of Coleridge's humour (III, 312-3), and anecdotes (IV, passim).

1066   J. M. B. 'The Life and Correspondence of S. T. Coleridge'. Notes and Queries, VII, 282, 368.
Note with comment by 'Theta' on appropriate biographer for Coleridge.

1067   _____. 'Passage in Coleridge'. Notes and Queries, VII, 330, 393.
Query with reply by I. H. M. concerning variant reading.

1853–J. M. G.

1068   J. M. G. 'Samuel Taylor Coleridge'. <u>Notes and Queries</u>, VII,
        280.
            Marginalia from Parr's <u>Spital Sermon</u> quoted and dis-
        cussed.
            G. Whalley (NCBEL, III, 221) attributes this to John
        Matthew Gutch.

1069   LANDOR, WALTER SAVAGE. 'To the Reverend Charles Cuthbert Sou-
        they on his Father's Character and Public Services'. <u>The</u>
        <u>Last Fruit Off an Old Tree</u>. London: Edward Moxon,
        pp. 332–8.
            Wordsworth and Coleridge judged (pp. 334–5) inferior to
        Scott and Southey.

1070   MOORE, THOMAS. <u>Memoirs, Journal, and Correspondence</u>. Ed.
        Lord John Russell. 8 vols. London: Longman <u>et al</u>.
            Numerous anecdotes in IV–VIII, <u>passim</u>, of Coleridge's
        conversation, and opinions of him held by Scott, Jeffrey
        and others. Moore's authorship of 'A Vision by the Author
        of <u>Christabel</u>' (1826) q.v. acknowledged (V, 100).

1071   [RAYMOND, HENRY JARVIS]. 'Samuel Taylor Coleridge'. <u>New York</u>
        <u>Daily Times</u>, No. 535 (4 June), p. 2.
            Review of <u>Works</u> (1853) acknowledges Coleridge's contri-
        bution to literature. Discusses Coleridge's character
        which, of all poets, was 'the worst we know'.
            Attribution: Duffy

1072   S. Y. 'Coleridge's Christabel'. <u>Notes and Queries</u>, VII, 206,
        292–3; VIII (1853), 11–2, 111–2; IX (1854), 455, 529.
            Interchange by S. Y., J. M. B., A. B. R., J. S. Warden,
        and Ingleby concerning authorship of Moir's 1819 parody of
        <u>Christabel</u> and Niven's of 1815.

1073   SHEDD, W. G. T. 'Introductory Essay'. <u>Complete Works of</u>
        <u>Samuel Taylor Coleridge</u>. 7 vols. New York: Harper and
        Bros., I, 9–62. Reprinted as 'Coleridge as Philosopher and
        Theologian' in his <u>Literary Essays</u>. New York: Charles
        Scribner's Sons (1878), 271–344; <u>Dickinson's Theological</u>
        <u>Quarterly</u>, VI (1880), 72–92; 182–98.
            Exposition as much of Shedd's own theological views as
        of Coleridge, but important in showing Coleridge's value
        and appeal to a learned, intelligent and sympathetic 19th-
        century figure. For Shedd, Coleridge's value less in in-
        complete system than in his record of intellectual and
        spiritual struggle, in his account of a 'man thinking',
        one who found way to theism rather than pantheism. Turning
        back from Schelling to Kant, Coleridge was close to Jacobi.

(SHEDD, W. G. T.)
Reviewed: Harper's New Monthly Magazine [New York], VI
(1853), 568-70. See also 1096.

1854

1074   A. B. 'Wordsworth, Coleridge and Southey'. Archiv [Herrigs]
        [Braunschweig], XVI, 1-71.
        Biography and paraphrases.

1075   The Poetical Works of Coleridge and Keats with a Memoir of
        Each. 4 vols in 2. [S. T. Coleridge, I]. Boston: Hough-
        ton Mifflin.
        The memoir (I, xxix-cxi) added to this reprint of the
        1852 edition is by Charles Eliot Norton, adapted from his
        1847 North American Review article, and follows the 'mel-
        ancholy record' of Coleridge's life with a discussion of
        his 'genuine and original' poetic achievement and his re-
        markable' influence on the next generation.

1076   ANON. 'Coleridge as a Theologian'. British Quarterly Review,
        XIX, 112-59.
        Comments on Coleridge's relation to Boehme, Bruno,
        Schelling, and Kant. Argues that Coleridge's equation of
        terms of contemporary German metaphysics with Christian
        doctrine are invalid. Praises Coleridge's good heart while
        attacking his theology.

1077   _____. 'Coleridge, Samuel Taylor'. Encyclopaedia Britannica.
        Eighth edition. 21 vols. Edinburgh: Adam & Charles
        Black, VII, 109-12.
        Brief biographical survey stresses illness, opium, and
        lack of will. Notes influence in England and America.

1078   _____. 'The Oracles of God...By...Irving'. Eclectic Review,
        5th Series VIII, 4.
        Flattering characterization of Coleridge among celebri-
        ties at Irving's chapel.

1079   _____. 'Fine Arts'. Guardian, No. 469 (19 Nov), p. 921.
        Flattering critique of Allston's portrait of Coleridge.

1079a   _____. 'Town and Table-Talk on Literature, Art, &c.' Illus-
        trated London News, XXV, No. 69 (15 July), p. 35.
        Announcement of discovery of Collier's notes.

SAMUEL TAYLOR COLERIDGE: AN ANNOTATED BIBLIOGRAPHY

1854-ANON.

1080 ANON. 'Wordsworth'. Presbyterian Quarterly Review [Phila-
delphia], III, 69-88.
Substantial discussion of mutual influence of Wordsworth
and Coleridge.

1081 BAILEY, ELIZABETH RAINIER. 'Lines, on Viewing the Cottage at
Clevedon, for some time the Residence of the Poet, Cole-
ridge'. Lady Jane Grey, and Other Poems. 2 vols. London:
Longman et al., II, 146-7.

1082 COLLIER, J. PAYNE. 'Coleridge's Lectures on Shakespeare and
Milton in 1812'. Notes and Queries, X, 1, 21-3, 57-8,
117-9.
Four notes describe background of Coleridge's lectures,
with extracts from Collier's shorthand report, suggest
Mishna as source for Coleridge's four classes of readers.
J M G[utch] quotes Cottle and Dibdin in support of Collier's account (X, 106-7), and 'Eirionnach' (X, 373) asks
about similar notes.

1083 CURRY, REV. DR. [DANIEL]. 'Coleridge'. Methodist Quarterly
Review [New York], XXXVI, 34-57.
Review of Works (1853), chiefly devoted to expositions
of Coleridge's theology and philosophy which are seen as
far more significant than his poetry and criticism.

1084 DE QUINCEY, THOMAS. 'Conversation'. Letters to a Young Man.
Boston: Ticknor, Reed, and Fields, pp. 127-59.
In this edition, De Quincey added to earlier article a
'second paper' discussing (pp. 151-4) Coleridge's monologues and Mme. de Staël's view of them.

1085 ÉTIENNE, L. 'Poètes contemporains de l'Angleterre: Coleridge
ses amis, ses imitateurs. Charles Lamb - Charles Lloyd -
Hartley Coleridge'. Revue contemporaine [Paris], XIII,
79-123.
Coleridge considered as a philosophical and psychologi-
cal poet. Shares with George Fox a 'mysticisme sensuel'.
The meditative pattern of Fears in Solitude is that of a
Quaker meeting.

1086 GUNNING, HENRY. Reminiscences of the University, Town and
County of Cambridge, from the year 1780. 2 vols. London:
G. Bell.
Account (I, 299-300) of Coleridge's behaviour at the
1793 trial of Frend.

150

1087 HOLLAND, JOHN, and JAMES EVERETT. Memoirs of the Life and
      Writings of James Montgomery. 7 vols. London: Longman
      et al.
          Coleridge's 1812 lectures compared (II, 337-9) with
      Campbell's.

1088 J. M. 'Coleridge's Unpublished Manuscripts'. Notes and
      Queries, X, 146.
          Query on Coleridge's marginalia on Boehme.

1089 JAMESON, MRS. [ANNA]. Commonplace Book of Thoughts, Memories,
      and Fancies, Original and Selected. London: Longman
      et al.
          Tieck's reaction to Coleridge's death (pp. 71-2).

1090 J. R. G. 'Story of Coleridge'. Notes and Queries, X, 153.
          Familiar anecdote.

1091 [LITTLEJOHN, A. H.]. 'Works of Samuel Taylor Coleridge'.
      Church Review [New Haven, New York], VI, 489-511.
          Attacks popular derogatory views and theological ob-
      jections.
          Attribution: Haney

1092 PATMORE, P. G. My Friends and Acquaintances. 3 vols. Lon-
      don: Saunders and Otley.
          Discussion (II, 139-54) of political apostasy of Cole-
      ridge, Wordsworth, and Southey.

1093 PEASE, REV. AARON G. 'Associate Alumni'. Semi-Centennial
      Anniversary of the University of Vermont. Burlington:
      Free Press Print.
          Creed for graduates includes belief in Coleridge.

1094 THOMSON, MRS. [KATHERINE]. Recollections of Literary Charac-
      ters and Celebrated Places. 2 vols. London: Richard
      Bentley.
          Childhood reminiscence (II, 57-60) of Coleridge telling
      of Mary of Buttermere. Later impression of lecture.

1095 TRAHERNE, J. M. 'Remarks on the Moravians, by the Late Samuel
      Taylor Coleridge'. Gentleman's Magazine, New Series XLII,
      360-3. Reprinted Littell's Living Age [Boston], 2nd Se-
      ries VII (1854), 476-8.
          Transcript of and notes on marginalia in Southey's
      copy.

1096   [TURNBULL, R.]. 'Coleridge as a Thinker'. Christian Review
        [New Haven], XIX, 319-42.
            Coleridge ranked with Berkeley, Schelling, De Quincey,
        and below Plato and Bacon. Criticizes Shedd's 1853 intro-
        duction.
            Attribution: Potter Collection.

                              1855

1097   ANON. 'Third Gallery of Portraits...By George Gilfillan.'
        Christian Examiner [Boston], LVII (1855), 453-7.
            Review of Gilfillan (1845) compares Coleridge with P. T.
        Barnum.

1098   _____. 'The Complete Works of Samuel Taylor Coleridge'.
        Presbyterian Quarterly Review [Philadelphia], IV, 80-103.
            Comprehensive assessment with emphasis upon distinction
        of fancy and imagination, versification, and religious and
        subjective aspects of Coleridge's poetry.

1099   No entry.

1100   [BRAE, ANDREW EDMOND]. Literary Cookery. With reference to
        Coleridge and Shakespeare. London: John Russell Smith.
            Attack on Collier's credibility, centering on disputed
        date for one of Coleridge's lectures.
            Attribution: B. Mus. Cat.

1101   C. V. L. G. [LE GRICE, CHARLES VALENTINE?]. 'Coleridge's Re-
        ligious Musings'. Notes and Queries, XII, 226, 371.
            C. V. L. G.'s query answered by J. Y.

1102   FITZPATRICK, WILLIAM JOHN. 'Coleridge's Lectures'. Notes and
        Queries, XII, 80, 322-3.
            Florence G. Edgeworth answers query concerning 1812
        lecture.

1103   [HANNAY, JAMES]. 'Table-Talk'. Quarterly Review, XCVIII,
        1-31. Reprinted Eclectic Magazine [New York], XXXVIII
        (1856), 1-18.
            Coleridge's Table-Talk described as monologue, 'cloudy,
        with mystic magnificence', but with evidence of 'substan-
        tial thought'.
            Attribution: WI.

1104   INGLEBY, C. MANSFIELD. 'Coleridge's Marginalia on Raleigh's
        History of the World'. Notes and Queries, XII, 5-6.
        Description and text of Coleridge's notes.

1105   KÖPKE, RUDOLPH. Ludwig Tieck. 2 vols. Leipzig: F. U. Brock-
        haus.
        Account (I, 375-6) of Tieck's 1817 visits with Coleridge
        and their discussions of Shakespeare.

1106   LE GRICE, CHARLES VALENTINE. 'To the Memory of Coleridge and
        Charles Lamb'. Gentleman's Magazine, New Series XLIII,
        263. Reprinted anonymously Littell's Living Age [Boston],
        2nd Series IX (1855), 82.
        Poem.

1107   MADDEN, R. R. Literary Life and Correspondence of the Count-
        ess of Blessington. 3 vols. London: T. C. Newby.
        Includes two letters from Landor (II, 362, 370) on
        withdrawal of Coleridge's pension, praising him as second
        only to Shakespeare and Milton. Disraeli (III, 91-2) com-
        ments on authorship of the 1834 Quarterly article.

1108   REED, HENRY. Lectures on English Literature from Chaucer to
        Tennyson. Philadelphia: Parry and McMillan; London:
        Shaw.
        Brief discussion (pp. 266-9) of Christabel and its in-
        fluence on Scott, Shelley, and Byron.

1109   [ROSENWALD, VICTOR] V. R. 'Coleridge (Samuel Taylor)'.
        Nouvelle Biographie Générale. 46 vols. Paris: Firmin
        Didot Frères (1852-66), XI, 126-9.
        Sympathetic sketch largely derived from Penny Cyclo-
        paedia (1837).

1110   [STANLEY, ARTHUR PENRHYN]. 'Archdeacon Hare'. Quarterly Re-
        view, XCVII, 1-28. Reprinted in his Essays, Chiefly on
        Questions of Church and State. London: John Murray
        (1870), pp. 536-71.
        Supports Hare's 1842 assessment of Coleridge (pp. 19,
        23).

1111   [VALENTINE, M.]. 'Samuel Taylor Coleridge'. Evangelical Re-
        view [Gettysburg], VII, 85-102.
        Chiefly on Coleridge's character with discussion of re-
        action to Enlightenment and introduction of German philos-
        ophy to England. As poet, Coleridge far above average but
        not in first rank.
        Attribution: Poole

1856-Seven Lectures

1856

1112   Seven Lectures upon Shakespeare and Milton, By the Late S. T.
       Coleridge...with an introductory preface by J. Payne Col-
       lier. London: Chapman and Hall. cxx, 275 pp.
            Shorthand notes of Coleridge's lectures. Diary excerpts
       (pp. xlv-lix) describe Coleridge's conversation on Shake-
       speare. Reviewed: [Charles Wentworth Dilkes]. Athenaeum,
       No. 1513 (25 Oct 1856), pp. 1299-1301 (attribution: Fahne-
       stock); Saturday Review, III (1857), 156-60; Westminster
       Review, New Series XI (1857), 319-20. See also 1114, 1115,
       1135, 1171.

1113   ANON. Recollections of the Table-Talk of Samuel Rogers, to
       which is added Porsoniana. London: Edward Moxon.
            Describes Coleridge's talk (pp. 203-4).

1114   _____. 'Seven Lectures on Shakespeare and Milton'. Examiner,
       No. 2543 (25 Oct), pp. 677-8. Reprinted Littell's Living
       Age [Boston], 2nd Series XV (1856), 698-702.
            Account of rediscovery of Collier's notes on 1811-12
       lectures, with letters from Wordsworth and Lamb.

1115   _____. 'Seven Lectures on Shakespeare and Milton'. Gentle-
       man's Magazine, CCI, 600-1; CCII (1857), 158-64.
            Coleridge the most comprehensive intellect since Milton.
       Collier's notes, clearly authentic. Sequel offers uniform-
       ly favourable discussion of lectures VI and VII.

1116   _____. 'Julius Charles Hare'. Methodist Quarterly Review
       [New York], 169-97; 329-51.
            Coleridge's influence on Hare discussed and seen as un-
       fortunate.

1117   [CALVERT, GEORGE HENRY]. 'Göttingen in 1824'. Putnam's
       Monthly Magazine [New York], VII, 595-607. Reprinted in
       his First Years in Europe, Boston: Lee and Shepard; New
       York: Charles T. Dillingham (1866), pp. 86-126.
            American student quotes tutor who knew Coleridge and
       thought him an 'idler' who did not learn German thoroughly
       and was already an opium addict.

1118   DE QUINCEY, THOMAS. 'Confessions of an English Opium-Eater'.
       Works. Edinburgh: James Hogg (1853-1860). 14 vols., V.
            Coleridge's attack on De Quincey's use of opium as
       stimulus provoked rejoinder (pp. 3-10) giving 'rheumatic
       toothache' as excuse. Coleridge described as opium's
       slave. Reviewed: Athenaeum, No. 1516 (22 Nov 1856),
       pp. 1427-8.

1119   EMERSON, RALPH WALDO. English Traits. Boston: Phillips,
        Sampson, and Company.
            Includes account of visit to Highgate, disappointment
        with an 'old and preoccupied' Coleridge, and Wordsworth's
        remarks on Coleridge's obscurity.

1120   [GILFILLAN, GEORGE]. History of a Man. Ed. George Gilfillan.
        London: Arthur Hall, Virtue, and Co.
            Discussion of Coleridge with Christopher North [John
        Wilson] (pp. 109-11), Cockburn (p. 147) and Carlyle
        (p. 152), concerning conversation, poems, plagiarisms, and
        use of opium.

1121   HARE, JULIUS CHARLES. Charges to the Clergy of the Archdea-
        conry of Lewes. Introduction by F. D. Maurice. 3 vols.
        Cambridge: Macmillan and Co. Introduction reprinted
        Julius Charles Hare. The Victory of Faith. London: Mac-
        millan and Co. (1874). Ed. E. H. Plumptre.
            Maurice's introduction ranks Coleridge among his chief
        teachers (p. xviii) and describes (p. xxiii) nature of his
        influence. Scattered remarks on Coleridge in Hare's notes
        passim, with special reference to Church and State (III,
        (246-8).

1122   [HORT, F. J. A.] F. J. A. H. 'Coleridge'. Cambridge Essays,
        1856. London: John W. Parker, pp. 292-351.
            Scholarly discussion and exposition of some central as-
        pects of Coleridge's intellectual development. Discusses
        use of Kantean terms and shows his essential Englishness.
        In spite of his debts, Coleridge Platonic rather than Neo-
        platonic. Important discussion of Coleridge on imagination
        and symbol, and briefly on positions in politics, theology,
        and moral philosophy.
            Attribution: Hort

1123   [JAYCOX, FRANCIS]. 'Prosings by Monkshood about the Essayists
        and Reviewers. VII -- Charles Lamb'. Bentley's Miscel-
        lany, XXXIX, 430-40.
            Coleridge should have had some definite daily employment
        as did Lamb.
            Attribution: WI.

1124   _____. 'Prosings by Monkshood, about the Essayists and Re-
        viewers. IX--Samuel Taylor Coleridge'. Bentley's Miscel-
        lany, XL, 208-20. Reprinted Eclectic Magazine [New York],
        XXXIX (1856), 394-402.
            Patchwork of anecdotes and references showing Coleridge
        as fragmentary writer of wide influence.
            Attribution: WI.

1125 [KINGSLEY, CHARLES] C. K. 'Hours with the Mystics. By Rob-
      ert Alfred Vaughan'. Fraser's Magazine, LIV, 315-28. Re-
      printed in his Miscellanies, 2 vols. London: Parker
      (1859), I [325]-356.
         Coleridge mentioned as one of the 'few mystic writers of
      this island' and for wide theological influence.

1126 MARTINEAU, JAMES. 'Personal Influences on Our Present The-
      ology: Newman-Coleridge-Carlyle'. National Review, III,
      449-94. Reprinted in his Essays Philosophical and Theol-
      ogical. 2 vols. Boston: William V. Spencer (1866), I,
      329-405.
         'Oxford', 'Cambridge', and 'Scottish' movements exempli-
      fied by Newman, Coleridge and Carlyle. Summarizes Cole-
      ridge's theological position and discusses influence on
      Hare and Maurice.

1127 MAYOR, J. E. B. 'The Common Soldier in Coleridge's 'Friend'.
      Notes and Queries, New Series II, 267.
         Identifies William Sedgwick as source for passage in
      The Friend.

1128 REMUSAT, CHARLES de. 'Deux controverses religieuses en Angle-
      terre. Deuxième partie. Coleridge--Arnold'. Revue des
      deux Mondes [Paris], V, 492-592.
         A careful discussion (pp. 504-17) of Coleridge's influ-
      ence on Broad Church movement, especially on Thomas Arnold.

1129 ROFFE, ALFRED. 'Coleridge'. Notes and Queries, New Series
      II, 369.
         Anecdote concerning Coleridge's request for musical
      setting for Glycine's Song.

1130 SCOTT, SIR WALTER. The Lay of the Last Minstrel. Edinburgh:
      Adam and Charles Black.
         Scott's introduction, dated 1830, and here first pub-
      lished, acknowledges debt to Christabel.

1131 SOUTHEY, ROBERT. Selections from the Letters of Robert Sou-
      they. Edited by his son-in-law John Wood Warter. 4 vols.
      London: Longman et al.
         Letters, supplementing edition of 1849-1850, q.v., in-
      clude (IV, 380-3) one on Coleridge after his death.

1132 VAUGHAN, ROBERT ALFRED. Hours with the Mystics. 2 vols.
      London: John W. Parker.
         Coleridge and Carlyle familiarized England with German
      philosophy (I, 93-4).

1133   W. B. 'Samuel Taylor Coleridge. Touching the Society of
       Friends'. British Friend [Glasgow], XVI, 177-8, 210-11.
       Takes issue with Coleridge's remarks in Table Talk.

                                    1857

1134   Rime of the Ancient Mariner. Illustrated W. W. Wehnert, E.
       Duncan, and Birket Foster. London: Sampson Low, Marston,
       Low and Searle; New York: D. Appleton. 51 pp. Re-
       viewed: [George Walton Thornbury], Athenaeum, No. 1518
       (29 Nov 1856), p. 1462 (attribution: Fahnestock).

1135   ANON. 'Shakespeareana: Collier and Coleridge'. Bentley's
       Miscellany, XLI, 90-5.
       Defence of Collier (1856), with note quoting Byron's
       contemptuous allusions to Coleridge's lectures.

1136   _____. 'Hazlitt and Coleridge: At the Hotel Dessin'. Cham-
       bers's Edinburgh Journal, 3rd Series VII, 103-6; reprinted
       Littell's Living Age [Boston], 2nd Series XVII (1857), 248-52.
       Imaginary conversation on Sterne.

1137   _____. 'Mr. Rigg on the Coleridgean Theology'. Monthly
       Christian Spectator, VII, 734-44.
       Review of Rigg (1857) calls Coleridge's theology 'popu-
       lar...influential and...pernicious'. Mentions influence on
       Maurice and Kingsley.

1138   _____. 'Coleridge and Wordsworth'. Peripatetic Papers. Ed.
       John M. Gilchrist. London: James Blackwood, pp. 202-4.
       Poem.

1139   _____. 'Modern Anglican Theology'. Record, No. 3335 (23
       Dec), p. 4. Expanded as Modern Anglican Neology. London:
       Wertheim, Macintosh, and Hunt (1858), 118 pp.
       Review of Rigg (1857) becomes extended attack on Cole-
       ridge and his followers for pantheism, mysticism, and
       various heresies.

1140   BRIGHAM, C. H. 'M. Remusat on Unitarians and Unitarianism'.
       Christian Examiner [Boston], LXII, 433-44.
       Coleridge's influence (p. 441) on the English Church as
       advocate of application of reason to dogma.

1857-E. W. S.

1141   E. W. S. 'The Essayist, Coleridge'. British Controversial-
       ist, 2nd Series IV, 35-40.
              Florid panegyric on Coleridge's genius. Coleridge
       lacked Milton's decisiveness.

1142   [HUTTON, R. H.]. 'William Wordsworth'. National Review, IV,
       1-30.
              Coleridge's criticism of Wordsworth used in comparison
       of the two.
              Attribution: WI.

1143   LEE, WILLIAM. The Inspiration of Holy Scripture. New York:
       Robert Carter & Brothers.
              Lectures correct passim errors in Coleridge's view of
       Biblical inspiration.

1144   LUDLOW, FITZ-HUGH. 'Ideal Men and Their Stimulants'. The
       Hasheesh Eater: Being Passages from the Life of a Pythag-
       orean. New York: Harper and Brothers, pp. 352-62.
              Coleridge's addiction explained by character, back-
       ground, and demands of his practical life.

1145   OWEN, ROBERT. The Life of Robert Owen Written By Himself.
       London: Effingham Wilson.
              Describes (pp. 36, 70) discussion with Coleridge in
       Manchester and a later meeting.

1146   REED, HENRY. 'Coleridge'. Lectures on the British Poets.
       2 vols. Philadelphia: Parry & McMillan; London: John
       Farquahar Shaw, I, 88-126.
              1841 lecture discusses influence of French Revolution
       and of W. L. Bowles, and gives uncritical summary of The
       Ancient Mariner and Christabel.

1147   RIGG, JAMES H. Modern Anglican Theology: Chapters on Cole-
       ridge, Hare, Maurice, Kingsley, and Jowett, and on the
       Doctrine of Sacrifice and Atonement. London: Heylin.
       424 pp.
              Attacks Coleridge and followers and discusses influence
       of Schelling and Plotinus. Reviewed: London Quarterly
       Review, IX (1857-58), 266-7. See also 1137, 1139.

1148   RUSKIN, JOHN. Elements of Drawing. London: Smith Elder.
              'Cast Coleridge at once aside, as sickly and useless'
       (p. 348).

1858

1149   A. B. R. 'Coleridge on "Hooker's Definition of Law"'. Notes
       and Queries, New Series, VI, 411.
           Takes issue with Coleridge's criticism in Literary
       Remains.

1150   ANON. 'Coleridge and the Personality of the Devil'. Chris-
       tian Reformer, New Series, XIV, 337.
           Note rejecting idea of a personal devil cited as evi-
       dence of Coleridge's theological weakness.

1151   DAVY, SIR HUMPHRY. Fragmentary Remains. Edited by his broth-
       er John Davy. London: John Churchill.
           Includes (pp. 72-114) correspondence with Coleridge.

1152   TIMBS, JOHN. 'Coleridge at Christ's Hospital and Cambridge'.
       School-Days of Eminent Men. London: Kent and Co.,
       pp. 271-3.
           Chiefly excerpts from published sources.

1859

1153   No entry.

1154   ALLIBONE, SAMUEL. 'Coleridge, Samuel Taylor'. Critical Dic-
       tionary of English Literature and British and American
       Authors. 3 vols. Philadelphia: Childs and Peterson;
       London: N. Trubner, I, 405-6.
           Biographical sketch.

1155   ANDREWS, ALEXANDER. The History of British Journalism. 2
       vols. London: Richard Bentley.
           Account of Coleridge, Stuart and Morning Post (II, 3-9),
       followed (II, 28-9) by Coleridge's effect on the Truce of
       Amiens, flight from Leghorn in 1806 and papal intervention.

1156   ANON. 'Life of Samuel Taylor Coleridge'. Poetical Works of
       Thomas Campbell and Samuel Taylor Coleridge, With Lives.
       Edinburgh: Gall & Inglis, pp. [iii]-xvii.
           Conventional biographical sketch, torn between pity and
       admiration.

1859-ANON.

1157 ANON. 'The Life of S. T. Coleridge'. Christian Observer,
      LVIII, 308–18, 374–85, 634–9.
          Belated review of Gillman (1838) and Cottle (1847), con-
      sists of an inaccurate biographical summary and extended
      eulogy. Reply, 'The Theology of Coleridge', argues Cole-
      ridge's responsibility for 'almost all' modern heresies.

1158 _____. 'Plagiarism and Literary Coincidences'. Eclectic Re-
      view, 6th Series, V, 517–26.
          Coleridge's plagiarisms explained by opium addiction.

1159 [BAGEHOT, WALTER]. 'Tennyson's Idylls'. National Review, IX,
      368–94.
          Coleridge and others classified (pp. 392–3) as 'intel-
      lectualized poets'. Coleridge will remain a critical prob-
      lem and psychological puzzle. Christabel and The Ancient
      Mariner discussed in terms of supernatural.
          Attribution: St John-Stevas

1160 BAYNE, PETER. 'Elementary Principles of Criticism'. Essays,
      Biographical, Critical, and Miscellaneous. Edinburgh,
      London: J. Hogg and Sons, pp. 144–201.
          Coleridge discussed passim and credited with having
      'indicated, in our country, the organic law on which a
      science of criticism must repose'.

1161 EIRIONNACH, pseud. 'Archbishop Leighton's Works'. Notes and
      Queries, New Series VIII, 41–4, 61–4, 507–9, 525–7.
          References to Coleridge on Leighton.

1162 GRINSTED, T. P. Relics of Genius: Visits to the Last Homes
      of Poets, Painters, and Players, with Biographical Sketch-
      es. London: W. Kent. Reprinted as Last Homes of Depart-
      ed Genius. London: George Routledge (1867).
          Conventional biographical sketch (pp. 191–3).

1163 GUTCH, J. M. 'Yorkshire Worthies, by Hartley Coleridge'.
      Notes and Queries, New Series VII, 207–8.
          Comparison of Hartley Coleridge with his father.

1164 HOOD, THOMAS. 'Literary Reminiscences. No. IV'. Hood's
      Own. London: Edward Moxon, pp. 545–68.
          Two meetings with Coleridge at Lamb's and description
      of conversation and appearance.

SAMUEL TAYLOR COLERIDGE: AN ANNOTATED BIBLIOGRAPHY

1165   MARSH, GEORGE P. Lectures on the English Language. New York:
       Charles Scribner; London: Sampson Low.
           Coleridge the only modern author whose style and syntax
       are discussed (pp. 115-6, 661).

1166   [MARTINEAU, JAMES]. 'John Stuart Mill'. National Review,
       IX, 474-508. Reprinted in his Essays, Reviews and Addres-
       ses. 4 vols. London: Longmans (1890-91), III, 489-536.
           Considers (pp. 476-8) Coleridge's influence on Mill,
       and Mill's 1840 essay.

1167   [WARD, JULIUS HAMMOND]. 'The Poet Percival'. Christian Ex-
       aminer [Boston], LXVII, 227-53.
           Compares James G. Percival with Coleridge (p. 248).
           Attribution: Cushing

1168   [WAYLEN, JAMES]. A History Military and Municipal of the An-
       cient Borough of the Devizes. London: Longman et al.
           Includes (pp. 503-8) account of Coleridge and Thomas
       Methuen.
           Attribution: Devizes copy

                              1860

1169   AMPHLETT, JAMES. The Newspaper Press. London: Whittaker
       and Co.; Shrewsbury: W. Wardle.
           Recollections of meetings with Coleridge and reprint of
       1812 article on Coleridge's lectures.

1170   ANON. 'Poets: Their Lives, Songs, and Homes. The Cole-
       ridges: A Family of Poets'. Englishwoman's Domestic Mag-
       azine, VIII, 302-5.
           Brief sketch.

1171   [BRAE, ANDREW EDMOND]. Collier, Coleridge, and Shakespeare.
       A Review, By the Author of Literary Cookery. London:
       Longman et al. 150 pp.
           Attacks authenticity of Collier's Seven Lectures (1856).

1172   COLE, OWEN BLAYNEY. Christabel Concluded. A Christmas Tale.
       Portishead: n.p., 20 unnumbered pages.
           Continuation of Christabel. Note suggests Beaumont's
       Book of the Genii (1701) as a source of the poem.

1860-FREILIGRATH

1173   FREILIGRATH, FERDINAND. 'Biographical Memoir of Samuel Taylor Coleridge'. Poems of Samuel Taylor Coleridge. Leipzig: Bernhard Tauchnitz, pp. vii-xxviii.
        Biographical sketch. Particular attention to Coleridge's visits to Germany and relation to German literature. Finds 'new metrical principle' in Christabel in old German poetry. Accepts Sara's defence of Coleridge but points out German originals of Hymn to the Earth, Fancy in Nubibus, and Something Childish but very Natural.

1174   [HINTON, JAMES]. 'Physiological Riddles (No. IV): Conclusion'. Cornhill Magazine, II, 421-31.
        Credits Theory of Life (pp. 426-7) with anticipation of most later knowledge of physiology.
        Attribution: WI.

1175   HOLMES, OLIVER WENDELL. 'The Professor's Story'. Atlantic Monthly [Boston], V-VII (1860-61). Reprinted as Elsie Venner: A Romance of Destiny. 2 vols. Boston: Ticknor and Fields (1861).
        Elsie Venner compared to Geraldine in Christabel.

1176   LESLIE, CHARLES ROBERT. Autobiographical Recollections. 2 vols. Ed. Tom Taylor. London: John Murray.
        Allston's pupil, who met Coleridge frequently, reports several conversations and lectures, the production of Remorse (II, 32-4) and Coleridge's appearance (II, 40-1).
        Reviewed: [Robert Cassie Waterston]. North American Review [Boston], XCII (1861), 113-33 (attribution: Cushing).

1177   M. D. W. 'Coleridgiana'. Athenaeum, No. 1691 (24 March), p. 409.
        Two marginal notes from Wieland's 'Comische Erzahlungen'.

1178   [SMITH, LEAPIDGE]. 'Reminiscences of an Octogenarian'. Leisure Hour, IX, 633-5.
        Personal recollections (pp. 633-4) by a school friend. Describes Coleridge's appearance and relations with Bowyer.
        Attribution: Snyder, Blunden

1179   [SOTHEBY, H. W.] H. W. S. 'Life and Writings of Thomas De Quincey'. Fraser's Magazine, LXII, 781-92; LXIII (1861), 51-69.
        Discusses De Quincey's criticism of Coleridge and argues for achievement in religion and ethics.
        Attribution: WI.

1861

1180 ANON. 'Our Weekly Gossip'. Athenaeum, No. 1750 (11 May),
      pp. 632-3; no. 1751 (18 May), p. 663; no. 1755 (15 June),
      pp. 797-8; no. 1766 (31 Aug), pp. 284-5.
          Notes by Freiligrath and Gillman on stage ms used for
      translation of Wallenstein.

1181 _____. 'Wallenstein's Camp'. National Magazine, IX, 3.
          Comments on Coleridge's translation.

1182 _____. 'On the Life and Poetry of Percy Bysshe Shelley'.
      Temple Bar, III, 538-51.
          Comparison of eloquence and intellect of Coleridge and
      Shelley.

1183 COLLIER, WILLIAM FRANCIS. 'Samuel Taylor Coleridge'. A His-
      tory of English Literature. London: Thomas Nelson,
      pp. 441-6.
          Biographical sketch. 'A great genius with a great
      infirmity'.

1184 [FITZHUGH, GEORGE]. 'Table Talk: Sydney Smith - Coleridge -
      Luther'. De Bow's Review [New Orleans and Charleston],
      XXX, 53-67.
          Accuses Coleridge (pp. 57-8) of lacking common sense:
      'there is hardly a wise, prudent, or practical suggestion
      in his whole works'.
          Attribution: Weatherford

1185 J. H. 'Pronunciation of Coleridge'. Notes and Queries, New
      Series XI, 69, 136-7, 178, 233, 334-5.
          Query and several replies.

1186 MAYOR, JOHN E. B. 'S. T. Coleridge'. Notes and Queries, New
      Series XII, 167.
          Praises Hort's 1856 essay.

1187 MELETES, pseud. 'S. T. Coleridge'. Notes and Queries, New
      Series XII, 324.
          Variant line of To A Young Ass shows change in Cole-
      ridge's politics and improvement in his poetry.

1188 THOMSON, MRS. [KATHERINE]. 'Samuel Taylor Coleridge and
      Charles Lamb'. Celebrated Friendships. 2 vols. London:
      James Hogg, II, 51-98.
          Conventional account. Reviewed: Westminster Review,
      New Series XXII (1862), 140-70.

1862-ANON.

1862

1189   ANON. 'Dinner Tables and Table Talkers'. <u>Eclectic Review</u>,
       New Series II, 213-33.
          Describes (pp. 227-8) character of Coleridge's
       conversation.

1190   [CHEEVER, DAVID WILLIAMS]. 'Seven Sisters of Sleep'. North
       American Review [Boston], XCV, 374-415.
          Review of books on opium uses Coleridge as (pp. 393-4)
       'a remarkable example'.
          Attribution: Cushing

1191   FITZGERALD, WILLIAM. 'Evidences of Christianity'. <u>Aids to</u>
       <u>Faith: A Series of Theological Essays</u>. Ed. William Thom-
       son. New York: D. Appleton and Company, pp. 53-94.
          Coleridge's skepticism over miracles the basis for an
       essay in their defence.

1192   GORDON, MRS. MARY. <u>Christopher North, A Memoir of John Wil-</u>
       <u>son. Compiled from family papers and other sources.</u> 2
       vols. Edinburgh: Edmonston & Douglas.
          Account (I, 207) of 1816 visit to Coleridge, and attri-
       bution of 1834 <u>Blackwood's</u> article.

1193   GRATTAN, THOMAS COLLEY. 'A Three Days' Tour With Coleridge
       and Wordsworth'. <u>Beaten Paths; And Those Who Trod Them</u>.
       2 vols. London: Chapman and Hall, II, 107-45.
          Account of meeting in Belgium in 1828 describes Cole-
       ridge's appearance, conversation, and abhorrence of De
       Quincey's <u>Confessions</u>.

1194   HERAUD, JOHN A. 'A New View of Shakespeare's Sonnets. An
       Inductive Critique'. <u>Temple Bar</u>, V, 53-66.
          Uses Coleridge's criticism of Shakespeare's sonnets.

1195   HORNE, THOMAS HARTWELL. <u>Reminiscences Personal and Biblio-</u>
       <u>graphical</u>. With Notes by Sarah Anne Cheyne. London:
       Longman <u>et al</u>.
          Describes (pp. 4-6) learning Greek from Coleridge during
       Christ's Hospital vacation, 1790.

1196   HUNT, LEIGH. <u>Correspondence of Leigh Hunt</u>. Edited by his
       Eldest Son. 2 vols. London: Smith, Elder and Company.
          Letters offering to review Coleridge's poems in 1818
       (I, 102-3), describing him in Highgate (I, 208), and later
       with Irving (I, 249-50).

1197   [JERDAN, WILLIAM]. 'Men I Have Known, Samuel Taylor Cole-
       ridge'. Leisure Hour, XI, 679-80. Reprinted with addi-
       tions in his Men I Have Known. London: George Routledge
       (1866), pp. 119-31.
            Account of meeting with Coleridge describes appearance,
       manner, and humour. Reprint adds Jerdan's role in obtain-
       ing Coleridge's Fellowship.

1198   [NEIL, SAMUEL] S. N. 'The Right Hon. and most Rev. Richard
       Whately, D. D.'. British Controversialist, Part 1, 1-12.
            Comment on the 'excursive brilliancy' of Coleridge's
       plan for Encyclopaedia Metropolitana.
            Attribution: Snyder

1199   OLIPHANT, MRS. [MARGARET]. The Life of Edward Irving. 2
       vols. London: Hurst and Blackett.
            Notes (I, 204-5) Irving's dedication to Coleridge and
       gives account (II, 136) of meeting in 1830.

1200   S. C. 'Name Wanting in Coleridge's Table-Talk'. Notes and
       Queries, 3rd Series I, 52.
            Duplicates Lewes's request in 'Passage' (1851).

1201   [SHACKFORD, CHARLES CHAUNCY]. 'Unity of Life'. North Ameri-
       can Review [Boston], XCIV, 136-53.
            Coleridge's view in Theory of Life representative of
       major modern movement. Although borrowed from Schelling,
       it belongs equally to Coleridge.
            Attribution: Cushing

1202   [SHEPHERD, RICHARD HERNE] R. H. S. 'Coleridge's notes on
       Colquhoun'. Philobiblion [New York], I, 65-6.
            Marginalia in Colquhoun's Treatise on Indigence (1806).

1203   TAINE, H[IPPOLYTE]. 'La Poésie Moderne en Angleterre. I.
       Les Précurseurs et les Chefs d'École'. Revue des deux
       Mondes [Paris], XLI, 332-81. Reprinted in his Histoire de
       la littérature Anglaise. Deuxième Édition Revue et Corri-
       gée. 4 vols. Paris: Hachette (1863-4), III (1863),
       [417]-520. Translated Henri Van Laun. History of English
       Literature. 2 vols. Edinburgh: Edmonston and Douglas
       (1871), II, 223-70.
            Cites Coleridge's pantisocracy and unitarianism as in-
       stances of Romantic revolt.

1862–WHEWELL

1204   WHEWELL, WILLIAM. 'Reason and Understanding – S. T. Cole-
        ridge'. Lectures on the History of Moral Philosophy.
        Cambridge: Deighton, Bell, and Co. Lecture XIV,
        pp. 118-30.
            Lecture, added in this edition, complains that Coleridge
        reverses proper meanings of Reason and Understanding.

                                1863

1205   Coleridge's Rime of the Ancient Mariner. Illustrated by J.
        Noel Paton. London: Art Union, 12 pp., twenty plates.
        Reviewed: Art Journal, XXVI (1864), 91.

1206   ANON. 'Literary Miscellanies'. Eclectic Magazine [New York],
        LVIII, 140.
            Apocryphal, humorous anecdote about Coleridge's horse-
        manship.

1207   _____. 'Robert Southey'. New Review [Dublin], I, 399-416.
        Unitarianism and 'outrageous Republicanism' of 'the man of
        Opium' exercised pernicious but temporary influence on
        Southey.

1208   _____. 'Stray Thoughts on Coleridge'. New Review [Dublin],
        II, 99-114.
            Homage to Coleridge 'who first awakened the dormant
        mind within us'. Criticizes views on Biblical inspiration.
        Praises Hymn before Sunrise in comparison with German
        original.

1209   ARNOLD, MATTHEW. 'Heinrich Heine'. Cornhill, VIII, 233-49.
        Reprinted in his Heinrich Heine. Philadelphia: Frederick
        Leypoldt (1863), pp. 3-52; Essays in Criticism. Boston:
        Ticknor and Fields (1865), pp. 140-173; London: Macmillan
        and Co. (1865), pp. 151-86.
            Some Romantics confronted the modern spirit; some with-
        drew. Coleridge took to opium (p. 242).

1210   CAMPBELL, J[AMES] D[YKES]. 'Coleridge's Early Poems, Pub-
        lished 1796'. Notes and Queries, 3rd Series III, 106-7.
            Variant lines from 1796 poems.

1211   DANIEL, GEORGE. 'Recollections of Charles Lamb'. Love's Last
        Labour Not Lost. London: Basil Montagu Pickering,
        pp. [1]-31.
            Coleridge and his conversation in 1817 (p. 7).

1212   KOK, A. S. English Poetry...With Introductory Remarks, Bio-
         graphical Sketches, and Explanatory and Critical Notes.
         Schoonhoven, Netherlands: S. E. Van Nooten.
             School text. Brief inaccurate account of Coleridge.

1213   LISLE, GWYNNE. 'The Essayist, Samuel Taylor Coleridge'.
         British Controversialist, 3rd Series X, 369-77.
             Coleridge's life and philosophy provides 'a good study·
         for young men'. Highest rank as poet and critic, but Aids
         gives him 'lasting place in our literature'.

1214   A PROTESTANT, pseud. 'Coleridge on Popery'. Christian Ob-
         server, New Series No. 306 (June), pp. 469-70.
             Biographia testifies against popery.

                               1864

1215   No entry.

1216   [ARNOLD, MATTHEW]. 'Joubert, or, A French Coleridge'. Na-
         tional Review, XVIII, 168-90. Reprinted Littell's Living
         Age [Boston], LXXX (1864), 462-75; in his Essays in Criti-
         cism. Series 1. London, Cambridge: Macmillan (1865),
         pp. 265-307. Frequently reprinted.
             Joubert was, like Coleridge, a great talker, desultory
         and incomplete writer, conservative by antipathy to shallow
         modern liberalism, and motivated by ardent impulse to find
         truth.

1217   [BROWN, JOHN TAYLOR]. 'Bibliomania'. North British Review,
         XL, 78-92. Reprinted in his Spare Hours Second Series.
         Boston: Ticknor and Fields (1866), 341-81.
             Coleridge's annotations in Joan of Arc and Frere's
         'Prospectus'.

1218   COLQUHOUN, JOHN CAMPBELL. 'Life of Samuel Taylor Coleridge'.
         Scattered Leaves of Biography. London: William Macintosh,
         pp. 223-70.
             Coleridge portrayed as man of genius who made his way
         through error and weakness to become exponent and exemplar
         of pure Christian faith.

1219   DE VERE, AUBREY. 'Coleridge'. Infant Bridal and Other Poems.
         London: Macmillan, pp. 91-3.
             Poem.

1864-FOWLER

1220   FOWLER, FRANK. 'Coleridge'. Last Gleanings. London: Samp-
        son Low, and Marston, pp. 167-200.
            Lecture, chiefly biographical, delivered in Sydney be-
        fore posthumous publication.

1221   GARNETT, R[ICHARD]. 'Letters from Coleridge to William God-
        win'. Macmillan's Magazine, IX, 524-36. Reprinted
        Littell's Living Age [Boston], 3rd Series, XXV, 275-85.
            Unpublished letters with editorial notes.

                                1865

1222   BERKELEY, THE HONOURABLE GRANTLEY F[ITZARDINGE]. My Life and
        Recollections. 4 vols. London: Hurst and Blackett.
            Short account (IV, 12-13) of Coleridge's conversation.

1223   COTTERELL, G. 'S. T. Coleridge'. Notes and Queries, 3rd Se-
        ries VII, 433-4.
            Describes mss formerly belonging to Cottle and now in
        Cotterell's possession, including annotated sheets of Re-
        ligious Musings and Departing Year.

1224   EIRIONNACH, PSEUD. ' Mr. Eden's Edition of Bishop Taylor's
        Works'. Notes and Queries, 3rd Series VIII, 383-6.
            Defends Taylor against Coleridge's charge of political
        time-serving.

1225   GREEN, JOSEPH HENRY. Spiritual Philosophy Founded on the
        Teaching of the Late Samuel Taylor Coleridge. Ed. John
        Simon. 2 vols. London; Cambridge: Macmillan. Reviewed:
        Athenaeum, No. 2022 (28 July 1866), pp. 107-8.
            Green's posthumously published attempt to develop Cole-
        ridge's philosophical manuscripts, fragments, and notes
        into a coherent work. Simon's introductory memoir dis-
        cusses Green's relations with Coleridge.

1226   HALL, S. C. and MRS. S. C. HALL. 'Memories of the Authors of
        the Age'. Art-Journal, XXVII, 49-59. Illustrations. Re-
        printed Atlantic Monthly [Boston], XV (1865), 213-21;
        Eclectic Magazine [New York], New Series I (1865), 657-69;
        Book of Memories of Great Men and Women. London: Virtue
        and Co. (1867), pp. 27-48. Partially reprinted Harper's
        New Monthly Magazine [New York], XXXIX (1869), 530-1.
            Sympathetic and tactful biographical sketch, account of
        meetings with Coleridge at Highgate, and general descrip-
        tion of conversation.

1227   HURST, JOHN F. History of Rationalism. New York: Charles
        Scribner and Co., 623 pp.
            Chapter XX discusses Coleridge and Carlyle as, respec-
        tively, philosophical and literary rationalists, 'devout
        and reverent', but influence on Hare, Maurice, and Kingsley
        unhealthy.

1228   JEWITT, LLEWELLYN. The Wedgwoods. London: Virtue Brothers.
            A brief account (pp. 377-9) of Coleridge's friendship
        with Wedgwoods and of Wedgwood annuity.

1229   MASSON, DAVID. Recent British Philosophy. London, Cambridge:
        Macmillan; New York: Appleton (1866).
            Lecture includes Coleridge among century's major philos-
        ophers, emphasizes popularization of Kant and Schelling,
        ties to Anglo-Platonism and traditional Anglicanism
        (pp. 5, 10, 54, 160, passim).

1230   O. 'The Essayist. The Genius of Coleridge'. British Contro-
        versialist, 3rd Series XIII, 42-54.
            Anecdotes of Coleridge's youth with discussion of musi-
        cal language and descriptive power of The Ancient Mariner.

1231   [PHILLIPS, GEORGE SEARLE] January Searle, pseud. 'Gossip
        About Some Men of Letters'. Ladies' Repository [Cincin-
        nati], XXV, 355-7.
            Splendour of Coleridge's conversation attributed to
        opium.

1232   [SHAIRP, JOHN CAMPBELL]. 'Samuel Taylor Coleridge'. North
        British Review, XLIII, 251-322. Reprinted Littell's Living
        Age [Boston], 3rd Series XXX (1866), 81-99, 161-82. Re-
        printed with revisions in his Studies in Poetry and Philos-
        ophy. Edinburgh: Edmonston and Douglas (1868), pp. 116-
        266.
            Biographical sketch, with discussion of intellectual de-
        velopment and exposition of views of England's greatest
        19th century thinker. Coleridge's relation to Hartley, di-
        vergence from Kant, opposition to Paley, and influence
        discussed. Reviewed: no. 1270.

1233   STIRLING, JAMES HUTCHISON. The Secret of Hegel. 2 vols.
        London: Longman et al. Reprinted without plagiarism note
        Edinburgh: Oliver and Boyd; London: Simpkin, Marshall
        (1898), p. 19.
            Long note (I, 28-9) dismisses all claims for Coleridge's
        significance as philosopher, critic, or theologian.

1234   TURNER, CHARLES EDWARD. 'Wordsworth and Coleridge'. <u>Our</u>
<u>Great Writers</u>. 2 vols. St. Petersburg: A. Munx, <u>II</u>,
189–220, 419–20.
    Brief biography with long poetic extracts, of interest
as text-book by lecturer at Imperial Alexander Lyceum of
St. Petersburg.

1866

1235   ANON. 'Our Literary Table. <u>The Friend</u>'. <u>Athenaeum</u>, No. 1997
(3 Feb), p. 171.
    Sketch of contemporary reactions to Coleridge's work.

1236   _____. 'The Friend'. <u>British Quarterly Review</u>, XLIII, 606.
    Brief notice. Revival of interest in Coleridge a hope-
ful sign for philosophy.

1237   BAYLY, EMANUEL H. 'The Devil's Walk'. <u>Notes and Queries</u>, 3rd
Series IX, 197–8.
    Query and reply concerning composition of <u>Devil's</u>
<u>Thoughts</u>.

1238   [BERNAYS, ERNEST LEOPOLD] Meta, <u>pseud</u>. 'Coleridge's Poems'.
<u>Marlburian</u>, No. 17 (13 Sept), pp. 187–9; No. 18 (26 Sept),
pp. 197–8.
    Coleridge honoured as thinker, but unjustly neglected as
poet.
    Attribution: Marlborough College archives

1239   CALVERT, GEORGE H. 'To Coleridge'. <u>Anyta and Other Poems</u>.
Boston: E. P. Dutton, p. 159.
    Sonnet.

1240   DALLAS, E[NEAS] S[WEETLAND]. <u>The Gay Science</u>. 2 vols. London: Chapman and Hall.
    Indebted to Coleridge's remarks on poetic pleasure (I,
109–11), while rejecting his views on imitation (I, 81–8)
and imagination (I, 192–3). Reviewed: [John Skelton].
<u>Fraser's Magazine</u>, LXXIV (1866), 771–86 (attribution:
<u>WI</u>.).

1241   FITZGERALD, PERCY. <u>Charles Lamb; His Friends, His Haunts,</u>
<u>and His Books</u>. London: R. Bentley.
    Frequent references to Coleridge. Reviewed: [Mortimer
Collins]. <u>British Quarterly Review</u>, XLV (1867), 335–56
(attribution: <u>WI</u>.).

1242   [PATER, WALTER HORATIO]. 'Conversations, Letters and Recol-
        lections of S. T. Coleridge'. Westminster Review, New Se-
        ries XXIX, 106-32.
              Pater's first published paper. First part revised and
        combined with 'Samuel Taylor Coleridge' (1880) as 'Cole-
        ridge' in Appreciations, (1889); latter part revised as
        'Coleridge As A Theologian' in Sketches and Reviews (1919),
        q.v. for annotations. Reviewed: [R. H. Hutton]. Specta-
        tor, No. 1959 (13 Jan 1866), 37-9 (attribution: Tener).

1243   [PROCTER, BRYAN WALLER] Barry Cornwall, pseud. Charles Lamb:
        A Memoir. London: Edward Moxon & Co. Portrait by
        Northcote.
              Procter, who knew Coleridge in his later years, in-
        cludes, passim, numerous references especially to conversa-
        tion, achievements, and contemporary reputation. Reviewed:
        [Mortimer Collins]. British Quarterly Review, XLV,
        335-56 (attribution: WI.).

1244   [THOMSON, JAMES] B. V., pseud. 'The Poems of William Blake',
        National Reformer, VII, 22-3, 42-3, 52-4, 70-1. Reprinted
        in his Biographical and Critical Studies, London: Reeves
        and Turner (1896), pp. 240-69.
              Concludes with discussion of mystical simplicity in
        several poets including (p. 70) Coleridge.

1245   UNEDA, pseud. 'Coleridge's Rhyme'. Notes and Queries, 3rd
        Series X, 330, 401.
              Anecdotes by Uneda and H. A. Kennedy involving poetic
        jeu d'esprit.

                            1867

1246   ALGER, WILLIAM ROUNSEVILLE. The Solitudes of Nature and of
        man; or, The Loneliness of Human Life. Boston: Roberts
        Brothers.
              Part IV includes (pp. 276-7) quotations from Coleridge
        and comment on his spiritual isolation.

1247   ANON. 'Introduction of German Philosophy into the United
        States'. Church Review [New Haven, New York], XIX,
        400-17.
              Review article on Aids and Cousin's introduction to the
        History of Philosophy attacks 'rationalistic philosophy',
        condemns Coleridge's metaphysics and discusses influence
        on younger theologians, especially Marsh.

1867–ANON.

1248   ANON. 'Talk About Talking'. Harper's New Monthly Magazine
       [New York], XXXIV, 318–22.
          Evaluates Coleridge's conversation (p. 321).

1249   BARNETT, JOHN FRANCIS. The Ancient Mariner, Cantata Written
       by S. T. Coleridge. Composed expressly for the Birmingham
       Triennial Musical Festival. London: Novello, 143 pp.

1250   BIRKS, T[HOMAS] R[AWSON]. 'Notes on Coleridge's Confessions
       of an Inquiring Spirit'. The Victory of Divine Goodness.
       London, Oxford, and Cambridge: Rivingtons, pp. 65–146.
          According to Birks, Sara Coleridge's notes were in re-
       sponse to these criticisms.

1251   [FRISWELL, JAMES HAIN]. 'Poets of the Present Century.
       Scott, Wordsworth and Coleridge'. Essays on English Writ-
       ers, by the Author of 'The Gentle Life'. London: Sampson
       Low, Son, and Marston, pp. 328–37.
          Biographical and bibliographical sketch.

1252   HAZLITT, W. CAREW. Memoirs of William Hazlitt. 2 vols. Lon-
       don: Richard Bentley.
          Includes recollections of Coleridge, with extracts from
       Hazlitt.

1253   HUNT, LEIGH and S. ADAMS LEE. 'An Essay on the Sonnet'.
       Book of the Sonnet. 2 vols in one. Boston: Roberts, I
       [3]–91.
          In this Anglo-American collection, Hunt praises Cole-
       ridge as critic (pp. 83, 86–7) and prefers his poetry to
       Wordsworth's.

1254   KINDT, HERMANN. 'Coleridge at Rome in 1806'. Notes and Que-
       ries, 3rd Series XII, 281.
          Notes reference to Coleridge as guest of George Augus-
       tus Wallis in letters of Gottlieb Schick.

1255   [LYTTON, EDWARD GEORGE]. 'Charles Lamb and Some of his Com-
       panions'. Quarterly Review, CXXII, 1–29. Reprinted in
       his Miscellaneous Prose Works. 3 vols. London: Richard
       Bentley (1868), I, 95–134; Quarterly Essays, London:
       Routledge and Sons (1875), pp. 86–118.
          Includes long defence of Coleridge (pp. 21–8), discus-
       sion of influence on Lamb, Hazlitt, Hunt, and Scott, and
       importance of his opposition to Bentham.

1256 O'HAGAN, THOMAS. 'Coleridge'. The Afternoon Lectures on Literature and Art, Delivered in the Theatre of the Museum of Industry, ...Dublin. London: Bell and Daldy. Fourth Series, pp. 231-78. Reprinted in his Occasional Papers and Addresses. London: Kegan Paul, Trench, and Co. (1884), pp. 199-240.
      Popular informative lecture on Coleridge's work and influence.

1257 [ROGERS, HENRY]. 'Life and Letters of the late Rev. A. C. Simpson, LLD.' British Quarterly Review, XLVI, 143-79.
      Memoir of a life-long admirer with extracts from his otherwise unpublished letters. An account of Coleridge's influence on Simpson and friends (pp. 169-73) includes anecdotes of Coleridge.
      Attribution: WI.

1258 SMITH, W. J. BERNHARD. 'Coleridge's Christabel'. Notes and Queries, 3rd Series XII, 430; 4th Series I (1868), 43.
      Comment with replies from J. Bouchier and J. H. C. on relation of Christabel to Scott's 'Bridal of Tremain'.

1259 STIRLING, JAMES HUTCHISON. 'De Quincey and Coleridge upon Kant'. Fortnightly Review, XIII, 377-97. Reprinted in his Jerrold, Tennyson and Macaulay. Edinburgh: Edmonston and Douglas (1868), pp. 172-224.
      Important attack on Coleridge's pretensions to philosophic originality in relation to Schelling. His claims are 'ludicrous'.

1260 [WYMAN, FREDERICK F.?] Pips, pseud. 'Meeting of the Justices. The Hon'ble G--C-----L on the Water-Supply'. Lyrics and Lays. Calcutta: Wyman Bros., pp. 118-20.
      Parody of The Rime of the Ancient Mariner.
      Attribution: Huntington Library copy note gives Wyman or W. H. Abbott, Jr. On basis of work, Wyman more probable.

1868

1261 ALCOTT, A. BRONSON. 'Coleridge'. Radical [Boston], IV, 294.
      Flattering assessment.

1262 ANON. 'Mr. Coleridge'. Spectator, No. 2076 (11 April), pp. 427-8.
      Article on John Duke Coleridge, then a rising M.P., finds him sharing S. T. Coleridge's intellectual qualities.

1868-DAY

1263   DAY, HORACE B. The Opium Habit. New York: Harper and
        Brothers.
                Account of Coleridge (pp. 133-78) based on Cottle and
        Gillman.

1264   [LABOUCHÈRE, PETER ANTHONY]   P. A. L.   'The Drama at Here-
        ford: Dramatic Costumes'.   Notes and Queries, 4th Series
        I, 464-5, 576-7.
                Describes dinner with Coleridge and Charles Mathews.
        LaBouchère secretary to Joshua Bates, American and founder
        of the Boston Public Library. Includes in sequel a letter
        from Coleridge to Mrs. Bates, reprinted by LaBouchère in
        1872.

1265   MACDONALD, GEORGE. England's Antiphon. London: Macmillan
        and Co.
                Effusive comment (pp. 307-11) on Wordsworth and Cole-
        ridge as 'seer' and 'sage'. Hymn Before Sunrise great hymn
        of praise.

1266   [MOZLEY, JOHN RICKARDS]. 'The Poems of Samuel Taylor Cole-
        ridge...1854'. Quarterly Review, CXXV, 78-106. Reprinted
        Littell's Living Age [Boston], 4th Series X (1868), 515-29.
                Prefers later to earlier poems. But Coleridge the only
        instance since Milton of a man past middle age writing
        poems of the first rank. Compares Coleridge with Words-
        worth, and both with Byron and Shelley. Defends Cole-
        ridge's prose against charges of plagiarism.
                Attribution: WI.

1267   [PROWSE, WILLIAM JEFFERY] W. J. P. 'Coleridge, Samuel Tay-
        lor'. Hood's Comic Annual for 1868. London: Published at
        the Fun Office, p. 45.
                Parody of The Ancient Mariner satirizes Coleridge as
        talker.
                Attribution: Kitchin

1268   VARNHAGEN VON ENSE, KARL AUGUST LUDWIG PHILIPP. Aus dem
        Nachlass Varnhagen's Tagebücher. Edited by B. L. Assing.
        15 vols., X, Hamburg: Hoffman and Campe.
                Account of Tieck's 1853 remarks on Coleridge and his
        views of Shakespeare (p. 8).

1869

1269 AINGER, ALFRED. 'Coleridge and Daniel'. Notes and Queries,
      4th Series III, 577.
          Identifies epigraph from Daniel in Aids.

1270 ANON. 'Shairp's Studies in Poetry and Philosophy'. Christian
      Observer, LXVIII 344-55.
          Second half of review devoted to discussion of Words-
      worth and Coleridge as religious writers. Coleridge's
      tenets 'defective and dangerous'.

1271 CLOUGH, ARTHUR HUGH. Poems and Prose Remains. Ed. [Blanche
      Athena] Clough. 2 vols. London: Macmillan.
          Letter of 1845 (I, 103) includes description of meeting
      of Jowett and Stanley with Schelling who praised Coleridge
      and regretted charges of plagiarism.

1272 [DORAN, JOHN]. 'Christabel, and the Lyrical and Imaginative
      Poems of S. T. Coleridge. Arranged and Introduced by Al-
      gernon C. Swinburne'. Athenaeum, No. 2182 (21 Aug),
      p. 237.
          Swinburne over-enthusiastic. Christabel charming,
      though violating common sense. Last stanzas of Separation
      are from Cotton's 'Chlorinda'.
          Attribution: Fahnestock

1273 E. R. 'A Poetical Sphinx'. Victoria Magazine, XIII,
      26-40.
          Explication of Christabel, offers only summary.

1274 [FRISWELL, J. HAIN]. 'Poets of the Present Century'. Essays
      on English Writers. London: Sampson Low, Son, and Mars-
      ton, pp. 328-37.
          Biographical sketch, general praise of Table Talk and
      Coleridge's 'reverential philosophy'.

1275 HOWITT, WILLIAM. The Northern Heights of London, or Histori-
      cal Associations of Hampstead, Highgate, Wiswell Hill,
      Hansey, and Islington. London: Longmans et al.
          A description of Coleridge's tomb (p. 294) and life at
      Highgate (pp. 310-17).

1276 ROBINSON, HENRY CRABB. Diary, Reminiscences, and Correspon-
      dence. Ed. Thomas Sadler. 2 vols. London: Macmillan.
          Extensive recollections of Coleridge from 1810 until
      death. Reprinted with many additions by Edith Morley
      (1938). Reviewed: British Quarterly Review, L (1869),

1869-ROBINSON

(ROBINSON, HENRY CRABB)
343-68; North British Review, L (1869), 357-80; [Augustus de Morgan] A. de M. Theological Review, VI (1869), 376-400 (attribution: WI.).

1277 SWINBURNE, ALGERNON CHARLES. 'Coleridge'. Christabel and the Lyrical and Imaginative Poems of S. T. Coleridge. London: Sampson, Low and Co.; New York: Scribner, Welford and Co., pp. v-xxiii. Reprinted in his Essays and Studies. London: Chatto and Windus (1875), 259-75.
Enthusiastic survey of Coleridge's poems, of which the best are 'neither explicable nor communicable' through criticism. Reviewed: Notes and Queries, IV (1869), 307-8. See also 1272.

1870

1278 ANON. 'Modern Metaphysicians. Joseph Henry Green'. British Controversialist, XXIV, 81-95, 321-35.
Summary of Green's Spiritual Philosophy and discussion of Coleridge's influence.

1279 _____. 'Chaumoni at Sunrise'. Dwight's Journal of Music [Boston], XXX, 257. Reprinted as 'Coleridge A Plagiarist'. Littell's Living Age [Boston], CVI (1870), 319.
Translation of Friederike Brun's poem with note on Coleridge's indebtedness.

1280 BEETON, S[AMUEL] O[RCHART], Ed. Great Book of Poetry from Caedmon to Tennyson. London: Ward Lock and Tyler. Unpaged.
Brief biographical notice with poems.

1281 [CALL, W. M.]. 'Unpublished Letters Written by Samuel Taylor Coleridge'. Westminster Review, New Series XXXVII, 341-64; New Series XXXVIII (1870), 1-24.
Letters to Dr. Brabant, with editorial comment.
Attribution: J. D. Campbell in Huntington Library copy, p. 342.

1282 C. K. P. 'Rough Notes on Coleridge's Lectures'. Notes and Queries, 4th Series V, 335-6. Reprinted in Coleridge's Miscellaneous Criticism, ed. Raysor, 1936, pp. 8-10.
H. H. Carwardine's notes on lecture of 27 January 1818.

176

Samuel Taylor Coleridge: An Annotated Bibliography

1283 COLLINS, MORTIMER. 'Coleridge's Country'. Belgravia, New
Series II, 197-203. Reprinted Eclectic Magazine [New
York], New Series I, 621-5. Reprinted Pen Sketches by a
Vanished Hand. 2 vols. London: Richard Bentley and Son
(1879), II, 108-20.
Slight derivative discussion.

1284 C. W. S. 'Coleridge'. Notes and Queries, 4th Series VI, 392.
Query and reply concerning Coleridge's projected
writings.

1285 HODDER, GEORGE. Memories of My Time. London: Tinsley Brothers.
Describes (pp. 101-2) Gillman's house, and recollections
of Coleridge's talk by landlady of Lion and Sun.

1286 INGLEBY, C[LEMENT] M[ANSFIELD]. 'On Some Points connected
with the Philosophy of Coleridge'. Transactions of the
Royal Society of Literature. 2nd Series IX, 396-433.
Discusses Coleridge's poetic and philosophical 'plagiarisms', prints Coleridge's marginal notes on Henry More and
William Law. See Ingleby's 'Many-sided Minds' (1872) for
his later more sympathetic views.

1287 _____. 'On the Unpublished Manuscripts of Samuel Taylor Coleridge'. Transactions of the Royal Society of Literature.
2nd Series IX, 102-34.
Sharp criticism of J. H. Green for failure to make
available unpublished manuscripts left in his care. Comments on recorded but unavailable annotated volumes.

1288 MOKROCHEIR. 'Letters, Conversations, and Recollections'.
Notes and Queries, 4th Series VI, 500.
Query and response concerning edition.

1289 METHUEN, THOMAS ANTHONY. Autobiography, with a Memoir of his
eldest Son, Thomas Plumptre Methuen. London: Hatchards.
Repeats anecdotes printed 1845, with fuller account of
first meeting with Coleridge.

1290 NICHOLLS, J. F. 'Capt. Thomas James'. Bristol Biographies.
Bristol: privately printed, pp. 76-7.
Suggestion that James's account of Arctic voyage may
have been source for The Ancient Mariner, further developed
by Ivor James (1890), q.v.

1291   SMITH, GODWIN. 'Ecclesiastical Crisis in England'. North
        American Review [Boston], CX, 151–208.
            Coleridge noted as 'only' real theologian in the English
        Church.

1292   WHATELY, EDWARD. 'Personal Recollections of the Lake Poets'.
        Leisure Hour, XIX, 651–3.
            Version of Wordsworth's account of origins of The An-
        cient Mariner and of Coleridge's contribution to 'We Are
        Seven'.

1293   WIELAND, W. J. 'The Ancient Mariner; A New Version'. Tom
        Hood's Comic Annual, IV, 80–2. Illustrations.
            Parody.

                                1871

1294   Poetical Works of Samuel Taylor Coleridge. Edited with a
        critical memoir by William Michael Rossetti. London: E.
        Moxon. xxxii, 424 pp. Illustrated by Tho[ma]s Seccombe.
        Memoir reprinted William Rossetti. Lives of Famous Poets.
        London: E. Moxon Son & Co. (1878), pp. [237]–55.
            Biographical memoir (pp. ix–xxvii) criticizes Cole-
        ridge's lack of character, finds insufficient substance in
        the poetry.

1295   COLLIER, JOHN PAYNE. An Old Man's Diary, Forty Years Ago.
        2 vols. London: Thomas Richards.
            Anecdotes of Coleridge (I, 61–2, 90, 100) and comments
        (II, 80–2) on Coleridge's relation with wife.

1296   COLLINS, MORTIMER. ['Silas Tomkin Comberbatch']. Marquis and
        Merchant. 3 vols. London: Hurst and Blackett, III,
        206–7.
            Doggerel on Coleridge at Reading.

1297   DUNKIN, A. J. 'Parodies'. Notes and Queries, 4th Series
        VII, 105, 261.
            Query and reply by Stephen Jackson concerning 'Christa-
        bess' (1816).

1298   FIELDS, JAMES T. 'Barry Cornwall'. Yesterdays with Authors.
        23rd edition [1882]. Boston: Houghton, Mifflin,
        pp. [353]–419.
            Reports Procter's 1851 recollections of Coleridge
        (pp. 359–60), mentioning many names but few details.

1299   HUTTON, RICHARD HOLT. Essays Theological and Literary. 2
        vols. London: Strahan.
            Coleridge unfavourably compared with Wordsworth. His
        criticism of Wordsworth largely mistaken (II, 109, 123-4).

1300   JONES, HENRY BENCE. The Royal Institution. London: Longmans
        et al.
            Gives accounts (pp. 277, 284-5, 342) of Coleridge's
        proposed lectures for 1806, and lectures of 1808-9. Prints
        correspondence with Davy (pp. 333-7).

1301   J. R. B. 'Great Men Alluded to by Arnold in a sermon'. Notes
        and Queries, 4th Series VII, 209.
            Query and editorial reply concerning reference by Thomas
        Arnold.

1302   L'ESTRANGE, A. G. The Literary Life of the Reverend William
        Harness. London: Hurst and Blackett.
            Includes (pp. 142-4) recollections of Coleridge at
        Gillman's.

1303   LOWELL, JAMES RUSSELL. 'Chaucer'. My Study Windows. Boston:
        James R. Osgood and Company, pp. [227]-89.
            Coleridge (pp. 267-8) is praised for 'natural fineness
        of ear', but found ignorant of Elizabethan pronunciation.

1304   METEYARD, ELIZA. A Group of Englishmen (1795-1815). Being
        Records of the Younger Wedgwoods and Their Friends. Lon-
        don: Longmans et al.
            Discusses Wedgwoods' relations with Coleridge and in-
        cludes new material on their financial assistance.

1305   [OLIPHANT, MARGARET]. 'A Century of Great Poets, from 1750
        Downwards. No. IV-Samuel Taylor Coleridge'. Blackwood's
        Magazine, CX, 552-76. Reprinted Littell's Living Age
        [Boston], 4th Series XXIII (1871), 643-61; Eclectic Magazine
        [New York], New Series XV (1872), 138-57.
            Half biographical sketch, half critical discussion
        chiefly devoted to The Ancient Mariner, Christabel, and
        Love, Coleridge's three 'real and great poems'. Considers
        Coleridge a seer, and The Ancient Mariner a 'visionary
        voyage' from the visible to the invisible and back, an
        'unconscious allegory'. Christabel interpreted as 'Chris-
        tian romance'.
            Attribution: Coghill

1871-ROSSETTI

1306   ROSSETTI, W[ILLIAM] M[ICHAEL]. 'Shelley in 1812-1813'. Fort-
        nightly Review, New Series IX, 67-85.
            Includes comparison of Shelley's 'Devil's Walk' with The
        Devil's Thoughts (p. 73).

1307   [TOWLE, G. M.] G. M. T. 'Letter of Coleridge's'. Harper's
        New Monthly Magazine [New York], XLIII, 444-6.
            1817 letter to R[est] F[enner] 'full of poetic sensi-
        bility and sensitiveness'.

1308   WHIPPLE, EDWIN PERCY. 'Wordsworth'. Life and Literature.
        Boston: James R. Osgood, pp. [253]-302.
            Lecture includes comparison with Coleridge.

1309   YOUNG, JULIAN CHARLES. A Memoir of Charles Mayne Young, Tra-
        gedian, with Extracts from his Son's Journal. 2 vols.
        London, New York: Macmillan. Reprinted as 'Coleridge and
        Wordsworth'. Personal Reminiscences of Chorley, Planche,
        and Young. Ed. Richard Henry Stoddart. New York: Scrib-
        ner, Armstrong (1874), pp. 191-203.
            Includes (I, 173-86) important account of 1828 visit to
        Mrs. Aders in Godesberg during which Coleridge, Wordsworth
        and Dora Wordsworth were guests. Describes conversations
        with Coleridge and Wordsworth, a discussion between Cole-
        ridge and Schlegel, and compares Coleridge and Wordsworth
        as talkers and in their attitudes towards nature.

                            1872

1310   ALCOTT, A. BRONSON. Concord Days. Boston: Roberts Brothers.
            Two expressions (pp. 136-7, 246-9) of admiration and
        obligation. Coleridge 'the most stimulating of modern
        British thinkers'.

1311   BUCKLE, HENRY THOMAS. Miscellaneous and Posthumous Works.
        Ed. Helen Taylor. 3 vols. London: Longmans et al.
            Notes for an unwritten essay on 'the influence of German
        literature in England' (II, 217-9) mention Coleridge as
        guilty of 'great carelessness' but not intentional
        plagiarism.

1312   [FIELD, LEON C.]. 'Prince of Conversationalists'. Ladies
        Repository [New York], XXXII, 377-9.
            A biographical sketch emphasizing Coleridge's amazing
        effect on contemporaries, especially through conversation.
            Attribution: WPA Index to Early American Periodicals.

1313　FITZHOPKINS. 'Coleridge: Rabelais'. Notes and Queries, 4th
　　　　Series X, 225.
　　　　　　Query.

1314　FRERE, JOHN HOOKHAM. Works of the Right Honourable John Hook-
　　　　ham Frere. 2 vols. London: Basil Montagu Pickering. Re-
　　　　vised with additions, by W. E. Frere. 3 vols. London:
　　　　Basil Montagu Pickering (1874). Reviewed: no. 1320.
　　　　　　Volume I contains admiring comments on Coleridge's phi-
　　　　losophy and poetry.

1315　HARE, AUGUSTUS J. C. Memorials of a Quiet Life. 2 vols.
　　　　London: Strahan.
　　　　　　Brief account (II, 85-7) of J. C. Hare and Coleridge,
　　　　and of Coleridge's death (II, 93-4).

1316　HOLLAND, SIR HENRY. Recollections of Past Life. London:
　　　　Longmans et al.
　　　　　　Recalls (pp. 205-6) Coleridge as 'eloquent but intoler-
　　　　able' talker and criticizes his 'misty dogmas'.

1317　INGLEBY, C. M. 'Many-Sided Minds, Samuel Taylor Coleridge'.
　　　　British Controversialist, 3rd Series XXVII, 239-61; XXVIII,
　　　　81-98. Reprinted in his Essays. London: Trubner (1888),
　　　　pp. 190-250.
　　　　　　Culmination of Ingleby's various essays and notes on
　　　　Coleridge. Part one, 'the poet', begins with bibliography,
　　　　annotated genealogy, and scholarly biographical sketch.
　　　　Discussion of The Ancient Mariner, Christabel, and Love,
　　　　presents Coleridge as 'seer' whose 'inner vision of the
　　　　inward world' was 'simply provoked by outward objects'.
　　　　Part two, 'the divine', argues that Coleridge's philosophy
　　　　though fragmentary and derivative, had practical value.

1318　[LABOUCHÈRE, PETER ANTHONY] P. A. L. 'S. T. Coleridge'.
　　　　Notes and Queries, 4th Series IX, 358.
　　　　　　Slightly different version of Labouchère (1868), q.v.

1319　McVICKAR, WILLIAM A. Life of the Reverend John McVickar.
　　　　New York: Hurd and Houghton.
　　　　　　Recounts visit to Highgate in 1830, quotes Scott's opin-
　　　　ion of Coleridge, and gives circumstances of McVickar's
　　　　article in The Churchman (1833) and of his edition of Aids
　　　　to Reflection (1839).

1872-MERIVALE

1320   [MERIVALE, HERMAN]. 'The Works of John Hookham Frere'. Edin-
       burgh Review, CXXXV, 472-501.
          Suggests Frere may have influenced Kubla Khan which re-
       viewer misdates as 1816.
          Attribution: WI.

1321   MITFORD, MARY RUSSELL. Letters of Mary Russell Mitford:
       Second Series. Ed. Henry Fothergill Chorley. 2 vols.
       London: R. Bentley and Son.
          Letter of 1819 (I, 41) discusses Peacock's treatment of
       'my poor dear friend' in Nightmare Abbey.

1322   YONGE, CHARLES DUKE. 'Coleridge'. 'Three Centuries of Eng-
       lish Literature.' London: Longmans et al., pp. 269-77.
          Biographical sketch. Love quoted entire as Coleridge's
       'most perfect' lyric.

                              1873

1323   Aids to Reflection. Rev with a copious index...and transla-
       tion of the Greek and Latin quotations by Thomas Fenby.
       Liverpool: Edward Howell. xx, 395 pp.
          Adds biographical sketch and note on value of the work.

1324   Osorio. A Tragedy. As originally written in 1796. London:
       John Pearson.
          Includes R. H. Shepherd's 'monograph', q.v. (1873).

1325   ANON. 'Literary Notes'. Academy, IV, 363.
          Note on relation of Remorse and Osorio.

1326   _____. 'Rime of the Modern Shipowner'. Fun, New Series
       XXVII, 100.
          Parody.

1327   COLERIDGE, SARA. Memoir and Letters of Sara Coleridge. Ed.
       by her daughter [Edith Coleridge]. 2 vols. London:
       Henry S. King.
          Contains Sara's autobiographical memoir written as a
       letter to her daughter, and letters from 1833 onwards.
       Reviewed: [Richard Copley Christie?]. Athenaeum, No.
       2385 (12 July 1873), pp. 39-40 (attribution: Fahnestock);
       New York Times, No. 6894 (22 Oct 1873), p. 2; Spectator,
       No. 2361 (27 Sept 1873), p. 1213; Lippincott's Magazine
       [Philadelphia], XIII (1874), 390-1. See also 1345.

1328   DEVEY, J.   A Comparative Estimate of Modern English Poets.
          London: E. Moxon.
             Compares Coleridge and Wordsworth as poets (pp. 104-11).

1329   GIBBON, CHARLES.   The Casquet of Literature.   4 vols.   London:
          Blackie.
             Includes (III, 137) brief inaccurate biographical intro-
          duction to The Ancient Mariner.

1330   HALL, FITZ-EDWARD.   Modern English.   London: Trubner and Co.,
          New York: Scribner, Armstrong, and Co.
             Draws frequent examples of usage from Coleridge, and
          discusses his attitude to coinages (pp. 70-7).

1331   [KNIGHT, JOSEPH].   'Coleridge's Osorio.   Athenaeum, No. 2396
          (27 Sept), pp. 391-2.
             Brief textual history of Osorio with discussion of Cole-
          ridge's lyric and dramatic gifts.   The three major lyrical
          poems are 'the most absolutely dream-like compositions in
          literature'.
             Attribution: Fahnestock

1332   MILL, JOHN STUART.   Autobiography.   London: Longmans et al.
             Describes associations with 'the Coleridgians' (pp. 128,
          152), reading Coleridge (p. 153) who influenced Maurice and
          Sterling (p. 155), the times (p. 161); with general charac-
          terization of Mill's 1840 essay on Coleridge (p. 219).
          Quotes from Dejection and Work without Hope to describe own
          depressions (pp. 134, 140).

1333   MORLEY, HENRY.   'Samuel Taylor Coleridge'.   First Sketch of
          English Literature.   London: Cassell, Petter, & Galpin,
          pp. 876-9, 885.   Revised as A Manual of English Literature,
          thoroughly Revised by Moses Coit Tyler.   New York: Sheldon
          and Company (1879), pp. 623-4.
             Biographical sketch with chronology of work.

1334   NICHOLS, W. L.   The Quantocks and their Associations.   Bath:
          Printed for Private Circulation.
             Paper read to Bath Literary Club with familiar biograph-
          ical information on Coleridge and Wordsworth.

1335   PITMAN, ISAAC.   A Memorial of Francis Barham.   London: Fred.
          Pitman; Bath: I. Pitman, J. Davies; Truro: J. R. Nether-
          ton.
             Prints in phonetic alphabet three pieces by Barham con-
          cerning Coleridge (pp. 174-5, 224-8, 292-306).   Sees Cole-

1873-PITMAN

(PITMAN, ISAAC)
ridge's views similar to Barham's 'Alism', criticizes am-
bivalence in mysticism, and adapts ideas from Church and
State.

1336   SHEPHERD, R. H. 'A Monograph on Coleridge's Osorio'. Published in 1873 edition of Osorio (pp. v-xxii).
Discusses relation of Remorse to Osorio, but chiefly
concerned with production and critical reactions.

1874

1337   The Poetical Works of Samuel Taylor Coleridge. Ed. with an
introductory memoir by William B. Scott. London, New York:
G. Routledge. xxviii, 420 pp. Maclise frontispiece.
The memoir (pp. ix-xxviii) a derivative biographical
sketch.

1338   ANON. 'The Rime of the Ancient Statesman'. A Relic of the
Past Not By S. T. Coleridge. Cambridge: Henry W. Wallis.
15 pp.
Parody.

1339   BAILEY, JOHN EGLINGTON. The Life of Thomas Fuller, D. D.
London: Basil Montagu Pickering.
Several references to Coleridge passim. Notes (p. 498)
that last stanza of Lines Suggested by Berengarius derives
from Fuller's Abel Redivivus.

1340   BASCOM, JOHN. Philosophy of English Literature. New York:
Putnam.
Comments passim on nature and importance of Coleridge's
intellectual achievements.

1341   BROOKE, STOPFORD A. 'Coleridge'. Theology in the English
Poets. London: Henry S. King, pp. 60-92.
Discussion of Coleridge's early revolutionary enthusiasm, of his poetry of nature, and conception of relation
of nature to God and man.

1342   [DENNIS, JOHN] J. D. 'English Lyrical Poetry'. Cornhill
Magazine, XXIX, 698-719.
Coleridge foremost in lyric, especially in versifica-
tion.
Attribution: WI.

SAMUEL TAYLOR COLERIDGE: AN ANNOTATED BIBLIOGRAPHY

1343 [FRERE, SUSAN] S. F. 'On the Poet Coleridge'. The Works of
      the Right Honourable John Hookham Frere in Verse and Prose.
      3 vols. London: Basil Montagu Pickering, I, 269.
          Poem written by Frere's niece, giving, according to him,
      'perfect description' of Coleridge.

1344 LEBRETON, ANNA LETITIA. Correspondence of William Ellery
      Channing D. D. and Lucy Aikin, from 1826 to 1842. Boston:
      Roberts Brothers.
          Letters of 1834-1836 contain detailed discussion of
      Table Talk and Literary Remains expressing warm admiration,
      with some reservations.

1345 [MERIVALE, LOUISA]. 'Memoir and Letters of Sara Coleridge'.
      Edinburgh Review, CXXXIX, 44-68.
          Discusses Sara's editorial work and compares her theo-
      logical views with Coleridge's.
          Attribution: WI.

1346 'THE RUSTIC', pseud. 'The Fight of the Fifth November'.
      Shotover Papers [Oxford], I, 162.
          Undergraduate parody.

1347 RUSSELL, WILLIAM CLARK. 'Samuel Taylor Coleridge'. Book of
      Table-Talk. With Notes and Memoirs. London: George
      Routledge and Sons, pp. 280-91.
          Excerpts from Table-Talk prefaced by brief biography and
      description of Coleridge's conversation.

1348 STEPHEN, LESLIE. 'Mr. Maurice's Theology'. Fortnightly Re-
      view, XXI, 595-617.
          Maurice acted under a general impulse from Coleridge
      rather than a theological system (pp. 595-6), and was part
      of reaction against theology of preceding generation.

1349 TIMBS, JOHN. 'Samuel Taylor Coleridge'. Anecdote Lives of
      the Later Wits and Humourists. London: Richard Bentley
      and Son, pp. 85-126.
          Selection of previously published anecdotes.

1350 TOWLE, GEORGE M. 'Some Unpublished Letters of Samuel Taylor
      Coleridge'. Lippencott's Magazine [Philadelphia], XIII,
      697-710.
          Prints and explains letters of 1816-18 to Coleridge's
      publishers.

1874-WORDSWORTH

1351   WORDSWORTH, CHRISTOPHER. Social Life at the English Universi-
        ties in the Eighteenth Century. Cambridge: Bell.
           Excerpts from diary of Wordsworth's brother (1793) de-
        scribe Coleridge at Cambridge discussing Wordsworth and
        Bowles.

1352   WORDSWORTH, DOROTHY. Recollections of a Tour Made in Scotland
        A. D. 1803. Ed. J. C. Shairp. Edinburgh: Edmonston and
        Douglas.
           Coleridge mentioned often in first part of journal.
        Preface (pp. ix-xliv) describes Racedown meeting (p. xv).

                                1875

1353   ANON. 'Notes on Stillingfleet. By S. T. Coleridge'. Athe-
        naeum, No. 2474 (27 March), pp. 422-3.
           Marginalia from Poole's copy of Stillingfleet's Origines
        Sacrae (1675).

1354   _____. 'Wordsworth's Prose Writings'. Athenaeum, No. 2502
        (9 Oct), pp. 467-9.
           Mentions Wordsworth's contributions to The Friend.

1355   _____. 'Rime of the Ancient Premier'. Funny Folks, No. 36
        (14 Aug), p. 45.
           Parody.

1356   BALSTON, CHARLES. 'S. T. Coleridge's "Lay Sermon"'. Notes
        and Queries, 5th Series IV, 289, 377.
           Query concerning a quotation and an allusion answered
        by Ed. Marshall and C. P. E.

1357   BELL, G. C. 'Coleridge and Lamb'. Blue, III, 87-8.
           Describes Coleridge memorial sculpted by Woolner.

1358   BOUCHIER, JONATHAN. 'Coleridge's Knowledge of French'.
        Notes and Queries, 5th Series IV, 126, 312, 375-6.
           Two notes with intervening comment by William Black on
        Coleridge's knowledge of French.

1359   BRANDES, G[EORG MORRIS COHEN]. Naturalismen I England. Vol-
        ume IV of Hovedstromninger I Det 19de Aarhundreds Littera-
        tur. 6 vols. (1872-1890). Kjobenhavn: Gyldendal; vol.
        IV translated as Der Naturalismus in England. 4 vols. in
        2. Berlin: F. Duncker (1872-1896). Translated by Mary
        Morison as Naturalism in England. London: William
        Heinemann (1905).

                                186

(BRANDES, G[EORG MORRIS COHEN])
Chap. VII (pp. 111-131) on Coleridge offers somewhat
inaccurate account of his shift from radicalism to conservatism. Christabel 'first English poem permeated by the
genuine romantic spirit'. The Ancient Mariner praised for
realistic description, but criticized for 'romantic extravagance' and compared unfavourably with Moritz Hoffman's
'Der Camao'.

1360 CHILDERS, R. 'An Unpublished Letter of Coleridge'. Academy,
VII, 167-8. Reprinted Littell's Living Age [Boston], 5th
Series X, 191-2.
Prints 1814 letter to John Kenyon. Note (ibid., p. 215)
points to internal evidence that it was written in Bath.

1361 CLARKE, MARY COWDEN. 'Coleridge'. Gentleman's Magazine,
CCXXXIX, 324-7. Reprinted Littell's Living Age [Boston],
5th Series XII, 124-6. Reprinted in her Recollections of
Writers. London: Sampson Low and Company; New York: Charles
Scribner's Sons (1878), pp. 30-5, 63-4 and partially in My
Long Life. London: T. Fisher Unwin; New York: Dodd, Mead
and Company (1896), pp. 97-8.
Reports conversations at Ramsgate and Highgate, and
Coleridge's appearance. Brief account of lecture on The
Tempest.

1362 DILKE, SIR CHARLES WENTWORTH. The Papers of a Critic. 2
vols. London: John Murray.
Contains (I, 32) harsh comments about Coleridge in
Malta, obtained from a 'Mr. Underwood' in Paris.

1363 MOREHEAD, CHARLES, ED. Memorials of the Life and Writings of
the Reverend Robert Morehead, D. D. Edinburgh: Hamilton,
p. 102.
1799 letter from Jeffrey expresses enchantment with
'Lyrical Ballads' and praises The Ancient Mariner.

1364 MORGAN, NICHOLAS. The Skull and Brain: Their Indications of
Character and Anatomical Relations. Longmans et al.
A phrenological study using Coleridge among primary examples. Claims to have Coleridge's death mask and now
lost 1828 head cast.

1876–The Rime of the Ancient Mariner

1365   The Rime of the Ancient Mariner. London: Doré Gallery. 12
       p. 39 plates. Illustrated by Gustave Doré. Reprinted:
       New York: Harper Brothers (1877). Reviewed: Godey's
       Lady's Book and Magazine [Philadelphia], XCIV, 92.
       First appearance of Doré's illustrations.

1366   ANON. 'The Poetical Works of Coleridge and the Poetical Works
       of Shelley'. Academy, X, 563.
       Considers Religious Musings Coleridge's best poem.

1367   _____. 'Ye Rime of Ye Ancient Dowager'. Figaro, No. 686
       (23 Feb), p. 13.
       Parody, directed at Henry Irving.

1368   _____. 'Editor's Literary Record'. Harper's New Monthly Mag-
       azine [New York], LIV, 148.
       The Ancient Mariner (1876 edition) is seen as lawless,
       wild, and weird.

1369   BROOKE, REV. STOPFORD A. English Literature. London: Mac-
       millan and Co. Frequently reissued.
       Christabel, Kubla Khan, The Ancient Mariner, and Love
       (pp. 152-3) characterized by 'exquisite music' and 'imag-
       inative phantasy', and unique in our language.

1370   FORMAN, H. BUXTON. 'The Ancient Mariner'. Notes and Queries,
       5th Series V, 175.
       Query concerning sheets of Sibylline Leaves.

1371   FROTHINGHAM, OCTAVIUS BROOKS. Transcendentalism in New Eng-
       land. New York: G. P. Putnam's Sons.
       General account of basis for Coleridge's appeal to next
       generation in England and America with simplistic summary
       of his metaphysics (pp. 76-104).

1372   AN HABITUATE. Opium Eating. An Autobiographical Sketch.
       Philadelphia: Claxton, Remsen and Haffelfinger.
       After harrowing account of experiences as Civil War
       prisoner, the author describes his treatment with and ad-
       diction to opium. Chapters IX and XV and appendices dis-
       cuss Coleridge and De Quincey, defend Coleridge against
       critics and insist that Coleridge's achievements, despite
       addiction, give the author his only hope.

1373   HAYDON, BENJAMIN ROBERT. Benjamin Robert Haydon: Correspond-
       ence and Table-Talk. Ed. Frederic Wordsworth Haydon. 2
       vols. London: Chatto and Windus.

(HAYDON, BENJAMIN ROBERT)
Haydon's recollections of Coleridge's conversation (I,
110) and an account of his first meeting with Coleridge
after a 17 years lapse (II, 93).

1374   J.   'The Coleridge Family'.   Notes and Queries, 5th Series VI,
245.
This and sequel by 'Jabez' (p. 317) identify three books
written by Coleridge's father.

1375   JEWELL, ALFRED.   'The Ancient Mariner'.   Notes and Queries,
5th Series V, 89.
Request for variant stanzas answered by H. B. Forman
(pp. 174-5), 'W. M. T.' (p. 175), and 'J. W. E.'

1376   J. W. E.   'The Ancient Mariner'.   Notes and Queries, 5th Series V, 212.
A description of 1802 copy of Lyrical Ballads and various illustrations.   Responses by A. J. M., W. J. Bernard
Smith (p. 458) and Katherine Halliday (VI, 74-5).

1377   [KLIPSTEIN, AUGUST?].   'Characteristics of the Lake-School-
Poets'.   Jahresbericht über die höhere Burgerschule
[Freiburg i. Schlesien], II, 3-12.
Summarizes characteristics of Lake Poets as a group, but
notes Coleridge's distinction in 'the terrible and the
wonderful'.
Attribution: Haney

1378   LAMB, CHARLES.   The Life, Letters and Writings of Charles
Lamb.   Ed. Percy Fitzgerald.   6 vols.   London: E. Moxon.
Many references to Coleridge, especially in Lamb's correspondence (I, 287-429), (II, 1-25), and Fitzgerald's account (I, 207-14) of meeting.

1379   PAUL, C. KEGAN.   William Godwin: His Friends and Contempo-
raries.   2 vols.   London: Henry S. King.
Includes (II, 1-16) Godwin's correspondence with
Coleridge.

1380   SCHILLER, JOHANN CHRISTOPH FRIEDRICH VON.   Briefwechsel
zwischen Schiller und Cotta.   Herausgeben von Wilhelm Vol-
mer.   Stuttgart: J. G. Cotta.
Many letters from 1799-1800 (pp. 351, 395-8) concerning
translation of Wallenstein, with (pp. 406-8) description of
its various editions.

1876-THOMPSON

1381   THOMPSON, ROBERT ELLIS. 'Professor George Allen, LL. D.'.
       Penn Monthly [Philadelphia], VII, 562-83.
           Obituary. Allen came under influence of Coleridge
       through Marsh and (p. 564) read proof-sheets of Marsh's
       editions of Coleridge. Career was molded by the
       Coleridgeans.

1382   TODHUNTER, ISAAC. William Whewell. An Account of His Writ-
       ings. 2 vols. London: Macmillan and Co.
           Whewell (II, 195-6) objects to Hare's 1834 suggestion of
       a Coleridge Prize Essay at Cambridge.

                                1877

1383   La Chanson du Vieux Marin. Trans. A. Barbier. Paris: Li-
       braire Hachette. Illustrated by Gustave Doré.
           Poor translation preceded by inaccurate biography.

1384   Poetical and Dramatic Works. Ed. with a Memoir by R. H. Shep-
       herd. 4 vols. London: Pickering. Reissued with 16 p.
       supplement, London: Macmillan (1880).
           'Memoir' (I, ix-cxii) discusses textual problems and
       earlier editions.
           Reviewed: Academy, XI (1877), 247; [Richard Garnett],
       Athenaeum, No. 2583 (25 April 1877), p. 538 (attribution:
       Fahnestock). See also 1397, 1535.

1385   ANON. 'A Wily Card-Sharper'. Truth, I, 142-4.
           Parody.

1386   ARMSTRONG, EDMUND J. 'Coleridge'. Essays and Sketches. Ed.
       George Francis Armstrong. London: Longmans et al., pp.
       38-94.
           A well-informed but uncritical undergraduate prize
       essay--defends Coleridge 'as a man'.

1387   ARMSTRONG, GEORGE FRANCIS. Life and Letters of Edmund J.
       Armstrong. London: Longmans et al.
           Discusses (pp. 33-7) Coleridge's great influence on
       Armstrong.

1388   BOWRING, SIR JOHN. Autobiographical Recollections. London:
       Henry S. King and Co.
           Brief discussion of Coleridge, Southey, and Wordsworth
       (p. 356).

                                190

1389   [BOYLE, G. D.] G. D. B. 'Coleridge, Samuel Taylor'. Encyclopaedia Britannica. Ninth Edition. 25 vols. Edinburgh:
Adam and Charles Black, VI, 135-8.
     Affirms Coleridge's place as poet and concentrates on
his critical, philosophical, and political ideas. Apostrophe to 'the greatness of the services which he rendered
to philosophy and religion'.

1390   G. B. 'Lessing and Coleridge'. Notes and Queries, 5th Series
VIII, 164, 200, 276.
     Notes by 'B. B.', anonymous writer, and 'J. W. W.' on
relation of Names to Lessing's 'Die Namen', John Barnett's
musical setting, a variant version in Cottle, and possible
plagiarisms from Lessing.

1391   GREEN, T. H. 'A Critical Account of the Philosophy of Kant.
By Edward Caird'. Academy, 297-300.
     The last generation understood Kant chiefly through
Coleridge's erroneous impression (p. 297).

1392   HARINGTON, J. D. 'Coleridge. A Lecture Delivered at Kes-
wick'. Transactions of the Cumberland Association for the
Advancement of Literature and Science. Part II. Carlisle:
G. and T. Coward, pp. 191-210.
     Sketch of Coleridge's life and condensed summary of his
main ideas.

1393   H. G. C. 'Samuel Taylor Coleridge'. Notes and Queries, 5th
Series VII, 366; 5th Series VIII (1877), 97, 255; 8th Series VI (1895), 445.
     Four notes by 'H. G. C.' and John Pickford on Cole-
ridge's Kisses and the Latin original.

1394   J. 'Coleridge and Rabelais'. Notes and Queries, 5th Series
VIII, 289, 319.
     Query and reply by W. T. M. on location of Coleridge's
estimate of Rabelais.

1395   [λ], pseud. 'Epilogue to Coleridge's Tragedy, "Remorse"'.
Notes and Queries, 5th Series VIII, 348.

1396   LYNCH, THOMAS P. 'Samuel Taylor Coleridge'. Argonaut [San
Francisco], I, 134-50.
     Conventional biographical narrative notes quantity as
well as the importance of his work, his prose will outlive
his poetry.

1397   MacCARTHY, D. F. 'Unnoted Variations in the Text of Cole-
         ridge'. Athenaeum, No. 2596 (28 July), pp. 112-3.
              Variant readings not included in 1877 Pickering edition.

1398   MARTINEAU, HARRIET. 'Coleridge'. Autobiography. With Memo-
         rials by Maria Weston Chapman. 3 vols. London: Smith,
         Elder, I, 396-9.
              Harsh retrospective account of reverent pilgrimage to
         Highgate. Description of Coleridge and conversation.

1399   NODAL, J. H. 'Coleridge in Manchester'. Manchester Literary
         Club. Papers, III, 141-7.
              Recounts Coleridge's visits to Manchester in 1793 and
         suggests Owen's possible influence on Pantisocracy.

1400   _____. 'Coleridge in Manchester'. Notes and Queries, 5th
         Series VI, 161-2.
              Suggests Owen's possible influence on Pantisocracy.
         Hyde Clarke claims (VII, 217) Fulton more likely.
         O., J. W. W. (VII, 376) and John Bailey (VII, 311) give
         dates of Coleridge's Manchester visits.

1401   PERRY, THOMAS SARGEANT. 'German Influence in English Litera-
         ture'. Atlantic Monthly [Boston], XL, 129-47.
              Assesses Coleridge's role in introducing German philos-
         ophy to England (pp. 130-5, 137).

1402   PROCTER, BRYAN WALLER. Autobiographical Fragment and Bio-
         graphical Notes. Ed. [Coventry Patmore] C. P. London:
         George Bell and Sons.
              Impressions (pp. 137-48) of Coleridge's appearance,
         learning, and conversation.

1403   QUESNEL, LEO. 'Les Poètes Modernes de l'Angleterre. Cole-
         ridge'. La Revue Politique et Littéraire [Paris], 2nd Se-
         ries XIII, 219-24.
              Sympathetic biographical and critical sketch. Discusses
         French and German translations.

1404   SHAW, THOMAS B. 'Samuel Taylor Coleridge'. A Complete Manual
         of English Literature. Ed. with notes and illustrations,
         by William Smith, with a sketch of American Literature by
         Henry T. Tuckerman. New York: Sheldon & Company, pp.
         425-7.
              Brief biography, with longer account of his literary
         character and works, with emphasis on Shakespearean lec-
         tures and Wallenstein. The Ancient Mariner 'wild, mysti-
         cal, phantasmagoric'. Love receives usual star-billing.

1405 VENABLES, EDMUND. 'Coleridge's Fly-Catchers'. Athenaeum, No.
      2614 (1 Dec), p. 699.
          Recalls and describes Coleridge's notebooks from visits
      with Hare. Remembers passages on Gospels and Old Testament
      miracles.

1406 WARD, C. A. 'Job's Luck'. Notes and Queries, 5th Series VII,
      367.
          Query concerning possible sources in John Owen and
      Cocquard.

                            1878

1407 ANON. 'The Ancient Mariner--The Wedding Guest's Version of
      the Affair from his Point of View'. Funny Folks.
          Parody. Reprinted Hamilton, V, 116-7. Original not
      located.

1408 _____. 'A Frantic Englishman'. Truth, III, 624-6.
          Parody of The Ancient Mariner.

1409 [BETHAM-EDWARDS, MATILDA BARBARA] M. B. E. 'Letters of Cole-
      ridge, Southey, and Lamb to Matilda Betham'. Fraser's Mag-
      azine, New Series XVIII, 73-84. Reprinted Littell's Living
      Age [Boston], 5th Series XXIII (1878), 416-26; and in her
      Six Life Studies of Famous Women. London: Griffith & Farran
      (1880), pp. 240-57.
          Brief account of Matilda Betham and letters of 1808-09,
      of which two from Mrs. Coleridge and one from Southey de-
      scribe Coleridge's appearance.

1410 DOWDEN, EDWARD. 'The Transcendental Movement and Literature'.
      Studies in Literature 1789-1877. London: C. Kegan Paul and
      Co., pp. 44-84.
          Brief comments on Coleridge, especially influence on
      Victorian theology.

1411 HARRISON, W. H. 'Notes and Reminiscences. Coleridge'. Uni-
      versity Magazine, XCI, 537-8.
          Coleridge's appearance and manner at lecture Harrison
      attended as a boy.

1412 MOZLEY, J. B. Essays Historical and Theological. 2 vols.
      London: Rivingtons.
          Brief reference (p. xxviii) to Coleridge's 'uncandid
      use' of Jeremy Taylor in Aids.

1413   ST. QUENTIN, pseud. 'Three Friends of Mine: De Quincey,
       Coleridge, and Poe'. Canadian Monthly and National Review
       [Toronto], XIII, 359-65.
         A purple effusion on 'friends' known through books.

1414   TOWNSEND, A. CATO. 'Samuel Taylor Coleridge at Highgate'.
       Aesthetic Review, Nos. 11, 12 (Dec - Jan 1878), 172-4.
       Highly inaccurate sketch.

1879

1415   ANON. 'Personal Reminiscences...By An American Friend'.
       Complete Works of Charles Lamb. Philadelphia: William T.
       Amies, pp. xxi-xxxii.
         Sentimental fictionalized biography of Coleridge. No
       first-hand material.

1416   BAYNE, PETER B. Lessons from my Masters, Carlyle, Tennyson,
       and Ruskin. London: James Clarke.
         Discusses Carlyle's view of Coleridge's influence on
       Sterling.

1417   DESHLER, CHARLES D. Afternoons with the Poets. New York:
       Harper and Brothers.
         Includes brief discussions of Coleridge's sonnets (pp.
       216-20) and Bowles's influence (pp. 180-3).

1418   DOWDEN, EDWARD. 'Waifs and Strays of S. T. Coleridge and
       Wordsworth'. Academy, XV, 523.
         Notes omission from 1877 Pickering edition.

1880

1419   The Poetical Works of S. T. Coleridge, Reprinted from the
       early editions, with memoir, notes, etc. The Lansdowne
       Poets. London: Frederick Warne and Company.
         Conventional biography and critical hyperboles on Cole-
       ridge's 'magic wand of genius', and 'ecstatic vision'.

1420   ANON. 'Coleridge Books in Professor Green's Library'. Athe-
       naeum, No. 2757 (28 Aug), pp. 273-4.
         Lists annotated books now in the British Museum.

1421   CALVERT, GEORGE H. 'Coleridge'. Coleridge, Shelley, Goethe, Biographic Aesthetic Studies. Boston: Lee and Shepard, pp. 11-123.
          Biographical account with (p. [9]) sonnet 'to Coleridge'. Calvert's tutor at Göttingen, Benecke, remembered Coleridge as an opium eater (p. 77).

1422   CHURCH, R[ICHARD] W[ILLIAM]. 'William Wordsworth'. English Poets. Selections with Critical Introductions by Various Writers. Ed. Thomas Humphry Ward. 4 vols. London, New York: Macmillan and Company, IV, 1-15.
          Coleridge's superiority to Wordsworth as interpreter of Wordsworth's poetry. Reviewed: B[asil] L. G[ildersleeve]. American Journal of Philology [Baltimore], II (1881), 105-6.

1423   FITZPATRICK, W. J. 'Samuel Taylor Coleridge'. Notes and Queries, 6th Series II, 42-3, 153.
          Query and reply by 'R. R.' on relation of Love to 1799 'Introduction to the Tale of the Dark Ladie'.

1424   GARRIGUES, GERTRUDE. 'Coleridge's Ancient Mariner'. Journal of Speculative Philosophy [St. Louis], XIV, 327-38.
          Reading of poem as allegory of mental and spiritual voyage. Fall and salvation through renunciation.

1425   H. K. 'Coleridge's Epigram'. Notes and Queries, 6th Series I, 77, 279.
          Query, and replies by A. P. A., R. R. and William Pengelly.

1426   INGRAM, J. H. 'Coleridge's Nom de Guerre'. Notes and Queries, 6th Series II, 148.
          Query on correct form of name assumed in Dragoons. Wilmott Dixon (p. 259) and William Platt (p. 477) offer incorrect answers.

1427   JONES, WILLIAM. Credulities Past and Present. London: Chatto and Windus.
          Coleridge's albatross, harbinger of good fortune (p. 12). His spectre-barque and dread crewman (p. 85) discussed as instances of bird-omens and apparitions at sea.

1428   LATHROP, GEORGE PARSONS. 'Coleridge as Poet and Man'. Atlantic Monthly [Boston], XLV, 483-98.
          Discusses nature of Coleridge's sensibility and argues that his imagination works upon inner experience rather than nature, history, or fable.

1880-PATER

1429   PATER, WALTER HORATIO. 'Samuel Taylor Coleridge'. The Eng-
        lish Poets. Selections with Critical Introductions by
        Various Writers. Ed. Thomas Humphry Ward. 4 vols. Lon-
        don, New York: Macmillan and Company, IV, 102-14.
            Introduction combined with part of Pater's 1866 review
        of Cottle to form essay 'Coleridge' in Appreciations
        (1889), q.v. for annotation.
            Reviewed: Athenaeum, No. 2278 (22 Jan 1881), pp. 127-8.

1430   PEABODY, ELIZABETH PALMER. Reminiscences of Rev. William El-
        lery Channing. Boston: Robert Brothers.
            Washington Allston's brother-in-law met Coleridge in
        1823 (pp. 70, 76-7), was deeply impressed: 'the study of
        him is good for the mind' (p. 143).

1431   POLLOCK, FREDERICK. Spinoza. His Life and Philosophy. Lon-
        don: C. Kegan Paul & Co.
            Discusses (pp. 399-403) Coleridge's view of Spinoza and
        his role in creating audience for his works.

1432   STEPHENS, JAMES BRUNTON. 'The Power of Science'. Miscella-
        neous Poems. London: Macmillan and Co., pp. 134-41.
            Parody of Love.

1433   WATTS, W. THEODORE. 'Thomas Chatterton'. English Poets.
        Selections with Critical Introductions by Various Writers.
        Ed. Thomas Humphry Ward. 4 vols. London, New York: Mac-
        millan and Company, III, 400-21.
            Coleridge shows Romantic characteristics popularized by
        Chatterton.

                                1881

1434   ARNOLD, MATTHEW. Poetry of Byron. Chosen and arranged by
        Matthew Arnold. London: Macmillan and Co.
            Coleridge's poetry (pp. vii-xxi) is 'equal, if not su-
        perior, to anything of Byron or Wordsworth,' although a
        'poet and philosopher wrecked in a mist of opium'.

1435   CARLYLE, THOMAS. Reminiscences. Ed. James Anthony Froude.
        2 vols. London: Longmans, Green and Co.
            Several brief judgmental comments on Coleridge, with
        longer account of visits with Coleridge, Irving, and
        Montagu (I, 230-2). Reviewed: William Wallace, Academy,
        XIX (1881), 181-2; Athenaeum, No. 2786 (19 Nov 1881), pp.
        387-9.

SAMUEL TAYLOR COLERIDGE: AN ANNOTATED BIBLIOGRAPHY

1436 CONWAY, MONCURE D. 'English Lakes and their Genii'. Harper's New Monthly Magazine [New York], LXII, 161–77.
Comments (p. 162) on Anti-Jacobin caricatures of Coleridge, Lamb, and Lloyd. Compares Lloyd with Coleridge.

1437 DOWDEN, EDWARD. 'S. T. Coleridge's France: An Ode'. Academy, XIX, 395.
Gives textual variant and a source in Samson Agonistes.

1438 ____. 'S. T. Coleridge's Monody on the Death of Chatterton'. Academy, XIX, 374.
Notes 1794 publication of poem.

1439 FORMAN, H. BUXTON. 'Coleridge's Editors and Critics. Athenaeum, No. 2782 (19 Feb), p. 264.
Note on text of recent editions.

1440 GILFILLAN, GEORGE. Sketches Literary and Theological. Ed. Frank Henderson. Edinburgh: David Douglas.
'Coleridge' (pp. 1–5) an appreciation of Coleridge's influence on the author. 'Coleridge on Thomas Campbell' (pp. 41–5) defends Campbell against Coleridge's criticism in Literary Remains.

1441 [HASELL, ELIZABETH JULIA]. 'A Talk about Odes'. Blackwood's Magazine, CXXIX, 783–802.
Discusses examples by Coleridge.
Attribution: WI.

1442 ROSSETTI, DANTE GABRIEL. 'Samuel Taylor Coleridge'. Ballads and Sonnets. London: Ellis and White, p. 315.
Sonnet.

1443 SCHIPPER, J[AKOB]. Englische Metrik in historicher und systematischer Entwickelung Dargestellt. 2 vols. Bohn: Strauss.
Illustrative discussion of numerous Coleridge poems, plans, translations. Fuller comments on metre of Christabel (II, 245–8).

1444 SCOTT, WILLIAM BELL. 'Inedited Poems by S. T. Coleridge'. Athenaeum, No. 2778 (22 Jan), p. 133; No. 2779 (29 Jan), pp. 163–4; No. 2782 (19 Feb), p. 246.
Exchange between Scott, R. H. Shepherd and H. B. Forman on publication of Mad Monk, To Miss Brunton, and Tears of a Grateful People.

1881-SHAIRP

1445   SHAIRP, JOHN CAMPBELL. 'Modern English Poetry'. Aspects of Poetry, Being Lectures Delivered at Oxford. Oxford: Clarendon.
        Draws on Coleridge's criticism of Wordsworth, and finds qualities of Christabel innovative.

1446   TAYLOR, SIR HENRY. 'Carlyle's Reminiscences'. Nineteenth Century, II, 33-8.
        Compares (p. 34) Carlyle's impressions of Coleridge's talk with four long excerpts from diary of 1824 and 1829 giving his own more favourable impressions.

1447   THRUPP, FREDERICK. The Antient Mariner and the Modern Sportsman. London: James Martin. 27 pp.
        Uses poem to attack blood sports.

1882

1448   ANON. 'The January Magazines'. Argus [Melbourne], No. 11158 (24 March), p. 7.
        Summary of Helen Zimmern's 1882 article, notes Coleridge's anti-French prejudice.

1449   _____. 'Coleridge's Flycatchers'. Oracle, VI, 274.
        Query and reply concerning Coleridge's notebooks.

1450   _____. 'S. T. Coleridge and Mary Evans'. Oracle, VI, 234.
        Query and reply.

1451   _____. 'Rime of the Potent Minister'. Punch, LXXXII, 129.
        Parody.

1452   _____. 'A Shrivelled Londoner'. Truth, XII, 620-2.
        Parody of The Ancient Mariner.

1453   BRANDL, A[LOIS]. 'Coleridge's Early Commonplace-Book'. Academy, XXII, 152.
        Description of notebook and plan to publish.

1454   CAINE, T. HALL. Recollections of Dante Gabriel Rossetti. London: E. Stock.
        Extensive account (pp. 146-66) of discussions with Rossetti concerning Coleridge whom both warmly admired. Aspects of Christabel considered in some detail.

1455 CLIFF, DAVID YENDELL. 'Coleridge's Marginalia'. Bibliographer, II, 86.
Marginalia from Tabulae Linguarum, 1793.

1456 COTTERILL, H. B. 'Coleridge'. An Introduction to the Study of Poetry. London: Kegan Paul, Trench and Co., pp. 179-207.
Biographical sketch. Brief comments on several poems. Christabel interpreted as allegory of human nature.

1457 FENTON, G. L. 'Spiritual Philosophy, By the Late Joseph Henry Green'. Notes and Queries, 6th Series VI, 186-7.
Query (repeated in 1884 and 1893) concerning Green's interpretation of Coleridge.

1458 FOX, CAROLINE. Memories of Old Friends, Being Extracts from the Journals and Letters of Caroline Fox. Ed. Horace N. Pym. London: Smith Elder and Co.
Friend of Derwent, Hartley, and Sterling, reports second-hand anecdotes.

1459 FROUDE, JAMES ANTHONY. Thomas Carlyle: A History of the First Forty Years of His Life, 1795-1835. 2 vols. London: Longmans et al.
Several harsh references to Coleridge in letters.

1460 GRAVES, ROBERT PERCIVAL. Life of Sir William Rowan Hamilton. 3 vols. Dublin: Hodges Figgis and Co.
Hamilton, a friend of Wordsworth and admirer of Coleridge. Account of meeting with Coleridge, 'personal notes' on him, letters from Coleridge to Hamilton, and from Wordsworth, Viscount Adare, and Aubrey de Vere concerning Coleridge.

1461 GREGORY, J. H. 'Coleridge's Marginalia'. Argus [Melbourne], No. 11159 (25 March), p. 10.
Reports annotated copy of Swedenborg. Authenticity denied by Higham (1899).

1462 O. 'On the Centenary of the Entry into Christ's Hospital of Samuel Taylor Coleridge'. Blue, X, 168.
Poem to Coleridge, 'Knight of Gentleness and Truth'.

1463   OLIPHANT, MRS. MARGARET. The Literary History of England in
       the End of the Eighteenth and Beginning of the Nineteenth
       Century. 3 vols. London: Macmillan and Co.
           Chapter VI-VII (I, 199-248) in part revision of author's
       1871 essay, but include more comparison with Southey and
       Wordsworth.

1464   SCHERR, J. History of English Literature. Translated from
       the third German edition by M. V. London: Sampson Low,
       Marston, Searle, and Rivington.
           Chapter on 'the Lake School' (pp. 208-18), discusses
       importance to literary relations between England and Ger-
       many of visit of Coleridge and Wordsworth. The Ancient
       Mariner exemplifies Coleridge's fondness for the wild and
       strange.

1465   SWINBURNE, ALGERNON CHARLES. 'After Looking into Carlyle's
       Reminiscences'. Sonnets of Three Centuries: A Selection.
       Ed. Hall Caine. London: Elliot Stock, pp. 208-9. Re-
       printed in Tristram of Lyonesse and Other Poems. London:
       Chatto and Windus (1882), pp. 214-6.
           Sonnet speaks of Coleridge, Wordsworth and Lamb 'whose
       names and words endure for ever'.

1466   WELSH, ALFRED H. Development of English Literature and Lan-
       guage. 2 vols. Chicago: S. C. Griggs and Company; Lon-
       don: Trubner Co.
           A conventional description of Coleridge (II, 277-80)
       with extracts illustrating 'weird', 'awful', 'inexpress-
       ible', 'gorgeous' quality of poems.

1467   [ZIMMERN, HELEN]. 'Coleridge Marginalia, Hitherto Unpub-
       lished'. Blackwood's Magazine, CXXXI, 107-25. Reprinted
       Littel's Living Age [Boston], CLII, 356-69.
           Description of annotations, in volumes acquired by
       British Museum from Green's library.
           Attribution: WI.

                                    1883

1468   Lectures and Notes on Shakspere and Other English Poets. Now
       first collected by T. Ashe. Bohn's Libraries. London:
       George Bell and Sons. xi, 552 pp.
           Preface based on reports of Collier and Crabb Robinson.
       Reviewed: Nation [New York], XXXIX (1884), 420-1; and
       Nos. 1470, 1487, 1492.

1469 ANON. 'Coleridge at Clevedon'. Oracle, X, 690.
      Query and reply.

1470 _____. 'Coleridge as Thinker and Critic. Lectures and Notes
      on Shakspere. By S. T. Coleridge'. Spectator, No. 2896
      (29 Dec), pp. 1700-1.
          Argues, contra Arnold, Coleridge's superiority to
      Joubert, compares him with Goethe, but rejects his inter-
      pretation of Hamlet.

1471 [AUSTIN, E.]. E. A. 'Coleridge and Swedenborg'. Morning
      Light, VI, 517-8.
          Describes William Mason's rejection of Coleridge's offer
      to write life of Swedenborg.

1472 BELL, CHARLES D. 'Samuel Taylor Coleridge'. Churchman, IX,
      93-114. Reprinted in his Some of Our English Poets. Lon-
      don: Elliot Stock (1895), pp. 205-44.
          Biographical sketch concludes (pp. 108-14) with a gen-
      eral discussion of the poems.

1473 CAINE, T. 'Coleridge'. Cobwebs of Criticism. London: El-
      liot Stock, pp. 54-87.
          Contrasts critical attacks during Coleridge's lifetime
      with posthumous eulogies. Defends Coleridge against
      charges of egotism and obscurity.

1474 CAMPBELL, J. DYKES. 'Lessing and Coleridge'. Notes and Que-
      ries, 6th Series VIII, 195.
          Continues discussion of Names begun by 'G. B.' in 1877.
      Describes ms version of the poem and incorrectly identifies
      its original place of publication. He is corrected by John
      Pickford (pp. 395-6) and 'R. R.' (p. 396).

1475 DENNIS, JOHN. Heroes of Literature. English Poets. A Book
      for Young Readers. London: Society for Promoting Chris-
      tian Knowledge.
          A biographical account of Coleridge (pp. 322-5) based
      on Shepherd (1877).

1476 HALL, S. C. 'Recollections of Authors I Have Known'. Retro-
      spect of a Long Life From 1815-1883. 2 vols. London:
      Richard Bentley & Son, II [2]-11.
          Describes visits to Highgate and Coleridge's
      conversation.

1883-HAVERFIELD

1477   HAVERFIELD, F.   'Coleridge and Spenser'.   Notes and Queries,
          6th Series VIII, 206.
             Passage in Christabel resembles lines from The Faerie
          Queene, and has been 'copied' by Byron in Childe Harold.

1478   INGLEBY, C. M.   'A Passage in Christabel'.   Academy, XXIII,
          99.
             Refutes Hall Caine's 1882 interpretation of Christabel,
          line 424.   Further argument by H. T. Mackenzie Bell (p.
          116) and Samuel Waddington (p. 135).

1479   SHORLAND, GEORGE LIVERMORE.   'Coleridge'.   Times, No. 30831
          (28 May), p. 4.
             Letter concerning neglect of Coleridge's tomb and pro-
          posed bust in Westminster Abbey.

1480   SIMPSON, A. L.   'The Poem and David Scott's Illustrations'.
          The Rime of the Ancient Mariner, Illustrated by David
          Scott, R. S. A. With a life of the artist by A. L. Simpson.
          London: T. Nelson and Sons, pp. 35-62.
             Detailed discussion of Scott's plates.   Considers Scott
          'the Coleridge of British painters'.

1481   STEPHENS, W. R. W.   Memoir of the Right Hon. William Page
          Wood, Baron Hatherley.   2 vols.   London: Richard Bentley
          and Son.
             Diary for 1828-29 describes visits to Coleridge and com-
          ments on his opinions.

                              1884

1482   The Poems of Samuel Taylor Coleridge.   With a Prefatory No-
          tice, Biographical and Critical.   Ed. Joseph Skipsey.
          Canterbury Poets.   London: Walter Scott. viii, 294 pp.
             Prefatory notice (pp. [9]-31) a conventional account.

1483   The Table Talk and Omniana of Samuel Taylor Coleridge.   Ed.
          T. Ashe.   London: George Bell and Sons.   xix, 446 pp.
             Adds items from Allsop (1836) to 'Table-Talk', and mar-
          ginalia from Southey's Omniana.   Reviewed: Academy, XXVI
          (1894), 427; Nonconformist and Independent, New Series No.
          254 (6 Nov 1884), pp. 2-3; Athenaeum, No. 2984 (3 Jan
          1885), p. 13.

1484   'Unpublished Letters from Samuel Taylor Coleridge to the Rev.
        John Prior Estlin. Communicated by Henry A. Bright.'
        Philobiblon Society. Miscellanies, XV, 1-117.
            Correspondence between 1796 and 1814.

1485   A. 'Coleridge as a Dramatist'. Theatre, New Series III,
        135-40.
            Compares Remorse to Heine's Almansor as romance, and
        discusses individual characters.

1486   ANON. 'Notes'. Critic [New York], I, 35.
            Announcement by Hall Caine of a (never published) edi-
        tion of Coleridge's prose.

1487   _____. 'Coleridge as a Poetical Critic'. Nation [New York],
        xxxix, 420-1.
            Acid criticism of Lectures and Notes on Shakspere
        (1883). Qualified praise of Coleridge as critic.

1488   _____. 'Coleridge's Intellectual Influence'. Spectator, No.
        2938 (18 Oct), pp. 1370-1. Reprinted in Littell's Living
        Age [Boston], 5th Series XLVIII (1884), 433-6; Eclectic
        Magazine [New York], New Series XXXIX (1884), 823-5.
            Challenges Traill's 'slighting estimate'. Argues that
        Coleridge's influence was great, but exerted chiefly
        through scattered comments.

1489   _____. 'Mr. Traill's Coleridge'. Spectator, No. 2938
        (18 Oct), pp. 1374-5.
            Criticizes Traill's weak treatment of Coleridge's
        thought.

1490   _____. 'Parodies of Portions of The Ancient Mariner'. Truth,
        XVI, 421-2.
            Eleven prize-winning parodies.

1491   _____. [Remorse]. Under the Clock: A Weekly Journal for
        Playgoers. No. 14 (30 April), p. 5.
            Account of Beck's recital of Thicke's version of Remorse
        in 1884.

1492   _____. 'Belles Lettres'. Westminster Review, CXXI, 594-618.
            Lectures and Notes on Shakspere (1883) show sureness
        of judgment and philosophical method.

1493   ATKINS, KATE.   'Notes of a Lecture on Coleridge by the Hon.
       Roden Noel'.   Cheltenham Ladies College Magazine, No. 60
       (Feb), pp. 269-76.
           Reports enthusiastic but superficial lecture on Cole-
       ridge's poetry and thought.

1494   [BADGLEY, JONATHAN]   Uncle Jonathan, pseud.   Walks in and
       Around London.   London: C. H. Kelly.
           Conventional account of Coleridge (pp. 140-4) at High-
       gate.
           Attribution: NUC Pre-1956 Imprints.

1495   BIRRELL, AUGUSTINE.   'Truth-Hunting'.   Obiter Dicta.   First
       Series.   London: E. Stock, pp. 98-124.
           Lamb compared with Coleridge (p. 105) 'whose fame is in
       all the churches' but who was 'an unlovely character'.

1496   [BRADLEY, EDWARD]   Cuthbert Bede, pseud.   'Coleridge's Re-
       morse'.   Notes and Queries, 6th Series IX, 466.
           Notes Beck's recent performances.
           Attribution: See Bradley (1852).

1497   CAMPBELL, J. DYKES.   'A Sonnet by S. T. Coleridge: A Passage
       in the Biographia Literaria'.   Athenaeum, No. 2949 (3 May),
       pp. 566-7.
           Textual variant on Sonnet to Miss Barbour.

1498   CLARKE, F. L.   'Lamb and Coleridge'.   Golden Friendships.
       Sketches of the Lives and Characters of True and Sincere
       Friends.   London: W. Swan Sonnenschein and Co., pp.
       160-88.
           Sentimental account.

1499   COLERIDGE, ERNEST HARTLEY.   'Notes and News'.   Academy, XXVI,
       292, 432.
           Announces preparation of biographical memoir of Cole-
       ridge and requests information concerning letters.   In
       reply, Brandl asserts his priority and regrets E. H. Cole-
       ridge's decision.

1500   COOKE, GEORGE WILLIS.   'The Influence of Coleridge'.   Critic
       [New York], New Series II, 13-14.
           Coleridge a major and living influence, especially in
       theology.   Lists materials concerning Coleridge which
       should be made available.

1501   COX, THOMAS. 'Hartley Coleridge'. Notes and Queries, 6th Se-
       ries IX, 389.
          Query concerning Coleridge and Hartley. Replies by
       J. H. Nodal (pp. 473-4) and J. D. Campbell (p. 474).

1502   DÖHN, RUDOLF. 'Samuel Taylor Coleridge'. Das Magazin für die
       Literatur des Ind- und Auslandes [Berlin], LIII, 449-51.
          Biographical sketch written for fiftieth anniversary of
       Coleridge's death.

1503   FENTON, G. L. 'Green's Spiritual Philosophy'. Notes and Que-
       ries, 6th Series X, 454.
          Repeats his 1882 query, q.v.

1504   FROUDE, JAMES ANTHONY. Thomas Carlyle. A History of His Life
       in London 1834-1881. 2 vols. London: Longmans et al.
          Sustained journal references to Table Talk and charac-
       terization of Coleridge (I, 45-6).

1505   G. G. 'Coleridge's Tomb'. Notes and Queries, 6th Series X,
       108.
          Thinks mistakenly that he remembers seeing Coleridge's
       face through a glass plate set in the coffin.

1506   [GATHORNE-HARDY, GATHORNE, EARL OF CRANBROOK] Cranbrook.
       'Christopher North'. National Review, III, 151-60.
          'Memorandum of Conversations' (written 1843) includes
       Wilson's comments on Remorse and Wallenstein, Coleridge's
       conversation, and his explanation of Coleridge's break with
       Wordsworth.
          Attribution: WI.

1507   GRAY, JOHN M. David Scott. Edinburgh, London: William
       Blackwood. Illustrations.
          Discussion and description (pp. 16, 17) of Scott's il-
       lustrations to The Ancient Mariner (pl. 11, 12). Compari-
       son with Paton's.

1508   HAZLITT, W. CAREW. 'Coleridge Abroad'. Offspring of Thought
       in Solitude. London: Reeves and Turner, pp. 1-22.
          Coleridge in Germany and Malta.

1509   HIGGINSON, THOMAS WENTWORTH. Margaret Fuller Ossoli. Ameri-
       can Men of Letters. Boston: Houghton, Mifflin and Company.
          Brief accounts of her reading Coleridge (p. 69), writing
       on him (pp. 290-2) and hearing (p. 223) from Miss Martineau
       gossip concerning his family.

1884-HOFFMAN

1510 HOFFMAN, FREDERICK A. Poetry. Its Origins, Nature, and History. 2 vols. London: Thurgate and Sons.
Fulsome evaluation of Coleridge's genius (I, 375-91).
The Ancient Mariner and Kubla Khan have a 'mystic unreal
character'. Love poetry combines Petrarch and Shakespeare.

1511 [HUTTON, RICHARD HOLT]. 'Truth-Hunting'. Spectator, No. 2927
(2 Aug), pp. 1008-9.
Reply to Birrell (1884), defends Coleridge and describes
his influence and England's intellectual debt.
Attribution: Tener

1512 LE BRETON, ANNA LETITIA AIKIN. Memories of Seventy Years.
Ed. Mrs. Herbert Martin. London: Griffin and Farrar.
Account of meeting with Coleridge in 1804 (pp. 77-8).
Mrs. Martin recalls another meeting, where Coleridge talked
on female characters in Shakespeare.

1513 RUSSELL, A[DDISON] P[EALE]. 'The Conversation of Coleridge'.
Characteristics, Sketches and Essays. Boston: Houghton
Mifflin, pp. 1-22.
Collection of reprinted accounts.

1514 STRACHEY, EDWARD. 'Coleridge and Mr. Traill'. Spectator, No.
2940 (1 Nov), pp. 1437-8.
Letter challenges Traill's underestimation of Coleridge's intellectual influence.

1515 THICKE, FRANK E. Remorse, Arranged for the Modern Stage.
Frome: J. Wheller. 55 pp.
Text of recitation given by Beck in 1884, with his
programme notes.

1516 TRAILL, H. D. Coleridge. English Men of Letters. London:
Macmillan and Co. xi, 211 pp.
Concise survey of Coleridge's life and work presents him
as major critic and during annus mirabilis unique if limited poet. Lower estimate of Coleridge's metaphysics and
theology. Unfavourable comparison with Wordsworth on critical and moral grounds. Adopts Carlyle's view of conversation and influence. Short section of Green's Spiritual
Philosophy. Reviewed: Hall Caine. Academy, XXVI (1884),
263-5; Critic [New York], New Series II (1884), 278-9; Nation [New York], XXXIX (1884), 549; Saturday Review, LVIII
(1884), 601-2; Spectator, No. 2938 (18 Oct 1884), pp.
1374-5.

1517   W. M. 'Coleridge the Poet at Clevedon'. Notes and Queries,
          6th Series IX, 115-6.
              Query concerning dates. Replies from C[lement] M.
          I[ngleby], George Potter, and Edward Malan.

1518   WATTS, ALARIC ALFRED [JR.]. Alaric Watts. A Narrative of
          His Life. 2 vols. London: Richard Bentley.
              Accounts of Coleridge by Mrs. Watts and J. Anster. Re-
          port of Wordsworth's view of Christabel as 'an indelicate
          poem'. Text of letters from Coleridge to Watts.

1519   WATSON, LUCY E. 'Mr. Traill's Coleridge'. Spectator, No.
          2940 (1 Nov), p. 1480.
              Gillman's granddaughter challenges Traill's assertion
          that Coleridge was an opium addict to the end. Cites Mrs.
          Gillman and evidence of post-mortem.

                        1885

1520   Miscellanies Aesthetic and Literary, To which is added the
          Theory of Life. Collected and arranged by T. Ashe. Lon-
          don: George Bell and Sons. Bohn's Libraries. ix, 442pp.
          Reviewed: Critic [New York], V (1885) 104; Saturday Re-
          view, LX (1885), 357-8.

1521   Poetical Works of Samuel Taylor Coleridge. Edited with Intro-
          duction and Notes by T. Ashe, B.A. 2 vols. London:
          George Bell and Sons. Frontispiece, Vol. I, Drawing by
          Hancock; Vol II, Greta Hall. Aldine Edition. I, clxxxvi,
          1-212; II, xiii, 1-409 pp.
              Long biographical memoir (xv-cxxvi), detailed but dif-
          fuse account of bibliography of poems (cxxxviii-clxxxvi)
          and discussion (cxxvi-cxxxviii) of 'Coleridge as a poet'.
          Enumerates Coleridge's poetic virtues, considers skill in
          versification. Shortcoming is 'unidealized' autobiography.
          Reviewed: Athenaeum, No. 3003 (16 May 1885), p. 629; T.
          Hall Caine, Athenaeum, No. 3011 (11 July 1885), pp. 48-9;
          Spectator, No. 2981 (15 Aug 1885), pp. 1076-7. See also 1691.

1522   ANON. 'Notes'. Critic [New York], VI, 263.
              Lists names of those at unveiling of Coleridge memorial.

1523   _____. 'Mr. Lowell's Address on Coleridge'. Literary World
          [Boston], XVI, 188-9.

1885–ANON.

1524   ANON. 'Coleridge's Bust Unveiled'. New York Times, XXXIX,
       No. 10508 (8 May), p. 1.
       Account of ceremony in Westminster Abbey.

1525   _____. 'The Admiralty Goose; or, The Modern Mariner'. Punch,
       LXXXVIII, 249.
       Political satire.

1526   _____. 'Samuel Taylor Coleridge'. Pictorial World, No. 143
       (21 May), pp. 133–5.
       Sketches of Poets' Corner, Thorneycroft bust and North-
       cote portrait. Describes Coleridge's memorial and compares
       him with Shakespeare.

1527   _____. 'News of the Week'. Spectator, No. 2967 (9 May),
       p. 599.
       Note of Coleridge's memorial with account of Lowell's
       speech.

1528   _____. 'The Canonization of Coleridge'. Saturday Review.
       LIX, 607; Reprinted Critic [New York], V (1885), 261–2.
       Lowell's speech at Westminster Abbey compared with
       those of Lord Coleridge, Lord Houghton, and Canon Farrar.
       Coleridge, 'one of the most remarkable men England has
       produced, deserved canonization'.

1529   _____. 'Coleridge and Westminster Abbey'. Times, No. 31434
       (30 April), p. 9.
       Notice concerning unveiling of Coleridge memorial.

1530   _____. 'Ye Ancient Father Thames'. Truth, XVIII, 178–9.
       Parody involving the shocking state of the river.

1531   ARDEN, MAURICE. Undercurrent and Afterglow. An Elegy of
       England. London: G. Bell & Sons; Clifton: J. Baker and
       Son.
       Six poems (pp. 75, 85–94) on Coleridge.

1532   BONAR, JAMES. 'Coleridge's Notes to Malthus'. Notes and
       Queries, 6th Series XII, 206, 274, 412.
       Notes with comment from Edmond Tew (p. 274) show Sou-
       they's 1803 review of Malthus consists largely of Cole-
       ridge's marginalia.

1533   BROWNING, ROBERT. 'Sketch of A Conversation between Cole-
       ridge and Kenyon'. Academy, XXV, 104.
       Text of Kenyon's account, now in Browning's possession,
       of Coleridge's differentiation among aesthetic terms.

1534 [CAMPBELL, J. D.] J. D. C. 'Coleridge and Leigh Hunt'.
     Notes and Queries, 6th Series XI, 65.
          Brief discussion of Hunt's failure to publish anything
     on occasion of Coleridge's death.

1535 CAMPBELL, J. DYKES. 'Coleridge, Lamb, Leigh Hunt, and Others
     in The Poetical Register'. Athenaeum, No. 2994 (14 March),
     pp. 344-5.
          Variants in Coleridge's poems.

1536 COURTHOPE, WILLIAM JOHN. 'The Liberal Movement in English
     Literature. V--Poetry, Music, and Painting: Coleridge
     and Keats'. National Review, V, 504-18. Reprinted The
     Liberal Movement in English Literature, London: John Mur-
     ray (1885), pp. 159-94.
          Coleridge's best poetry characterized by musical rather
     than logical unity. Coleridge combines 'isolated weird and
     romantic images in a sharp elfin metre'.

1537 DAVIES, J. LLEWELYN. 'The Bust of Coleridge'. Spectator,
     No. 2968 (16 May), pp. 641-2.
          Information on Dr. Mercer's financing of Coleridge
     memorial.

1538 DAWSON, GEORGE. 'The Poetry of S. T. Coleridge'. Biographi-
     cal Lectures. Ed. George St. Clair. London: Kegan Paul,
     Trench & Co., pp. 308-57.
          Lecture, delivered some years earlier, finds Coleridge
     inferior to Wordsworth and Shelley. But best poetry pro-
     duces effects like those of music. The Ancient Mariner a
     dream with effect like ghost story.

1538A DARRELL, JOYCE. 'Christobel'. Argosy, XL, 46-67, 123-42.
          Modern dress conclusion to Christabel in prose.

1539 AN ENGLISHMAN. 'Lowell and Coleridge'. Spectator, No. 2968
     (16 May), p. 642.
          Compares patriotic feelings of Coleridge and Lowell.

1540 FAHIE, J. J. 'Songs of the Pixies'. Notes and Queries, 6th
     Series XI, 324.
          Gives identity of fairy queen in Songs of the Pixies.

1541 HUTTON, LAURENCE. 'Samuel Taylor Coleridge'. Literary Land-
     marks of London. London: T. Fisher Unwin, pp. 56-60.
          Collection of anecdotes, mostly from published sources.

1885–KING

1542   KING, ALICE. 'Samuel Taylor Coleridge'. Argosy, XL, 116–22.
         Conventional biographical sketch.

1543   LOWELL, JAMES RUSSELL. 'Mr. Lowell on Coleridge'. Times,
         No. 31441 (8 May), p. 4. Reprinted Critic [New York], VI
         (1885), 249–50; in his Democracy and Other Addresses, Bos-
         ton, New York: Houghton Mifflin (1887), pp. 89–103.
            Eulogistic address includes general praise of Coleridge
         as critic and poet.

1544   MASON, EDWARD T. 'Samuel Taylor Coleridge'. Personal Traits
         of British Authors. New York: Charles Scribner's Sons,
         pp. [55]–109.
            Sympathetic sketch of 'the most distinguished talker of
         his time'. Largely extracts.

1545   'MODERN SHARP', pseud. 'Ye Ancient Mariner'. W. Hamilton
         gives Detroit Free Press (31 Jan 1885), which proves incor-
         rect. Correct reference not found.

1546   PATTISON, MARK. Memoirs. Ed. Mrs. Pattison. London: Mac-
         millan and Company.
            Influenced (p. 164) by Aids while Oxford undergraduate
         in 1837.

1547   [PROTHERO, ROWLAND]. 'English Men of Letters...Coleridge. By
         H. D. Traill'. Edinburgh Review, CLXII, 301–51. Reprint-
         ed Littell's Living Age [Boston], CLXVII (1885), pp. 515–
         41.
            Less review than independent biographical essay with
         concise discussions of Coleridge's various roles as poet,
         critic, metaphysician, and theologian.
            Attribution: WI.

1548   RHYS, ERNEST. 'A Little Academe'. Gentleman's Magazine,
         CCLIX, 371–89.
            Cottage at Nether Stowey, Alfoxden and unveiling of
         memorial.

1549   STEVENSON, ROBERT LOUIS. 'On Style in Literature: Its Tech-
         nical Elements'. Contemporary Review, XLVII, 548–61. Re-
         printed as 'On Some Technical Elements of Style in Litera-
         ture' in his Later Essays. 28 vols. Edinburgh: Longmans
         et al. (1895), III, 236–60.
            Brief analysis (p. 558) of sound patterns in first five
         lines of Kubla Khan.

1550   TAYLOR, HENRY. Autobiography of Henry Taylor 1800-1875. 2
        vols. London: Longmans et al.
            Character of Wulfstan the Wise in his play Edwin the
        Fair (I, 165) is modeled on Coleridge. Comments (I,
        188-91) on Wordsworth and Coleridge, both of whom he knew.

1551   TRAILL, H. D. 'A Pious Legend Examined'. Fortnightly Review,
        New Series XXXVII, [223]-33.
            Answer to Strachey (1884) and Tulloch (1885), both q.v.
        Challenges their conclusions on Coleridge's religious
        importance.

1552   TULLOCH, JOHN. 'Coleridge and His School'. Movements of Re-
        ligious Thought in Britain during the Nineteenth Century.
        London: Longmans et al., pp. 1-40.
            Coleridge's theological influence was pervasive and
        admirable.

1553   _____. 'Coleridge as a Spiritual Thinker'. Fortnightly Re-
        view, New Series XXXVII, 11-25. Reprinted Eclectic Maga-
        zine [New York], CIV (1885), 305-15; Littell's Living Age
        [Boston], 5th Series, XLIX (1885), 557-66.
            Discusses Coleridge's importance as 'spiritual' influ-
        ence and impact of Aids and Confessions on nineteenth
        century religious ideas.

1554   TYRER, C. E. 'The Genius of Coleridge'. Manchester Quarter-
        ly, XV, 201-38.
            Divides Coleridge's poems into three chronological pe-
        riods. Argues there is little in first to prepare for
        second.

1555   [WATTS-DUNTON, THEODORE] T. H. 'Poetry'. Encyclopaedia
        Britannica. 9th Edition. Edinburgh: Adam and Charles
        Black, XIX, 256-73. Reprinted in his Poetry and the
        Renascence of Wonder. London: Herbert Jenkins (1916),
        pp. [3]-232.
            Coleridge discussed among the 'pure lyrists', Shelley,
        Keats, Hugo and others.

1886

1556   ANON. 'A Prize Declamation entitled "The Desire of Posthumous
        Fame is Unworthy a Wise Man". By S. T. Coleridge'. Chan-
        ticleer [Cambridge], No. 2 (Lent Term), pp. 29-32.
            Description of Coleridge's prize-winning Latin declama-
        tion with brief account of its background.

1886-ANON.

1557 ANON. 'Highgate Literary and Scientific Institution'. North
      Middlesex Chronicle, No. 920 (6 March), p. 6; No. 921
      (13 March), p. 3; No. 922 (20 March), p. 6.
          Account of lectures by Henry Morley on Coleridge at
      Highgate, emphasizing use of opium.

1558 _____. 'Lay of Modern Millinere'. Punch, XC, 57.
          An imitation with gloss and drawings, protesting the use
      of feathers in hats.

1559 BAILEY, JAMES. 'The Rime of the Antient Missionere'. York-
      shire Weekly Post [Leeds], No. 12320 (24 Dec), p. 12.
          Parody.

1560 BRANDL, ALOIS. Samuel Taylor Coleridge und die Englische
      Romantik. Strassburg: Karl J. Trubner. xiii, 437 pp.
      Index. Trans. Lady Eastlake. London: John Murray (1887).
      Frontispiece. Vandyke Portrait. Reprinted New York:
      Haskell House (1966).
          Biography. Chapter on Coleridge in Germany of some
      continuing value. Work as a whole contains errors which
      are much compounded in the translation. Reviewed: C. H.
      Herford, Academy, XXX (1886); XXXI (1887), 321-2, 376,
      416; Athenaeum, No. 3112 (18 June 1887), pp. 791-4; [Mar-
      garet Oliphant, Alexander Allardyce, R. K. Douglas],
      Blackwood's Magazine, CXLII (1887), 235-53 (attribution:
      WI.); Murray's Magazine, I (1887), 863; Pall Mall Gazette,
      XLVI, No. 7030 (28 Sept 1887), pp. 2-3; [Coventry Patmore],
      St. James's Gazette, XIV, No. 2190 (13 June 1887), p. 7;
      Spectator, No. 3101 (3 Dec 1887), pp. 1660-1. See also
      1582, 1793.

1561 DOWDEN, EDWARD. The Life of Percy Bysshe Shelley. 2 vols.
      London: Kegan Paul, Trench and Co.
          Notion that Raisley Calvert rather than Coleridge was
      'noticeable man with large grey eyes' in Wordsworth's
      'Castle of Indolence' (p. 210) and general view of Cole-
      ridge (p. 225) criticized by Hall Caine in Academy (1886,
      371-4). Caine answered by Dowden (Academy, 1886, 395-6)
      and restated his case in next issue (p. 412).

1562 JOHNSON, CHARLES F. 'Coleridge'. Temple Bar, LXXVIII, 35-54.
      Reprinted in his Three Americans and Three Englishmen. New
      York: Thomas Whittaker (1886), pp. 41-87; Eclectic Maga-
      zine [New York], CVII (1886), 778-90.
          Psychological interpretations of The Ancient Mariner,
      Christabel, and Wanderings of Cain. Coleridge's opposition
      to 18th century materialism, philosophical relevance, and

(JOHNSON, CHARLES F.)
literary criticism reveal own insight rather than merely
German influence.

1563 LEE, EDMUND. Dorothy Wordsworth. The Story of A Sister's
Love. London: James Clarke & Co. Revised edition, 1894.
Coleridge's life in relation to, and through the eyes
of, the Wordsworths. Reviewed: Athenaeum, No. 3070
(28 Aug), pp. 266-7.

1564 NICHOLSON, CORNELIUS. Wordsworth and Coleridge: Two Parallel
Sketches. A Lecture Delivered at Ambleside. June 1886.
[Ambleside]: n. p. 28 pp.
Coleridge 'the most powerful thinker of his day'. Cole-
ridge spiritualistic, naturalistic.

1565 [PATMORE, COVENTRY]. 'Great Talkers. I. Coleridge'. St.
James's Gazette, XII, No. 1802 (13 March), pp. 6-7. Reprinted in his Courage in Politics and Other Essays, London: Oxford University Press (1921), pp. 70-4.
Favourable evaluation of Table-Talk, especially Coleridge's enduring political comments.

1566 TIMBS, JOHN. Anecdotes About Authors and Artists. London:
Diprose & Bateman.
Anecdotes of Coleridge, all included in his 1874
collection.

1887

1567 Rime of the Ancient Mariner. Illustrations by Gustave Doré
and Sir Joseph Noel Paton. Ed. Alfred Trumble. New York:
Pollard & Moss.
Contains two essays on composition and reception of poem
and on illustrations, contrasting Doré's 'gypsy freedom'
with Paton's supposed 'ripe knowledge'.

1568 [ABBOTT, EVELYN]. 'Peacock'. Temple Bar, LXXX, 35-52.
Sharp defence of Coleridge's poetry and revival of phi-
losophy and theology, against Peacock's caricature of Mr.
Flosky in Nightmare Abbey (pp. 39-40).
Attribution: WI.

213

1569   AINGER, ALFRED. 'Coleridge's Ode to Wordsworth'. Macmillan's
       Magazine, LVI, 81-7. Reprinted Littell's Living Age [Bos-
       ton], 5th Series, LIX (1887), 42-7; in his Lectures and Es-
       says. 2 vols. London: Macmillan (1905), II, 95-113.
           Notes relation between Coleridge's Dejection and Words-
       worth's Intimations Ode. Coleridge's ode thought to be
       addressed to Wordsworth.

1570   ANON. Literary Celebrities. London, Edinburgh: W. & R.
       Chambers.
           Sketch of Wordsworth (pp. 7-73) includes relations with
       Coleridge.

1571   _____. 'The Old Meeting, Birmingham'. Birmingham Daily Post,
       No. 9013 (18 May), p. 4. Reprinted Hanson (1938), p. 445.
           Report of 1796 canvassing visit to Birmingham.

1572   _____. 'Coleridge and Swedenborg'. Morning Light, X, 325-6.
           Comment on Coleridge's opinions of Swedenborg.

1573   BLEIBTREU, KARL. Geschichte der Englischen Literatur. Leip-
       zig: Wilhelm Friedrich.
           Negative view of Coleridge as 'sleep walker' whose poems
       'dissolve into a dream world'. Considers German influence
       and Coleridge's conservatism.

1574   BOURNE, HENRY R. FOX. 'Coleridge Among the Journalists'.
       Gentleman's Magazine, CCLXIII, 472-87. Reprinted in his
       English Newspapers. Chapters on the History of Journalism.
       2 vols. London: Chatto and Windus (1887), I, 264-5,
       296-304, 309-12. Partially reprinted Queries Devoted to
       Literature [Buffalo, New York], IV (1888), 139-40.
           Accounts of Coleridge's work for The Morning Chronicle,
       The Morning Post and The Courier. Largely drawn from
       Stuart's 1838 articles in Gentleman's Magazine.

1575   CABOT, JAMES ELLIOT. A Memoir of Ralph Waldo Emerson. 2 vols.
       Boston, New York: Houghton, Mifflin and Co.
           Emerson letter (I, 161-2) and lecture (II, 723-4) show
       Coleridge's increasing influence.

1576   CAINE, HALL. Life of Samuel Taylor Coleridge. London: Wal-
       ter Scott. 154 pp.
           Often inaccurate account without critical comment or
       documentation. Extensive primary and secondary bibliogra-
       phy by John P. Anderson (pp. i-xxi). Reviewed: George
       Cotterill, Academy, XXXI (1887), 122-3; Athenaeum, No. 3096
       (26 Feb 1887), p. 286; Literary World [New York], XVIII

(CAINE, HALL)
(1887), 219; Spectator, No. 3061 (26 Feb 1887), pp. 293-5;
and nos. 1582, 1593.

1577   [CAINE, THOMAS HALL] T. H. C. 'Coleridge'. Celebrities of
       the Century. Ed. Lloyd C. Sanders. London: Cassell & Co.
          Conventional biographical sketch, pp. 210-2; Reviewed:
       Academy, XXXI (1887), 122-3.

1578   CAMPBELL, J. DYKES. 'Christabel'. Notes and Queries, 7th
       Series IV, 368, 412-23.
          Two notes and replies by J. M. Cowper (VI [1888], 130)
       and 'C. C. B.' (VI [1888], 194), concerned with possible
       origins of the name 'Christabel'.

1579   _____. 'Coleridge's Lectures of 1811-12'. Notes and Queries,
       7th Series III, 6-7.
          Hunt's Examiner contains well-reported notes on lectures
       IX and XIV, not included in Ashe (1883).

1580   CAMPBELL, J. D. 'London Magazine'. Athenaeum, No. 3104
       (23 April), p. 546.
          Criticism and correction of Wotton (1887), q.v.

1581   DOUGLAS, EILDON. 'Coleridge's Ode "Dejection"'. Academy,
       XXXI, 398.
          Identifies Wordsworth as 'Lady' in Dejection.

1582   [EASTLAKE, ELIZABETH]. 'Samuel Taylor Coleridge'. Quarterly
       Review, CLXV, 60-96.
          Sketch of Coleridge's life and survey of his work, al-
       though ostensibly review of biographies, including her
       translation of Brandl (1886).
          Attribution: WI.

1583   GARNETT, RICHARD. 'Coleridge'. Atalanta, I, 106-10.
          A general estimate in journal for 'Young Ladies'.

1584   GRESWELL, WILLIAM. 'Coleridge and the Quantock Hills'. Mac-
       millan's Magazine, LVI, 413-20.
          Descriptions of the Quantocks, Alfoxden, and Nether
       Stowey. Brief comments on Coleridge's poems with Quantock
       setting.

1585   [HIGHAM, CHARLES] Bibliophile, pseud. 'Coleridge and Sweden-
       borg'. Morning Light, X, 361.
          Questions understanding of Swedenborg displayed in Table
       Talk.

SAMUEL TAYLOR COLERIDGE: AN ANNOTATED BIBLIOGRAPHY

1887-HOLMES

1586   HOLMES, OLIVER WENDELL. 'Our Hundred Days in Europe'. At-
       lantic Monthly [Boston, New York], LX, 213-25. Partially
       reprinted as 'The Great Dogmatists' in Critic [New York],
       XI (1887), 71.
           Comments on contemporary adulation of Coleridge.

1587   JESSOPP, AUGUST. 'Books that Have Helped Me'. Forum [Phila-
       delphia], IV, 29-37.
           Describes impact, in 1844, of Coleridge's prose writings,
       especially Aids, which came as 'a new revelation'.

1588   KNIGHT, WILLIAM. Memorials of Coleorton. 2 vols. Edinburgh:
       David Douglas.
           Correspondence between the Beaumonts and Coleridge,
       Wordsworth, Southey and Scott.
           Reviewed: Hall Caine. Academy, XXXII (1887), 399-400;
       Athenaeum, No. 3134 (19 Nov 1887), pp. 667-9; Critic [New
       York], XI (1887), 334; Saturday Review, LXIV (1887),
       710-11; Spectator, No. 3101 (3 Dec 1887), pp. 1656-7. See
       also 1595, 1598.

1589   LOCKHART, C., tr. Wallenstein: A Dramatic Poem. London,
       Edinburgh: Blackwood.
           Attacks Coleridge in introduction. Reviewed: no. 1601.

1590   MASON, JAMES. 'A Gallery of Illustrious Literary Characters'.
       Leisure Hour, XXXVI, 690-5.
           Discussion of Goethe, Carlyle, and Coleridge with ex-
       tracts from favourable and unfavourable contemporary
       opinions.

1591   MORRILL, JUSTIN S. 'Samuel Taylor Coleridge'. Self-
       Consciousness of Noted Persons. Boston: Ticknor and Co.
           Discusses Coleridge (p. 138) as self-centered
       monologist.

1592   OLIVER, EDWIN. 'Our Regimental Mess. (With An Apology to
       Coleridge.)' Squibs. London: London Literary Society,
       pp. 43-5.
           Parody.

1593   [PATMORE, COVENTRY]. 'Coleridge'. St. James's Gazette, XIV,
       No. 2115 (16 March), p. 7. Reprinted in his Courage in
       Politics and Other Essays. London: Oxford University
       Press (1921), pp. 84-8.
           Review of Caine (1887). Coleridge's poems are of almost
       unapproachable perfection. Considers Coleridge's influence
       in politics and religion. Compares him with Newman.

216

1594   ____. 'Crabbe and Shelley'. St. James's Gazette, XIV, No.
        2091 (16 Feb), p. 6. Reprinted in his Principle in Art.
        London: George Bell and Sons (1898), pp. 123-8.
           Shelley and Crabbe diverge from Coleridge's 'true poetic
        reality'.

1595   ____. 'Memorials of Coleorton'. St. James's Gazette, XV,
        No. 2341 (6 Dec), p. 7. Reprinted in his Courage in Poli-
        tics and Other Essays. London: Oxford University Press
        (1921), pp. 92-7.
           Letters show Coleridge's admirable morality and justify
        separation from his wife.

1596   SAUNDERS, FREDERICK. 'Coleridge'. The Story of Some Famous
        Books. London: Elliot Stock, pp. 135-41.
           Brief, derivative discussion of The Ancient Mariner,
        composition of Kubla Khan, Coleridge's use of opium, and
        originality of Hymn Before Sunrise.

1597   [STEPHEN, LESLIE] L. S. 'Coleridge, Samuel Taylor'. The
        Dictionary of National Biography. London: Smith, Elder
        and Company. 63 vols. and supplements (1885-1909). XI,
        302-17.
           A concise, judicious, documented biographical account,
        followed by relatively brief evaluations of Coleridge's
        work and influence. Coleridge best in poetry of dreams.
        Acknowledges intellectual influence, sees philosophical
        contribution as introduction of German metaphysics to
        England.

1598   [WOODBERRY, GEORGE EDWARD]. 'Wordsworths and the Beaumonts'.
        Nation [New York], XLV, 487-9. Revised as 'The Coleorton
        Papers'. Atlantic Monthly [Boston], LXI (1888), 270-4; as
        'Sir George Beaumont, Coleridge, and Wordsworth' in his
        Studies in Letters and Life. Boston, New York: Houghton,
        Mifflin and Co. (1891), pp. 188-208. Reprinted in his
        Makers of Literature, New York: Macmillan (1900); Burt
        Franklin (1970), pp. 250-70.
           Discusses Coleridge's character as seen mainly in 1803
        letters to Beaumonts. 'Marred by disease and moral feeble-
        ness' he produced nothing of value after this date.

1599   [WOTTON, MABEL E.] M. E. W. 'With An Old Magazine'. Temple
        Bar, LXXIX, 567-74.
           1807 meeting of Henry Cary with Coleridge, who admired
        his Dante translation.
           Attribution: WI.

1888

1600   ANON.   'Samuel Taylor Coleridge'.   Co-operative News and Jour-
       nal of Associated Industry, XIX, 400–41.
           'Lecture' for a home study course.

1601   _____.   'Belles Lettres'.   Westminster Review, CXXIX, 660–5.
           Defends Coleridge against Lockhart's 1887 charges of ex-
       cessive liberties as translator.

1602   BARNETT, JOHN FRANCIS.   The Ancient Mariner (Der alte Matrose).
       London: Novello, Ewer and Co. vi, 231 pp.
           Cantata with text by Freiligrath.

1603   [CAMPBELL, J. DYKES] J. D. C.   'Coleridge on Cary's Dante'.
       Athenaeum, No. 3141 (7 Jan), p. 17.
           Account of Coleridge's 1817 meeting with Cary.   Prints
       part of marginalia to Cary's Paradiso.

1604   _____.   'Coleridge Marginalia Hitherto Unpublished'.   Athe-
       naeum, No. 3154 (7 April), p. 435; No. 3165 (23 June),
       pp. 795–6.
           Brief description, with extracts, of annotations in
       Grew's Cosmologia Sacra (1701) and Jahn's History of the
       Hebrew Commonwealth (1829).   Notes Coleridge used Jahn in
       Church and State.

1605   CAMPBELL, J. DYKES.   'Coleridge's Remorse'.   Notes and Que-
       ries, 7th Series VI, 385.
           Notes variant stage directions to Act V of Remorse in
       Shepherd's 1877 edition.

1606   _____.   'The 1828 Edition of Coleridge's Poems'.   Athenaeum,
       No. 3150 (10 March), pp. 307–8; No. 3151 (17 March),
       pp. 339–40; No. 3153 (31 March), p. 405; No. 3154 (7April),
       p. 437.
           Exchange with Ashe and Cobden-Sanderson concerning
       textual authority of 1829 edition.

1607   [CAMPBELL, J. D.] J. D. C.   'Scott on Coleridge's Wallen-
       stein'.   Notes and Queries, 7th Series VI, 308, 491.
           Request with further information in a second note for
       explanation of Coleridge's reference in Friend to Scott's
       praise of Wallenstein.   Answered by Bouchier (p. 372) and
       Yardley (7th Series VII, 73–4).

SAMUEL TAYLOR COLERIDGE: AN ANNOTATED BIBLIOGRAPHY

1608 GRAVES, R. T. 'Coleridge's Opium-Eating'. Athenaeum, No.
3143 (21 Jan), pp. 85-6.
Recalls Wordsworth's opinion that Coleridge first used
opium for pain.

1609 GROVE, G[EORGE]. 'Coleridge's Notes'. Athenaeum, No. 3155
(14 April), pp. 470-1; No. 3158 (5 May), 566-7. Partially
reprinted Littell's Living Age [Boston], 5th Series LXII
(1888), 380-2.
Some supposedly unpublished verses and notes, with a reply by J. D. Campbell.

1610 HAMILTON, WALTER. 'Samuel Taylor Coleridge'. Parodies of
Works of English and American Authors. 6 vols. London:
Reeves and Turner, V, 107-37.
Fifty-three parodies chiefly of The Ancient Mariner or
Christabel, some discussion and historical background.

1611 KNIGHT, WILLIAM. Principal Shairp and His Friends. London:
John Murray.
Discusses Coleridge and his life-long influence on
Shairp (pp. 114, 208, 245, and passim).

1612 LINTON, ELIZA LYNN. 'Irresponsibilities of Genius'. Fortnightly Review, New Series XLIV, 521-36.
Scathing attack on Coleridge for opium and family neg-
lect, contrasted with Thomas Colley Grattan, Disraeli, and
Wordsworth.

1613 LLOYD, JOHN H. History, Topography, and Antiquities of Highgate. Highgate: on behalf of the Literary Fund. Portrait
by G. Dawe.
Describes (pp. 318-44) Coleridge's tomb and places as-
sociated with him. Reminiscences and anecdotes. Modest
bibliography.

1614 OLIPHANT, MARGARET. Memoir of the Life of John Tulloch. London and Edinburgh: Blackwood.
Tulloch a constant reader of Coleridge, where his
thought always started (pp. 437-8).

1615 PITMAN, ROBERT C. 'Books That Have Helped Me'. Forum [Phila-
delphia], IV, 604-11.
Aids has power (pp. 604-5) to make ideal life real.

1616   SANDFORD, MRS. HENRY. Thomas Poole and His Friends. 2 vols.
       London, New York: Macmillan and Co.
       Written by Poole's cousin, book gives detailed account
       of his life-long friendship with Coleridge. Includes
       Poole's poem to Coleridge (I, 125-6) and many letters. Re-
       viewed: Academy, XXV (1888), 105-6; Athenaeum, No. 3192
       (29 Dec 1888), pp. 871-3; [Margaret Oliphant], Blackwood's
       Magazine, CXLV (1889), 431-3 (attribution: WI.); Book Mart
       [New York], VI (1889), 529-36; Critic [New York], XV
       (1889), 1; Gentleman's Magazine, CCLXVI (1889), 431-5; Lon-
       don Quarterly Review, New Series XII (1889), 229-40, re-
       printed Littell's Living Age [Boston], 5th Series LXVIII
       (1889), 213-9; Nation [New York], XLVIII (1889), 181-2;
       Spectator, No. 3163 (9 Feb 1889), p. 202-3. See also 1623,
       1633.

1617   STEPHEN, LESLIE. 'S. T. Coleridge'. Reflector, I, 300-9.
       Reprinted in his Hours in a Library, 3 vols. London:
       Smith, Elder & Co. (1892), III, 339-68.
       Lecture takes Coleridge and Bentham as the 'two centres
       of intellectual light in England'. Traces Coleridge's in-
       tellectual biography, and blames opium for lack of
       accomplishment.

1618   TAYLOR, HENRY. Correspondence of Henry Taylor. Ed. Edward
       Dowden. London: Longmans et al.
       Taylor's description of Coleridge and letter from Sou-
       they concerning Table Talk.

1619   TRENCH, RICHARD CHENEVIX. Letters and Memorials. Ed. M[aria]
       Trench. 2 vols. London: Kegan Paul and Co.
       Letters to Sterling, Maurice and Kemble (I, 134, 165) on
       Coleridge's influence.

1620   TROLLOPE, T. A. 'Marginalia by S. T. Coleridge'. Notes and
       Queries, 7th Series VI, 501-2.
       Excerpts from Coleridge's marginalia in Fuller's Wor-
       thies. 'R. R.' requests (VII, 35) unexcerpted version.

1621   WAUGH, FRANCIS G. 'Lines by Coleridge'. Athenaeum, No. 3144
       (28 Jan), p. 116; No. 3145 (4 Feb), p. 147; No. 3146
       (11 Feb), p. 179.
       Hitherto unpublished poem To a Child followed by minor
       controversy over accuracy of transcription.

1889

1622   Critical Annotations by S. T. Coleridge. Being Marginal Notes
       Inscribed in Volumes Formerly in the Possession of Cole-
       ridge. Ed. William F. Taylor. Harrow: William F. Taylor.
       48 pp. Frontispiece. James Northcote.
           Introductory remarks (pp. 1-4) emphasize the value of
       marginalia for an unprejudiced reading of Coleridge's
       thoughts. Prints marginalia from eighteen titles in the
       British Museum.

1623   AINGER, ALFRED. 'Nether Stowey'. Macmillan's Magazine, LIX,
       254-63. Reprinted in his Lectures and Essays. 2 vols.
       London: Macmillan (1905), II, 67-94.
           Review of Sandford (1888). Discusses composition of The
       Ancient Mariner and possible influence of Burger's 'Wild
       Huntsman'.

1624   ANON. Some References to a Few of the Works of the Late Rev.
       A. G. Mercer, D. D. Newport, R. I.
           Reprints (pp. 22-64) newspaper articles on bust of Cole-
       ridge which Mercer presented to Westminster Abbey.

1625   _____. 'Religious Opinions of S. T. Coleridge'. Church Quar-
       terly Review, XXVII, 315-31.
           Review of Memorials of Coleorton and Eastlake transla-
       tion of Brandl. Disentangles 'the religious thinker from
       ...the poet, philosopher, politician, scholar and conversa-
       tionalist'. Traces Coleridge's religious growth and
       influence.

1626   BOYCE, ANNE OGDEN. Records of a Quaker Family. London:
       Samuel Harris and Co.
           Copies of The Friend rare in Quaker families, but one in
       Jonathan Priestman's library (pp. 225-6). Brief history of
       The Friend (pp. 277-8).

1627   [BROWNE, RICHARD CHARLES]. 'Charles Lamb's Letters'. Temple
       Bar, LXXXV, 33-51.
           Lamb's relations with Coleridge and his criticism of
       Coleridge's poetry.
           Attribution: WI.

1628   No Entry.

1629   [CAMPBELL, JAMES DYKES] J. D. C. 'Coleridge's "Epitaph on an
        Infant"'. Notes and Queries, 7th Series VII, 149; VIII,
        156, 334, 474, 518.

1630   CLAYDEN, P[ETER] W. Rogers and His Contemporaries. 2 vols.
        London: Smith Elder, and Co.
            Two accounts (I, 9-10, 87) of meetings between Coleridge
        and Samuel Rogers.

1631   COLERIDGE, E. H. and MARY STUART. Letters from the Lake
        Poets, Samuel Taylor Coleridge, William Wordsworth, Robert
        Southey, to Daniel Stuart. London: West, Newman and Co.
        463 pp.
            Letters from Coleridge (pp. 1-322), account of visit,
        1834 (pp. 322-6), and list of subscribers to The Friend
        (pp. 451-63).

1632   COLLIER, WILLIAM FRANCIS. A History of English Literature
        in a Series of Biographical Sketches. London: T. Nelson.
        Revised edition.
            Inaccurate and cliché-ridden account of Coleridge (pp.
        441-6), emphasizing 'dreaminess', 'sloth', and opium addic-
        tion. Praises Genevieve and Hymn Before Sunrise.

1633   [CROSSE, CORNELIA A. H.] Mrs. Andrew Crosse. 'Thomas Poole'.
        Temple Bar, LXXXVII, 354-70. Reprinted in her Red-Letter
        Days of My Life. 2 vols. London: Richard Bentley & Sons
        (1892), I, 63-121.
            Review of Sandford (1888), with anecdotes drawn from
        friends who knew Coleridge in Wiltshire.

1634   DOWDEN, EDWARD. 'Coleridge As A Poet'. Fortnightly Review,
        LII, 342-66. Reprinted Littell's Living Age [Boston], 5th
        Series LXVIII (1889), 131-45; in his New Studies in Litera-
        ture. London: K. Paul, Trench, Trubner and Co. (1895),
        pp. 313-54.
            An attempt to 'bring out the humanity' in Coleridge's
        major poems. Discusses Coleridge's use of Quantock scen-
        ery, social and political ideals, especially in France: An
        Ode and psychological realism of The Ancient Mariner,
        Christabel, and The Wanderings of Cain.

1635   GRESWELL, WILLIAM. 'Wordsworth and the Quantock Hills'. Na-
        tional Review, XIV, 67-83.
            Influence of the Quantocks on the poetry of Wordsworth
        and Coleridge.

1636   H. J. C. 'Marginalia by Coleridge'. Notes and Queries, 7th
       Series VII, 91-2.
             Single note from Xenophon's Memoirs of Socrates.

1637   HOWITT, MARY. An Autobiography. Ed. Margaret Howitt.
       2 vols. London: William Isbister.
             Random comments (I, 242-3) on Coleridge.

1638   JAMES, IVOR. 'Southey and Coleridge in Bristol'. Bristol
       Times and Mirror, No. 7601 (12 April), p. 6.
             Recalls loss of Bristol library register for years
       1795-8, with lists of borrowings.

1639   KNIGHT, WILLIAM. The Life of William Wordsworth. 3 vols.
       Edinburgh: William Paterson.
             Detailed biography gives interrelated lives of Coleridge
       and Wordsworth. Reviewed: Athenaeum, No. 3215 (8 June
       1889), pp. 719-21.

1640   MATHEWS, E. R. NORRIS. 'Southey and Coleridge in Bristol'.
       Bristol Times and Mirror, No. 7600 (11 April), p. 5; No.
       7609 (18 April), p. 6; No. 7621 (6 May), p. 3.
             Describes registers of Bristol Library Society, includ-
       ing list of the books borrowed by Coleridge, his letters to
       the librarian, George Catcott, and prospectus for 1795
       lectures.

1641   MUNZ, BERNARD. 'Samuel Taylor Coleridge'. Unsere Zeit [Leip-
       zig], No volume, pp. 500-15.
             Account of Coleridge's life and work based on Brandl
       (1886), emphasizes Coleridge's role as transmitter of Ger-
       man thought.

1642   PATER, WALTER HORATIO. 'Coleridge'. Appreciations. London:
       Macmillan and Co., pp. 64-106.
             Famous essay, composed of revised versions of parts of
       Pater's 1866 and 1880 articles, presents Coleridge as in-
       stance of unhealthy romanticism opposed to 'the Greek
       spirit'. Coleridge's concern with the absolute 'an effort
       of sickly thought'; his psychological insights reveal 'some
       tendency to disease'; and The Ancient Mariner and Christa-
       bel appeal to a Germanic taste for the supernatural.

1643   PRIMROSE KNIGHT, A, pseud. The Rime of the Ancient Senator...
       With Apologies to S. T. C. Reading: F. Blackwell.
             Political satire.

1889-SARRAZIN

1644   SARRAZIN, GABRIEL. La renaissance de la poésie Anglaise 1789-
       1889. Paris: Didier, Berin et Cie. xiv, 279 pp.
          Combines (pp. 117-46) sketch of Coleridge's biography
       and intellectual background with critical comments. Il-
       lustrated by translated passages. Coleridge ranks somewhat
       below Wordsworth and Tennyson.

1645   WARD, C. A. 'Coleridge'. Notes and Queries, 7th Series VIII,
       89.
          Familiar anecdote of visit by Wordsworth and Rogers.

1646   _____. 'The Devil's Walk'. Notes and Queries, 7th Series
       VIII, 161-2.
          A bibliographical history of the poem with comment
       (p. 258) by 'Cuthbert Bede' [Edward Bradley].

1890

1647   Lyrical Ballads. Reprinted from the First Edition (1798).
       Ed. Edward Dowden. London: David Nutt.
          Preface describes Coleridge's part in Lyrical Ballads
       and joint creation of The Ancient Mariner.
          Reviewed: Athenaeum, No. 3263 (10 May 1890), pp. 599-
       600; Richard Holt Hutton, Spectator, No. 3223 (5 April
       1890), pp. 479-80.

1648   ANON. 'The Late Mr. F. W. Cosens' Mss.' Athenaeum, No. 3273
       (19 July), p. 98.
          Announcement of dispersal of the Cosens Collection,
       several extracts from the Cottle and Thelwall correspond-
       ence with Coleridge, and evidence that Cottle (1837) had
       deliberately garbled a Coleridge letter.

1649   _____. 'Mysticism Versus Common-Sense. A French Criticism of
       Coleridge'. Review of Reviews, II, 596.
          English summary of Joseph Texte (1890), q.v.

1650   BAKER, JAMES. 'Books Read by Coleridge, and Southey'. Cham-
       bers's Edinburgh Journal, VII, 75-6. Reprinted in his
       Literary and Biographical Studies. London: Chapman and
       Hall (1908), pp. 211-18.
          Account of Bristol Library records.

224

1651   BEERS, HENRY A. From Chaucer to Tennyson, English Literature
       in Eight Chapters with Selections from Thirty Authors. New
       York: Chautauqua Library.
           Contains (pp. 173-6) brief mention of Coleridge as in-
       troducer of German thought to England, day dreamer, talker,
       'seminal mind'. Broad Church party traces origins to him.

1652   BROOKS, SARAH WARNER. English Poetry and Poets. Boston:
       Estes and Lauriat.
           An effusive appreciation (pp. 318-36) of Coleridge as
       'logician, metaphysician, critic, and rich imaginative
       poet'.

1653   [CAMPBELL, J. DYKES] J. D. C. 'Coleridge and the Anti-
       Jacobins'. Athenaeum, No. 3266 (31 May), pp. 703-4.
           Coleridge quoted in his own defence against charges in
       the Anti-Jacobin (1799).

1654   CAMPBELL, J. DYKES. 'Coleridge's Osorio and Remorse'. Athe-
       naeum, No. 3258 (5 April), pp. 445-6; No. 3374 (25 June
       1892), pp. 834-5.
           Comparison of Osorio and Remorse, with notes on textual
       changes during 1813.

1655   _____. 'Coleridge's Remorse'. Notes and Queries, 7th Series
       IX, 248; 7th Series XII (1891), 34.
           Request for information on performances of Remorse out-
       side London. Later note mentions lack of response but
       identifies performances at Boston and Bristol.

1656   _____. 'Lyrical Ballads'. Athenaeum, No. 3263 (10 May),
       pp. 599-600.
           Discusses reception of first edition, and especially of
       The Ancient Mariner.

1657   [CAMPBELL, J. DYKES] J. D. C. 'Unpublished Verses by Cole-
       ridge'. Athenaeum, No. 3255 (15 March), p. 34; No. 3279
       (30 Aug), p. 288.
           Text of To Matilda Betham, an account of its discovery,
       and identification of [Lady Rouse] Boughton (line 3).

1658   FARRAR, F. W. 'Formative Influences'. Forum [Philadelphia],
       X, 373-82.
           Milton and Coleridge most important influences on Far-
       rar's life.

225

1659   GRAY, A. 'Coleridge at Jesus, 1791-1794'. Chanticleer [Cam-
       bridge], No. 16 (Oct term), pp. 1-13.
       Coleridge Society paper draws on unexamined college
       records to fill in details of Coleridge's college years.

1660   HODGKINS, LOUISE MANNING. A Guide to the Study of Nineteenth
       Century Authors. Boston: D. C. Heath.
       Brief biography, followed by a list of poems, and ex-
       cerpts, and bibliography.

1661   JAMES, IVOR. 'The Source of The Ancient Mariner'. Cardiff:
       Daniel Owen, 88 pp.
       Primary source was The Strange and Dangerous Voyage of
       Captain Thomas James (1633). James's thesis attacked and
       defended in articles by John Taylor et al. (1890), q.v.
       Reviewed: Academy, XXXVII (1890), 132; and no. 1667.

1662   MOZLEY, ANNE, ED. Letters and Correspondence of John Henry
       Newman. 2 vols. New York, London: Longmans et al.
       Letters from Acland (1834) and to Froude (1836): 'poor
       Coleridge was not so bad a fellow, if well used' but 'too
       much of a philosopher' (II, 35, 138-9).

1663   NICHOLSON, J. G. F. 'Ten Sonnets on Coleridge's Ancient Mari-
       ner'. Universal Review, VIII, 387-91.
       Each sonnet based on a phrase from the poem.

1664   PFLEIDERER, OTTO. The Development of Theology in Germany
       since Kant and its progress in Great Britain since 1825.
       Translated from the manuscript by J. Frederick Smith.
       London: Swan Sonnenschein and Co. German edition: Die
       Entwicklung der Protestantischen Theologie. Freiburg
       (1891).
       Critical but sympathetic account of Coleridge's theology
       (pp. 308-11).

1665   REID, T. WEMYSS. The Life, Letters, and Friendships of Rich-
       ard Monckton Milnes, First Lord Houghton. 2 vols. London:
       Cassell and Co.
       Two meetings with Coleridge (I, 146; II, 432).

1666   SCOTT, SIR WALTER. Journal 1825-1832. Ed. D. Douglas. 2
       vols. Edinburgh: D. Douglas.
       Brief account of 1828 dinner (II, 164) where Coleridge
       discoursed on Samothracian Mysteries and Homer.

1667   TAYLOR, JOHN, et al. 'The Source of The Ancient Mariner'.
      Athenaeum, Nos. 3254-3257 (March 1890), pp. 307, 335-6,
      371-2, 405.
         Generally negative responses by Taylor, an anonymous re-
      viewer, J. D. Campbell, and Stuart M. Samuel to James
      (1890), q.v.

1668   TEXTE, JOSEPH. 'Le mysticisme littéraire: Samuel Taylor
      Coleridge'. Revue des Deux Mondes [Paris], CII, 342-77.
         Biographical sketch of Coleridge's early years and brief
      consideration of The Ancient Mariner. Chiefly discussion
      of low regard for Coleridge and English Romantics in
      France.

1669   WALPOLE, SPENCER. A History of England from the Conclusion of
      the Great War in 1815. 6 vols. London, New York: Long-
      mans et al. New and revised edition.
         Compares (I, 237-8) Coleridge's and Southey's changes
      from liberal to conservative.

1891

1670   'S. T. Coleridge on Mysticism'. Monthly Packet, New Series
      II, 377-85.
         Dialogue printed from Coleridge's ms. with introductory
      note by E. H. C.

1671   ANON. 'From A Philistine Book-Room'. Anti-Jacobin, I, 588.
         Account of two recently auctioned Coleridge letters.

1672   _____. 'A Forgotten Poem by Coleridge'. Anti-Jacobin, I,
      708-9.
         Rescues To Fortune, first collected in 1893.

1673   _____. 'Coleridge's Friend'. Athenaeum, No. 3337 (10 Oct),
      pp. 484-5.
         Comment on letter from Wordsworth concerning distribu-
      tion of The Friend.

1674   [CAMPBELL, JAMES DYKES] J. D. C. 'A Letter of Charles Lamb'.
      Athenaeum, No. 3320 (13 June), pp. 765-6; No. 3321
      (20 June), p. 797; No. 3322 (27 June), p. 830.
         Exchange between Campbell and C. A. Ward on Reflections
      and a Lamb letter.

1675   CAMPBELL, J. DYKES. 'Some Lectures Delivered by Coleridge in
        the winter of 1818-19'. Athenaeum, No. 3348 (26 Dec), pp.
        865-6; No. 3349 (2 Jan 1892), pp. 17-8.
            Evidence that Coleridge delivered two series in 1818-9.

1676   [CAMPBELL, J. DYKES] J. D. C. 'A Sonnet by S. T. Coleridge'.
        Athenaeum, No. 3331 (29 Aug), p. 290; No. 3333 (12 Sept),
        p. 352. Reprinted inaccurately Critic [New York], New
        Series XVI (1891), 203.
            Query on originality of Lady, To Death We're Doomed.
        Identified by Sidney Crompton as translation from Spanish
        and by J. W. M. as from Italian.

1677   CHANCELLOR, E. BERESFORD. Essays and Studies, Literary and
        Historical. London: Bemrose & Co. Portrait by Val R.
        Prince.
            Essays (pp. 1-83, 165-80) present biography chiefly
        through quotation from Coleridge's contemporaries and from
        his poems with descriptive and historical discussion of a
        few poems.

1678   CHURCH, RICHARD WILLIAM. The Oxford Movement: Twelve Years,
        1833-1845. London, New York: Macmillan & Co.
            Coleridge influenced Charles Marriott (p. 70), who dis-
        cussed him with Charles Badham.

1679   CLARKE, JAMES FREEMAN. Autobiography, Diary and Correspond-
        ence. Ed. Edward Everett Hale. Boston, New York: Hough-
        ton, Mifflin & Co.
            Describes (pp. 39-40) influence of Coleridge and Marsh
        during Harvard student days (1825-29).

1680   COMPTON, THEODORE. 'Recollections of the Poet Coleridge'.
        New Church Magazine, X, 356-60.
            Account by Compton's mother, Eliza Nevins, of visit to
        Coleridge in 1808, with letters concerning the visit from
        Coleridge and Sara.

1681   DAWSON, WILLIAM JAMES. The Makers of Modern English. New
        York: Thomas Whittaker.
            Sympathetic account (pp. 71-80) of Coleridge's influence
        and poetry. Considers prose inferior.

1682   DE QUINCEY, THOMAS. Memorials. Being Letters...Here First
        Published...From Coleridge, The Wordsworths...and Others.
        Ed. Alexander H. Japp. 2 vols. London: William Heine-
        mann; New York: United States Book Company.

(DE QUINCEY, THOMAS)
Correspondence with Coleridge (1808-1821) and references passim. Reviewed: Nation [New York], LII (1892), 242-3.

1683 GOODWIN, H. M. 'Coleridge As A Spiritual Philosopher'. New Englander and Yale Review [New Haven], LIV, 61-96.
Account of Coleridge's contemporary reputation and importance as opponent of the 'empirical school'. Exposition of Coleridge's intellectual development and metaphysical concepts.

1684 GROSER, HORACE G. 'Samuel Taylor Coleridge'. The Poets and Poetry of the Century. Ed. Alfred H. Miles. 10 vols. London: Hutchinson & Co., I, 435-52.
Biographical sketch and selection of poems. Discusses The Ancient Mariner. Blames opium for blighted hopes, and considers influence of Coleridge's conversation.

1685 [HANCOCK, ROBERT]. Portraits of English Poets from Drawings Made for Joseph Cottle of Bristol. Bristol: William George's Sons. 5 Reproductions.
Photogravures of Hancock's drawings of Coleridge and others.

1686 JUPP, RICHARD F. 'Coleridge and the Supernatural'. Spectator, No. 3269 (21 Feb), p. 275.
Notes possible echo of Christabel in Scott's 'Lady of the Lake'.

1687 NISBET, J. F. The Insanity of Genius and the General Inequality of Human Faculty Physiologically Considered. London: Ward and Downey.
Describes (pp. 115-9, 325-7) evidence of hereditary 'nerve disorder' and physical debility in Coleridge's family.

1688 PIKE, CLEMENT. 'Frederick Denison Maurice. His Influence on Liberal Theology'. Unitarian Review [Boston], XXXV, 118-26.
Coleridge's influence on Maurice and similarity of their views (pp. 121-3).

1689 SMILES, SAMUEL. A Publisher and His Friends. Memoirs and Correspondence of the Late John Murray. 2 vols. London: John Murray; New York: Charles Scribner's Sons.
Letters to Murray (1814-1817), I, 296-307.

1891-VAUGHAN

1690   [VAUGHAN, H. M.] Vaughan, E. 'Coleridgianum'. Chanticleer
        [Cambridge], No. 18 (Easter Term), pp. 22-4.
            Describes variants in ms. of To A Young Ass.
            Attribution: Letter from author to J. D. Campbell.

1691   [WATSON, WILLIAM]. 'Coleridge's Supernaturalism'. Spectator,
        No. 3268 (14 Feb), pp. 249-50. Reprinted in his Excursions
        in Criticism. London: Elkin Mathews and John Lane (1893),
        pp. 97-103.
            Examines relation between supernatural and actual in
        The Ancient Mariner and Christabel, in review of The Poeti-
        cal Works, 1885.

                            1892

1692   ANON. 'Coleridge and Lamb'. Bookworm, No. 50 (Jan), pp. 53-
        4.
            Notes sale of copy of Poems on Various Subjects (1797)
        with original ms. of preface.

1693   _____. 'Some Unpublished Correspondence of Washington All-
        ston'. Scribner's Magazine [New York], XI, 68-83.
            Two letters (pp. 72-4) to Allston.

1694   BAYNE, THOMAS. 'Burns and Coleridge'. Notes and Queries, 8th
        Series II, 164-5.
            Quotes 1798 letter from Burns to Miss Dunlop, which he
        thinks is 'strongly echoed' by The Eolian Harp. Suggestion
        reprinted (9th Series I [1898], 405-6), arousing a quibble
        from 'H. J. F.' (II [1898], 95), answered in II, 97.

1695   BROOKE, WILLIAM T. 'Unpublished Fragments of Coleridge and
        Lamb'. Newberry House Magazine, VI, 68-70.
            Coleridge's marginalia in Barclay's Argenis.

1696   [CAMPBELL, JAMES DYKES] J. D. C. 'Coleridge's Quotations'.
        Athenaeum, No. 3382 (20 Aug), pp. 259-60; No. 3384
        (3 Sept), p. 322.
            Categorizes Coleridge's misremembered quotations into
        instances of garbling, deliberate word-substitution, and
        new additions. Each indicates Coleridge's mental habits.
        Further comment by Thomas Bayne.

1697 _____. 'The Poets' Nightingales'. Athenaeum, No. 3370
(28 May), p. 697; No. 3371 (6 June), p. 727.
References to nightingales from Coleridge letters, poems
and a verse note. Identifies allusions to Drs. Mant and
D'Oyley. Waugh adds excerpt from unpublished letter.

1698 _____. 'Scott on Coleridge'. Athenaeum, No. 3394 (12 Nov),
pp. 664-5; No. 3397 (3 Dec), pp. 778-9. Reprinted Critic
[New York] XVIII (1892), 317.
Quotations from Scott's commendation of Love in unpublished letter. Several explanations of Scott's access to
poem and variants in Stoddard's recitation of Christabel.

1699 CARLYLE, THOMAS. 'Wotton Reinfred'. Last Words of Thomas
Carlyle. Ed. Richard Preuss. London: Longmans; New York:
Appleton.
Character of 'Dalbrook' (pp. 1-149) a satirical portrait
of Coleridge.

1700 CHENEY, JOHN VANCE. The Golden Guess. Essays on Poetry and
the Poets. Boston: Lee and Shepard.
Coleridge discussed in attempt to distinguish (pp. 3-42)
poetry from science and philosophy.

1701 DUFFY, C. GAVAN. 'Conversations and Correspondence with
Thomas Carlyle'. Contemporary Review, LXI, 120-50. Reprinted Littell's Living Age [Boston], 5th Series LXXVII
(1892), 531-50, and in his Conversations with Carlyle.
London: S. Low, Marston and Co. (1892).
In conversation here reported, Carlyle called Coleridge's writing 'vague and purposeless, and...intrinsically
cowardly' and Coleridge himself 'a poor, greedy, sensual
creature'.

1702 ESTE, pseud. 'Shelley the Atheist'. Notes and Queries, 8th
Series, I, 404, 484-5; 8th Series II (1892), 54-5.
Prior attribution to Shelley of line from Coleridge's
Hymn Before Sunrise elicits replies by Este, Bayne, and
Bouchier on relation of poem to Brun's original, and pro-
priety of calling it a lyric.

1703 FLAGG, JARED B. Life and Letters of Washington Allston. New
York: Charles Scribner's Sons. 435 pp.
Describes passim Allston's acquaintance with Coleridge.
Reviewed: Athenaeum, No. 3447 (18 Nov 1893), pp. 702-3.

1892-GOSSE

1704   GOSSE, EDMUND. 'Coleridge at Nether Stowey'. Illustrated
       London News, CI, 406.
           Opposes placing plaque on Coleridge's cottage, now a
       'squalid pothouse'.

1705   HAKE, GORDON. Memoirs of Eighty Years. London: Richard
       Bentley and Son.
           Work Without Hope an example of poetic perfection. Won-
       ders whether first line should read 'slugs leave their
       lair', or 'stags'.

1706   HUTTON, LAURENCE. 'Collection of Death Masks'. Harper's New
       Monthly Magazine [New York], LXXXV, 781-93. Coleridge
       mask, p. 783.
           Quotes descriptions by contemporaries of Coleridge's
       physical features.

1707   K. 'Literary Gossip'. Illustrated London News, CI, 275.
           Describes Coleridge's criticism of Burke.

1708   _____. 'Literature'. Illustrated London News, C, 362.
           Comment on first publication of Conciones, Plot Discov-
       ered, and Mad Monk.

1709   [LEWIN, WALTER]. 'James Russell Lowell'. Temple Bar, XCVI,
       88-95.
           Lowell criticized (pp. 93-4) for insufficient sympathy
       with Coleridge, although Coleridge an inspirer of Lowell's
       philosophy.
           Attribution: WI.

1710   MARTIN, SIR THEODORE. 'The Camp of Wallenstein'. Blackwood's
       Magazine, CLI, 231-56.
           Coleridge's omission from Wallenstein of Part I ex-
       plained (p. 231). Campbell, Athenaeum (27 Feb 1892),
       p. 286, rejects explanation.

1711   MATHER, J. MARSHALL. 'Coleridge, the Metaphysician'. Popular
       Studies of Nineteenth Century Poets. London, New York:
       Frederick Warne, pp. 52-73.
           Appreciation of Coleridge requires a feeling for dreams,
       the supernatural, and the psychological. The Ancient Mar-
       iner an allegory of the history of a soul.

1712   PAGE, JOHN LL. WARDEN. 'Coleridge and the Quantocks'. Eng-
       lish Illustrated Magazine, X, 334-7. Portrait.
           Describes Coleridge's cottage and identifies spots de-
       scribed in This Lime-Tree Bower.

1713   PRIDEAUX, W. F. 'Coleridge's Views on Church Establishment'.
       Notes and Queries, 8th Series II, 209, 257.
       Query with reply by F. Jarratt.

1714   STEDMAN, EDMUND CLARENCE. The Nature and Elements of Poetry.
       Boston, New York: Houghton, Mifflin.
       Coleridge mentioned passim. Cannot 'quite forgive the-
       ology and metaphysics' for Coleridge's 'loss to the highest
       field of poetic design' (p. 125).

1715   SWANWICK, ANNA. 'Samuel Taylor Coleridge'. Poets the Inter-
       preters of the Age. London, New York: George Bell & Sons,
       pp. 281-8.
       Brief general evaluation of Coleridge's intellectual in-
       fluence with short comments on a number of poems. Notes
       Coleridge's concern with French Revolution, attitude to-
       wards nature, and 'weird supernaturalism'.

1716   TALFOURD, SIR THOMAS NOON. Memoirs of Charles Lamb. Ed. and
       annotated Percy Fitzgerald. Engraving of Coleridge by W.
       Say, after Northcote, facing p. 34. London: W. W. Gib-
       bings.
       The close relations between Coleridge and Lamb from
       school days (p. 13) to death (pp. 284-5).

1717   WATSON, ROBERT A. and ELIZABETH S. George Gilfillan. London:
       Hodder and Stoughton.
       Contrasts Coleridge with Hall (pp. 129-30) and comments
       on Coleridge's criticism (pp. 288-9).

1718   WATSON, WILLIAM. 'On Coleridge's Christabel'. Spectator,
       No. 3334 (21 May), p. 711. Reprinted in his Lachrymae
       Musarum and Other Poems. London, New York: Macmillan
       (1892), pp. 46-7. Reprinted Littell's Living Age [Boston],
       5th Series LXXXI (1893), 66.
       Poem.

1719   WATTS, THEODORE. 'Apparent Pictures. I. Coleridge'. Athe-
       naeum, No. 3360 (19 March), p. 373. Reprinted as 'I see
       thee pine like her in golden story', in his The Coming
       Life...and Other Poems. London: John Lane (1898),
       pp. 217-8.
       Sonnet on Coleridge.

1892–WINTER

1720 WINTER, WILLIAM. 'At The Grave of Coleridge'. Shakespeare's
England. New York, London: Macmillan & Co., pp. 208–14.
New, revised edition, being republication of Trip to Eng-
land and English Rambles.
Thoughts expressed in purple prose.

1893

1721 Poetical Works. Ed. with a biographical introduction by James
Dykes Campbell. London: Macmillan and Co.
Campbell's biographical introduction (pp. xi–cxxiv) re-
vised as Samuel Taylor Coleridge (1894), q.v. Critical and
explanatory notes still of some value. Reviewed: Library
Review, II, pp. 215–7; [Richard Holt Hutton], Spectator,
No. 3390 (17 June 1893), pp. 804–6 (attribution: Tener).
See also 1724, 1726.

1722 Rime of the Ancient Mariner. By Samuel Taylor Coleridge. Il-
lustrated by J. Noel Paton, R. S. A. with an Introductory
Note by Francis H. Underwood. Boston: Lee and Shepherd.
57 pp.
Introductory note (pp. 4–10) summarizes action of poem.
'Every line bears witness to the keenness of his spiritual
sight'.
Reviewed: Peterson Magazine [New York, Philadelphia]
New Series II (1893), 1249.

1723 Selections From the Prose Writings. Ed. with introduction
and notes by Henry A. Beers. New York: Henry Holt. xxix,
146 pp.
Introduction and biographical sketch (pp. vii–xxix) directed at students.

1724 ANON. 'The Poetical Works of Samuel Taylor Coleridge'. Athenaeum, No. 3425 (17 June), pp. 756–60.
Criticizes Campbell's inattention to Cambridge years,
and notes influence of Frend and Hammond. The 'fusion' in
Coleridge's poems explained by associative powers rather
than by dream composition.

1725 _____. 'The Hazlitt Papers'. Athenaeum, No. 3447 (18 Nov),
pp. 697–8.
Marginalia from Lamb's copy of Daniel's Poems.

Samuel Taylor Coleridge: An Annotated Bibliography

1726   ANON. 'Samuel Taylor Coleridge'. <u>Church Quarterly Review</u>,
       XXXVII, 166-79.
           Review of <u>Poetical Works</u> (1893) attempts briefly to
       rectify Campbell's neglect of character of Coleridge's
       work and genius.

1727   No entry.

1728   BRIDGES, ROBERT. 'On Metrical Equivalence'. <u>Milton's Pros-
       ody</u>. Oxford. The Clarendon Press, pp. 67-72.
           Discussion (pp. 69-71) of the metrics of <u>Christabel</u>.

1729   [CAMPBELL, J. DYKES] J. D. C. "Coleridge on Quaker Prin-
       ciples'. <u>Athenaeum</u>, No. 3438 (16 Sept), pp. 385-6.
           Extracts from 1808 correspondence with Thomas Wilkinson
       concerning prospectus to <u>Friend</u>. Wilkinson's and Jeffrey's
       objections noted with Coleridge's alterations.

1730   _____. 'The Prospectus of Coleridge's Watchman'. <u>Athenaeum</u>,
       No. 3450 (9 Dec), p. 808.
           Announcement of Buxton Forman's discovery of original
       prospectus of <u>Watchman</u>, with description of contents,
       physical appearance and circumstances of discovery.

1731   DE QUINCEY, THOMAS. 'Conversation and Coleridge'. <u>Posthumous
       Works</u>. Ed. from the original mss. by Alexander H. Japp.
       2 vols. London: Heinemann, II, 7-57.
           De Quincey's last essay on Coleridge discusses manner
       and some topics of his conversation, defends Coleridge's
       plagiarisms as unintentional and trivial. Long discussion
       of influence of Coleridge's father. Reviewed: <u>Athenaeum</u>,
       No. 3452 (23 Dec 1893) pp. 873-4.

1732   [GRESWELL, WILLIAM] W. G. 'Coleridge and Nether Stowey'.
       <u>Athenaeum</u>, No. 3425 (17 June), pp. 765-6.
           Note on dedication ceremony at Coleridge's cottage in-
       cludes E. H. Coleridge's poetical inscription.

1733   HIGHAM, CHARLES. 'New Jerusalem Church'. <u>Notes and Queries</u>,
       8th Series IV, 258.
           Comment on Coleridge's notes on Swedenborg.

1734   _____. 'Coleridge and Swedenborg'. <u>Morning Light</u>, XVI,
       397-8.
           Notes acquisition by Swedenborgian Society of two anno-
       tated works (<u>Regnum Animale</u> and <u>Oeconomia Regni Animalis</u>).

1735 HOWARD, HENRY C. Christabel (concluded) With Other Poems.
       London: Kegan Paul, Trench, Trübner and Co.
       Poem (pp. 1-17).

1736 HUTCHINSON T[HOMAS]. 'Coleridgiana'. Academy, XLIII, 481,
       505.
            Notes on text and dating of To A Young Lady, Water Bal-
       lad, and Allegoric Vision, and on Coleridge's debts to
       Dorothy Wordsworth's Journal.

1737 LORD, ALICE E. The Days of Lamb and Coleridge. New York:
       Henry Holt.
            Historical romance on Lamb, Coleridge and their inti-
       mates. Combines historical material with imagined scenes
       and conversations.

1738 PANCOAST, HENRY S. 'Samuel Taylor Coleridge'. Representative
       English Literature. New York: Henry Holt and Company,
       pp. 343-54. Reprinted Introduction to English Literature.
       New York: Henry Holt and Company (1902), pp. 324-38.
            Sympathetic biographical account. Coleridge contrasted
       with Wordsworth and discussed as philosopher and poet.
       Background and moral significance of The Ancient Mariner.

1739 SCOTT, SIR WALTER. Familiar Letters. Edited by D[avid
       D[ouglas]. 2 vols. Edinburgh: D. Douglas.
            Letters (I, 280-2, 315) on Remorse and on his first
       hearing Christabel and introducing it to Byron.
       Attribution of editor: B. Mus. Cat.

1740 SYDNEY, WILLIAM CONNOR. 'The Cradle of the Lake Poets'.
       Gentleman's Magazine, CCLXXV, 590-605. Reprinted in Eclec-
       tic Magazine [New York], New Series LIX (1894), 119-28.
            Account of Nether Stowey and Alfoxden.

1741 THOMPSON, SILVANUS P. 'Samuel Taylor Coleridge on Quaker
       Principles'. Friends' Quarterly [Glasgow], XXVII, 355-60.
            History and text of letter written in response to criti-
       cism of prospectus for The Friend.

1742 WARD, C. A. 'Coleridge's Logic'. Athenaeum, No. 3427
       (1 July), p. 34; No. 3548 (26 Oct 1895), p. 571; No. 3562
       (1 Feb 1896), p. 149.
            Announcement of location of the manuscript volumes of
       History of Logic and Elements of Logic. Ward is later dis-
       turbed at the seeming lack of interest. Lucy Watson
       (Athenaeum, No. 3552, 23 Nov 1895, p. 719) denies this.

1743   _____. 'Transcendental Knowledge'. <u>Notes and Queries</u>, 8th
Series III, 64-5, 138.
     Query concerning fate of Green's library and Coleridge's
unpublished ms. elicits repetition of Fenton's 1882 query.

1744   YOUNG, H. S. 'Samuel Taylor Coleridge'. <u>Athenaeum</u>, No. 3436
(2 Sept) p. 322; No. 3437 (9 Sept), p. 356.
     Note on Coleridge's marginalia on Fulke Greville and use
of various stanzas.

1894

1745   <u>Passages From the Prose and Table Talk of Coleridge</u>. Ed. with
a prefatory note by W. H. Dircks. London: Walter Scott.
xiii, 261 pp.
     A prefatory discussion (pp. vii-xiii) of <u>Biographia
Literaria</u> and Coleridge's criticism of Wordsworth.

1746   No entry.

1747   ANON. 'Unpublished Letters of Wordsworth and Coleridge'.
<u>Athenaeum</u>, No. 3502 (8 Dec), p. 791.
     An announcement of Sotheby auction to include five let-
ters to Wrangham.

1748   _____. 'Ten Letters from Coleridge to Southey'. <u>Atlantic
Monthly</u> [Boston], LXXIII, 57-67.
     Brief biographical headnote precedes collection of let-
ters to Southey in 1800.

1749   _____. 'Notes and News'. <u>Poet-Lore</u> [Boston], VI, 167.
     Compares Coleridge's 'dull' letters with those of Edith
Thomas.

1750   _____. 'Some Literary Tendencies'. <u>Poet-Lore</u> [Boston], VI,
559-63.
     Coleridge probably model for Saltram in James's <u>The
Coxon Fund</u>.

1751   BATESON, H. D. 'The Rhythm of Coleridge's <u>Christabel</u>'. <u>Man-
chester Quarterly</u>, XIII, 275-86. Reissued for private
circulation (1896). Reprinted, with additions and corrections, Liverpool: Donald Fraser (1904).
     Classifies lines of <u>Christabel</u> in conventional metrical
categories.

1752   BEDDOES, THOMAS LOVELL. Letters of Thomas Lovell Beddoes.
        Ed. Edmund Gosse. London: E. Mathews and J. Lane; New
        York: Macmillan and Co.
            Describes (p. 105) a meeting with Coleridge's language
        tutor at Göttingen, who thought Coleridge's German weak.

1753   BENTON, MYRON B. 'Coleridge's Introduction to the Lake Dis-
        trict'. Atlantic Monthly [Boston], LXXIV, 95-102.
            Biographical potpourri, including survey of Coleridge's
        life in 1800, anecdotes, description of Greta Hall and the
        Quantocks, and unpublished letter of 1801 to John Tobin.
        Reviewed: R. Ackerman. Anglia. Beiblatt [Halle], V
        (1895), 335-6.

1754   CAMPBELL, JAMES DYKES. Samuel Taylor Coleridge. A Narrative
        of the Events of his Life. London: Macmillan and Co. xii,
        319 pp. Portrait by Peter Vandyke. Reprinted with a mem-
        oir of the author by Leslie Stephen. London: Macmillan
        and Co. (1896).
            Revised version of Campbell's biographical study in 1893
        edition of Poetical Works. Scholarly, but uncritical, this
        contains much hitherto unpublished and uncollected informa-
        tion. Reviewed: Critic [New York], XXV (1894), 154; Poet-
        Lore [Boston], VI (1894), 164-5, 167; Spectator, No. 3433
        (14 April 1894), p. 512; [Thomas Parsons] T. P. Weekly Sun
        IV (1894), unpaged; E. E. Dowden. Athenaeum, No. 3557
        (25 Dec 1896), pp. 128-9; Saturday Review, LXXXII (1896),
        138-9; Richard Le Gallienne. Retrospective Reviews. A
        Literary Log. 2 vols. London: John Lane; New York: Dodd
        Mead (1896), II, 57-61. See also 1763, 1826.

1755   _____. 'S. T. Coleridge'. Notes and Queries, 8th Series VI,
        5.
            Request for a transcript of a letter.

1756   CLINCH, GEORGE. 'Christ's Hospital'. Pall Mall Magazine,
        IV, 356-/2. Partially reprinted Critic [New York], XXV
        (1894) 310.
            Includes brief account of Coleridge.

1757   [COLERIDGE, ERNEST HARTLEY] E. H. C. 'Note on Coleridge'.
        Athenaeum, No. 3457 (27 Jan), p. 114.
            Discussion of prefatory note and date of early draft of
        Wanderings of Cain.

1758   CROSSE, MRS. ANDREW. 'Poet, Parson, and Pamphleteer'. Temple
       Bar, CIII, 25-45.
              An appreciation of Bowles (pp. 25-8) with reference to
       his influence on Coleridge.

1759   DENNIS, JOHN. 'S. T. Coleridge'. Leisure Hour, XLIII, 520-3.
              Quotes opinions of Coleridge's friends, blames opium
       and lack of character for 'comparative failure', judges
       poetry exquisite but hollow, approves criticisms and phi-
       losophy.

1760   DIXON, WILLIAM MACNEILE. English Poetry from Blake to Brown-
       ing. London: Methuen and Co. 204 pp. Second Edition,
       1896.
              Coleridge (pp. 74-83) in discussion of 'naturalism and
       supernaturalism'. Attention to The Ancient Mariner, Chris-
       tabel, seen as original, exquisite, but without 'sustain-
       ing, spirit-enriching power'.

1761   [GORDON, W. J.]. 'The Ancient Mariner in New South Wales'.
       Leisure Hour, XLIII, 633-5.
              Disagrees with Nicholls (1870) and Ivor James (1890).
       Attribution: English Catalogue of Books

1762   HAZLITT, W. CAREW. 'English and Scottish Book Collectors'.
       Bookworm, VII, No. 75 (Feb), 65-74, 145-9.
              Includes list of books with Coleridge's autograph.
       Supplement adds three more Coleridge titles.

1763   HUTCHINSON, T. 'Samuel Taylor Coleridge'. Academy, XLV,
       141-3.
              Review of Campbell (1894). Opium was responsible for
       Coleridge's flowering and decline.

1764   HUTCHINSON, THOMAS. 'Wordsworth's Castle of Indolence Stan-
       zas'. Fortnightly Review, New Series LVI, 685-704; Athe-
       naeum, No. 3503 (15 Dec), p. 829.
              An identification of Wordsworth and Coleridge in Castle
       of Indolence. Debate with Ernest Hartley Coleridge, who
       in Athenaeum of 24 Nov 1894 (pp. 716-7) challenges him.

1765   JAMES, HENRY. 'The Coxon Fund'. Yellow Book, II, 290-360.
       Reprinted in Terminations. London: William Heinemann
       (1895), pp. 65-162.
              Story, as James explained in his notebooks, is based on
       character of Coleridge. Reviewed: Poet-Lore [Boston], VI
       (1894), 559-63.

1894-LAMB

1766   LAMB, MARY. 'Why is he wandering on the sea?' Samuel Taylor
       Coleridge. A Narrative of the Events of His Life. By
       James Dykes Campbell. London, New York: Macmillan and
       Co., p. 194, note 2.
          Poem on death of John Wordsworth mentions Coleridge.

1767   LOWELL, JAMES R. Letters of James R. Lowell. Ed. Charles
       Eliot Norton. 2 vols. New York: Harper & Brothers.
          Letter of 1869 (II, 23-5) tells of reading Lay Sermons
       to hens to encourage them to lay eggs.

1768   MILLNER, RALPH. 'A Few Words About Coleridge, Byron, and
       Shelley'. Manchester Monthly, I, 264-5.
          Brief conventional estimate.

1769   MINTO, WILLIAM. 'Wordsworth - Coleridge - Southey'. The
       Georgian Era. Edinburgh, London: William Blackwood,
       pp. 170-84.
          Lecture, given in Aberdeen. High praise for Biographia
       Literaria, but views Coleridge as 'dreamy, speculative,
       aimless'.

1770   MURRAY, J. O. 'What the preacher may gain from a study of
       Coleridge'. Homiletic Review [New York], XXVIII, 387-94.
          Value found in most of Coleridge's work, but particular-
       ly in writing on pantheism, agnosticism, and ethics.

1771   PORTER, CHARLOTTE. 'The Import of Keat's Lamia in contrast
       with Coleridge's Christabel'. Poet-Lore [Boston], VI,
       32-40.
          Coleridge emphasizes repulsive side of the 'Lamia' myth,
       Keats the beautiful side.

1772   RADFORD, G[EORGE] H[EYNES]. 'Pantisocracy'. Shylock and
       Others. London: T. Fisher Unwin, pp. 119-50.
          Reconstruction of Coleridge and Southey at time of
       pantisocracy scheme, with an explanation of its failure.

1773   RAWNSLEY, HARDWICKE D. Literary Associations of the English
       Lakes. 2 vols. Glasgow: J. Maclehose & Sons.
          Numerous allusions to Coleridge, especially Vol I,
       Chapter II on Greta Hall.

1774   ROBERTSON, JOHN M. 'Coleridge'. Free Review, No. 4 (Jan),
       pp. 305-29. Revised: New Essays Towards A Critical Meth-
       od, London, New York: Bodley Head (1897), pp. 131-90.

1895-Letters of Samuel Taylor Coleridge

(ROBERTSON, JOHN M.)
>   Attributes achievements of annus mirabilis to opium.
>   Explains 'inferior quality' of Coleridge's other work by
>   'pathological' inadequacies.

1775   WRIGHT, WILLIAM ALDIS. 'Coleridge and Opium'. Academy, XLV,
>   170, 192.
>   Date of Coleridge's first use of opium six months ear-
>   lier than given by Hutchinson (1894). Hutchinson replies
>   (p. 192).

1776   WYLIE, LAURA JOHNSON. Studies in the Evolution of English
>   Criticism. Boston: Ginn and Company.
>   Coleridge's German sources and development as critic
>   (pp. 113-204). Mostly expository. Coleridge's theoretical
>   and practical criticism fails in achievement, but offers
>   'germ of a higher development'.

1895

1777   Anima Poetae, From the Unpublished Note-Books of Samuel Taylor
>   Coleridge. Ed. Ernest Hartley Coleridge. 2 vols. London:
>   William Heinemann; Boston, New York: Houghton Mifflin and
>   Company. xv, 352; xi, 271 pp.
>   Selection from Coleridge's notebooks. Reviewed: W. E.
>   Garrett Fisher. Academy, XLVIII (1895), 513-4; Book Buyer
>   [New York], Series 3, XII (1895), 729; Bookman [New York],
>   II (1895), 333-4; Critic [New York], New Series XXIV
>   (1895), 383-4; W. E. H. New Review, XIII (1895), 353-8
>   [possibly New Review editor, W. E. Henley]; Poet-Lore [Bos-
>   ton], VIII (1895), 100-5; J. B. Bury, Saturday Review,
>   LXXX (1895), 681-3; Spectator, No. 3513 (16 Oct 1895),
>   p. 550; Times, No. 34717 (25 Oct 1895), p. 14; Nation [New
>   York], LXII (1896), 185-6. See also 1785, 1791, 1797, 1837.

1778   The Golden Book of Coleridge. Ed. with an introduction by
>   Stopford A. Brooke. London: J. M. Dent.
>   Introduction traces Coleridge's development as poet, de-
>   scribes his particular sense of nature and the supernatur-
>   al. Compares Coleridge with Wordsworth and Shelley. Re-
>   viewed: Critic [New York] XXVII (1895), 97-9; Spectator,
>   No. 3507 (14 Sept 1895), p. 345.

1779   Letters of Samuel Taylor Coleridge. Ed. Ernest Hartley Cole-
>   ridge. 2 vols. London: William Heinemann; Boston, New
>   York: Houghton Mifflin and Co. I, xix, 444; II, vii,
>   448-813 pp. Portraits (Leslie, Kayser), illustrations.

1895-Letters of Samuel Taylor Coleridge

(Letters of Samuel Taylor Coleridge)
Introduction (I, i-x) surveys previous publications, explains principle of selection, and discusses Coleridge as
letter-writer. Reviewed: George Saintsbury, Bookman [New
York], I (1895), 394-6; Critic [New York], XXVII (1895),
97-9; Charles E. L. Wingate, Critic [New York], XXVII, (1895),
315-6; Daily Graphic No. 1685 (30 April 1895), p. 5; Dial
[Boston], XVIII (1895), 316-9; Independent [New York],
XLVII (1895), 1472-3; John Dennis, Leisure Hour, XLVI
(1895), 573-5; New York Times, No. 13653 (26 May 1895),
p. 27; Spectator, No. 3496 (29 June 1895), pp. 901-2;
Spectator, No. 3497 (6 July 1895), pp. 16-7; [E. S. Roscoe],
Edinburgh Review, CLXXXIII (1896), 99-128 (attribution:
WI.); London Quarterly Review, LXXXV (1896), 58-76. See
also 1782, 1783, 1783A, 1784, 1786, 1787, 1798, 1800, 1807, 1833 .

1780   The Rime of the Ancient Mariner and Other Poems. Boston:
        Houghton Mifflin and Co.   102 pp.
           Biographical sketch (pp. 5-8) with brief comments for
        students.

1781   ANON. 'Literary Gossip'. Athenaeum, No. 3512 (18 Feb),
        p. 220; No. 3514 (2 Mar 1895), pp. 281-2; No. 3517 (23 Mar
        1895), p. 379.
           Announces discovery of Coleridge letters connected with
        Lloyd family, transcript of Osorio, with alterations and
        glosses in Coleridge's hand, critical notes by Charles
        Lloyd approving comment presumably in hand of Bowles; and
        Coleridge note.

1782   _____. 'Samuel Taylor Coleridge'. Atlantic Monthly [Boston],
        LXXVI, 397-413.
           Review of Letters (1895). Surveys biographical content,
        argues that Coleridge's life neither lacked unity nor ended
        in failure, discusses his Neoplatonic, rather than Kantean,
        transcendentalism, and Coleridge's influence on Wordsworth,
        Hare, Maurice, and Newman.

1783   _____. [Letter of Samuel Taylor Coleridge]. Athenaeum, No.
        3532 (6 July), pp. 29-30.
           Letters (1895) too prolix and unselective. Should
        emphasize Coleridge's critical opinions and philosophical-
        theological speculations over his life. Values Letters
        only as psychological study.

1783A   _____. 'Unpublished Letters of Samuel Taylor Coleridge. Edit-
        ed by his grandson, Ernest Hartley Coleridge'. Illustrated
        London News, CII, 397-8, 437,463,500, 530,634, 698, 766; CIII, 42.
           Extracts illustrated by portraits, sketches, and photo-
        graphs. Concludes with letter from John Duke, Lord Cole-
        ridge on childhood visit to Highgate.

SAMUEL TAYLOR COLERIDGE: AN ANNOTATED BIBLIOGRAPHY

1784   _____. 'Coleridge's Letters'. London Quarterly and Holburn Review, LXXXV, 58-76.
     A biographical sketch based on letters, includes comparison in favour of Wordsworth. Comments on uniqueness of The Ancient Mariner.

1785   _____. 'The Soul of A Philosopher'. New Outlook [New York], LIII, 770-1.
     Review of Anima Poetae. Brief essay on Coleridge the philosopher, source of all Broad Church theology.

1786   _____. 'Coleridge'. Critic [New York], New Series XXIV, 97-100. Portraits (pp. 97-9) by Robert Hancock and J. Kayser.
     Contrasts selectivity of Letters (1895) with poor choice of poems and neglect of prose in Brooke's Golden Book of Coleridge (1895).

1787   _____. 'Coleridge's Letters'. Times, No. 34562 (27 April), p. 14.
     Coleridge's Letters 'will show...a strangely interesting figure', with 'incurable weakness of character'. Reply by Lucy Watson (1895) q.v.

1788   BENSON, ARTHUR CHRISTOPHER. 'At Nether Stowey'. Lyrics. London: John Lane; New York: Macmillan, pp. 93-6.
     Poem.

1789   CAMPBELL, J. DYKES. 'Coleridge at Highgate'. Sketch, X, 340.
     Describes Coleridge's room and memorial tablet. Illustrations.

1790   CHANCELLOR, E. BERESFORD. 'Samuel Taylor Coleridge, Poet'. Literary Types, London: Sonnenschein; New York: Macmillan, pp. 172-92.
     Discusses disparity between Coleridge's abilities and performance. In genius, 'nearer Shakespeare than any other', but in use made of genius, 'he remains...the most disappointing of all truly great men'. Coleridge's mind half-oriental and half German.

1791   DARMESTETER, MARY JAMES. 'Anima Poetae: Pensées Intimes de Samuel Taylor Coleride'. Revue de Paris, VI, 180-91.
     Challenges Coleridge's classification as Lake Poet, and describes progress from poet to philosopher, with translated selections from Anima.

243

1792   DODD, W[ILLIA]M. 'De Quincey on Coleridge'. Notes and Que-
       ries, 8th Series VII, 345-6.
           Facetious comment on De Quincey's description of Cole-
       ridge.

1793   EASTLAKE, LADY ELIZABETH. Journals and Correspondence. 2
       vols. Ed. Charles Eastlake Smith. London: John Murray.
           Comments (I, 55-6) on abilities revealed in Coleridge's
       Friend and (II, 286-7) difficulties in translating Brandl's
       Life (1886) which 'too clever for our English public'.

1794   GILLMAN, ALEXANDER W. The Gillmans of Highgate, With Letters
       from Samuel Taylor Coleridge, etc. London: Elliot Stock.
       53 pp. Illustrated with four portraits.
           Account of Coleridge at Highgate, his opium addiction
       and financial problems, and texts of several letters.

1795   GRESWELL, WILLIAM. 'The Witchery of the Quantock Hills'.
       Temple Bar, CIV, 523-36.
           Strained effort to find significance in accidental con-
       nections among Coleridge, Wordsworth, and Andrew Crosse
       with the Quantocks.

1796   HOGG, JAMES. De Quincey and His Friends. London: Sampson
       Low, Marston and Company.
           Recollections of De Quincey's comments on Coleridge's
       use of opium (p. 83) and of his conversation (p. 128).

1797   HUNTINGDON, TULEY FRANCIS. 'Leaves from Coleridge's Note-
       books'. Dial [Boston], XIX, 244-6.
           Anima Poetae recommended for striking passages and care-
       ful description of nature. Discusses mutual influence of
       Coleridge and Wordsworth.

1798   [HUTTON, RICHARD HOLT]. 'Glorifying the Slipshod Life'.
       Spectator, No. 3490 (18 May), pp. 679-80; No. 3491 (25 May)
       pp. 718-9; No. 3492 (1 June) p. 752.
           Recently published letters confirm wasted nature of
       Coleridge's life. Challenged by Julia Wedgwood and Alger-
       non Warren, but supported by editorial note.
           Attribution: Tener

1799   KEATS, JOHN. Letters of John Keats. Ed. H. Buxton Forman.
       London: Reeves and Turner.
           Letter of 1819 (pp. 282-333) describes meeting and con-
       versation with Coleridge.

SAMUEL TAYLOR COLERIDGE: AN ANNOTATED BIBLIOGRAPHY

1800   LANG, ANDREW. 'The Letters of Coleridge'. Contemporary Re-
        view, LXVII, 876-87. Reprinted Littell's Living Age [Bos-
        ton], 6th Series VII (1895), 279-87.
            Discusses Coleridge's strengths and weaknesses.

1801   LINDE (née DENNY), GERTRUDE M. 'A Letter of Coleridge's'.
        Athenaeum, No. 3525 (18 May), p. 643.
            Letter to Mary Evans.

1802   MITCHELL, DONALD G. English Lands, Letters and Kings. 4 vols.
        London: Sampson Low, Marston and Co.
            Flippant biographical sketch (III, 309-18).

1803   READE, A. ARTHUR. Provident British Authors. Notes About
        Their Investment in Life Assurance. Manchester. No
        publisher.
            Details of Coleridge's insurance (pp. 7-8) with brief
        comments.

1804   SAINTSBURY, GEORGE. 'Robert Southey'. Macmillan's Magazine,
        LXXI, 346-57. Reprinted in his Essays in English Litera-
        ture 1780-1860. 2nd Series. London: Percival and Co.;
        New York: Charles Scribner's Sons (1895), pp. [1]-37,
        415-7.
            Parallel biographical accounts of Southey and Coleridge
        in Bristol and Keswick (pp. 349-51).

1805   SHEPHERD, RICHARD HERNE. 'The Bibliography of Coleridge'.
        Notes and Queries, 8th Series VII, 361-3, 401-3, 443-5,
        502-3. Revised, corrected, and enlarged by Colonel W. F.
        Prideaux. London: F. Hollings (1900). x, 95 pp.
            Chronological list. Both original and revision contain
        many small errors.

1806   SMITH, NOWELL C. 'Coleridge and His Critics'. Fortnightly
        Review, LXIV, 340-54.
            Discusses attacks on Coleridge made during and after his
        lifetime. Suggests Campbell's biography and E. H. Cole-
        ridge's Letters have made just estimate possible.

1807   STEPHEN, LESLIE. 'Coleridge's Letters'. National Review,
        XXV, 318-27. Reprinted in Littell's Living Age [Boston],
        6th Series VI, 795-801.
            Letters contain 'some of the strangest [sermons] that
        ever a man preached upon himself' and display Coleridge's
        mind at work as do the marginalia. His 'great poems are
        dreams'.

1808   STODDART, ANNA M. John Stuart Blackie. 2 vols. Edinburgh,
       London: William Blackwood and Sons.
           Description of Coleridge in 1831 (I, 129).

1809   WATSON, LUCY E. 'S. T. Coleridge'. Times, No. 34598 (8 June)
       p. 14; reprinted with comments in Lancet, No. 3746 (15 June
       1895), p. 1527; reprinted in Alexander W. Gillman, The
       Gillmans of Highgate. London: Elliot Stock (1895),
       pp. 35-6.
           Angered by anonymous review of Letters in the Times
       (April 27), James Gillman's grand-daughter quotes his de-
       scription of Coleridge's post-mortem, which disclosed se-
       vere organic malformation.

1810   WEDGWOOD, JULIA. 'Samuel Taylor Coleridge'. Contemporary Re-
       view, LXVII, 548-68; reprinted in Littell's Living Age
       [Boston], 6th Series VI (1895), 387-401; in her Nineteenth
       Century Teachers and Other Essays. London: Hodder and
       Stoughton (1909), pp. 1-28.
           Coleridge's poetry and philosophy embody 'in an unusual-
       ly deep sense, revelation of a character'. Considers Cole-
       ridge's relation to his own time and to Victorian Period.

1811   WOLFE, THEODORE FRELINGHUYSEN. 'Literary Hampstead and High-
       gate'. Literary Pilgrimage Among the Haunts of Famous
       British Authors. Philadelphia: J. P. Lippincott Company,
       pp. 13-24.
           Essentially geographical survey mentions Coleridge where
       appropriate.

                              1896

1812   AITKEN, G. A. 'Coleridge on Gulliver's Travels'. Athenaeum,
       No. 3590 (15 Aug) p. 224.
           Coleridge's note from Wordsworth's copy.

1813   ANON. Catalogue of the Library of The Right Honourable Lord
       Coleridge, Lord Chief Justice of England. [London], West-
       minster: Sotheby, Wilkinson and Hodge.
           Seven Coleridge items recorded in lots 333-9 of sale of
       4, 8 May 1896.

1814   _____. 'Samuel Taylor Coleridge's Notes on Comic Literature:
       A Find'. Athenaeum, No. 3609 (26 Dec), pp. 906-7; No. 3612
       (16 Jan 1897), p. 86. Reprinted Cosmopolis, IX, X (1898)
       635-48, 52-7.

                              246

(_____.)
   Fifty-two Coleridge marginalia in Southey's copy of
Flögel's Geschichte der komischen Literatur. In response,
Lavens Mathewson notes Poole's copy of Raleigh's History of
the World similarly annotated.

1815   A. T. 'The Southey-Coleridge Sonnet'. Athenaeum, No. 3558
         (4 Jan) p. 18; No. 3559 (11 Jan), pp. 53-4.
         Note by A. T. with replies by W. Hale White and E. A. P.
       on authorship of Bala Hill.

1816   BAYNE, THOMAS. 'Coleridge and Lord Lytton'. Notes and Que-
         ries, 8th Series X, 47-8.
         Compares a Coleridge comment on Milton with one by
       Bulwer-Lytton on Hazlitt.

1817   _____. 'Coleridge on Wordsworth'. Notes and Queries, 8th
         Series IX, 186.
         Praises Coleridge's criticism of Wordsworth.

1818   BRANDL, A. 'Cowper's Winter Evening und Coleridge's Frost At
         Midnight'. Archiv für das Studium der neuren Sprachen und
         Literaturen [Braunschweig], XCVI, 341-2.
         Notes parallels between the two poems.

1819   _____. 'S. T. Coleridge Notisbuch aus den Jahren 1795-1798'.
         Archiv für das Studium der neuren Sprachen und Literaturen
         [Braunschweig], XCVII, 333-72.
         Detailed but inaccurate description and history
       (pp. 332-9) of Gutch Notebook with (pp. 340-72) extracts
       and comments.

1820   CLARKE, ARCHIBALD. 'Coleridge and Sainte-Beuve'. Notes and
         Queries, 8th Series IX, 485-6.
         Queries Coleridge's influence.

1821   DODGE, R. E. NEILL. 'An Allusion in Coleridge's First Advent
         of Love'. Anglia [Tubingen], XVIII, 132.
         Finds basis of poem in Sidney's Arcadia.

1822   FORSTER, MAX. 'Wordsworth, Coleridge, and Frederike Brun'.
         Academy, XLIX, 429-30.
         Prints Brun's poem so that reader may settle Coleridge's
       plagiarism issue.

1823   GOSSE, EDMUND. 'Walter Pater: A Portrait'. Critical Kit-
        Kats. London: W. Heinemann, pp. 239–73.
            Pater's 1866 essay on Coleridge is 'correct and cold'.
        Concerns Coleridge only as philosopher, neglecting role as
        'exquisite poet'.

1824   GRESWELL, WILLIAM. 'The Coleridge Cottage at Nether Stowey'.
        Athenaeum, No. 3570 (18 Mar), p. 413.
            Appeal for aid in purchasing cottage for use as Cole-
        ridge library.

1825   HORT, ARTHUR FENTON. Life and Letters of Fenton John Anthony
        Hort. 2 vols. London, New York: Macmillan and Co.
            References in diaries and letters suggest Coleridge's
        early influence (I, 96–7). Gives correspondence (I, 320–1)
        on composition of 1856 essay.

1826   [HUTCHINSON, THOMAS] T. H. 'The Late J. Dykes Campbell'.
        Academy, L, 114–5.
            Review of second edition of Campbell's biography, dis-
        cusses correction of errors in first edition.

1827   JERNINGHAM, LADY FRANCES (DILLON). The Jerningham Letters
        (1870–1896). 2 vols. Ed. Egerton Castle. London: Rich-
        ard Bentley and Son.
            Letter from Edward Jerningham to Lady Bedingfeld (I,
        314–18) describes Coleridge's 1808 lectures, which he at-
        tended, Coleridge's appearance, and problems with the Royal
        Institution.

1828   JOHNSON, R. BRIMLEY. Christ's Hospital Recollections of Lamb,
        Coleridge, and Leigh Hunt. London: George Allen. Illus-
        trated.
            Brief biographical note with facsimile of Coleridge's
        application for admission. Extracts from Coleridge's writ-
        ings on his schooldays.

1829   LÉGOUIS, EMILE. La Jeunesse de William Wordsworth 1770–1798.
        Paris: G. Masson. 490 pp. Trans. J. W. Matthews. The
        Early Life of William Wordsworth 1770–1798. London: J. M.
        Dent and Co. (1897).
            A detailed discussion of relation of Coleridge and
        Wordsworth up to 1798, their mutual influence, and efforts
        at collaboration.

SAMUEL TAYLOR COLERIDGE: AN ANNOTATED BIBLIOGRAPHY

1830 MILES, P. NAPIER. Hymn Before Sunrise for Baritone Solo, Chorus, and Orchestra. New York, London: Boosey and Co. Composed for Bristol Music Festival.

1831 MITCHELL, SILAS WEIR. 'Coleridge at Chamouny'. Collected Poems. New York: Century Co. Four stanzas (pp. 252-3) mourning Coleridge.

1832 MONKHOUSE, COSMO. 'The National Portrait Gallery'. Scribner's Magazine [New York], XX, 317-37. Hancock drawing, p. 326. Mentions (p. 330) Allston's portrait and describes Robert Hancock's 1796 drawing.

1833 P. 'Personalia: Coleridge, Arnold, Stevenson'. Poet-Lore [Boston], VIII, 100-05. Review of Letters (1895) which reveal Coleridge's weaknesses and show him like Arnold a self-centered conservative in contrast with Stevenson.

1834 [PROESCHOLDT, LUDWIG] Ldw. Pr. 'Coleridge, Samuel Taylor, Anima Poetae'. Literarisches Zentralblatt [Leipzig], No. 4 (25 Jan), pp. 131-2. Coleridge and Carlyle the most important English representatives of German thought.

1835 ROBERTS, W. 'Coleridge Mss'. Notes and Queries, 8th Series IX, 285. Queries location of mss from David Charles Read's library.

1836 SAINTSBURY, GEORGE. History of Nineteenth-Century Literature (1780-1895). New York, London: Macmillan and Co. Biographical sketch and general assessment of Coleridge (pp. 56-65). The Ancient Mariner, Christabel, Kubla Khan, and Love only first-class poems, but they inaugurated a new poetry and entitle Coleridge to rank of great poet.

1837 WATERER, CLARENCE. 'The Note-Books of Samuel Taylor Coleridge'. Westminster Review, CXLV, [526]-38. Review of Anima Poetae (1895) surveys Coleridge's life, comments on his introspection, analysis and original thought.

1838 WOODBERRY, GEORGE EDWARD. 'Samuel Taylor Coleridge'. Library of the World's Best Literature. New York: J. A. Hill & Company, VII, 3843-53. Reprinted in his Makers of Literature. New York: Macmillan (1900), pp. 27-50.

249

1896-WOODBERRY

    (WOODBERRY, GEORGE EDWARD)
        Analysis of Coleridge's character and temperament. Ex-
    tended discussion of kinds of unity in The Ancient Mariner
    and interpretation of poem as allegory of psychological
    states and moral facts. Christabel less successful since
    it mixes the supernatural with the actual.

1839   WRIGHT, W. H. KEARLEY. 'Samuel Taylor Coleridge'. West-
        Country Poets. Their Lives and Their Works. London:
        Elliot Stock, pp. 102-07.
        Biographical account.

1897

1840   The Ancient Mariner. Ed. Andrew J. George. Boston: Heath
        and Co. 150 pp.
        Biographical sketch (pp. v-xxxiv) emphasizes connection
    with and influence of the Wordsworths.

1841   ABBOTT, EVELYN. Life and Letters of Benjamin Jowett, M.A.
        2 vols. London: John Murray.
        Letter to Benjamin Brody (I, 98) describes meeting with
    Schelling, who discussed Coleridge and thought him unfairly
    attacked for plagiarism.

1842   ANON. 'A Literary Leather Man'. Shoe and Leather Record,
        No. 587 (27 Aug), pp. 550-6.
        Account of the interrelated lives of Coleridge and Poole
    from 1794.

1843   [COLERIDGE, SIR JOHN DUKE]. 'Coleridgeiana'. Temple Bar,
        CXI, 114-7.
        Biographical sketch with emphasis on familiar anecdotes.
        Attribution: WI.

1844   DALL, CAROLINE HEALEY. Transcendentalism in New England. A
        Lecture Delivered Before the Society of Philosophical En-
        quiry, Washington, D. C. May 8, 1895. Boston: Roberts.
        Partially reprinted George Willis Cooke. An Historical and
        Biographical Account to Accompany The Dial. 2 vols.
        Cleveland: The Rowfant Club (1902), II, 72-4.
        1877 letter from F. H. Hedge explains intentions of his
    1833 essay.

250

Samuel Taylor Coleridge: An Annotated Bibliography

1845   DE VERE, AUBREY. Recollections of Aubrey de Vere. New York,
      London: Edward Arnold.
        Admiring references to Coleridge, the subject of his
      first poem, comments by Wordsworth (pp. 123-4) and Sir Wil-
      liam Rowan Hamilton (p. 200), who thought Coleridge 'nearly
      the only Englishman of our time [who was] a philosopher'.

1846   DOWDEN, EDWARD. The French Revolution and English Literature.
      New York: Charles Scribner's Sons.
        Coleridge's attitudes towards French Revolution compared
      (pp. 172-84, 209, 228) with those of Wordsworth and
      Southey.

1847   EMERSON, EDWARD WALDO. 'John Sterling and a Correspondence
      Between Sterling and Emerson'. Atlantic Monthly [Boston]
      LXXX, 14-35. Reprinted with minor additions Correspondence
      between John Sterling and Ralph Waldo Emerson. Boston, New
      York: Houghton, Mifflin (1897), pp. 41-2, 52.
        Comments on Coleridge's influence on Sterling, and
      prints letters in which Sterling and Emerson discuss
      Coleridge.

1848   FORMAN, H. BUXTON. 'Coleridge's Notes on Flögel'. Cosmopolis,
      IX, 635-48, X (1898), 52-65.
        Marginalia in C. F. Flögel's Geschichte der komischen
      Literatur with Forman's commentary.

1849   GARNETT, R[ICHARD]. 'Sibylline Leaves'. Athenaeum, No. 3661
      (25 Dec), p. 885; No. 3662 (1 Jan 1898), p.24.
        Congratulates W. E. Henley for recognizing that Mutual
      Passion was modernized by Coleridge from Ben Jonson, and
      should not be printed among Coleridge's poems. W. Hale
      White adds publishing history of Coleridge's version.

1850   GOSSE, EDMUND. 'Popularity of Poetry'. Essays from the Chap-
      Book. London: Gay and Bird, pp. 89-98.
        Anecdote (pp. 94-5) of Coleridge's failure to make money
      from poetry.

1851   HAZLITT, W. CAREW. Four Generations of A Literary Family.
      2 vols. London, New York: George Redway.
        Brief mentions of Coleridge from 1798 (I, 79) to the
      painting of his portrait (I, 84-5) for Sir George Beaumont
      in 1803, in which he is described as looking like a con-
      demned man about to meet his fate.

1852   HAZLITT, WILLIAM CAREW. The Lambs, their lives, their
       friends, and their correspondence. London: Elkin Mathews;
       New York: Charles Scribner's Sons.
           Includes (pp. 112, 118, 134, 198, 212, 219-24) some of
       Coleridge's correspondence with Lamb.

1853   HERFORD, C. H. 'Samuel Taylor Coleridge'. The Age of Words-
       worth. London: G. Bell and Sons. 315 pp.
           Sketch (pp. 169-83) of first half of Coleridge's life,
       with impressionistic critical comments ('voluptuous',
       'dreamlike', 'mystic'). Compares Coleridge with Wordsworth
       and discusses mutual influence.

1854   HIGHAM, CHARLES. 'Coleridge and Swedenborg. A Hitherto Un-
       published Letter'. New Church Magazine, XVI, 106-12.
           Describes Coleridge's marginalia on Swedenborg and
       prints 1820 letters to Tulk.

1855   LANG, ANDREW. Life and Letters of John Gibson Lockhart. 2
       vols. London: John C. Nimmo; New York: Charles Scrib-
       ner's Sons.
           Brief account of Lockhart's reviews of Coleridge and two
       familiar anecdotes.

1856   LANDOR, WALTER SAVAGE. Letters and Other Unpublished Writings
       of Walter Savage Landor. Ed. Stephen Wheeler. London:
       Richard Bentley & Son.
           Describes (p. 161) visit to Highgate in 1832.

1857   MILL, JOHN STUART. 'Unpublished letter from John Stuart Mill
       to Professor Nichol'. Fortnightly Review, New Series LXI,
       [660]-78.
           Letter of 1834 (pp. 665-7) describes enthusiasm for
       Coleridge, especially Church and State. 'On the whole
       there is more food for thought--and the best kind of
       thought--in Coleridge than in all other contemporary writ-
       ers'. Coleridge more systematic than even Bentham.

1858   OLIPHANT, MRS. [MARGARET]. Annals of a Publishing House; Wil-
       liam Blackwood and his Sons, their Magazine and Friends.
       Edinburgh, London: Blackwood and Sons.
           Discusses (pp. 406-22) Blackwood's relations with Cole-
       ridge and includes several of their letters to each other.

1859   PALGRAVE, FRANCIS T. Landscape in Poetry. London, New York:
       Macmillan and Co.
           Discussion (pp. 196-203), with many examples, of Cole-
       ridge's descriptions of landscape.

SAMUEL TAYLOR COLERIDGE: AN ANNOTATED BIBLIOGRAPHY

1860 SCHNABEL, B. 'Ossian in der schönen Literatur Englands bis
      1832'. Englische Studien [Leipzig], XXIII, 366–401.
      Attempts by parallel passages to show (pp. 369–78) in-
      fluence of Ossian on some of Coleridge's early poems.

1861 STEPHEN, LESLIE. 'Wordsworth's Youth'. National Review,
      XXVIII, 769–86. Reprinted in his Studies of a Biographer.
      4 vols. London: Duckworth (1899–1902), I, 227–67.
      Comparison with Wordsworth shows Coleridge's unusual
      combination of poetical and reasoning faculties, justifica-
      tion of a creed by apparatus of dialectics.

1862 [TENNYSON, HALLAM]. Alfred Lord Tennyson. A Memoir by his
      Son. 3 vols. London, New York: Macmillan.
      Notes (I, 50) Tennyson's indifference to Coleridge's
      prose but devotion to his poetry, and gives his explanation
      of Coleridge's adverse criticism of his early poems.

1863 THOMPSON, FRANCIS. 'Academy Portraits XIII--S. T. Coleridge'.
      Academy, LI, 179–80. Portrait by Vandyke, p. 179. Re-
      printed Works of Francis Thompson, 3 vols. London: Burns
      & Oates Ltd. (1913), III, 181–9. Reprinted in one volume
      1949, 1969.
      Later work devoid of value, and character deplorably
      weak, but Coleridge, nevertheless, 'a poet's poet'.

1864 TWEEDIE, W. M. 'Christabel'. Modern Language Notes [Balti-
      more], XII, 191.
      Asks source of Dykes Campbell's reading of a line from
      Christabel.

1865 WHITE, W. HALE. 'Coleridge on Spinoza'. Athenaeum, No. 3630
      (22 May), pp. 680–1.
      Discussion of Coleridge's marginalia in Spinoza with
      several extracts.

1866 _____. A Description of the Wordsworth and Coleridge Manu-
      scripts in the Possession of Mr. T. Norton Longman. With
      Three Facsimile Reproductions. London: Longmans et al.
      vi, 72 pp.
      Letters and mss. related to second edition of Lyrical
      Ballads, including Coleridge's alterations in The Ancient
      Mariner, and facsimile of ms. of Love. Reviewed: Athe-
      naeum, No. 3636 (3 July 1897), pp. 31–2; No. 3713 (24 Dec
      1898), pp. 897–8; Saturday Review, LXXXIII (1897), 665–6.

1898–Lyrical Ballads by William Wordsworth

1898

1867   Lyrical Ballads by William Wordsworth and S. T. Coleridge
1798. Ed. with an introduction and notes by Thomas Hutchinson. London: Duckworth and Co.
Long bibliographical note and selection of critical notices, discussion of the origins of The Ancient Mariner,
and notes on individual poems. Reviewed: Notes and Queries, 9th Series II (1898), 19.

1868   The Poetry of Samuel Taylor Coleridge. Ed. with an introduction by Richard Garnett. The Muses Library. London:
Lawrence and Bullen. lii, 318 pp. Introduction pp. xiii-
lii. Introduction reprinted his Essays of an Ex-Librarian.
London: William Heinemann, New York: Dodd Mead (1901),
pp. 55–97.
Argues that 'Quintessential Poetry' of 1797-8 unpredict-
able from earlier work, though it owed something to Wordsworth's influence. Reviewed: Athenaeum, No. 3656 (20 Nov
1897), pp. 701-2; Commentary, CX (1897), 110; Literature,
II (1898), p. 142; Nation [New York], LXVI (1898), 225;
Sewanee Review [Tennessee], VI (1898), 251; Spectator, No.
3652 (25 June 1898), p. 888.

1869   The Raven. A Poem by Samuel Taylor Coleridge. With Illustra-
tions by Ella Hallward. With an Introduction by the Hon.
Stephen Coleridge. London: H. S. Nichols.
Brief, vacuous introduction.

1870   BYRON, GEORGE GORDON NOEL BYRON. Letters and Journals. 6
vols. Ed. Rowland E. Prothero. London: John Murray; New
York: Charles Scribner's Sons. Reprinted New York: Octa-
gon Books (1966).
Numerous references 1811-22 show Byron's shift from admiration to anger and contempt.

1871   COLERIDGE, ERNEST HARTLEY. Poems. London, New York: Bodley
Head. 107 pp.
Three poems (pp. 17, 76, 78-81) and three sonnets (pp.
43, 75, 77) on Coleridge by his grandson.

1872   CURRY, JOHN T. 'The Nightingale's Song: S. T. Coleridge and
John Skelton'. Notes and Queries, 9th Series I, 204-5.
Coleridge possibly influenced by Skelton's 'Crowne of
Laurell'.

1873   FORSTER, JOSEPH. 'S. T. Coleridge'. Great Teachers. London:
George Redway, pp. 101-137.
Conventional, ill-informed, biographical sketch.

1874   GOSSE, EDMUND. Short History of Modern English Literature.
       London: W. Heinemann.
           Chapter VIII primarily discussion of linked careers of
       Wordsworth and Coleridge (pp. 276-88). Coleridge also
       (pp. 109, 320) mentioned as critic.

1875   GUTHRIE, WILLIAM NORMAN. 'The Rime of the Ancient Mariner As
       Prophecy'. Sewanee Review [Tennessee], VI, 200-13.
           Discusses nature of Mariner's crime, argues that poem
       embodies philosophy of mystical love also found, less po-
       etically, in Religious Musings and Destiny of Nations.

1876   HAMMOND, ELEANOR P. 'The Artistic Devices of Coleridge's
       Ancient Mariner'. Poet-Lore [Boston], X, 425-9.
           Examines poem as 'deliberate piecing-together' of artis-
       tic devices to produce sequence of impressions.

1877   KINGSLEY, MAUD ELMA. 'Test Questions for "The Ancient Mari-
       ner"'. Journal of Education [Boston], LXVII, 37. Re-
       printed Boston: Almer Co. (1910).
           Explanation and advice for school teachers.

1878   LANG, ANDREW. Coleridge. Selections from the poets series.
       London: Longmans et al. xliii, 247 pp. Illustrated by
       Patten Wilson.
           Introduction (pp. xi-xliii) presents Coleridge as poet
       of 'dream and desire' who captured 'that indefinable emotion
       which is less articulately expressed in music'. Coleridge's
       theology product not of philosophy but of 'his incommuni-
       cable experience of prayer and rapture'.
           Reviewed: Academy, LV (1898), 152-3; Spectator, No.
       3675 (3 Dec 1898), p. 838; Bookman XV (1899), 144-5; Lit-
       erary World [Boston], XXX (1899), 59.

1879   LATHROP, GEORGE PARSONS. 'Some Forgotten Hawthorne Verses'.
       New York Times [Supplement: Saturday Review of Books].
       No. 15029 (12 March).
           Suggests The Ancient Mariner was model for Hawthorne's
       'Star of Calvary'.

1880   LUCAS, E. V. 'Coleridge and Charles Lloyd'. Charles Lamb and
       the Lloyds. London: Smith Elder & Co.
           Coleridge's relations with Lloyd and Lamb (Ch II-IV).

1881   MERIVALE, J[UDITH] A., ed. Autobiography and Letters of
       Charles Merivale, Dean of Ely. Oxford. Privately printed;
       reprinted London: E. Arnold (1899).
           Mentions influence of Coleridge, Wordsworth and Hare on
       Cambridge Apostles.

1898-NEWCOMEN

1882   NEWCOMEN, GEORGE. 'A Very Ancient Mariner'. New Ireland Re-
       view [Dublin], IX, 13-17.
          Account of circumstances of composition.

1883   SAINTSBURY, GEORGE. A Short History of English Literature.
       London: Macmillan and Company.
          Discusses (pp. 656-7) Coleridge's prose and poetry.
       Comments (p. 654) on pervasiveness of influence on poetry
       and criticism.

1884   SMITH, ELIZABETH GRANT. Memoirs of a Highland Lady. London:
       John Murray.
          Description (p. 385) of 'that poor mad poet, Coleridge'
       in 1823.

1885   STUCKEY, HARRY DYMOND. Coleridge in Somersetshire and
       Stuckey's Version for his Dramatic Recital of the Rime of
       the Ancyent Marinere. Bristol: B. H. Matthews.
          Popular biographical sketch with abridged text used by
       Stuckey for public reading in Somersetshire dialect.

1886   TEXTE, JOSEPH. 'William Wordsworth et la poésie lakiste en
       France'. Études de littérature Européene. Paris: Armand
       Colin et Cie, pp. 147-94.
          Argues (pp. 165-7) that Coleridge provided Wordsworth
       with a philosophy.

1887   TYLER, MOSES COIT. 'The Home and Grave of Coleridge'.
       Glimpses of England. New York, London: G. P. Putnam,
       pp. 216-22.
          1863 visit to Gillman's house and later to Coleridge's
       grave with gardener who had as a boy met Coleridge.

                              1899

1888   Coleridge's Poems. A Facsimile Reproduction of the Proofs and
       Mss. of Some of the Poems Edited by the Late James Dykes
       Campbell with Preface and Notes by W. Hale White. xii,
       134 pp. [London] Westminster: Archibald Constable and Co.
          Type-facsimile of Poems on Various Subjects, of versions
       of Dark Ladie, British Stripling's War Song and Lewti from
       British Museum. Reviewed: Bookman, XVI (1899), 162;
       Literature [New York] V (1899), 109-10.

1889　ANON. [A Facsimile Reproduction of the Proofs and Mss. of
Some of the Poems of Coleridge.]. Athenaeum, No. 3746
(12 Aug), pp. 213-4.
Early drafts of The Dark Ladie show Coleridge's attention to detail and rejection of imperfect material.

1890　CHAPMAN, EDWARD JOHN. 'The Snake Witch'. A Drama of Two
Lives...and Other Poems. London: K. Paul, Trench, Trubner
and Co., pp. 23-64.
Continuation of Christabel.

1891　COLERIDGE, ERNEST HARTLEY. 'The Lake Poets in Somersetshire'.
Royal Society of Literature. Transactions. 2nd Series XX,
105-31.
Biographical account of Wordsworth and Coleridge in
1797 with brief discussion of poetical innovations.

1892　FESTING, GABRIELLE. John Hookham Frere and His Friends. London: James Nisbet.
Chapter on 'Coleridge and Southey' (pp. 217-34) and several letters from Coleridge to Frere (1816 and 1827).

1893　HALDANE, E[LIZABETH] S[ANDERSON]. 'The Coleridge Plagiarism'.
James Frederick Ferrier. Edinburgh, London: Oliphant
Anderson & Ferrier, pp. 106-12.
Brief survey of controversy over Coleridge's plagiarisms
and of Ferrier's involvement.

1894　HANCOCK, ALBERT ELMER. The French Revolution and The English
Poets. New York: Henry Holt. Reissued Port Washington,
New York: Kennikat Press (1967).
Concluding chapter (pp. 157-94) discusses Coleridge's
early political ideas, distinguishing his attitude toward
French Revolution from his theoretical position.

1895　HIGHAM, CHARLES. 'Coleridge's Marginalia'. Notes and Queries, 9th Series IV, 536.
Notes Gregory's 1882 report of marginalia on Swedenborg
whose authenticity Higham later questions (1899).

1896　＿＿＿＿. 'Pseudo-Coleridge Marginalia'. Morning Light, XXII,
445.
According to E. H. Coleridge, marginalia in volumes of
Swedenborg owned by Swedenborg Society are not by Coleridge
as claimed by Gregory (1882).

1899-HUTCHINSON

1897   HUTCHINSON, T. 'Coleridge and the Poet Young'. Notes and
        Queries, 9th Series IV, 42-3.
            Identifies passages from Coleridge's marginalia as
        transcriptions from Young's Discourse on Lyric Poetry.

1898   KNOWLSON, T. SHARPER. 'Confessions of Enquiring Spirits. II.
        Coleridge's Confessions'. Great Thoughts, XXXII, 99-100.
            Friendly account of Coleridge's creed and its influence.

1899   MACKAIL, J[OHN] W[ILLIAM]. Life of William Morris. 2 vols.
        London: Longman, Green and Co.
            Morris, preparing 1896 Kelmscott edition of Coleridge's
        poems, wrote (II, 310) that Coleridge 'was a muddle-brained
        metaphysician, who...turned out a few real poems amongst
        the dreary flood which was his wont'.

1900   MATHER, J. MARSHALL. 'Six Great Books of the Century. I. The
        Confessions of an Inquiring Spirit'. Young Man, XIII,
        17-19.
            Confessions one of the 'six great formative books of the
        century' because of its 'unparalleled influence' on theolo-
        gy. Summarizes Coleridge's arguments and answers to pos-
        sible objections.

1901   MERCER, ALEXANDER GARDINER. Notes of an Outlook on Life. Ed.
        Manton Marble. London: George Bell & Sons.
            Selections from mss. of donor of memorial show his
        respect for Coleridge.

1902   PALGRAVE, GWENLLIAN F. Francis Turner Palgrave: His Journals
        and Memories of His Life. London: Longmans et al.
            Letters to his mother, pp. 28-9 (1843) describe his
        response to Table Talk.

1903   TOWLE, ELEANOR. 'Literary Courtships'. Fortnightly Review,
        New Series LXVI, 475-89. Reprinted Living Age [Boston],
        CCXXI (1899), 220-31.
            Brief account of Coleridge's courtship.

1904   TURK, WILLIAM. Completion of Coleridge's Christabel and Other
        Poems. Cincinnati: Editor Publishing Co.
            Title poem (pp. 1-46).

1905   TURNER, ALFRED T. 'Some Poets in Love'. Temple Bar, CXVII,
        507-30.
            Anecdotal biographical survey presents Mary Evans as
        love of Coleridge's life. Emphasizes Coleridge's irrespon-
        sibility as husband (pp. 526-30).

1906   WHITE, W. HALE. 'Poole's Correspondence in the British Mu-
            eum'. Athenaeum, No. 3748 (26 Aug), p. 292; No. 3759
            (11 Nov 1899), p. 655.
            Account of gift to British Museum of Coleridge letters
        and mss.

1907   YARNALL, ELLIS. 'Sara Coleridge and Her Brothers'. Words-
            worth and the Coleridges With Other Memories Literary and
            Political. New York, London: Macmillan, pp. 105-41.
            Gives recollections of Coleridge by Allston, Wordworth,
        Derwent C. and A. H. Hallam (pp. 124-5, 133-4, 138). Re-
        viewed: Athenaeum, No. 3738 (17 June 1899), pp. 752-3;
        J. W. Chadwick, Nation [New York], LXIX (1899), 135-6.

Author/Title Index

A.   653, 754, 802, 1485
A. B.   1074
A. B. C. D.   24
A. B. R.   1072, 1149
A. J. M.   1376
A. P. A.   1425
A. S.   284
A. T.   1815
'A. W. Schlegel on Shakespeare's Romeo and Juliet; with remarks on the
    characteristics of German criticism'   332
A. Z.   277
Abbott, Evelyn   1568, 1841
A'Beckett, Sir William   671
Academic [Liverpool]   349
Academical Lectures and Pulpit Discourses   864
'Academy Portraits XIII - S. T. Coleridge'   1863
Academy   1325, 1360, 1366, 1384, 1391, 1418, 1435, 1437, 1438, 1453,
    1478, 1483, 1499, 1516, 1533, 1560, 1576, 1581, 1588, 1616, 1661,
    1736, 1763, 1775, 1777, 1822; 1826, 1863, 1878
'Account of the Manuscripts of the late Sam Spitfire, Author'   105
Ackermann, R.   1753
Adams, Sarah Flower   611
Address Delivered in King's College, London   526
'Admirable Crichton'   704
'Admiralty Goose: or, The Modern Mariner'   1525
Aesthetic Review   1414
'After Looking into Carlyle's Reminiscences'   1465
Afternoon Lectures on Literature and Art   1256
Afternoons with the Poets   1417
'Age of Folly'   424
Age of Wordsworth   1853
Age Reviewed: A Satire   436
Aids to Faith: A Series of Theological Essays   1191
Aids to Reflection   454, 762, 830, 1323
'Aids to Reflection'   407, 408, 420, 421, 439, 494, 783
Aikin, A. L. See Le Breton.
Aikin, John   10, 11, 38, 39
Aikin, Lucy   382

Andrews, Alexander   1155
Anecdote Lives of the Later Wits and Humourists   1349
Anecdotes about Authors and Artists   1566
'Anecdotes of the Late Mr. Coleridge'   758
'Anecdotes of the Poet Coleridge'   758
Anglia [Tubingen]   1821
Anglia Beiblatt [Halle]   1753
Anima Poetae, From the unpublished note-books of Samuel Taylor Cole-
     ridge   1777
'Anima Poetae: pensées intimes de Samuel Taylor Coleridge'   1791
Annales Encyclopédiques [Paris]   258
Annals of a Publishing House   1858
'Annual Biography and Obituary'   623
Annual Biography and Obituary   635
Annual Register   28, 559
Annual Report of the Royal Society of Literature, 1835.   See Royal
     Society...Annual Report
Annual Review   87
'Annuals'   428
'Annuals for 1834'   539
Anster, John   628
'Answers to Correspondents'   738
Anti-Jacobin Review   46, 48, 49, 71, 179, 1671, 1672
Antient Mariner and the Modern Sportsman   1447
Anyta and Other Poems   1239
'Apparent Pictures. I. Coleridge'   1719
'Appeal Apologetic from Philip Drunk to Philip Sober'   453
Apollodorus   1060
Appreciations   1642
'April Voyage'   736
Aquinas, St. Thomas   1059
'Archbishop Leighton's Works'   1161
'Archdeacon Hare'   1110
Archiv für das Studium der neueren Sprachen und Literaturen [Braun-
     schweig]   1074, 1818, 1819
Arden, Maurice   1531
'Are The English a Musical People?'   989
Argonaut [San Francisco]   1396
Argosy   1538A, 1542
Argus [Melbourne]   1448, 1461
Ariel and Other Poems   1059
Armstrong, Edmund J.   1386
Armstrong, George Francis   1386, 1387
Arnold, Matthew   1209, 1216, 1434
Arnold Thomas   858
Art-Journal   1226
Art-Union   703
'Artistic Devices of Coleridge's Ancient Mariner'   1876
Ashe, Thomas   1468, 1483, 1520, 1521, 1606
Aspects of Poetry, being Lectures Delivered at Oxford   1445
Assing, B. L.   1268

269

Croker, John Wilson 127, 196
Croly, George 157
Crompton, Sidney 1676
Crosse, Cornelia A. H. (Mrs. Andrew) 1633, 1758
Crotchet Castle 515
Crowe, Eyre Evans 368
Culpepper, Ned 488
'Culpret Fay, and Other Poems' 700
Cunningham, Allan 543
Cunningham, Mr. 993A
Curry, Daniel 900, 1083
Curry, John T. 1872
Curtis, Reverend Thomas 970
Cyclopedia of English Literature 847

D. 328, 690A
D. L. 719
D. M. 4
D. M. S. 47
D. N. 327
D. S. 833
Daily Graphic 1779
Dalby, E. J. 442
Dall, Caroline Healey 1844
Dallas, Eneas Sweetland 1240
Dana, Richard Henry, Jr. 959
Dana, Richard Henry, Sr. 297, 448
Daniel, George 633, 1211
Darmesteter, Mary James 1791
Darrell, Joyce 1538A
'David Hume Charged by Mr. Coleridge with Plagiarism From St. Thomas
    Aquinas' 285
David Scott 1507
Davies, J. Llewelyn 1537
Davies, W. W. 1629
Davy, Sir Humphry 1151
Davy, John 1151
Dawson, George 1538
Dawson, William James 1681
Day, Horace 1263
Days of Lamb and Coleridge 1737
De Bow's Review [New Orleans and Charleston] 1184
'De Diabalo' 674
'De la Haine Litteraire' 516
De'Prati, Giocchino 732
'De Quincey and Coleridge upon Kant' 1259
De Quincey and His Friends 1796
'De Quincey on Coleridge' 1792
'De Quincey's Writings' 1026
De Quincey, Thomas 389, 390, 391, 507, 588, 720, 744, 768, 795,
    796, 866, 867, 914, 1084, 1118, 1682, 1731

AUTHOR / TITLE INDEX

Hamilton, Walter 1610
Hamilton, Sir William 891
Hammond, Eleanor P. 1876
Hancock, Albert Elmer 1894
Hancock, Robert 1685
Hanna, Rev. William 997
Hannay, James 1103
Harbinger [Boston] 759
Hardman, Joseph 498
Hare, Augustus 431, 1315
Hare, Julius Charles 332, 431, 453, 639, 825, 892, 938, 1121
Harington, J. D. 1392
Harper's Monthly Magazine [Boston] 958
Harper's New Monthly Magazine [New York] 1073, 1226, 1248, 1307,
   1368, 1436, 1706
Harrison, I. B. 638
Harrison, W. H. 1411
'Hartley Coleridge' 1501
'Hartley Coleridge's Lives of the Northern Worthies' 1022
Hasell, Elizabeth Julia 1441
Hasheesh Eater: being Passages from the Life of a Pythagorean 1144
Haunted Farmer 73
Haverfield, F. 1477
Hawthorne, Nathaniel 870
Haydon, Benjamin Robert 1373
Haydon, Frederic Wordsworth 1373
Hayward, A. 592
'Hazlitt and Coleridge: at The Hotel Dessin' 1136
'Hazlitt in Switzerland: a Conversation' 777
'Hazlitt Papers' 1725
Hazlitt, William Carew 1252, 1508, 1762, 1851, 1852
Hazlitt, William 159, 173, 197, 198, 199, 200, 206, 243, 244, 245,
   246, 247, 248, 249, 274, 275, 276, 277, 278, 333, 334, 335, 370,
   392, 402, 413, 466
'Hazlitt's Essays, Criticisms, and Lectures' 289
'Hazlitt's Lectures on the English Poets' 297
'Hazlitt's Table-Talk' 368
Headlong Hall 207
Heath, Charles 27
Heath, William 71
'Hebrew Tales...by Hyman Hurwitz' 434
Hedge, Frederic Henry 544, 1844
'Hegel's Aesthetics. Philosophy of Art' 954
'Heinrich Heine' 1209
Helen 663
Hemans, Felicia Dorothea 593
Henderson, Frank 1440
Henry, Caleb Sprague 815
Heraud, John Abraham 432, 488, 509, 527, 528, 529, 594, 595, 640,
   641, 642, 643, 696, 725, 751, 772, 773, 774, 775, 776, 913, 925,
   992, 1164

'Import of Keats's <u>Lamia</u> in contrast with Coleridge's <u>Christabel</u>'
1771
<u>Indicator</u> 299, 336
'Inedited Poems by S. T. Coleridge' 1444
'Infallibility of the Bible and Recent Theories of Inspiration' 1028
<u>Infant Bridal and Other Poems</u> 1219
'Influence of Coleridge' 1500
'Influence of German Literature' 832
Ingleby, Clement Mansfield 1034, 1035, 1036, 1063, 1064, 1072, 1104,
1286, 1287, 1317, 1478, 1517
Ingram, J. H. 1426
<u>Inquirer</u> 1062
<u>Insanity of Genius</u> 1687
<u>Inspiration of Holy Scripture</u> 1143
'Intelligence: Literary, Philosophical' 121
'Introduction of German Philosophy into the United States' 1247
<u>Introduction to English Literature</u> 1738
<u>Introduction to the Study of Poetry</u> 1456
<u>Introductory Discourse and the Lectures Delivered Before the American
Institute of Instructors</u> 608
'Introductory Essay' 1073
'Inventions of William Blake, Painter and Poet' 477
<u>Invocation, as Sung with Unbounded Applause by Mrs. Bland</u> 161
'Irresponsibilities of Genius' 1612
Irving, Edward 414
'Isabelle' 201

J. 596, 894, 1374, 1394
J. C. H. 332, 639
J. D. 1185, 1342
J. D. C. 1534, 1603, 1604, 1629, 1653, 1657, 1674, 1676, 1696, 1729,
1730
J. D. W. 957
J. E. 242
J. E. H. 838
J. H. 1185
J. H. C. 1258
J. H. R. 203
J. M. 1036, 1088
J. M. B. 1066, 1067, 1072
J. M. G. 1068, 1082
J. R. B. 1301
J. R. G. 1090
J. W. E. 1375, 1376
J. W. W. 1390, 1400
J. Y. 1101
Jabez 1374
Jackson, Ezekiel 105, 106
Jackson, Stephen 1297
Jacobsen, Friederich Johann 337

'Julius Charles Hare' 1116
Jupp, Richard F. 1686

K. 1707, 1708
Kaufman, A., Jr. 647
Keats, John 1799
'Keepsake Reviewed' 460
Kelly, Michael 161, 423
Kemble, John Mitchell 726
Kemperhausen, Philip 314
Kennedy, H. A. 1245
Kennedy, T. 853
Kershaw, J. H. 1000
Kindt, Hermann 1254
King 567
King, Alice 1542
King, Thomas E. 871
'King's Speech' 501
Kingdom of Christ 822
Kingsley, Charles 1125
Kingsley, Maud Elma 1877
Klipstein, August 1377
Knickerbocker [New York] 620, 672, 681, 1017
Knight, Charles 920, 953
Knight, Joseph 1331
Knight, William 1588, 1611, 1639
Knight's Quarterly Magazine 399
Knowlson, T. Sharper 1898
Köpke, Rudolph 1105
Kok, A. S. 1212
Koszul, A. 280, 290

L. 430
L. F. T. 826
L. M. C. 587
L. S. 1597
L'Estrange, A. G. 1302
Labouchere, Peter Anthony 1264, 1318
Lachrymae Musarum and Other Poems 1718
Ladies Companion [New York] 719
Ladies' Repository [Cincinnati] 1231
Ladies' Repository [New York] 1312
Lady Jane Grey, and Other Poems 1081
Lady's Magazine and Museum 580
'Lake Poets in Somersetshire' 1891
'Lake Reminiscences from 1808 to 1830. By the English Opium-Eater,
    No. V. Southey, Wordsworth, and Coleridge' 768
Lamb, Charles [Elia, pseud] 35, 204, 279, 338, 339, 510, 1378
Lamb, Mary 1766

'Lines by Mr. Coleridge on the Queen'   325
'Lines to S. T. Colridge' [sic]   36
'Lines' [on Coleridge's Cottage]   771
'Lines, on Viewing the Cottage at Clevedon, for some time the Resi-
    dence of the Poet Coleridge'   1081
'Lines, written at Bridgwater, in Somersetshire, on the 27th of July,
    1797'   82
Linton, Eliza Lynn   1612
Lions: Living and Dead   890
Lippincott's Magazine [Philadelphia]   1327, 1350
Lisle, Gwynne   1213
Literarisches Centralblatt [Leipzig]   1834
Literary and Biographical Studies   1650
Literary and Scientific Repository [New York]   324, 346, 350
Literary and Theological Review [New York]   570
'Literary Assize Court'   330
Literary Associations of the English Lakes   1773
Literary Celebrities   1570
Literary Chit-Chat   941
Literary Chronicle   321, 325, 441, 442
Literary Cookery. With Reference to Matter Attributed to Coleridge
    and Shakespeare   1100
'Literary Courtships'   1903
Literary Essays   1073
Literary Gazette [Philadelphia]   356
Literary Gazette   225, 226, 227, 228, 242, 262, 443, 748, 1045
'Literary Gossip'   1707, 1781
'Literary Hampstead and Highgate'   1811
Literary History of England in the End of the Eighteenth and Begin-
    ning of the Nineteenth Century   1463
'Literary Intelligence'   189
'Litterary Intelligence: Essays on His Own Times'   967
Literary Journal   93, 263
Literary Landmarks of London   1541
'Literary Leather Man'   1842
Literary Life and Correspondence of the Countess of Blessington   1107
Literary Life of The Reverend William Harness   1302
Literary Magnet   459
'Literary Memoirs of Living Authors'   43
Literary Memoirs of Living Authors of Great Britain   53
'Literary Miscellanies'   1206
Literary Miscellany [Cambridge, Mass.]   94
'Literary Notes'   1325
'Literary Notices'   570, 809
Literary Panorama   145, 187
Literary Phoenix [Birmingham]   467
Literary Pilgrimage among the Haunts of Famous British Authors   1811
'Literary Police Office, Bow Street'   384
Literary Recollections   495
Literary Recreations, or, Essays, Criticisms and Poems   1039
Literary Remains   392, 774

Q. 309
Quantocks and their Associations 1334
Quarterly Christian Spectator [New Haven] 609
Quarterly Essays 1255
'Quarterly Review and Lake Poets' 604
Quarterly Review 118, 127, 167, 190, 196, 210, 254, 355, 388, 432,
    434, 451, 506, 585, 648, 727, 794, 825, 839, 975, 1103, 1110,
    1255, 1266, 1582
Quarterly Theological Review 421
Queries Devoted to Literature [Buffalo, New York] 1574
Quesnel, Leo 1403
Quiz, Sam 347

R. 362, 374
R. A. 672
R. H. S. 1202
R. R. 1425
Radford, George Heynes 1772
Radical [Boston] 1261
'Rambler, Authors Continued' 522
Rapid, Robert 342
'Rationale of Verse' 940
Rattler, Morgan 686
Raven, A Poem by Samuel Taylor Coleridge with illustrations by Ella
    Hallward 1869
Rawnsley, Hardwicke D. 1773
Raymond, Henry Jarvis 1071
Raysor, T. M. 110
Reade, A. Arthur 1803
Real Devil's Walk. Not by Professor Porson 470
'Reason and Understanding according to Coleridge' 1035
'Reason and Understanding - S. T. Coleridge' 1204
Recent British Philosophy 1229
'Recent Poetical Plagiarisms and Imitations' 385
'Recent Shakespearian Literature' 806
Recollections of a Literary Life 1038
Recollections of a Tour Made in Scotland 1352
Recollections of an Actor 835
'Recollections of another of Mr. Coleridge's Lectures' 503
Recollections of Aubrey De Vere 1845
'Recollections of Authors I Have Known' 1476
'Recollections of Charles Lamb' 744, 1211
'Recollections of Coleridge' 682, 693, 701
Recollections of Dante Gabriel Rossetti 1454
Recollections of Literary Characters and Celebrated Places 1094
Recollections of Past Life 1316
'Recollections of the late William Linley' 629
'Recollections of the Poet Coleridge' 1680
Recollections of the Table-Talk of Samuel Rogers, to which is added
    Porsoniana 1113

AUTHOR / TITLE INDEX

Smith, Horace   127
Smith, J. E.   734, 981
Smith, J. Frederick   1664
Smith, James   127
Smith, Leapidge   1178
Smith, Nowell C.   1806
Smith, W. J. Bernard   1258, 1376
Smith, William   1404
Smith, William Henry   956, 982, 1005
Smyth, John   252
'Snake Witch'   1890
Social Life at the English Universities in the Eighteenth Century   1351
Solitudes of Nature and of Man   1246
'Some Account of Coleridge's Philosophy'   529
Some Account of the English Stage from the Restoration in 1660 to 1830   525
'Some Forgotten Hawthorne Verses'   1879
'Some Lectures Delivered by Coleridge in the Winter of 1818-1819'   1675
'Some Literary Tendencies'   1750
'Some Observations on the Biographia Literaria of S. T. Coleridge, Esq.'   256
Some of Our English Poets   1472
'Some Poets in Love'   1905
Some References to a Few of the Works of the late Rev. A. G. Mercer   1624
'Some Remarks on the Use of the Preternatural in Works of Fiction'   287
'Some Unpublished Correspondence of Washington Allston'   1693
'Some Unpublished Letters of Samuel Taylor Coleridge'   1350
'Songs of the Pixies'   1540
'Sonnet'   406
'Sonnet by S. T. Coleridge'   1676
'Sonnet by S. T. Coleridge: A Passage in the Biographia Literaria'   1497
'Sonnet in Reminiscence of the Poet Coleridge'   1037
'Sonnet on the late S. T. Coleridge'   960
'Sonnet to Coleridge'   492
Sonnets   492
'Sonnets'   690
Sonnets of Three Centuries: a Selection   1465
Sortain, Joseph   605
Sotheby, H. W.   1179
'Soul of a Philosopher'   1785
Source of 'The Ancient Mariner'   1661
'Source of the Ancient Mariner'   1667
Southern Literary Journal [Charleston, S. C.]   690
Southern Literary Messenger [Richmond, Va.]   517, 638, 654, 661, 700, 701, 818, 940, 1043
'Southey'   1005

Index of Proper Names

Persons and places referred to in annotations

INDEX OF PROPER NAMES

INDEX OF PROPER NAMES

Subject Index

It is the purpose of a subject index to direct a reader to the material which he needs without at the same time directing him to a great deal of material which is not useful for his purposes. For the material listed in this bibliography, a conventional alphabetical listing of subjects does not seem to serve that purpose. Modern critical and scholarly essays are inclined to focus on a few fairly clearly defined points. In the nineteenth century, we more commonly find either a wide-ranging essay or review-article incorporating a summary of biography, some general criticism of poetry and ideas, with more specific remarks on works or issues which interest the writer, or a note on a very narrow point, a few lines of a poem or a brief passage of prose. Our annotations reflect these different levels of generalization, and we feel that a usable subject index should so so as well.

We have therefore designed a schematic index based on a fairly broad outline of the material covered by this bibliography. The outline defines a few general areas of subject matter. Within each of these, as is illustrated below, are more numerous and more specific subdivisions. In dealing with an individual item, we have first indexed it under the most specific headings which would describe it as a whole, whether it is a general discussion of Coleridge and his works or a note on a line in "Christabel". If in addition, a substantial part of it was devoted to a more specific or specialized topic, we have included it in that more specific category as well. Listings in the more specific categories should not therefore be taken as inclusive, but should be supplemented by the more general categories under which they are subsumed. By this means, we have attempted to avoid the omission of brief items without including comprehensive items under virtually every subject heading and losing all distinctions.

We cannot pretend that the resulting index will instantly direct the user to all items in which a given subject is mentioned and will exclude all those in which it is not. We do believe that it may minimize the effort required.

Subject Index Outline

A. Summary Evaluations of Coleridge and his work. See also M1,
    N1, O1.
    1. Classified by type of publication. Brief, general
    2. comments from literary histories, critical essay
    3. memoirs, letters, etc. Reflect attitudes and responses
    4. of different periods and types of readers

B. Biographical studies, sketches, reminiscences
    1. Books and monographs. Because few in number and wide-
            ranging in content, these are generally excluded from
            more detailed categories below.
    2.-6. Biographical sketches classified by type of publication.
    7. Accounts of Coleridge in particular places. See also B13
    8. Obituaries
    9. Word portraits
    10. Word portraits, fictional
    11. Anecdotes
    12. Personal recollections. See also D.
    13. Personal recollections of Coleridge at particular places
    14. Humorous or satirical sketches
    15. Proposals for biographies
    16. Discussion of personal traits
            Appearance
            Character
          ┌─Health
          │ Manner of conversation
          │ Manner of lecturing
          │ Manner of preaching
          │ Use of alcohol
          └──Use of opium

C. Discussions of Coleridge's
        Academic achievement
        Admission to Christ's Hospital   Devoted to specific
        Annuity   biographical and factual
        Etc.   points

D. Reports and descriptions of conversation

E. Correspondence

F. Discussion or comparison of Coleridge and... See also I8, J, K
        Coleridge's intellectual or personal relations with
            specific individuals or institutions.

G. Discussion or criticism of Coleridge as...
        Professional and personal roles.

H. Discussion or criticism of Coleridge on...
        views on specific topics and individuals

I. Coleridge's influence
    1. General
    2.-7. Types (critical, literary, etc.)
    8. on individuals

SUBJECT INDEX OUTLINE

—J. Influence on Coleridge of [individuals and institutions] <u>See also</u> K. For specific titles, <u>see</u> Q————————————

—K. Discussions of plagiarism. <u>See also</u> J.
        general
        from specific authors

L. Discussions of criticisms of Coleridge by [individuals and journals]

M. Published works, general
    —1. General estimates. <u>See also</u> A
      2. Personal responses
      3. Characteristics
      4. Translations
      5. Editing

—N. Published works, poetry. <u>See also</u> Q.————————————
    —1. General estimates
      2. Characteristics
      3. Types
      4. Editing

O. Published works, prose. <u>See also</u> P, Q.————————————
    —1. General estimates
      2. Personal responses
      3. Characteristics
      4. Editing
    —Topics in prose-e.g. philosophy, theology-<u>see</u> G-philosopher; G-Theologian

P. Published works, other
    1. drama
    2. journalism

Q. Published works, individual [by title]— <u>See also</u> R————————
    Sub-headings for discussions of special topics————————
        and reviews of first publication

R. Discussions and reviews of collections and subsequent editions

S. Discussions and reports of lectures, notes, marginalia, manuscripts

T. Discussions and reviews of works on Coleridge [by title]

Subject Index

B. BIOGRAPHICAL STUDIES, SKETCHES, REMINISCENCES

B13 Personal recollections concerning Coleridge at (cont)
     Highgate, 551, 585, 587, 602, 603, 642, 652, 672, 693, 716,
          732, 752, 753, 770, 878, 884, 890, 933, 936, 969, 997,
          1031, 1061, 1119, 1196, 1226, 1264, 1285, 1302, 1319,
          1361, 1398, 1430, 1512, 1808, 1856
     Keswick, 86, 495
     Lamb's, 335, 1164
     Malta, 1362
     Manchester, 1145
     Nether Stowey, 82
     Racedown, 1352
     Ramsgate, 1361
     Rome, 895, 959
     Scotland, 1352
     Shrewsbury, 246
     Shropshire, 392, 905
     Thomas Bernard's, 691
     Wales, 8
     Wiltshire, 873, 1633
B14 Humorous or satirical sketches, 43, 46, 49, 105, 106, 123,
     203, 251, 257, 272, 283, 302, 326, 330, 342, 347, 348, 361,
     398, 436, 502, 515, 531, 563, 649, 699, 1267
B15 Proposals for biographies, 722, 1499, 1500
B16 Discussions of personal traits,
     Appearance, 3, 392, 430, 611, 876, 890, 969, 970, 978, 991,
          1120, 1164, 1176, 1178, 1193, 1197, 1361, 1398, 1402,
          1409, 1411, 1637, 1706, 1764, 1808, 1827, 1884
     Character, 200, 247, 256, 265, 306, 321, 332, 372, 383,
          430, 440, 532, 588, 602, 631, 679, 706, 708, 717, 723,
          736, 864, 867, 910, 913, 922, 932, 963, 968, 991, 1020,
          1022, 1071, 1076, 1077, 1091, 1111, 1141, 1144, 1183,
          1184, 1218, 1246, 1294, 1386, 1398, 1428, 1459, 1504,
          1591, 1598, 1612, 1642, 1699, 1701, 1774, 1787, 1800,
          1809, 1810, 1838, 1863
          Phrenological analysis of, 807, 1364
     Health, 403, 1608, 1809 (See also Use of opium)
     Manner of conversation, 320, 392, 395, 398, 551, 585, 602,
          610, 611, 613, 620, 622, 642, 644, 652, 688, 728, 770,
          788, 864, 866, 899, 969, 970, 978, 991, 997, 1013, 1022,
          1103, 1113, 1157, 1164, 1189, 1193, 1226, 1231, 1248,
          1285, 1309, 1312, 1316, 1347, 1398, 1402, 1435, 1446,
          1476, 1591, 1684, 1731
     Manner of lecturing, 3, 586, 876, 899, 1145, 1411
     Manner of preaching, 246, 392, 905, 1047
     Use of alcohol, 296, 358, 839
     Use of opium, 318, 319, 358, 388, 430, 588, 706, 717, 744,
          862, 866, 911, 913, 922, 963, 1002, 1023, 1077, 1117,
          1118, 1120, 1144, 1158, 1179, 1190, 1193, 1209, 1231,
          1263, 1372, 1421, 1434, 1519, 1557, 1596, 1608, 1612,
          1617, 1684, 1759, 1763, 1774, 1775, 1794, 1796

C. DISCUSSIONS OF COLERIDGE'S

SUBJECT INDEX

C. DISCUSSIONS OF COLERIDGE'S (cont)

Unfulfilled promise, 230, 354, 395, 402, 407, 412, 437, 455,
    544, 678, 781A, 922, 1790, 1799
Will, 560, 566, 578, 640

D. REPORTS AND DESCRIPTIONS OF CONVERSATION, 335, 342, 370, 418,
    466, 509, 546, 585, 589, 594, 602, 610, 611, 613, 618, 624, 641,
    642, 652, 693, 702, 728, 752, 757, 884, 890, 899, 1014, 1070,
    1084, 1211, 1243, 1276, 1285, 1347, 1506, 1512, 1513, 1565, 1796
        with Adams, Sarah F., 611
            Aikin, Anna L., 1512
            Berkeley, G. F., 1222
            Carlisle, 991, 1435
            Carlyon, 688
            Chalmers, T., 997
            Chasles, P., 969
            Clarke, M. C., 1361
            Collier, 1112
            Curtis, T., 970
            De Prati, 732
            De Quincey, 1731
            Decatur, S., 896
            Dibdin, T. F., 691
            Dicks, J., 890
            Galt, J., 770
            Gathorne-Hardy, 1506
            Grattan, T. C., 1193
            Hall, S. C., 1226
            Haydon, 1373
            Hazlitt, 333, 335, 370, 392, 466
            Heraud, J. A., 594
            Holland, H., 1316
            Hood, T., 1164
            Keats, 1799
            Kenyon, 1533
            Leslie, R., 1176
            McLellan, H. B., 602
            Martineau, Harriet, 1398
            Merivale, H., 652
            Methuen, T. A., 873
            Moir, D. M., 752
            Mudford, W., 603
            Owen, R., 1145
            Robinson, H. C., 1276
            Scott, D., 978
            Scott, W., 728
            Taylor, H., 1446
            Tieck, L., 1105
            Willard, Emma, 551
            Willmott, R. A., 702

D. REPORTS AND DESCRIPTIONS OF CONVERSATION (cont)
        Wordsworth, W., 1122
        Young, J. C., 1309

E. CORRESPONDENCE

    Selections from, 717, 748, 763, 913, 1179
        with Allsop, 672
            Allston, 1693
            Bates, Mrs., 1264
            Beaumont family, 1588
            Britton, J., 554
            Cary, H. F., 912
            Catcott, G., 1640
            Coleridge, Sara F., 626
            Collins, W. W., 936
            Cottle, 717, 913, 1648
            Davy, 1151, 1300
            De Quincey, 1682
            Edinburgh Review, 255
            Estlin, 1484
            Evans, Mary, 1801
            Fenner, 1307
            Flower, B., 553
            Frere, 1892
            Godwin, 1221, 1379
            Hamilton, W. R., 1460
            Heath, C., 553
            Kenyon, 1360
            Lamb, 735, 942, 1041, 1114, 1378, 1852
            Lloyd family, 1781
            Martin, H., 670
            Mathews, C., 753
            Methuen, 873
            Mudford, 603
            Murray, 1689
            Poole, 1616, 1906
            publishers, 1350
            Scott, David, 978
            Southey, 1748
            Stuart, 758, 1631
            Taylor and Hessey, 555
            Thelwall, 1648
            Tulk, 1854
            Watts, 1518
            Wilkenson, T., 1729, 1741
            Wordsworth, W., 1114
            Worship, W., 1697
            Wrangham, 1747

F. DISCUSSION OR COMPARISON OF COLERIDGE AND (See also I, J, K)

F.   DISCUSSION OR COMPARISON OF COLERIDGE AND (cont)

F. DISCUSSION OR COMPARISON OF COLERIDGE AND (cont)
    Pindar, 29
    Plato, 856, 957
    Pollock, R., 448
    Poole, T., 1616, 1842
    Price, Dr., 351
    Procter, B. W., 352
    Racine, 177
    Robespierre, 12
    Rogers, S., 1630
    Royal Institution, 1300
    Saltram in James's "The Coxon Fund" 1750
    Schelling, F. W. J., 856
    Schick, G., 1254
    Schiller, J. C. F., 66, 68, 77, 393, 1180
    Schlegel, A. W., 314, 815A, 886, 1020, 1309
    Scott, D., 949, 1480
    Scott, W., 180, 287, 352
    Shakespeare, 159, 177, 346, 355, 915, 1526
    Shelley, P. B., 467, 915, 1182, 1266, 1594, 1778
    Southey, R., 69, 78, 229, 247, 399, 909, 913, 970, 975, 990,
        1069, 1463, 1669, 1772, 1804, 1892
    Spenser, W., 552
    Spinoza, B., 1431
    Sterling, J., 1061, 1332
    Sterne, L., 1016
    Stevenson, R. L., 1833
    Stuart, D., 758, 1155, 1631
    Swedenborg, E., 462, 478, 816, 939
    Taylor, W., 841
    Tennyson, A., 653, 825, 1040, 1159
    Tholuck, F. A. G., 496
    Thomas, Edith, 1749
    Vico, G., 732
    Wallis, G. A., 1254
    Wedgwood family, 1228, 1304
    White, J. B., 947
    Wilson, J., 458, 1192
    Wordsworth, Dorothy, 1563
    Wordsworth, W., 237, 242, 278, 303, 346, 363, 367, 442, 664,
        714, 795, 824, 849, 865, 987, 1009, 1026, 1046, 1080, 1142,
        1253, 1265, 1266, 1299, 1308, 1309, 1328, 1334, 1422, 1463,
        1506, 1563, 1564, 1570, 1635, 1639, 1677, 1778, 1797, 1829,
        1853, 1861, 1874, 1886
    Young, C. M., 1309
    Young, E., 1897

SUBJECT INDEX

G. DISCUSSION OR CRITICISM OF COLERIDGE AS

Art critic, 721
Conservative, 275, 625, 734, 1359, 1573
Conversationalist. See B16; D
Critic, 101, 116, 120, 260, 265, 284, 294, 297, 314, 424, 624,
    631, 653, 727, 737, 787, 801, 806, 810, 823, 855, 902, 944,
    953, 954, 1002, 1060, 1115, 1160, 1194, 1213, 1233, 1253,
    1422, 1445, 1470, 1487, 1492, 1516, 1547, 1717, 1776, 1874
Dragoon, 580, 650, 1038, 1426
Dramatist, 2, 4, 5, 134, 141, 142, 157, 167, 177, 221, 308, 365,
    397, 419, 469, 637, 943, 1010, 1331
Dreamer, 921, 1022, 1023, 1573, 1632, 1642, 1652, 1711, 1769,
    1807, 1853, 1878
Heretic, 793, 1157
High churchman, 734, 829
Humorist, 882
Journalist. See P-journalism.
Lake poet, 84, 93, 99, 125, 142, 149, 167, 180, 220, 270, 323,
    349, 371, 391, 458, 519, 557, 803, 835, 864, 1004, 1377,
    1791
Lecturer, 3, 119, 586, 863, 876, 899, 1145, 1411
Letter writer, 1779
Metrist, 206, 813, 898, 940, 1303, 1443, 1751
Monologuist, 1084
Mystic, 476, 477, 856, 897, 1085, 1125, 1132, 1244, 1305, 1317,
    1875
Philosopher, 113, 250, 412, 441, 444, 546, 574, 585, 588, 624,
    625, 631, 634, 657, 677, 685, 690A, 754, 760, 762, 791, 800,
    802, 805, 822, 824, 845, 863, 872, 885, 897, 929, 957, 973, 1023,
    1061, 1073, 1083, 1096, 1122, 1179, 1229, 1232, 1233, 1261,
    1317, 1389, 1489, 1547, 1564, 1568, 1617, 1738, 1782, 1810,
    1857. See also I5.
Poet, 489, 657, 863, 865, 883, 1342, 1428, 1435, 1516, 1521,
    1555, 1568, 1593, 1738. See also N1.
Radical, 3, 12, 14, 15, 23, 25, 31, 43, 46, 48, 49, 55, 56, 64,
    106, 309, 1341
Rationalist, 1227, 1247
Theologian, 420, 421, 454, 457, 496, 532, 550, 561, 609, 616,
    645, 652, 668, 689, 756, 762, 764, 775, 778, 793, 808, 829,
    856, 857, 863, 873, 886, 892, 900, 923, 928, 932, 939, 947,
    952, 963, 988, 1007, 1028, 1062, 1073, 1076, 1083, 1091,
    1126, 1132, 1137, 1139, 1147, 1157, 1218, 1232, 1233, 1247,
    1270, 1291, 1382, 1516, 1547, 1551, 1553, 1625, 1785, 1900
    See also I7.
Translator, 9, 66, 68, 70, 393, 400, 426, 432, 483, 585, 592,
    597, 767, 826, 972, 1010, 1181, 1380, 1601, 1710

Subject Index

H. DISCUSSION OR CRITICISM OF COLERIDGE ON

Agnosticism, 1770
Allston, 602
Apocalypse, 997
Ball, A., 291
Beaumont and Fletcher, 786
Biblical inspiration, 668, 809, 815, 947, 961, 986, 1028, 1143, 1208
Biblical interpretation, 1140
Blackwood's Magazine, 369
Bowles, 1351
Burke, 243, 1707
Caliban, 276
Campbell, 1440
Catholicism, 1121, 1214
Chalmers, 602
Church and state, 521, 749, 773, 802, 845, 871
Church of England, 625, 874
Classes of readers, 568
Claude Lorraine, 721
Crashaw, 894
Davy, 720
De Quincey, 1193
Defoe, 1006
Devil, 1150
Dissenters, 619
Domestic affection, 1612
Education, 118, 331, 526, 726, 916
Elizabethan pronunciation, 1303
Epic, 585
Ethics, 1770
Faith, 774, 897
France's future, 1063
French Revolution, 1846, 1894
Genius, 686
German philosophy, 647, 1401
Gnosticism, 641
Goethe's Faust, 585, 855
Gospels, 1405
Greek grammar, 992
Greek mysteries, 1666
Hamlet, 311, 1470
Homer, 728, 1666
Hooker, 1149
Hume, 285, 888
Imagination, 1098, 1122, 1240
Imitation, 110, 1240
Ireland, 958
Irving, E., 602, 1697
Jacobinism, 276

Subject Index

O. DISCUSSIONS OF PUBLISHED WORKS, PROSE   (See also P, Q)

    1   General estimates of,
          1793-1834,
              British, 72, 497, 549
              American, 189, 474, 570
          1835-99,
              British, 802, 921, 988, 1236
              American, 853, 919, 983, 1466
    2   Personal responses to,
          1835-99,
              British, 857
              American, 1344, 1587, 1615
    3   Characteristics of,
          obscurity, 113, 168, 408, 420, 421, 439, 444, 474, 475,
              499, 608, 609, 631, 654, 840, 1083
          style, 7, 17, 113, 216, 235, 408, 499, 520, 544, 631,
              675, 819, 821, 901, 1165
    4   Editorial problems, 1486

P. DISCUSSIONS OF PUBLISHED WORKS, OTHER
    1   Drama, 221, 1010, 1331 (See also G-dramatist: Q)
    2   Journalism, 758, 958, 1155, 1574, 1577

Q. DISCUSSIONS OF PUBLISHED WORKS, INDIVIDUAL

"Advent of Love",
    influence on Sidney's Arcadia, 1821
Aids to Reflection,
    reviewed, 407, 408, 420, 421, 439, 441, 494, 544
    general estimates of,
        contemporary,
            British, 434
            American, 523
        1835-99,
            British, 760, 986, 1213
            American, 756, 840, 842, 1247
    epigraph to, 1269
    exposition or analysis of, 454, 529, 762, 1083
    influence of on theology, 1553
    McVickar's edition of, 1319
    references in, 977
    sources of, 1412
"Allegoric Vision",
    sources of, 1736
"Bala Hill",
    interpretations and criticism of, 1815
"Ballad of the Dark Ladie",
    textual variants in, 1889

Q.   DISCUSSIONS OF PUBLISHED WORKS, INDIVIDUAL (cont)
<u>Biographia Literaria</u>,
       reviewed, 215, 216, 217A, 225, 230, 235, 236, 237, 241, 243,
           256, 294, 544
       general estimates of,
           contemporary,
               British, 464
           1835-99,
               British, 1422, 1445
       biographical accuracy of, 309
<u>Blessed are ye who walk beside all waters</u> [second Lay Sermon],
       reviewed, 214, 218, 224, 231, 234, 238
       general estimates of,
           contemporary,
               British, 253, 254
"British Stripling's War Song",
       first publication of, 937
"Christabel",
       reviewed, 179, 183, 185, 186, 187, 189, 191, 195, 197, 204,
           205, 206, 208, 212, 233, 336
       general estimates of,
           contemporary,
               British, 182, 192, 193, 202, 265, 267, 287, 318, 345,
                   371, 442, 458, 522, 524, 536, 595, 605, 1518
               American, 350, 468
               French, 437
           1835-99,
               British, 885, 927, 943, 979, 1004, 1039, 1272, 1445
               American, 614, 719, 803, 1108, 1146
       compared with,
           Burns's "Tam O'Shanter", 204
           "Christobell, a Gothic Tale", 595
           Hogg's "Lady Isabelle", 196
           Keats's "Lamia", 1771
           Scott's "Eve of St. John", 971
           Scott's "Lay of the Last Minstrel", 287
           Spenser's <u>Faerie Queene</u>, 971, 1477
           Tupper's "Geraldine", 761
       influence on,
           American poets, 889
           Byron, 1108
               <u>Childe Harold's Pilgrimage</u>, 385, 404, 1477
               "Siege of Corinth", 188, 193, 404
           Scott, W., 883, 1108, 1258, 1698, 1739
               <u>Lady of the Lake</u>, 1686
               "Lay of the Last Minstrel", 453, 1130
           Shelley, 1108
       influenced by,
           Chatterton, 1433
           German poetry, 312
           Goethe, 652

"Christabel" (cont)
    interpretations of, 205, 301, 453, 607, 825, 1032, 1273,
        1454, 1456, 1463, 1478, 1562, 1634
    metrics of, 204, 206, 883, 889, 940, 1443, 1728, 1751
    sources of, 1172, 1173
    text of, 1698, 1864
    miscellaneous,
        Geraldine compared with Elsie Venner, 1175
        Geraldine's nature, 971
        indecency of, 197, 281, 1518
        name of, 1578
        recitation of, 495
        romanticism of, 1359
        Shelley's reaction to, 524
        supernaturalism in, 1691
Conciones ad Populum,
    reviewed, 12, 14, 17, 25
Confessions of an Inquiring Spirit,
    reviewed, 809, 811, 815, 819, 1028
    general estimates of,
        1835-99,
            British, 947, 986, 1250, 1898
            American, 1143
    exposition or analysis of, 1900
    influence of on theology, 1553, 1900
    influenced by Lessing, 945, 947, 965
Death of Wallenstein,
    reviewed, 66, 68, 70, 77, 79A
"Dejection, an ode",
    general estimates of,
        contemporary,
            British, 605
    compared with,
        Wordsworth's "Ode: Intimations of Immortality", 1569
    miscellaneous,
        "lady" identified as Wordsworth, 1581
"Devil's Thoughts",
    compared with,
        Goethe's Faust, 674
        Shelley's "Devil's Walk", 1306
    bibliographical history of, 1646
    authorship of, 490, 491, 789
    composition of, 263
    text of, 1327
"Eolian Harp",
    influenced by Burns, 1694
"Epitaph on an Infant",
    authorship of, 1629
"Essay on Faith",
    reviewed, 774

371

Q. DISCUSSION OF PUBLISHED WORKS, INDIVIDUAL (cont)
"Lines suggested by the Last Words of Berengarius",
sources of, 1339
"Lines written at the King's Arms, Ross",
general estimates of,
contemporary,
British, 27
"Love",
general estimates of,
contemporary,
British, 458, 462A, 522, 552, 1698
American, 88
French, 455
1835-99,
British, 941, 1039
compared with,
Tennyson's "Gardener's Daughter", 1020
"Mad Monk",
publication of, 1444
"Monody on the death of Chatterton",
reviewed, 11, 28
general estimates of,
contemporary,
British, 24, 91
American, 96
text of, 1438
Moral and Political Lecture delivered at Bristol,
reviewed, 7
"Mutual Passion",
sources of, 1849
"Names",
influenced by Lessing's "Die Namen", 1390
music for, 1390
text of, 1474
"Nightingale"
reviewed, 62
general estimates of,
contemporary,
British, 124
personal responses to,
contemporary,
British, 239
influenced by Skelton's "Crowne of Laurell", 1872
"Ode on the Departing Year",
reviwed, 29, 30, 32, 34, 37
personal responses to,
contemporary,
British, 117
"On a Cataract",
influenced by Stolberg, 710

Q. DISCUSSION OF PUBLISHED WORKS, INDIVIDUAL (cont)
   "On a late connubial Rupture in high Life",
      timeliness of, 325
   On the Constitution of the Church and State,
      reviewed, 473, 475, 497, 499
      general estimates of,
         contemporary,
            British, 521
         1835-99,
            British, 1121
      compared with,
         Arnold's Fragment on the Church, 871
      influence of on J. H. Green, 526
      influenced by Jahn's History of the Hebrew Commonwealth,
         1604
      interpretation or analysis of, 749, 802
   "On the Principles of Genial Criticism",
      publication of, 1000
   Osorio,
      compared with Remorse, 1324, 1331, 1336, 1654
      rejection of, 656
   "Pains of Sleep",
      reviewed, 179, 183, 191, 195, 206, 212, 233
   Piccolomini,
      reviewed, 66, 68, 70, 77
      manuscripts of, 1180
   Plot Discovered,
      reviewed, 12, 15, 17, 25
   "Poet's Answer",
      reviwed, 460
   "Religious Musings",
      reviewed, 11, 13, 28
      general estimates of,
         contemporary,
            British, 253, 403, 580, 605
         1835-99,
            British, 1366
      compared with Homer, 1023
      composition of, 738
      text of, 998
   Remorse,
      reviewed, 129, 130, 132, 134, 135, 136, 137, 138, 139, 140,
         141, 142, 143, 144, 145, 146, 147, 148, 149, 150, 151,
         153, 154, 156, 157, 158, 159, 160, 162, 162A, 167, 226
      general estimates of,
         contemporary,
            British, 173, 174, 177, 282, 308, 324, 334, 365, 397,
               419, 469, 525, 1739
           American, 396
           French, 418
      characterization in, 1482

"Rime of the Ancient Mariner" (cont)
    metrics of, 875, 898
    sources of, 1049, 1290, 1661, 1761
    translations of,
        French, 418
        German, 1602
    miscellaneous,
        and blood sports, 465, 1447
        artistic devices in, 1876
        debated in Cambridge Union, 465
        dialect reading of, 1885
        illustrators of, 1376, 1567
        reception of, 1567
        recitation of in France, 516
        Scott's illustrations of, 585, 1480
        supernaturalism in, 329, 1691
        superstition in, 772
    editing of, 668
"Separation",
    sources of, 1272
"Something childish but very natural",
    sources of, 1173
Statesman's Manual,
    reviewed, 198, 200, 219, 232
    general estimates of,
        contemporary,
            British, 246, 248
        1835-99,
            American, 957, 1767
"Tears of a grateful People",
    publication of, 1444
"Three Graves",
    reviewed, 108, 227
"To a young Ass",
    text of, 1187, 1690
"To a young Lady",
    date of, 1736
"To Fortune",
    text of, 1672
"To Matilda Betham",
    discovery of, 1657
"To Miss Barbour",
    text of, 1497
"To Miss Brunton",
    publication of, 1444
"To Mr. Pye",
    sources of, 980
"Two round Spaces on the Tombstone",
    propriety of, 548

R. DISCUSSIONS AND REVIEWS OF COLLECTIONS, SUBSEQUENT EDITIONS, ETC.
    (cont)
    Christabel, Kubla Khan, The Pains of Sleep (1816), 179, 180,
        183, 185, 186, 187, 189, 191, 195, 197, 204, 205, 206, 208,
        233, 336, 349
    Essays on his own Times (1850), 967
    Fears in Solitude, 56, 57, 60, 64
    Friend (1865), 1235
    Golden Book of Coleridge (1895), 1786
    Keepsake (1828), 446
        (1829, 1830), 460
    Lectures and Notes on Shakspere (Ashe, 1883), 1470, 1487, 1492
    Letters (1895), 1782, 1783, 1783A, 1784, 1786, 1787, 1798, 1800,
        1807, 1833
    Literary Remains (1836), 679, 705, 727
        (1838), 740, 742
        (1839), 769, 774, 775, 790
    Lyrical Ballads (1798), 38, 39, 41, 54, 58, 59, 61, 62, 65
        (1800), 67, 71, 75, 80, 1867
        (1802), 83
    Notes. Theological and Political (1853), 1056
    On the Constitution of the Church and State (1839), 773
    Poems on Various Subjects (1796), 11, 13, 16, 19, 20, 21, 22,
        23, 28
    Poems (1797), 32, 42, 45
    Poems (1803), 87, 97
    Poetical Works (1828), 442, 443, 444, 445, 469, 1606
    Poetical Works (1829), 479, 544, 1606
    Poetical Works (1834), 565, 567, 569, 574, 585, 586, 605, 606,
        607, 662
    Poems (1854), 1266
    Poetical Works (Chandos, 1875), 1366
    Poetical and Dramatic Works (1877), 1397, 1535
    Poetical Works (1885), 1691
    Poetical Works (1893), 1724, 1726
    Seven Lectures upon Shakspere and Milton (1856), 1100, 1114,
        1115, 1135, 1171
    Sibylline Leaves (1817), 216, 220, 227, 230, 295, 322, 327
    Table-Talk (1835), 613, 614, 616, 619, 620, 622, 624, 625, 627,
        638, 641, 644, 646, 648, 652, 655, 660, 677, 683, 769, 858,
        877, 1184, 1504, 1565, 1902
    Table-Talk (1851), 1103
    Works (1853), 1048, 1052, 1054, 1055, 1058, 1071, 1083, 1091,
        1096, 1098

S. DISCUSSIONS AND REPORTS OF LECTURES, NOTES, MARGINALIA, MANU-
    SCRIPTS

    S1 Lectures,
        (1808),
            reports of, 118
            descriptions of, 1094, 1300

SUBJECT INDEX

S3 Marginalia (cont)
    "Osorio", 1781
    Parr's Spital Sermon, 1068
    Pepys Diary, 1024
    Petvin's Letters concerning the Mind, 1053
    Procter's Dramatick Sketches, 665
    Raleigh's History, 1104
    Raleigh, 1814
    Reynolds's God's Revenge against Murder, 1053
    Selden's Table Talk, 912
    Southey's Joan of Arc, 1217
    Southey's Omniana, 1484
    Spinoza, 1865
    Stillingfleet's Origines Sacrae, 1353
    Swedenborg, 820, 1461, 1733, 1739, 1854, 1896
      Oeconomia Regni Animalis, 816
    Swift's Gulliver's Travels, 1812
    Tabulae Linguarum, 1455
    Vaughan's Life of Wycliffe, 857
    Wieland, 1177
    Wilson's Defoe, 1006
    Xenophon's Memoirs of Socrates, 1636
S4 Notebooks,
  selections from, 1777
  descriptions of, 1405, 1449, 1453, 1819, 1937

T. DISCUSSIONS AND REVIEWS OF WORKS ON COLERIDGE
Allsop,
  Letters [etc.] (1836), 612, 673, 680, 682, 685, 689, 694, 701
  Letters [etc.] (1864), 1242
Brandl, Coleridge and the English Romantic School (1886), 1582, 1793
Caine, Life of Coleridge (1887), 1582, 1593
Campbell, Coleridge (1894), 1726, 1826
Carlyle, Life of Sterling (1851), 994
Carlyon, Early Years and Late Reflections (1836-58), 844
Coquerel, Histoire abrégée de la littérature anglaise (1828), 440
Cottle,
  Early Recollections (1837), 706, 708, 723, 727
  Reminiscences (1847), 909, 910, 922, 934, 955, 1157
Foster,
  Contributions to the Eclectic Review (1844), 861
  Essays (1828), 861
Gilfillan, Gallery of Literary Portraits (1845), 1097
Gillman, Life of Coleridge (1838), 769, 802, 866, 1157
Hazlitt, Spirit of the Age (1825), 417
Hogg, Poetic Mirror (1816), 182, 196
James, Source of 'The Ancient Mariner' (1890), 1667
Knight, Memorials of Coleorton (1887), 1595, 1598

379

Index of Parodies, Satires, Fictional Portraits, Coleridgeiana

Index of Parodies, Satire, Fictional Portraits, Coleridgeiana

Poems, to Coleridge 35, 36, 50, 79, 89, 211, 411, 433, 542, 583,
        780, 985, 992, 1106, 1219, 1239, 1442, 1616, 1831
Portraits 836, 1712, 1794
     by Allston 1832
       Arnald 684, 743
       Dawe 1613
       deathmask 1796
       Hancock 717, 1011, 1521, 1685, 1786, 1832
       Kayser 1786
       Leslie 727
       MacLise 546, 1337
       Northcote 788, 1243, 1716
       Nye 1020
       Phillips 610
       Thorneycroft 1526
       Vandyke 717, 1560, 1863
       Wedgwood 455
       Wivell 782, 1043
Satires 46, 48, 49, 100, 103, 105, 106, 114, 123, 170, 207, 245,
   251, 257, 272, 283, 296, 302, 319, 326, 330, 342, 347, 348, 384,
   435, 436, 515, 563, 650, 835, 837